THE LATICS
The Official History of Wigan Athletic F.C.

By:
Dean Hayes

Published by:
Yore Publications
12 The Furrows, Harefield,
Middx. UB9 6AT.

British Library Cataloguing-in-Publication Data.
A catalogue record for this book
is available from the British Library.

ISBN 1 874427 91 7

Printed and bound by The Bath Press

Dedication

For Mum and Dad Walker

With Love

THE LATICS

THE OFFICIAL HISTORY OF WIGAN ATHLETIC F.C.

DEAN HAYES

Acknowledgements

The Author wishes to thank the following for their help in producing this book:
Dave Twydell (Yore Publications), members of staff at Wigan Athletic F.C. especially Gordon Allan, The Football League, The Football Association, The History Shop at Wigan Library and the Wigan Observer.

Thanks to individuals are due to Ronnie King, Colin Walls, Ben Hayes, and special thanks to my wife Elaine who devoted considerable time and effort in helping with copy and proof-reading.

Thanks are also given for permission to use the many illustrations which were kindly supplied by Wigan Athletic F.C., with the original source of the majority of these coming from the Wigan Observer. Unfortunately copies of original photographs were frequently not traced, and therefore in these cases reliance had to be placed on newspaper and programme cuttings etc. In view of their importance these were included despite the inferior quality of same. Apologies are offered to the owner(s) should the use of any illustrations in this book have inadvertently infringed copyright.

Contents

INTRODUCTION

Wigan Athletic hold a unique place in the history of organised football. The story of the growth of the game in the town and in Lancashire in general, is a source of much interest and fascination.

Publication of this book coincides with the club's 64th anniversary. It is designed to fill a gap in the available club literature and be, so to speak, the Latics' own 'bible'. It is hoped that it will entertain and amuse supporters as well as satisfy the growing army of amateur football statisticians. It might even settle a friendly argument or two, over who did what and when.

The story of Wigan Athletic concerns and belongs, to the townsfolk. When the club does well the town and its people seem to thrive. When the Latics do badly, Wigan seems to decline somewhat in stature.

During my research it became obvious as to why football facts and figures are a source of argument and frustration. Even when every effort has been made to get the details right, they could be wrong, for in many cases there are no means of double checking. Discrepancies often do not come to light until a player's career tally is added up - and this may be years after the circumstances of disputed goals have been forgotten. Everything possible, however, has been done to ensure the facts in this volume are correct.

Though there are many Football League clubs who have a longer and more illustrious history than Wigan Athletic, the Latics history is one that has enough intrigue, success, failure and emotional highs and lows. Wigan supporters have a football club in whose history they can be proud and in whose future they can look forward to.

Dean Hayes
Bamber Bridge
September 1996

THE HISTORY OF WIGAN ATHLETIC: 1932 -1996

During the past 100 years, five attempts have been made to establish the game of football in Wigan - Wigan County, Wigan United, Wigan Town, Wigan Borough and Wigan Athletic.

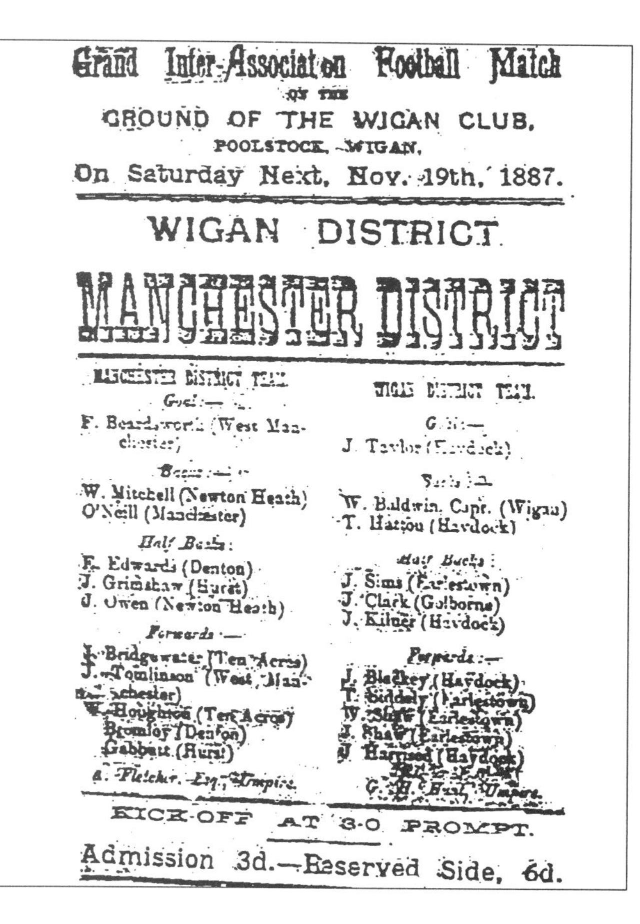

Grand Inter-Association Football Match
ON THE
GROUND OF THE WIGAN CLUB,
POOLSTOCK, WIGAN,
On Saturday Next, Nov. 19th, 1887.

WIGAN DISTRICT
v.
MANCHESTER DISTRICT

MANCHESTER DISTRICT TEAM.	WIGAN DISTRICT TEAM.
Goal:—	Goal:—
F. Beardsworth (West Manchester)	J. Taylor (Haydock)
Backs:—	Backs:—
W. Mitchell (Newton Heath)	W. Baldwin, Capt. (Wigan)
O'Neill (Manchester)	T. Hatton (Haydock)
Half Backs:	Half Backs:
F. Edwards (Denton)	J. Sims (Earlestown)
J. Grimshaw (Hurst)	J. Clark (Golborne)
J. Owen (Newton Heath)	J. Kilner (Haydock)
Forwards:—	Forwards:—
J. Bridgewater (Ten Acres)	J. Bleakey (Haydock)
J. Tomlinson (West Manchester)	T. Siddaly (Earlestown)
W. Houghton (Ten Acres)	W. Shaw (Earlestown)
Bromley (Denton)	J. Shaw (Earlestown)
Gabbott (Hurst)	J. Harrison (Haydock)
A. Fletcher, Esq., Umpire.	G. H. Hunt, Umpire.

KICK-OFF AT 3-0 PROMPT.

Admission 3d.—Reserved Side, 6d.

The very earliest beginnings of football in Wigan.

Wigan County began playing in the Lancashire League in 1897-98 at Springfield Park. The first football match played there was between Wigan County and Burton Swifts on Wednesday 1 September 1897 when the result was a 1-1 draw. The County's first League match was against Southport Central at Springfield Park when around 4,000 spectators saw County win 5-1. The team which beat Southport Central consisted: Menham; Holmes, Molyneux Stevenson, Greer, Sharp; J.Gordon, P.Gordon, Sharples, Morris and Snodgrass. Although the County fared badly in League matches, they had a remarkable run of successes in both the Lancashire Senior Cup and the FA Cup. In the latter competition, they defeated Fleetwood Rangers 1-0, Hurst Ramblers 4-3, Blackburn Park Road 2-1 and Nelson 4-0 at Springfield Park after a draw at Nelson.

In the first round proper, the County were drawn to meet Manchester City at Ardwick. As City occupied second place in the Second Division of the Football League, County's prospects seemed none too bright. Wigan County players were sent to Lytham for special training and City trained at Matlock. The match which was played on 29 January 1898, was more keenly contested than the City supporters anticipated. A few minutes from the end, the Wigan goalkeeper, who had given a masterly display, made his only mistake. He made a weak clearance, which allowed City to score the only goal of the match.

In the Lancashire Senior Cup, Wigan County beat Rochdale 2-0 at Springfield Park and Bacup away 1-0 before losing to Newton Heath, another Second Division club, at Clayton by 6-0.

On 3 January 1898, Preston North End played County in a friendly game at Springfield Park and won 3-2 whilst Liverpool sent a team to play County at Springfield Park in aid of the Wigan Cricket Club's new ground fund. County won 4-1. Andy Gara of Ashton-in--Makerfield, an Irish international, played for County against North End. Wigan County also played Sunderland at Springfield Park with the Wearsiders winning 2-1.

Meanwhile County had got seriously in arrears with their Lancashire League prog-ramme and they finished ninth, winning eleven and drawing five of their twenty-six matches; New Brighton were the League Champions.

In the following season, County finished sixth in the Lancashire League but had one success, winning the Rawcliffe Cup by defeating St Helens Recs. at Chorley 2-0. The County team was: Mackay; Wilde, Nellors; Evans, D.Fitzsimmons, Clibborn; Atherton, Fielding, Gordon, T.Fitzsimmons and Otty. When they returned to Wigan they were conveyed round the town in a wagonette headed by a brass band. Season 1899-1900 proved to be the last for Wigan County. Only four League matches were won and nine drawn out of 28.

Another club was formed in season 1900-01. The new team was named Wigan United and their matches, in the Lancashire League were played on the West End ground during the early part of the season.

In November the club began to play at Springfield Park, but little success was gained in League games and the club ended the season second from bottom.

Wigan United however beat Blackburn Rovers Reserves in the first round of the Rawcliffe Cup 2-1 and defeated Chorley in the second round 4-2. In the third round they were drawn away to Stalybridge, but as the ground was waterlogged they refused to play. The referee did not agree with their decision and allowed the home team to dribble the ball down the field and place it into an empty net !

In season 1901-02, both Wigan United and Wigan Rugby Club played at Springfield Park, each using the ground on alternate Saturdays. On 29 March 1902, Edinburgh St Bernards played United at Springfield Park, winning 2-0. That season, United finished third in the Lancashire League behind Darwen and Southport Central.

United won only one League match in 1902-03. Their solitary victory was earned in the last month of the season. They began their fixtures at Springfield Park, but early in January 1903 it was announced that owing to the expiration of their lease there, United would play all their remaining fixtures away. It did not come as any surprise when it was learned that Wigan United failed to function the following season.

With Wigan County and Wigan United having failed to establish soccer in the town, another effort was made in season 1905-06. The club was formed in December 1905 and was named Wigan Town. They were admitted to what was known as the Combination, in which such clubs as Chester, Birkenhead, Crewe, Wrexham, Druids, Rhyl and Bangor were members. Wigan took over the fixtures of Middlewich, who had disbanded. George Robey, the comedian, brought a team of crack players to oppose Wigan Town in aid of the Chief Constable's Clog and Stocking Fund, and George himself played !

Despite the fact that the club fared badly, it was stated that there was a great possibility of Wigan Town being in the Second Division of the Football League the following season and that first class players had been signed. The club finished at the bottom of the League table, having gained only six points; two having been deducted for playing an ineligible man.

Season 1906-07 opened with a victory over Wrexham and though several other League successes were recorded, Adlington beat Town in the first round of the Lancashire Junior Cup. A rumour at this time that the club had ceased to exist was strongly denied by the management but soon afterwards there was a bombshell. For it was alleged that they neglected to observe orders of the Football Association with regard to penalties inflicted by the Emergency Committee because of alleged wrong treatment of certain players, and the Wigan Town Club was suspended sine die. However, the ban was soon removed and the Town continued to do well in their League programme.

On Saturday 9 March 1907, Sheffield United brought a very strong team to Springfield Park and beat Town 6-2. Aston Villa also came to Wigan later in the season, but heavy rain spoiled the gate. The result was a 1-1 draw. It was also announced that Wigan Town intended to make an application for admission to the Lancashire Combination the following season, since travelling expenses in the English Combination were very heavy. The application was successful.

The following season saw Town have trouble with three of their professional players - O'Hara, Dean and Sutton - and they were given free transfers. Matters continued to go badly and on 3 April 1908 the club had difficulty in raising a team to visit Colne. The players arrived late and the start was delayed by fifty minutes, but they were still defeated 12-0 ! An effort was made to raise money to help to keep the club in existence and a letter was addressed through the press, *'To the working men of Wigan and District'.* This was an appeal for 1,000 supporters of Association football in Wigan to subscribe 1/- (5p) a week, which would mean that *'the club would be placed on a good foundation.'* The club finished second from the bottom of the League table and it was not surprising therefore to find that Wigan Town did not continue to function in season 1908-09.

WIGAN UNITED A.F.C.

A TOWN'S MEETING

WILL BE HELD IN THE OLD COUNCIL CHAMBER
BOROUGH COURTS, KING STREET.
ON THURSDAY 7th OCTOBER, 1920, at 7 p.m.

to consider the re-organisation of the above club in accordance with the decision of the Football Association.
All season ticket holders and supporters are earnestly requested to attend.

BUSINESS IMPORTANT
W. Ashworth,
Hon-Secretary
48, Market St. Wigan

This resurrection failed!

Wigan Borough became founder-members of the Football League Third Division (North), which was formed in the summer of 1921. Mr H.S.Bamlett, a former League referee, who had had considerable experience as a club manager, was engaged in that capacity. Boro's first match in the League was away to Nelson. Within seconds of the kick-off, Nelson scored and so wrote themselves into the record books as scorers of the first ever goal to be scored in the Division. However, the Boro' were not too intimidated and goals from Hodges and Twiss gave them a 2-1 win. The Wigan Borough team was: Bromilow; Bibby, Jenkinson; Woodward, Hobson, Williams; Campbell, Hodges, Twiss, Brodie and Knight. The Boro's next success in League games was on 8 October when they defeated Walsall 4-2 at Springfield Park. It seemed likely that they would be beaten in their next home match with Halifax Town who were leading 3-1 and with just ten minutes to go. Then Freeman the international centre-forward, who had only just been signed by Boro' crashed the ball into the net. A few minutes later, Boro' were awarded a penalty and Carlisle the centre-half scored. Then with the end drawing near, Chesser scored the winning goal for the home side to effect a remarkable turn around.

Wigan Boro' A.F.C., Ltd.

Members Football Association, Lancashire Association,
Football League, Liverpool County Combination.

Official Programme.

Saturday, August 26th, 1922 PRICE 2d

Telegrams -"Cabs, Wigan. Telephone 611 Wigan.

Middleton and Wood, Ltd.

Complete
Funeral Furnishers.

3, King St. West, Wigan

Acknowledged to be the most reasonable in Town for the very best.

We have the Finest Fleet of Cha-as in the North.

Bookings for all away matches. Famous Fiat Cars at your disposal.

Ring up 611 and you can have one at your door in two minutes.

There was a crowd of 7,000 present for the season opener versus Ashington.

The Boro' finished fourth from bottom of the League with 31 points from 38 matches. Stockport County who won the League, beat Boro' in a second round replay of the Lancashire Cup, and the same club knocked them out of the Manchester Senior Cup. The top scorer for the season was Freeman with 13 goals. Carlisle scored five goals from penalties, but all the penalties awarded against the Boro' were saved!

Ashington were beaten 6-1 in the opening game of the 1922-23 season, with Dennison scoring four of the goals. That same season saw the club record their biggest win, of 9-1 over Lincoln, and almost win promotion to Division Two. Unfortunately they faded towards the end of the season and finished fifth as Nelson took the title. However, they did reach the second round proper of the FA Cup before losing at home to Queen's Park Rangers 4-2 in front of a then record crowd of 25,000. The Boro' team in that game was: Hunter; Fare, Currie; Findlay, Whitfield, O.Williams; Jones, Spencer, A.Williams, Dennison and Stevenson. On 2 October 1922, Cardiff City and Newcastle United played a match at Springfield Park in aid of the Whitehaven Pit Disaster Fund. The attendance was 15,000 and Cardiff won 4-0.

When Nelson, the League leaders, came to Springfield Park on 17 February 1923, there was another crowd of 15,000 to see Boro' win 3-1 with goals from Fare, Dennison and Glover. The last named was an inside-forward secured from Southport.

In season 1923-24, the Boro' defeated Nelson, the Second Division club, in the fifth qualifying round of the FA Cup after a draw at Nelson. Northampton Town came to Springfield Park in the last qualifying round and the Boro' were soundly defeated 6-0. There were over 18,000 spectators and the gate receipts were £1,000.

The Boro' reached the semi-final of the Manchester Senior Cup having beaten Hurst 2-1 and Bury 2-1 after a draw. In the semi-final they played Manchester City at Springfield Park and were beaten 1-0. Wolverhampton Wanderers won the Third Division Championship. The Boro' who were tenth in the table gained a point in each match against the Wanderers.

With the exception of the Manchester City Senior Cup, Wigan Boro' did not have much success in cup-ties in season 1924-25, when they finished eleventh in the League table and Darlington won promotion. In the Lancashire Cup, Nelson beat the Boro' 4-0 at Nelson and Bradford knocked them out of the FA Cup at Springfield Park by 1-0. In the Manchester Senior Cup, the Boro' defeated Oldham Athletic 3-1 in the first round and Manchester North End 1-0 in the second round, but lost 2-1 to Bury in a closely fought semi-final at Springfield Park.

The 1925-26 season was fairly uneventful as the Boro' finished sixth from bottom of the League as Grimsby Town won promotion. After beating Nelson 3-0 and

Crewe 2-1 in the first two rounds of the FA Cup, they went down 5-2 to a strong Stoke side in the third round. Wigan Boro' had however, discovered a very good forward in Dickinson, a local player who created a record by scoring 32 goals in all matches.

Four leading Borough players

The Boro' started the 1926-27 season in disastrous fashion. After beating Nelson 2-1 at home, they did not win another match until 16 October when they defeated Hartlepool United 3-0. Meanwhile they had lost seven League games, drawn two and been beaten by Southport in the Lancashire Cup, and at the end of the season they were fifth from bottom of the League.

They beat Barrow in the first qualifying round of the FA Cup but then lost to Crewe in the next round. They did well to defeat both Oldham Athletic and Manchester City in the Manchester Senior Cup, but lost to Manchester United in the semi-final by 1-0. Dickinson was again the club's most prolific scorer with 34 goals in League and Cup ties.

In 1927-28, the club finished third from bottom of the League with Bradford winning the championship. Rhyl knocked Boro' out of the FA Cup and Manchester City beat them in the semi-final of the Manchester Cup. Although Dickinson did not maintain his great goalscoring records of the previous two seasons, he was still top scorer with 19 goals. He was later transferred to Nottingham Forest.

Wigan Borough's best season was 1928-29 when they finished fourth in the League. They also had some considerable success in cup-ties. They reached the third round of the Lancashire Cup and the semi-final of the Manchester Senior Cup for the third season in succession. But their greatest triumph was in the FA Cup. After beating Ashington and Grantham, both at Springfield Park, they were drawn against Sheffield Wednesday in the third round at Springfield Park. The Boro' went down 3-1 in front of record attendance of 30,443. The Wigan team in that match was: Preedy; Moran, Dennis; Humpish, Wilson, Potter; Hughes, Welsh, Lievesley, Cockle and Lindsay.

After their successful season it was disappointing to find the Boro' again occupying a lowly place in the Third Division (North) in 1929-30. They finished fifth from the bottom and Port Vale secured promotion. The only gratifying feature of an otherwise uneventful campaign was the fact that Boro' won the Manchester Senior Cup by defeating Manchester City 3-2 after extra-time.

Season 1930-31 opened successfully with five victories out of the first six matches, but in the second half of the season the team fared badly and although their League position was tenth, there were signs that the Boro' would not survive long unless the gates improved considerably.

Though they acquired some fine players, notably Frank Barson, the former Manchester United and England centre-half, Boro' always had difficulty in raising the transfer fees and in fact, towards the end of that 1930-31 season, the financial situation became so critical that difficulty was experienced even in finding the players' wages.

The club's dire financial straits were exaggerated somewhat by the appallingly low gates the club had been getting since the defeat at home to Accrington Stanley on Boxing Day. Before that match, Wigan Borough were in mid-table, but following Barson's dangerous tackle in the 83rd minute, resulting in him being dismissed, the defence collapsed. It was Barson's last game for the Boro' for he like so many others, was sold to aid the club's fight for survival. But results were going against the Boro' and as their League position crumbled, so the crowds dwindled. Just 600 paid to watch the final home game of the season against Gateshead.

To avoid the embarrassment of League suspension the club had sold its stars. Full-back Moran went to Tottenham Hotspur and outside-left Welsby joined Sunderland, and although additional sums of money were raised through the early selling of season tickets, the tactics proved merely to be delaying ones.

At the tenth Annual General Meeting on 10 August 1931, which was only moderately attended, a discussion of the club's finances was the main item of business. There were pleas to reduce expenditure, to repay loans and to raise money by selling advertising space on the stands and hoardings on the ground.

The club's *'financial depression'* had manifested itself in a number of ways - unpaid transfer fees, arrears of wages, rates and taxes. Perhaps most significant, the shortage of money had debarred the directors from paying transfer fees for new players. To strengthen the playing staff, a number of professionals given free transfers by their clubs were snapped up. Moon arrived from Barrow, Sharp from Crewe and Wade from West Ham United. Also, in an effort to augment the staff, invitations were made for local amateur footballers to join the club's professionals. In spite of all these ominous signs, there were good attendances at the pre-season public practice matches and it seemed to local reporters that the club might have a *'serviceable team'* which might be a force in the League.

The first match of the season saw Boro' share in a bit of soccer history when they played before a crowd of 13,000 at Chester, for whom this was the first match in the Football League. Boro' collected a most welcome £100 from the £700 gate receipts, but went down 4-0.

The following Wednesday, they salvaged some pride when they beat Hull City 3-1 before drawing with Hartlepool United. Defeat at home to Lincoln City was followed by away losses at Crewe and Lincoln and by mid-September only New Brighton and Rochdale were below Boro' in the League. Worse was to follow. Defeats by Halifax and Darlington put Boro' next to bottom.

Injuries and a loss of form contributed to this poor record. It was necessary to supplement the inadequate first team squad by the regular use of Cockle, the player-coach of the reserve side. The gloom was only temporarily lifted by victory over Gateshead, a side striving to get back into the Second Division, and including Billy Walsh, an ex-Boro' forward.

Meanwhile off the field, strenuous efforts were being made by interested parties to improve the alarming financial situation. Fewer spectators were watching a losing side and expenditure exceeded income. The Football League issued an ultimatum, demanding that the club put its affairs in order. So it was, that the Boro' officials appealed to the Wigan public for help in the difficult and slow process of resuscitating the club's resources. However, there was little response and on Monday 28 September 1931, a shareholders' meeting was convened to consider the *'grave crisis'* - the worst in the club's history. The major problems were listed - a large wage bill, total liabilities of £30,000, and very low gates. An air of depression hung over the club and this was made worse by further defeats in the League.

The crisis intensified somewhat during October, and the League Management Committee insisted that the position of the club be cleared up to their satisfaction. The club's Honorary Secretary, Frank Platt, prepared a scheme for the reconstruction of the club; this scheme proposed the resignation of the club's current directors and the seeking of a much wider financial base, by the offer of 10/- shares to the general public of Wigan, who were asked to demonstrate that they wanted a League Club.

The Football League Committee approved the scheme, but there was a poor response to the share offer. Despite the appeals for active support, the majority of Wigan football followers did not seem to acknowledge the seriousness of the club's financial affairs and the only alternative seemed to be the ending of Wigan Borough AFC.

On Monday 26 October 1931, Wigan Borough resigned from the Third Division (North), when the directors expressed their inability to meet the present and future commitments of the club. The Football League's decision was to declare that all Boro's results for that season were void and a new club would be elected in their place the following year.

Boro's last Football League games was played on Saturday 24 October 1931 against Wrexham at the Racecourse Ground. They were defeated 5-0. Boro's team that day was: Mittell; Hartley, Wade; Hallam, Martin, Hurst; Cherry, Kilourhy, Valentine, Oakes and Moon. Their League record for the 1931-32 season up until their time of resignation read:

P.	W.	D.	L.	F.	A.	Pts.
12	3	1	8	12	33	7

The team did make just one more appearance before going into voluntary liquidation, when in a last desperate attempt to fulfil their reserve team fixtures in the Lancashire Combination, they played Southport and won 2-1. Wigan Borough's epitaph was fittingly written by the Club's Honorary Secretary, Frank Platt. It read: *'From the information I have gleaned from the books of the club, I have no hesitation in saying that the Association Football public of Wigan have shown once again, that they have no desire to maintain League football in Wigan.'*

Even with the collapse of Wigan Borough, the town's die-hard soccer enthusiasts were already plotting the rebirth of a town team. On 9 May 1932, Wigan's Mayor, Councillor W.A.Hipwood, presided over a public meeting held at the Queen's Hall.

Councillor Hipwood told the packed hall that Wigan was noted throughout the country for the quality of its sporting representation and had in fact turned out some of the finest sportsmen in the world. He called on the town to keep that reputation intact by ensuring that an Association Football team as well as the Rugby League team, carried the town's sporting banner.

Fortunately, the call was well received and a committee was appointed on the spot. It was chaired by Mr J.Howarth JP, and the other serving members were Mr C.Ostick (Vice-Chairman), Mr J.H. Farrimond (Secretary), Mr J.W.Roberts, Mr A.Roberts, Rev Father Greenhous, Mr J.Heywood, Mr J.Worswick, Mr J.Greenhalgh, Mr H.Bury and Mr R.Farrimond, and the Club was to be called Wigan Athletic.

J. HOWARTH, J.P.
President

Springfield Park was purchased for £2,850 from the owners of the Woodhouse Lane Dog Track, and one interesting clause in the agreement stated that the ground must never be used for Greyhound racing.

The club then had to find a league to play in. Their first application to join the Cheshire League was unsuccessful along with those of Glossop, Prescot Cables and Northern Nomads. Aiming high, they applied for what was to be the first of numerous unsuccessful attempts to join to the Football League - not surprisingly they failed on this first try to poll a single vote.

Just as things appeared to be taking their usual unlucky course for a Wigan team, Manchester Central resigned from the Cheshire League and Wigan Athletic were elected in their place, whilst the reserve team joined the West Lancashire League. However, even then their problems were not fully overcome as the Chairman and Secretary of the club were summoned to appear before a Lancashire FA commission on 31 July 1932 at Lytham St Annes. With the memory of Wigan Borough's collapse still fresh in the minds of the FA, the Latics had some convincing to do before the association were prepared to grant them the necessary affiliation.

Jack Farrimond - Secretary

Also present at the Commission was the club's first ever manager; Charlie Spencer, who had a wealth of League experience, having played centre-half for Newcastle United, Manchester United and gained international honours with England, winning two caps. His first managerial appointment had been with a moderately successful Tunbridge Wells side, but now he took over the new Wigan club as player-manager, earning the then above average wage of £6 per week.

With the opening game of the season scheduled for 27 August, the pressure was now on Spencer. He managed to employ a team of fulltime professionals, earning between £3 and £4 per week, and to weld them into some form of playing unit. Wigan Athletic faced Port Vale Reserves in this, their first ever match at Springfield Park. A crowd of 5,106 paid £161 to watch a rather inauspicious beginning, as Latics went down 2-0 after a goalless first-half.

Playing in red and white shirts with black shorts and socks, this first Latics team was: Abbott; O'Dell, Callaghan; Allon, Spencer, Wake; Chambers, Smith, McCabe, Henderson and Murphy.

By the following Wednesday, Spencer had whipped the Latics into shape and they beat Tranmere Rovers Reserves 5-1 with goals from Smith, who scored Latic's first-ever goal, and two apiece from Chambers and McCabe. It was the omen for an incredible first season for the Latics, as they finished fifth in the League and reached the semi-finals of the Cheshire League Challenge Cup before losing 3-1 at Springfield Park to Manchester North End.

The outstanding match of the campaign was against unbeaten League leaders Northwich Victoria on 22 October 1932, when Latics won 9-0. Even that scoreline looked likely to be beaten the following match when Congleton Town trailed 7-0 shortly after half-time. Fortunately for Congleton, the Latics didn't get the chance of adding to their score, for on that bitterly cold day, the match was abandoned. Congleton had been reduced to six men - their other players having been taken off with exposure! Nevertheless, Latics won the rearranged match 6-2.

From such high scoring games, William Chambers became Latics top scorer with 60 goals, followed by

McCabe with 43. The Latics scored 121 goals in the League and only conceded 54. The club's first season's success was merely a foretaste of that to come. With practically a new team for the following season, Charlie Spencer's side were invincible at home, winning all 21 of their home fixtures and romped away with the Cheshire County League Championship.

They finished with 66 points, five points ahead of former champions Macclesfield Town. Scott and Felton who formed a brilliant left-wing pair, scored 27 and 24 goals respectively. In the Lancashire Junior Cup, the Latics were beaten by Lancaster Town 4-3 at Lancaster after a draw at Springfield Park. Scott played in all 42 games and Felton in 41. The Latics had some success in the FA Cup. In the preliminary and qualifying rounds, they beat Great Harwood, Horwich RMI, Lytham and Dick Kerrs, before losing at Altrincham.

Before the 1934-35 season got underway, inside-right Stan Bentham was transferred to First Division Everton at a record fee for a Cheshire League club. Beaten at home for the second successive season, the Latics again took the League title but this time only on goal average from Altrincham and Stalybridge Celtic, who both finished with the same number of points. Centre-forward Jack Roberts' haul of 66 goals in all competitions set a scoring record that was to stand for thirty years until Harry Lyon equalled it in season 1964-65.

The club had a remarkable run of success in the FA Cup. In the first qualifying round, they defeated Nelson 3-1 at Springfield Park; in the second qualifying round they ousted Morecambe 5-0 at Morecambe; Dick Kerrs were beaten 5-1 in the third qualifying round at Springfield Park and Northwich Victoria fell to the Latics 4-0 in the fourth qualifying round, which was also at home. The Latics had the distinction of entering the first round proper where they drew Carlisle United away. Obviously a home tie would have been preferable, but who really cared, certainly not the Latics supporters who travelled in their droves over the Cumbrian border.

It was a journey they were never to forget, as two goals from Armes and Roberts, with one apiece from Scott and Robson, saw Latics crush Carlisle 6-1, before a crowd of 3,196. Next it was the turn of Torquay United as Latics claimed a home draw in the second round of the FA Cup. The Devon side too were humbled by the Latics, losing 3-2 in front of an ecstatic Springfield Park crowd of 20,000, with Roberts 2, and Scott finding the back of the net. Millwall were the next to take to the Springfield Park stage with a near record attendance of 25,304 watching the game in which Latics were finally humbled by 4-1, with Roberts netting for the third consecutive cup game.

The Latics also reached the final of the Lancashire Junior Cup, but were beaten 3-2 by Fleetwood in a match played at Deepdale. Latics best team in that eventful season was: Caunce; Robinson, Talbot; Patterson, Watson, Tufnell; Armes, Robson, Roberts, Felton and Scott. With the taste of success in their veins, the Latics did not stop there.

Season 1935-36 was another successful campaign. Under manager Charlie Spencer, they went on to win their third consecutive Cheshire League title by a clear thirteen points; they also won the Lancashire Junior Cup and the Cheshire League Challenge Cup. In the former they defeated South Liverpool 3-0 at Anfield in the Final after a goalless draw at Deepdale, and Crewe Alexandra were beaten in the Final of the Cheshire League Cup at Springfield Park 4-1. The Latics also reached the final of the Lancashire Senior Cup but were beaten by Blackpool at Bloomfield Road by 6-2.

During the season, Latics lost three of their star players of the previous seasons. Sammy Armes moved to Leeds, Edward Taylor Felton went to Huddersfield and Jack Roberts was transferred to Port Vale in exchange for JRM Wilson. For the first time in three seasons, Latics lost a home game, going down 2-1 to Chester Reserves. Two games were also abandoned, one at Stalybridge after 83 minutes when fog thwarted the Latics, who were leading 6-1 at the time and also the crunch game with Altrincham when the referee stopped play after 76 minutes following a crowd invasion after he had turned down two penalty appeals!

It was around this time that Secretary Jack Farrimond left the club, to take up the post of rate collector for the Wigan Corporation, which he did with some sadness. Indeed, manager Charlie Spencer who also owned a confectionary shop in Blackpool was foremost in organising Mr Farrimond's honeymoon during a very busy August Bank Holiday week!

There was little success to record in the 1936-37 season with Latics finishing a disappointing eighth in the Cheshire League and beaten 5-1 by Burton Town in the first round of the FA Cup. They did top Group 'A' of the Northern Midweek League and were matched against Group 'B' winners Blackpool in the play-off which was held over until the following season. During the 1936-37campaign, manager Charlie Spencer left for Grimsby Town. During his period of management, the Latics had won practically every honour open to a non-League side at that time.

The new manager was to be Frank Hancock who Charlie Spencer had signed from Millwall after the third round FA Cup defeat in 1935. When Spencer left Springfield Park, he promised to bring his full League side to Wigan for a friendly match to assist with Latics finances, as the Mariners at the time were a successful First Division outfit. Before this took place, however, the Second World War was looming dangerously over Britain, and at the time this promise was never fulfilled.

The club dropped further down the League in 1937-38, to finish eleventh. But they beat Lytham, Chorley, Leyland Motors and Northwich Victoria in the qualifying rounds of the FA Cup before succumbing to South Liverpool at Springfield Park in the first round proper by 4-1. Duncan Colquhoun's hat-trick against Lytham in the 7-0 win was a historic first.

Towards the latter end of 1938, the Latics experienced a mediocre time with attendances greatly reduced due to the imminence of war and the economic depression of the time. Finishing seventh in the Cheshire League in season 1938-39, the Latics reached the third qualifying round of the FA Cup before being beaten at Chorley 5-1 after a draw at Springfield Park. They were beaten 3-0 in the Lancashire Junior Cup Final by South Liverpool at Anfield. The season's top scorer was Thomas with 50 goals.

Players were now no longer so easy to acquire as they had been. Nevertheless the Club instituted a policy of recruiting local youngsters and were soon fielding a young and promising side who at the advent of war, in 1939, had won all four of their opening League fixtures. Former Blackpool player Bill Hanna, an Irishman captained the team which comprised: Littler; Robey, Topping; Rimmer, Hanna, Rainford; Appleton, Thomas, Liggins, Cole and Teers.

The club placed high hopes on inside-forward Cole, a player whose football future looked secure before his tragic death on the beaches of Dunkirk. The Cheshire League was automatically suspended at the outbreak of war and so the Latics played friendlies and took some part in the wartime league.

The war years were dead years at Springfield Park. The ground was completely closed apart from regular spot checks from the few directors who were available, and obviously the condition of the pitch and the ground in general became fairly dilapidated.

The old wooden stand which covered the length of the pitch needed major repairs and the popular side shelter needed completely re-roofing. When the war in Europe ended in 1945, this repair work had to be completed - mostly by local volunteers - before the Cheshire League re-started in August of that year.

The 1945-46 season was a disaster - the Cheshire League re-opened in a small way to allow each club to gradually find their feet after six years of war. Every club was restricted to a £2 wage limit as many of the players were not even demobilised and only expenses could be paid to men in the forces. Wigan did, however, employ a player-manager in Jimmy Milne, but with the restrictions, he was set a difficult task and the Latics finished that season at the bottom of the Cheshire League. A strip of blue and white was adopted, replacing the old red and white mainly because the sports shop could only supply the blue!

The Cheshire League then passed a decision which completely shocked the whole town. In a sensational meeting of the League's Committee, Wigan Athletic's application for re-election was defeated. In a fight between Latics and Ashton United, Ashton took the re-election honours by 16 votes to 8 and the Wigan club that had been virtually invincible before the war found itself ejected to make way for Winsford United. Latics chairman Mr Arthur Horrocks made a statement to the effect that 'this might mean the end of Association Football in Wigan for some time'.

This statement stirred the members of the Wigan Board, who saw the League Committee's decision as very short-sighted and were determined to fight it. Mr Horrocks thought he should resign in the face of such public criticism, but the Board gave him an overwhelming vote of confidence and it was agreed that his remarks had been taken out of context and misinterpreted as defeatism. Though he was voted off the Wigan Board by the shareholders later that year he was to make a triumphant return the year after.

Fortunately, the club's pride was salvaged as they, along with Accrington Stanley, were elected to the Lancashire Combination. The club's debut season in the Lancashire Combination was a dream as Duncan Colquhoun, a star of the Latics side of the 1930s, returned to take over the position of player-coach with Jimmy Milne leaving for Morecambe. Building a team from virtually scratch, Colquhoun harnessed the local talent to produce a side that astounded everyone by taking the League title by two points from Nelson. The top of the table read:

	P.	W.	D.	L.	F.	A.	Pts.
Wigan Athletic	42	25	9	8	72	37	59
Nelson	42	24	9	9	84	67	57

Latics Championship team was: Woolley; Ball, Parkinson; Shirley, Howcroft, Finch; Brown, Taylor, Barker, North and Miller.

During the season, full-back Johnny Ball was sold to Manchester United for a fee of £2,000. He was later to captain Bolton Wanderers and also gained a place in the England XI.

In 1948-49, the Latics lost their League title, finishing 15 points behind champions Netherfield. The following season, the Latics finished runners-up in the Lancashire Combination and beat the previous season's champions 7-0 at home with goals from Cunliffe 3, Lomax 2. Shirley and Pollard. At the end of that campaign, Latics, with Tom Finney guesting, played Grimsby Town in a friendly. They went down 5-3 in front of a 16,000 crowd.

The club's consistency over the previous few years almost rewarded them in 1950 with Football League status, and it was the closest the Latics came until 1978. The Football League Management Committee decided to enlarge both sections of the Third Division - North and South - with two additional clubs joining each Division.

Wigan Athletic once again applied for admission. In an effort to support their application, the club commissioned journalist Ivan Sharpe of the Sunday Express to edit a booklet outlining the Latic's achievements. He produced a superb brochure which was distributed to the voting clubs just before the meeting.

The result of the first vote gave the Latics some hope. Shrewsbury Town were elected with 30 votes, Wigan and Workington tied on 19 while Scunthorpe came in last with 17. The rules of the vote demanded that the three non-elected clubs were still in the running. Again the vote was tied, but this time however, Scunthorpe United picked up added support, tying with Wigan on 15 apiece with Workington on 14. A third vote was therefore necessary but it was the underdogs Scunthorpe who were elected to the Football League with 30 votes while the Latics could only finally muster 18. This failure was felt even more the following year when Workington were voted in replacing New Brighton. Yet despite all these disappointments, the Latics continued to knock on the League's door, backing their demands with yet another Lancashire Combination title in 1950-51. Under manager Bob Pryde, the Latics took the title on goal average from Nelson. Harry Parkinson, Latic's long-serving defender finally missed a game after 210 consecutive appearances.

Lancashire's Australian-born Ken Grieves who kept goal for Latics in 1951/52.

With Bob Pryde leaving in January 1952, the Latics slipped to finally finish in 4th position. That season also saw the Latics play St Mirren in a friendly at Springfield Park, with the home side winning 2-1. Guesting for the Latics were Bolton players, Nat Lofthouse, Johnny Ball and Malcolm Barrass. The latter two were later to become Wigan managers.

Although the 1952-53 season was a great one in terms of football success - in that the Latics won the Lancashire Combination, being unbeaten at home, and the Lancashire Junior Cup - it also brought disaster for the club. Towards the end of the season, Latic's main stand was raised to the ground by fire, causing £7,000 worth of damage.

Yet despite some enthusiastic fund raising by the club's supporters, it took nearly a year to raise sufficient money to build a replacement. It is highly probable that the fire cost the Latics their chance of Football League membership at the end of that season for the flames not only attacked the main stand, but also the dressing - rooms and baths. Even so, the Latics quality of football was recognised and the club did amass 17 votes. During that season, Billy Lomax overtook Horace Thomas's record of goals for the club.

The season of 1953-54 will be remembered as one of the most remarkable in the club's history. The club completed a unique treble by retaining the Lancashire Combination Championship(the third in four years), winning the Lancashire Junior Cup and the Lancashire

Combination Cup. In a wonderful season, Latics, under Ted Goodier, took the League title by 15 points from Netherfield, but not content in winning every non-League honour open to them, the club also had high hopes of winning the FA Cup !

Scarborough were the first team to be defeated in the Cup, the Yorkshire side going down 4-0 at Springfield Park in front of a crowd of 12,692, where goals from Lomax, Livesey, Hindle and Lyon took the Latics through to the second round. Drawn at home to Hereford United, who were one of the South's top non-League clubs, a record crowd of 27,526 saw Wigan win 4-1. This record still stands to this day as the largest attendance ever recorded for a game between two non-League clubs outside of Wembley finals. Rewarded for this second round victory with an away draw against the mighty Newcastle United, the non-League Lancashire Combination club were to face a star-studded First Division team at the height of their footballing powers.

The Magpies team sheet was filled with names that became legends - six internationals and a brace of Cup medal winners and years of League experience. Latics fielded a team of almost relative unknowns: Lomas; Lindsay, Parkinson; Lynn, Mycock, Banks; Butler, Livesey, Lomax, Lyon and Hindle. The attendance at St James' Park of 52,222 made it the largest crowd to watch a game involving the Latics.

Newcastle took the lead after 27 minutes when Dave Mycock sliced a clearance to Ivor Broadis who made no mistake from close range. Latics equalised seven minutes into the second-half through Jack Lyon. With just a quarter of an hour to go, Wigan took the lead when Hindle crossed for Livesey to crack the ball home. The Wigan fans were still celebrating when Jackie Milburn launched himself from the kick-off on a solo run which resulted in a brilliant goal. Both teams pushed hard for the winner and Latic's Hindle had a goal disallowed for offside, but it wasn't to be and a replay was necessary.

The second match got off to a very unsporting start when Stan Seymour, the Newcastle chairman refused to let his team change in Wigan's makeshift dressing rooms, calling the accommodation 'crude'. It was a very insensitive remark, especially as the Latic's supporters and directors were working hard in their attempts to repair the damage caused by the fire. Newcastle team eventually changed in the Corporation baths! The game started evenly but after 13 minutes, Newcastle went ahead when Mitchell's cross found Keeble's head. Mycock tried to clear the danger but only helped the ball into the net.

Newcastle's Monkhouse miskicks at a packed St.James' Park. Wigan defenders, Parkinson, Lomas, Lindsay and Mycock look on.

Action in the Newcastle cup-tie replay. Note the framework of the new Stand taking shape.

The visitors went 2-0 up in the 34th minute when after Broadis and Mitchell's shots were blocked, White forced the ball home. Within a minute the Latics had pulled a goal back. Livesey beat several defenders before passing to Lomax who smacked home a left-footed shot that gave Ronnie Simpson in the Newcastle goal no chance whatsoever.

Early in the second-half, Lyon lobbed the ball over Simpson's head. The Newcastle 'keeper caught the ball whilst stepping back and appeared to land over his line but the referee ruled against the Latic's appeals and play continued. Newcastle went further ahead in the 71st minute when Milburn crossed for Broadis to score. Nine minutes from time, Wigan pulled another goal back when Lomax received a ball from Livesey, who had just evaded a lunging tackle by Brennan to shoot home.

So the Latics went out of the FA Cup in great style, but they had certainly given the First Division outfit a nasty scare. Unfortunately, the successes of that memorable season in no way impressed the League AGM as the Latics failed to poll sufficient votes. In fact, despite the stirring performances, the Latics only polled two more votes than those received the previous season.

Kenny Banks wins the ball in the Newcastle replay.

In October 1954, manager Ted Goodier was sacked and replaced by Walter Crook. The Latics finished third in the Lancashire Combination and won the Liverpool non-League Senior Cup and Makerfield Cup.

In the Lancashire Combination Cup, Stubshaw Cross were defeated 12-0 with Corfield 4, Vincent 3, Hindle 2, Davis, Lindsay (penalty) and Penk scoring. Goalscoring legend Billy Lomax moved to Nelson on Christmas Eve after scoring 186 goals in Wigan colours. Walter Crook had been replaced by player-manager Ron Suart, who himself left at the end of the 1955-56 campaign. Latics star Harry Penk, aged 20, signed for Portsmouth in September for £2,500 later playing for Plymouth Argyle and Southampton.

The following season saw the Latics slip four places down the League to finish 10th, with new manager Billy Cooke departing in November. He was replaced on a temporary basis by the club captain Angus McLean. The Latics centre-half in this season was Les Rigby who was later to manage Wigan and take them to Wembley in the 1973 FA Trophy Final.

There was an improvement in 1957-58 as the Latics moved up to 4th place in the Lancashire Combination. Towards the end of the season, Manager and former player Sam Barkas was replaced by Trevor Hitchen. Hitchen then joined Southport in August and left-half John Bramwell, who had impressed in his 82 League outings for the club, was sold to Everton for £3,400.

Latics had a disastrous season in 1958-59, finishing 18th in the Lancashire Combination and winning just one away game, 1-0 at Horwich RMI. Player-manager Malcolm Barrass (ex-Bolton Wanderers and England) resigned on New Years Day 1959 and was replaced by former player Jimmy Shirley who was himself replaced at the end of the season by Pat Murphy, who became full-time manager. In the Lancashire Junior Cup-tie replay against Crompton Recs, Fred Taberner scored six of Latic's goals in a 7-2 away win. The team's improvements continued and in 1959-60, the Latics ended the season as runners-up. In February 1960, Latics chartered a plane to fly to Scotland to play Stirling Albion in a friendly. This didn't go as well as hoped for, since they lost 5-1, and the trip home became a saga when the plane broke down and the party were forced to hitch home on separate flights as they became available. At the end of the season, full-time manager Pat Murphy was sacked.

The first match of the 1960-61 season at Lytham was a thriller, won 6-5 by Latics who despite being a goal down after 20 seconds, led 3-1 after only six minutes! Manager Allenby Chilton, the ex-Manchester United and England centre-half was sacked on 15 December 1960 and replaced by player-coach Johnny Ball - the club's 12th manager in ten years.

After finishing 3rd in the Lancashire Combination, the club's management became all too aware of the general stagnation of the Club and the League in which they were competing.

The Latics had won the League and Combination Junior and Senior Cups many times, and a situation was beginning to arise where the successful clubs were getting bigger and winning all the honours, while the smaller clubs struggled to make ends meet at the foot of the table.

Given this situation and the implications which were beginning to present themselves, the Latics board of directors decided to apply for election into the Cheshire League, where the football was altogether stronger and the competition much fiercer than in the Lancashire Combination. The application was accepted with the Latics competing for the first season in 1961-62 under the management of Johnny Ball. Utilising some of the talents which he had learned under Duncan Colquhoun, Ball led the Latics to fifth in the table in what by Wigan's standards was only a moderately successful season. The annual Football League application was submitted at the end of a particularly long and arduous season only to read Wigan 5 votes, Oxford United 31 votes. The Manor Ground club were elected at the expense of Accrington Stanley.

John Higgins, former Bolton Wanderers centre-half, and Latics Captain from 1961-63.

Johnny Ball's team were to finish the 1962-63 season in 7th position. The home League game against Winsford United developed into a brawl and the referee - who had given 40 free-kicks, booked four Wigan players and sent off Latic's inside-left Bill Bradbury - waved his arms in a gesture of resignation and called the teams into the dressing room.

Only 64 minutes had been played and his action sparked off angry scenes amongst the 3,782 crowd (Latic's biggest of the season), and there was a half-hour demonstration outside the main stand by hundreds of fans. As the referee had already been buffeted as he strode up the passageway towards the dressing-rooms, there was a distinct possibility of more violence when he left the ground. But eventually he made a safe and unobtrusive exit, leaving by a side door with an escort of two police inspectors and a constable!

Having qualified for the first round proper of the FA Cup, the Latics faced a goalkeeper crisis before the tie at Gateshead and trainer Wilf Birkett had to don the number one jersey. Though he gave of his best, the Latics went down 2-1.

Manager Johnny Ball resigned on 11 September 1963 following the club's 4-1 home defeat to Macclesfield Town. Though they ended the season in 12th place, the Latics beat Winsford United 9-0 and Stafford Rangers 8-2 at Springfield Park. When Latics visited Winsford United on 25 September 1963, their goalkeeper Jeff McKay had to face four spot-kicks just before half-time. He saved the first three but was finally beaten by the fourth. This remarkable penalty incident was probably unique in the annals of the Cheshire League. The game ended in a 2-2 draw.

Allan Brown, the former Luton Town and Scottish international became player-manager on 6 April, whilst former Bolton winger Geoff Sleight was later to represent Australia in the 1966 World Cup qualifying matches.

In 1964-65, the club chalked up the honours as though they were going out of fashion, clinching the Cheshire League Championship with the following record:

P.	W.	D.	L.	F.	A.	Pts.
42	32	3	7	121	46	67

The Latics also claimed the Cheshire League Cup (beating Runcorn in the final), and the Liverpool non-League Senior Cup (beating New Brighton in the final). The team also went through an unbeaten run of 29 games between 5 December 1964 and Easter Monday 1965, at the time, a club record.

Another record smashed that season was one held by Jack Roberts for twenty-nine years, that of top individual goalscorer. His record had seemed unassailable until, that was, the arrival of Harry Lyon. One of the greatest players ever to wear the blue and white of Wigan Athletic, he amassed the amazing total of 66 goals in 196465 - over half the team's total - scoring six in one League match for another club record. Also that season, Carl Davenport who had scored 45 goals in competitive matches, was surprisingly the only player released by the Latics.

Despite losing only two League games, Allan Brown's side were pipped for the Cheshire League title by Altrincham. Goal king Harry Lyon notched 61 goals, even playing in goal in two Cup Finals and was only beaten once by a Swindells penalty. Latics new striker, Bert Llewellyn didn't have a bad season either, scoring 58 times.

If the League Championship was lost, then at least the Latics had excellent cup results including a good FA Cup run to compensate, and it was out of one of these matches that a legend grew up about 'the Lyon'. Drawn against Doncaster Rovers at Belle Vue, the Latics were 1-0 up at half-time thanks to Harry Lyon who headed the visitors into the lead from a Graham Stanley corner. On the hour, disaster struck with full-back Stuart Houghton having to go off injured. Lyon dropped back to play at full-back, but Doncaster pushed forward and scored two goals in quick succession to take the lead to 2-1. Not to be intimidated, the Latics went in search of an equaliser and with just two minutes remaining, Crompton scored their second goal.

The replay at Springfield Park was a thrilling game. Played on the following Wednesday, the game kicked off at 2pm because there were no floodlights at that time. In the early stages, the Latics looked the more dangerous team, but in the 19th minute, Harry Lyon was stretchered off with a suspected broken ankle. But fifteen minutes later Harry came hobbling back, fortified by pain killers plus a drop of whisky, and his ankle, which proved to be a torn ligament, was heavily strapped. All the 7,133 spectators gazed in amazement and wondered if Lyon would manage at all.

However, minutes later, it was Doncaster who were stunned as the incredible 'Lyon Heart' headed Wigan into the lead and shortly afterwards smashed in a second goal with his injured left foot to make it 2-0. He then proceeded to grab his hat-trick with another header and though Rovers scored a late consolation goal through Ogden, it was Harry Lyon's game. Unfortunately, Lyon couldn't do it every game and Latics were beaten in the next round at Chester, where after being 1-0 up through Bert Llewellyn, went down 2-1 through goals by Holmes and Morris. Much of the credit for Chester's performance in this match went to their young goalkeeper who made some outstanding saves. The 'keeper was Dennis Reeves, who later went on to play for the Latics during one of the club's most successful periods.

The 1966-67 season saw the introduction of substitutes, with Allan Brown being Latic's first. The club now had the services of Joe Hayes, ex-Manchester City, and it was the Maine Road club who officially opened the new £15,000 floodlights in October before a crowd of 10,119.

Two weeks later, player-manager Allan Brown resigned to take over at Luton Town. This coincided with Latics first League defeat after a run of 52 consecutive unbeaten games going back to 15 September 1965, as the Latics lost 2-0 at Buxton.

This season also saw the Latics hold Tranmere Rovers to a 1-1 draw at Prenton Park, with Harry Lyon scoring Wigan's goal. Rovers won the game at Springfield Park but it was a game marred by controversy. Played in a blinding snow storm, the League side were winning by the only goal of the game when, in the dying seconds, Alf Craig fired in a terrific shot that almost broke the back of the Tranmere net. The Wigan fans went wild, some thinking that the Latics had equalised, but others because the referee had disallowed the goal, claiming that he had blown for full-time before the ball entered the net. A cruel story was passed around the ground after the match that the referee had a 10 o'clock train to catch and did not want to miss it by playing extra-time! In the same match, Wigan 'keeper Halsall saved a penalty from the formidable Roy Parnell.

During that 1966-67 season, the Latics played a staggering 86 first-team matches - a club record that will never be beaten. However, the reward for all the hard work was the winning of five trophies - The Northern Floodlit League and Knockout Cup, the Liverpool non-League Cup, the Lancashire FA Floodlight Cup and the Case Trophy for the Cheshire League runners-up.

After Alf Craig had had a short spell in charge of team affairs, Harry Leyland was appointed as Allan Brown's successor. Under Leyland, the great Harry Lyon gradually faded after giving the Latics tremendous service, although he did go on to play a prominent part as centre-half or full-back in Wigan's first Northern Premier League season in 1968-69.

In 1967-68, the Latics slipped to eighth in the Cheshire League and in February of that season, manager Harry Leyland was sacked. His replacement Allan Saunders lasted just 32 days but was to sign five players including the late Ian Gillibrand, who was one of the greatest defenders ever to play for the Latics. Saunders also released Derek Houghton who had played over 500 games in ten seasons for the club. He was exchanged for Altrincham's Norman Sykes. Scot Ian McNeill became manager in May.

Latic's Goalkeeper Dennis Reeves in action

Also during that season, the Latics entertained a Port Vale side that included 52 year old Stanley Matthews in a friendly. Vale were later expelled from the Football League after making illegal payments, but they were reinstated the following month.

In 1968-69, the Northern Premier League was formed. It was created for two reasons - firstly, it was decided by a collection of clubs that the north needed a 'super league' for the non-League teams in the area who were too strong for their respective leagues and were tending to monopolise them. And secondly, after a number of disappointed visits to the FA Headquarters, non-League clubs had realised that there would be far greater chance of Football League status if the contenders came from a proven competition. There were at the same time, similar moves afoot in the south.

Wigan Athletic were amongst the founder-members, and in 1968-69 competed in the opening season of the North-ern Premier League. It marked the beginning of a new era of success for the club.

New manager Ian McNeill immediately stirred fresh interest by building a side of mainly Scotsmen like himself. It was not however, a team full of 'Jocks' for between the sticks was the ex-Manchester United goalkeeper Dave Gaskell, now representing his home town team.

So the season opened with a new league, a new manager and a new team. The whole town waited expectantly. The season began on a successful friendly note with a 4-4 thriller against Raith Rovers at Springfield Park with Alan Ryan grabbing two of the goals.

Now it was down to league business, and the club's opening fixture saw them play away to Scarborough. Billy Sutherland and Alan Ryan scored to give the Latics a 2-0 victory in their first Northern Premier League match.

It proved to be a good omen for the future, for the Latics finished as runners-up to Macclesfield Town. The squad captained by Norman Sykes (for the first half of the season before being deposed by Dave Gaskell) was as follows: Gaskell; Cairns; Lyon; Sutherland; Turner; Sykes; Gillibrand; Lynn; Sealey; Ryan; Cairney; Hill and Shaw.

Despite proving their worth in the league, the club failed to qualify for the first round proper of the FA Cup, having been dismissed 2-0 at Altrincham, Jackie Swindells blasting two penalties past Gaskell for the home side.

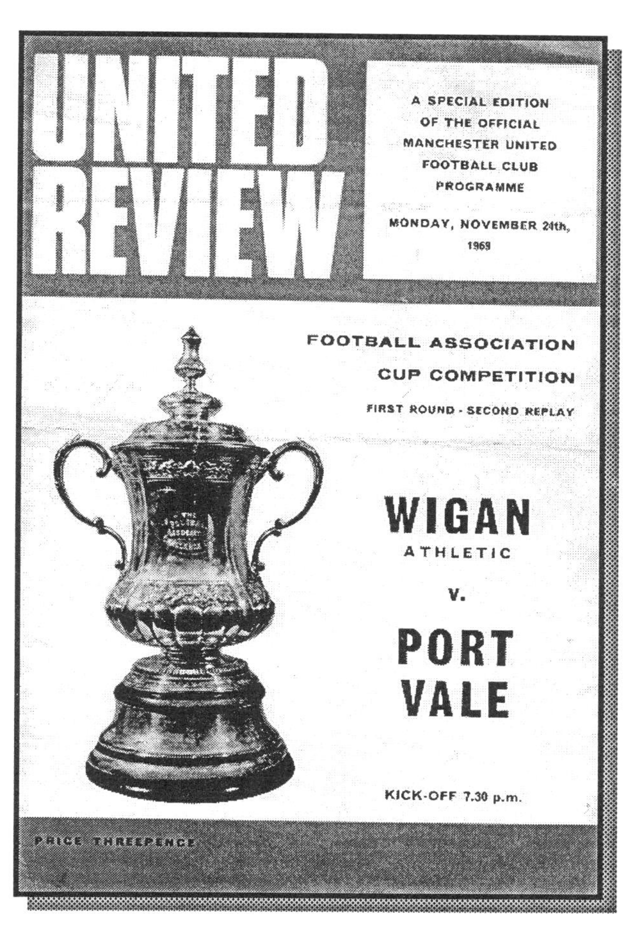

If the league provided a close and exciting finish, then the FA Cup was not to be outdone. After fighting their way into the first round proper, Latics drew Port Vale at Springfield Park. There followed two struggles of epic proportions; first Port Vale held Latics to a 1-1 draw, then Latics held Port Vale 2-2 at Vale Park (Sutherland scored for Latics in the first tie, while Fleming and Fielding notched the goals in the second). The second replay was held at Old Trafford and the spectators saw a game fit for such a fine stadium. Refusing to be overawed by the setting, the Latics forced Port Vale into extra-time, but after battling so gallantly, lost the match by a solitary goal in the last minute of the extra period!

In the first-half of the season, the Latics were rocked by a crisis. Manager Ian McNeill left the club following a disagreement with Arthur Horrocks the Club chairman, and returned to his native Scotland. Latic's physiotherapist and club scout Duncan Colquhoun was appointed as caretaker manager - a position he held until January 1970 when Gordon Milne was appointed player-manager.

Though the Latics won the Northern Floodlit League Cup they were dumped out of the Lancashire Junior Cup by Great Harwood after a second replay. Lancashire cricketer Jack Simmons was then a Great Harwood player and he figured prominently in all the matches. Dave Gaskell's consistency earned him a lot of attention and not surprisingly he returned to League football with Wrexham. It wasn't all doom and gloom for the Latics, as they took Dennis Reeves in part-exchange.

The 1969-70 season once again saw a two-horse race between Wigan and Macclesfield with the Moss Rose club once again snatching the title. But it was a close run race with everything hinging on the last match of the season.

Macclesfield visited South Shields; if the home side had won by three clear goals then the league title would have gone to the Latics. The Silkmen held on to the title however, by going down 3-1 and pipping the Latics to the post in a photo-finish with a goal average of 1.756 compared to Wigan's 1.750.

Despite all the changes on the managerial front, the 1969-70 season saw some memorable occasions. One was that of Harry Lyon's single match goalscoring record being broken. This happened in a Lancashire Floodlit Cup match against Darwen at Springfield Park, a game that the Latics won 11-1. Tony McLoughlin had returned, following a three month suspension after having been caught playing Sunday League football for an amateur side, and scored seven of Wigan's goals. The others were netted by Fleming 2, Fielding and Hill (penalty).

The season also saw the Latics entertain Metallist of Khartrov from Russia, in what was the club's first friendly match against foreign opposition. Despite goals from Sutherland and Fleming, the Latics went down 3-2 in front of a 3,992 crowd.

This is the game where the assistant secretary of Khartrov was Mikhail Gorbachev - now a Latics fan !

The team's last two good seasons were also rewarded after a fashion by the Football League, as Wigan polled 18 votes in favour of their League application. Unfortunately, they were not enough as Cambridge United were elected in place of Bradford Park Avenue. At least the Latics could take home some consolation in the fact that they polled one more vote than the deposed Yorkshire side.

As if to prove yet again that the Football League were missing something by not allowing the club in, Wigan Athletic turned in one of their finest seasons' performances ever in 1970-71. During the close season, Gordon Milne the Latics boss had signed former Everton and England winger Derek Temple from Preston North End for a paltry £4,000. Best remembered as the player who scored the winning goal in the 1966 FA Cup Final against Sheffield Wednesday, he was a class player and a great crowd puller. Another bargain buy that summer was Geoff Davies from Northwich Victoria. Combining well with Temple and Jim Fleming, Davies produced one of the finest feats of goalscoring seen at Wigan Athletic. By the end of October he had netted 20 times - more than he had scored the entire previous season at Northwich, and by the end of the campaign he had scored 42 goals including seven hat-tricks.

The crowds poured into Springfield Park and on Boxing Day, the match against League leaders Stafford Rangers attracted a crowd of 8,107, a number which still stands as a Northern Premier League record. The Latics beat Rangers 4-1 with goals from Milne, Fleming(pen), Oates and Davies. After this result, the Latics went from strength to strength and went on to win the Northern Premier League title at their third attempt. In fact, they only lost two of their 42 League matches. The club also won the Lancashire Floodlit Cup and were runners-up in the Lancashire Challenge Trophy. The Latics only big failure in a magnificent season came in the FA Challenge Trophy when they went down 1-0 at home to Hillingdon Borough.

However, the Latics more than made amends for this defeat, in the FA Cup. In the fourth qualifying round, they beat Skelmersdale United 5-0 at Springfield Park after the first meeting of the two clubs had ended all square at 1-1. Latics got through the first round proper by beating South Shields 2-0 after holding them to a 1-1 draw on their own ground. Drawn at home to Peterborough United in the second round, a crowd of 17,180 were treated to an exciting game. Derek Temple who had scored in both the South Shields games put the ball into the Peterborough net but the effort was disallowed when Oates was adjudged offside. However, the crowd did not have long to wait with Geoff Davies opening the scoring for Wigan with a diving header. Ernie Moss levelled the scores from close range early in the second-half when the Latics defence failed to clear the ball. At 1-1 it looked all set for a replay, but in the final minute the referee awarded the Latics a penalty after handball by a Peterborough defender. Jimmy Fleming placed the ball on the spot and made no mistake in beating the Peterborough 'keeper. As the final whistle went, thousands of Wigan fans, young and old flooded onto the pitch to celebrate yet another FA Cup giant-killing.

The third round draw took Latics to Maine Road and a tie against Manchester City on 2 January 1971. City were the holders of the Football League Cup and the European Cup Winners' Cup and were at the time riding high in the First Division. The Latics side that day was: Reeves; Turner, Sutherland, Milne, Coutts, Gillibrand, Temple, Todd, Davies, Fleming, and Oates, with Ledgard as substitute. City boasted a forward line of three England players in Summerbee, Bell and Lee. A remarkable crowd of 46,212 spectators paid to see the match to record City's largest home gate of the season.

The first-half was goalless as Wigan defended in numbers and gave City no room for creative movement. The Latics stuck to the same tactics in the second-half but as the game wore on they were increasingly probing a sometimes panicky City defence. Then after 72 minutes, Reeves the Wigan 'keeper, miskicked a goal kick straight to Neil Young some 30 yards out. He beat Turner, pushed the ball to Summerbee, who in turn fed Bell and he made no mistake to put City 1-0 up. The Latics pressed forward in search of an equaliser but it wasn't to be. The tie was the BBC 'Match of the Day' that evening and the Latics performance sent the commentator into raptures. The press too were stirred into sensational headlines.

It had been a magnificent season for the club and optimism in the town was high that surely the FA could not possibly refuse the Latics League status. The mood of optimism was captured perfectly by the Wigan Observer, '*Unless soccer has gone insane, I will challenge all-comers to argue that Wigan are not now a certainty to be in the Football League by the end of May.*'

The Football League meeting was held at the Cafe Royal. Lincoln City, Barrow, Hartlepool United and Newport County applied for re-election. All got it with 47, 38, 33 and 33 votes respectively; Hereford came next with 22, whilst Wigan polled the terribly disappointing total of 14. In Wigan the news was seen as an insult to both the club and the town as a whole. There had to be a scapegoat and Ken Cowap, the club chairman had the blame laid firmly at his feet. Prior to the meeting, Mr Cowap had distributed a gift of a £2 Parker pen to each voting representative. It seemed as if that small gesture of goodwill and publicity rebounded and was construed as an attempt to unfairly influence the voting. Whether or not it did affect the voting was debatable - yet the club picked up four fewer votes than the previous season, though they had achieved such fantastic results. The following year when Hereford United were admitted to the Football League, they made everyone a present of a china bull and it did not affect their vote tally!

Geoff Davies beats former Latics 'keeper Halsall in the 1971/72 season victory over Morecambe

The 1971-72 season was something of an anti-climax as the club finished a rather disappointing third in the Northern Premier League. They were also dismissed by Barnet in the third round of the FA Challenge Trophy at Springfield Park by 2-1 (with both Joe Fletcher and Jim Fleming missing penalties, although Fletcher did score one). The FA Cup provided a little excitement as Latics defeated Third Division Halifax Town 2-1 in the first round with goals from Oates and Sutherland. Drawn away to Wrexham in the next round, the game was heading for a goalless draw with just 12 minutes left when the Welsh side wrecked Latics hopes with four late goals!

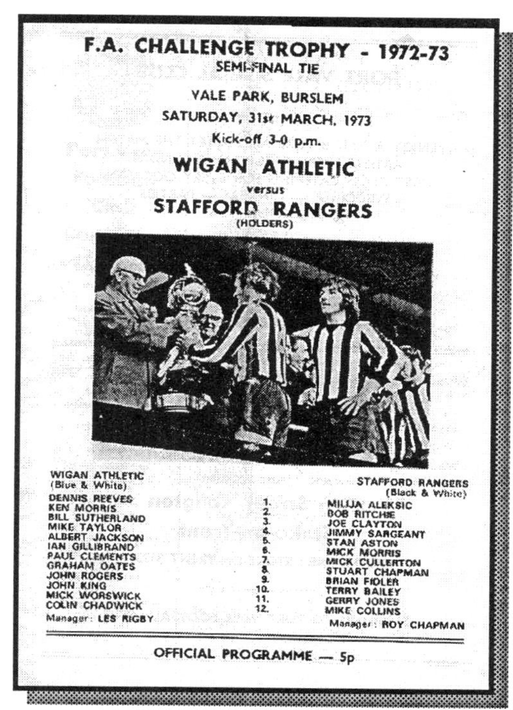

F.A. CHALLENGE TROPHY - 1972-73
SEMI-FINAL TIE
VALE PARK, BURSLEM
SATURDAY, 31st MARCH, 1973
Kick-off 3-0 p.m.

WIGAN ATHLETIC
versus
STAFFORD RANGERS
(HOLDERS)

WIGAN ATHLETIC (Blue & White)		STAFFORD RANGERS (Black & White)
DENNIS REEVES	1.	MILIJA ALEKSIC
KEN MORRIS	2.	BOB RITCHIE
BILL SUTHERLAND	3.	JOE CLAYTON
MIKE TAYLOR	4.	JIMMY SARGEANT
ALBERT JACKSON	5.	STAN ASTON
IAN GILLIBRAND	6.	MICK MORRIS
PAUL CLEMENTS	7.	MICK CULLERTON
GRAHAM OATES	8.	STUART CHAPMAN
JOHN ROGERS	9.	BRIAN FIDLER
JOHN KING	10.	TERRY BAILEY
MICK WORSWICK	11.	GERRY JONES
COLIN CHADWICK	12.	MIKE COLLINS
Manager: LES RIGBY		Manager: ROY CHAPMAN

OFFICIAL PROGRAMME — 5p

En-route to Wembley in 1973

Realising that their annual application to the Football League would probably meet with a similar fate to its predecessors, the club caused a sensation by applying (with South Shields) for election to the Second Division of the Scottish League. Needless to say the Scottish Management Committee rejected both clubs applications. The Latics had once again grabbed the headlines, but it certainly did them no good at the Football League AGM as they polled no votes whatsoever as Hereford United replaced Barrow in the Fourth Division.

During the course of that 1971-72 season, Gordon Milne's talents as a manager had been recognised, for he had been appointed England Youth team manager, and it only seemed a matter of time before a Football League team demanded his managerial services. First Division Coventry City were the club to snap him up and he left Springfield Park to join the Highfield Road club under the General Managership of Joe Mercer. The years under Gordon Milne's direction had been amongst Wigan Athletic's most successful - it was a pity that all his hard work did not bring the club entry into the Football League.

Milne's successor was Les Rigby, a Physical Education Lecturer at Wigan Technical College. His track record was quite impressive, for he had managed one of the Cheshire League's top sides, Rossendale United, but unfortunately, he struggled to keep Milne's successful side together. Geoff Davies went to Chester, Bobby Todd to Scarborough and Jim Fleming back to Scotland, whilst Derek Temple retired.

Replacements were found from Bangor City with centre-half Albert Jackson and centre-forward Tony Marsden joining the Latics, whilst Chorley provided

Micky Worswick, Netherfield, Mickey Taylor and Oldham Athletic, Paul Clements, a former England amateur international.

The newcomers at Springfield Park fitted in well and the club finished the 1972-73 season in the Northern Premier League in third place. In the FA Cup, the club were defeated at Grimsby 2-1 with Graham Oates scoring Latics goal from the penalty spot. The season is best remembered as Wigan's Wembley season and it was a fantastic run in the FA Challenge Trophy that earned them a well- deserved place in the final.

Burton Albion were the first to taste the Latics magic. Micky Worswick with a hat-trick and goals from Clements and Fletcher combined to crush the visitors 5-0. South Liverpool were no match in the second round going down 2-0 with Oates and Worswick the scorers. Romford followed by the same scoreline in round three, whilst the fourth round tie against Morecambe saw 300 minutes of football played before the tie was resolved. Latics were held to a goalless draw at Springfield Park and then drew 1-1 at Morecambe before a goal from Graham Oates, the seasons top scorer in the second replay at Ewood Park, took the Latics through to the semi-final.

The semi-final produced another replay. Latics met Stafford Rangers at Vale Park but neither team could find the net and the tie ended goalless. The replay at Oldham's Boundary Park seemed to be heading the same way until Oates broke the deadlock to give Wigan a one goal victory.

Once again the familiar sight of the blue and white army was to be seen, as thousands of Wigan supporters converged on the twin towers of Wembley. Several special trips were arranged and it was a fantastic and unforgettable experience for the 24,000 spectators. The atmosphere at Wembley was electric, even though the stadium was only a quarter full.

That day the teams lined up as follows:
Scarborough: Garrow; Appleton, Shoulder, Dunn, Siddle, Fagan, Donoghue, Franks, Leask, Thompson, Hewitt, Sub: Barmby:
Wigan Ath: Reeves; Morris, Sutherland, Taylor, Jackson, Gillibrand, Clements, Oates, Rogers, King, Worswick: Sub: McCunnell

It had been a long season with over sixty games played and it showed in Latics performance. Just 11 minutes into the game Scarborough scored through Leask.

Action from the 1973 F.A. Trophy Final.

The Yorksire team defended stoutly but Wigan deserved their equaliser, although they almost left it too late. John Rogers' shot from 20 yards somehow found its way through half a dozen players and then between the goalkeeper's legs - just 15 seconds from time! The game went into extra-time, but four minutes from the final whistle, Thompson hit Scarborough's second goal. There were no last minute comebacks and so Latics finished with losers' medals.

In March 1974, Latics lost manager Les Rigby when he resigned due to the Wigan Board insisting on a full-time manager to run the club, and Les didn't want to leave his Physical Education job at Wigan Technical College. Kenny Banks took over as caretaker-manager until the season's end, and saw the team lift the Lancashire Challenge Trophy against Skelmersdale United 4-1 at Southport's Haig Avenue ground. In the Northern Premier League, the Latics finished second as Boston United won their last game of the season to pip them for the League title by one point. Les Rigby was eventually replaced by Brian Tiler, the former Rotherham United and Aston Villa player, and under his guidance the Club continued to dominate the non-League competition.

In 1974-75, the Latics won the Northern Premier League for a second time, gaining a record number of points in doing so (72). The final match of that season was against old rivals Scarborough and Latics gained revenge for their Wembley defeat, beating them 2-0 to clinch the League title from runners-up Runcorn. There were some wonderful scenes at Springfield Park that Monday night. John King collected the trophy and displayed it to the crowd and the players pulled off their shirts and threw them to the hoards of waiting Latic fans.

The club's 1974-75 playing record was:

P.	W.	D.	L.	F.	A.	Pts.
46	33	6	7	94	38	72

The club also did their traditional giant-killing act in the FA Cup, disposing of Shrewsbury Town. A goal from King at Gay Meadow brought the Third Division club to Springfield Park for a replay where goals from Albert Jackson and Tommy Gore were enough to see the visitors out of the Cup. Gore's goal was from fully 35 yards.

The following round saw Latics at home to Mansfield Town. Again they held the Third Division team to a 1-1 draw in front of a crowd of 15,560, but Mansfield were too strong at home and won the replay 3-1. The only disappointment that season came in the FA Trophy when the Latics lost at home to Bedford, who were on paper probably the weakest side left in the competition!

In February of the following season, 1975-76, manager Brian Tiler left the club for America and Portland Timbers. For a month the club were managerless, then in April 1976, Ian McNeill returned to Springfield Park. That season was not a happy one for Wigan as they finished the campaign in 6th place, the first time they had ever finished outside the top three in the history of the Northern Premier League. Attendances plunged and only 730 watched the goalless draw at home to Great Harwood. The Latics did reach the final of the Lancashire Challenge Trophy only to lose 2-1 to a last minute goal against Chorley. After beating Matlock Town 2-1 in the first round of the FA Cup, the Latics travelled to Hillsborough but went down 2-0 to a strong Sheffield Wednesday side. However, there was general unrest within the Club and the team was suffering.

By the beginning of the 1976-77 season, the Club were £100,000 in debt and McNeill was forced to make a mass clearout of players whilst others were seeking transfers. The difficulties mounted as results on the field grew more and more disappointing, and at one stage the Latics languished at the very foot of the table. Matlock, who Latics had defeated in the previous season's FA Cup, did the double over them in the League and knocked them out of the FA Cup. The great giant-killers were humbled 2-0. Attendances at Springfield Park slumped even further and for the 3-0 win over Gainsborough Trinity, only 647 loyal supporters paid through the turnstiles. As financial difficulties began to increase, Director Graham Gorner resigned, as did Chairman Ken Cowap.

Ken Cowap

History it seemed was repeating itself. A cash appeal was made to supporters. Wigan Athletic seemed doomed to follow in the path of Wigan Borough, Wigan United, Wigan Town and Wigan County. Until the arrival of the new Chairman that was. Arthur Horrocks, who had resigned as Wigan chairman in 1972 to take over as chairman of Fourth Division Southport returned to his first love Springfield Park. The earlier argument between Horrocks and McNeill was discussed then truly forgotten as the two men set about rebuilding the club.

A new optimism filled Springfield Park, the team spirit returned, and performances and results began to improve. The team finished 14th in that season of 1976-77, a very creditable performance given the disastrous beginnings. They also won the Lancashire Junior Cup, beating Chorley 1-0 at Victory Park with Joe Hinnigan scoring the winner. Latics last match of the season saw them beat South Liverpool 3-0, but the match had to be switched to Runcorn as the BBC were doing 'It's a Knockout' final on the South Liverpool ground !

The club received some good news in that the FA were willing to lift a ban which had been placed on the Club applying for membership of the Football League. The ban was based on financial considerations with the League applying a 'vetting' system on potential applicants. The Club could not, however, apply that season due to the new Northern Premier League agreement which stated that only the champions would be nominated for Football League membership.

Also interesting that year was the Club's application to build a greyhound track at Springfield Park in an attempt to alleviate financial problems. The idea was rejected however, and the original condition remained in the early bill of sale for Springfield Park, that the only whippets on the field would be fast wingers!

Yet despite the club's remaining financial difficulties and the relatively unimpressive season, the air of optimism about the Club remained. Director Jack Farrimond, who had been connected with Wigan Athletic Football Club since 1932 when he was the club's first secretary, had always forecasted that promotion to the Football League would come when the club least expected it, although few, if any, would have predicted that exactly twelve months after finishing their worst ever season, the Latics would find themselves in League Division Four. Besides finishing in their lowest ever position, the Latics had also been knocked out of the FA Cup in an early qualifying round and had been beaten in the FA Challenge Trophy 3-2 by Wimbledon at Plough Lane. Wimbledon went on to gain election to the League, and in those days it was generally considered an impossibility for the FA to admit new clubs in consecutive seasons.

There were many in the town and connected with the club who believed that the stigma of Wigan Borough's past would never leave the Club. It was thus ironic that following the 'certainties' of 1954 and 1971, Wigan Athletic should be admitted to the Football League when the odds on them doing so were at there longest for many years.

In the close season of 1977, the popular Maurice Whittle became available on a free transfer from Oldham Athletic. Whittle had signed a contract with North American club Fort Lauderdale but was not due to honour it until February 1978. A shrewd move by manager McNeill brought the man back to his home town and Whittle made an immediate impact on the strength of the Wigan team when he eventually signed in October 1977. His steadiness and class in the middle of the park gave the Latics a new and unbeatable confidence that was reflected in an unbeaten run which stretched from early October 1977 to January 1978.

Given the Northern Premier League's new policy of 'winners only need apply', a successful League season was the key to the door of the Football League. Although the League provided the technicalities and qualifications for entry, it was the FA Cup which again brought Wigan Athletic to the notice of the general public and it was without doubt, their fine run to the third round that clinched the successful nomination. The run began with a 3-0 victory at Liverpool club Marine in the fourth qualifying round. Going into the hat for the first round proper, Latics drew Fourth Division strugglers York City at Springfield Park.

A crowd of 6,289 saw the Latics play their opponents into the ground. Though the victory margin was only 1-0 with Wilkie scoring the goal, the Minstermen left Springfield Park very much aware that they had been let off a humiliating defeat.

The Latics reward was a second round home tie against Sheffield Wednesday who were then a Third Division club and managed by the former Republic of Ireland team manager Jack Charlton. After Wednesday had spent the first half-an-hour on all-out attack, Wigan had the ball in the net courtesy of Micky Moore, but it was disallowed for offside. Latics began to control the game from midfield and went ahead when Maurice Whittle fired home a free-kick after Worswick had been hacked down on the edge of the box. The Owls went all-out for an equaliser and in injury time, Ridger Wylde headed home what looked like the equalising goal, but fortunately for the Latics, the linesman's flag shot up for offside - the Latics were in round three.

The most famous of English managers, Sir Alf Ramsey, was in charge of Birmingham City, whom the Latics visited in the third round of the FA Cup, in what was arguably the most important game ever played in the history of the club. Though beaten 4-0, Wigan left the field to tumultuous applause. Their football attracted the attention of Sir Alf Ramsey, who visited the dressing-room after the match to congratulate the team.

Exciting days at Springfield Park again

Within a few weeks of the Birmingham City match, Micky Moore signed for Port Vale for a fee of £4,000 and Maurice Whittle flew off to keep his appointment with Fort Lauderdale Strikers in the NASL. Replacements were found in Frank Corrigan, signed from Northwich Victoria, and Peter Houghton who was snapped up from South Liverpool. Meanwhile the 1977-78 season drew to its climax, and Boston United's lead at the top of the table, had at one time looked unassailable. But even if the Lincolnshire side had won the title with a 100% record, they could not have applied for Football League status, for the Football League Management Committee decided that their ground was not up to the required standards.

The Northern Premier League reached a decision and that was the club finishing second in the competition would get, as a consolation prize, a crack at applying for Football League status. The decision gave the Latics everything to fight for. The battle was between three clubs - Bangor City, Scarborough and Wigan Athletic. The Welsh club had the wind taken out of the sails, when it was discovered that their ground, like that of Boston United, did not meet the Football League's requirements and neither did Scarborough's! Scarborough, however, were certain to appeal against the League's decision and in fact, were strongly tipped to win it.

The last few matches of the 1977-78 season arrived and still the runners-up place was undecided. Latics had to beat Bangor City at Springfield Park to put Scarborough out of the running. With 85 minutes gone, the Latics were a goal down and all hopes of finishing in second place seemed to have disappeared. Then new boy Frank Corrigan equalised and with almost the last kick of the game, John Wilkie added a second to make it 2-1 to the Latics. Scarborough's fate was sealed - the result put the Yorkshire club out of the race.

Wigan were, however, still uncertain of the prize, for it now all rested on their last game of the season at Matlock. Bangor City's last match took them to East Lancashire and a match against Great Harwood. An easy victory was predicted for the Welsh side, so in theory it was all down to the Latics.

The Wigan team came through in fine style, Peter Houghton scoring the only goal of the game in what was to be the club's last Northern Premier League match. Meanwhile, poor Bangor City received a 7-2 thrashing from underdogs Great Harwood. Ironically, this proved to be Great Harwood's last ever game as they unfortunately folded during the close season.

The final League positions at the end of that 1977-78 season were as follows:

	P.	Pts.
1. Boston United	46	71
2. Wigan Athletic	46	65
3. Bangor City	46	62
4. Scarborough	46	62

It was a close finish, but Wigan's second place was enough to earn them the Northern Premier League's nomination.

It seemed just a matter of formality that the Latics would apply once again for Football League status and for the 35th time would be rejected. The Wigan Board however, were not defeatist. They and their manager Ian McNeill visited each one of the 44 clubs entitled to vote - all the First and Second Division clubs - using what was later called 'the personal touch' to canvas support for the Latics.

A well-produced straightforward brochure was circulated, informing all of Latics claim for League status. All the representatives of the English Football League met at the Cafe Royal in London on 2 June 1978.

The Football League at last! (Left) the first game, and (right) the first home match

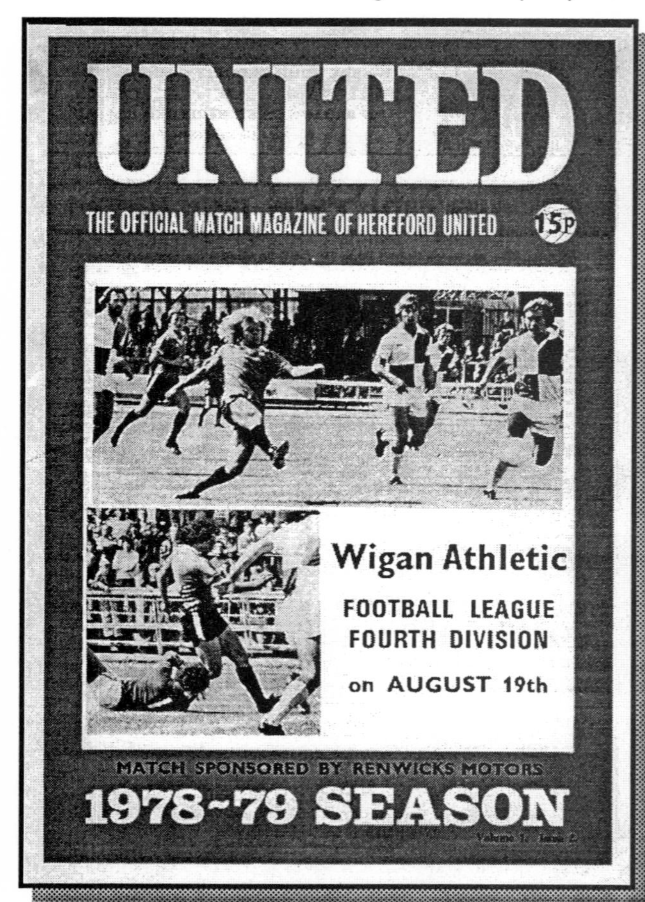

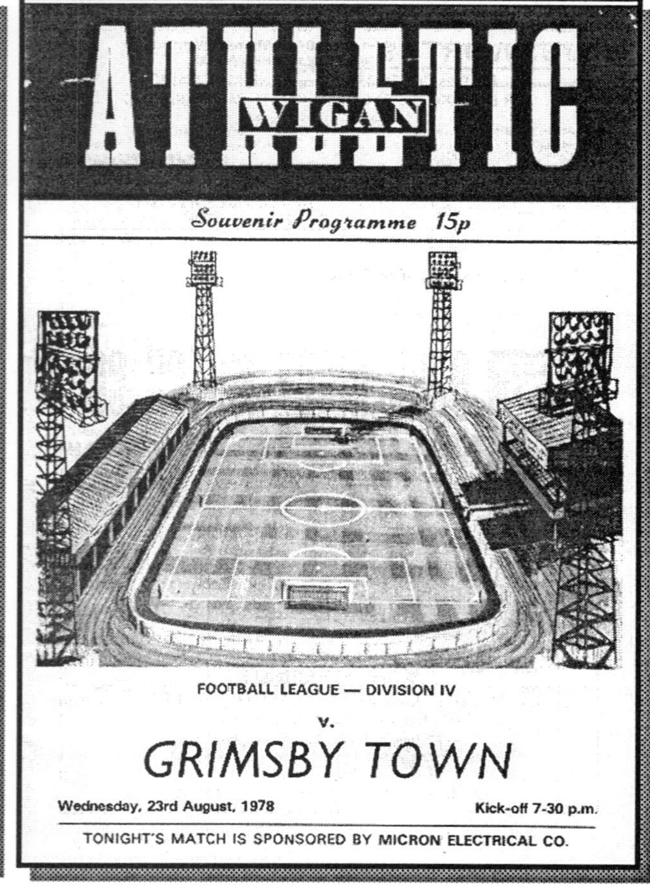

Neil Davids, injured and substituted at Reading

The first poll gave York City 49 votes (re-elected), Rochdale 39 votes (re-elected) and Hartlepool United 33 votes (re-elected). Southport and Wigan Athletic tied on 26 votes, whilst the Southern League's representatives, Bath City polled 23 votes.

The re-vote resulted in Wigan being elected by 29 votes to 20, so after 34 disappointments, Wigan Athletic were at last elected to the Football League. The club's representatives at the meeting, namely Arthur Horrocks, Jack Farrimond and Ian McNeill immediately returned to Springfield Park to be greeted by numerous jubilant supporters. Now the club were in the League, there was much to do and it had to be done within the space of two months.

Ground improvements were carried out by staff and numerous volunteers to whom the club were forever grateful, and manager Ian McNeill had the responsibility of producing a team to at least keep their heads above water in the Fourth Division.

For 91 Football League clubs, Saturday 19 August 1978 was merely another season's kick-off day. For Wigan Athletic it was the beginning of an era. No other club in the League could possibly have looked forward for so long to that day - after 34 unsuccessful applications and 34 disappointments, the great quest had been achieved.

The town of Wigan buzzed with excitement on that Saturday morning. Outside the gas showrooms, the traditional coach departure point, the Latics supporters gathered, each one well aware that history was being made. It seemed that everyone was going to Hereford by coach, car, train or transit. Over three thousand Wigan fans made that historic journey and the roar that greeted the team as captain Ian Gillibrand proudly led them on to the Edgar Street ground could have been heard in Wigan - the Latics were in the League!

Determined to prove their League status, the Latics swarmed all over the opposition and had the ball in the net in the 18th minute courtesy of Peter Houghton, only for the referee to disallow it for offside. Hughes, the Hereford 'keeper, made a fine point blank save from Wilkie and then beat Corrigan in a race to a fine through ball by Gore. In the final minute, Jeff Wright nearly snatched a winner for Latics with a long range shot which Hughes only just got his fingers to. Latics had made an impressive League debut, and the fans travelled home happy with the point, some of them making a party of it and not arriving back until Sunday lunch-time!

Latics first home game in the League saw Grimsby Town visit Springfield Park, with very few people giving odds on the Mariners returning home with even a point after losing their opening game. There were 9,227 spectators in the ground for the game, many of them there out of curiosity. The Springfield Park ground was littered with the scarves of a number of the surrounding teams, with the cherry and white of Wigan Rugby League team being predominant. Unfortunately the Latics were destroyed, beaten 3-0 by an experienced Grimsby team who punished the League's new boys with a series of organised attacks.

Latics first substitute in the Football League was Alan Crompton who came on for Neil Davids in the second-half of Latics third game of the season at Reading, which the Elm Park side won 2-0. The Latics first goalscoring substitute was Derek Brownbill who scored the fourth goal in the club's remarkable 5-3 win over Port Vale on Good Friday 1979. Latics first goal in League football came in their fourth game at home to Newport County and was scored by Joe Hinnigan after 331 minutes of League football unfortunately Latics lost 3-2. The club had to wait until their sixth match for their first League win, a 3-0 victory over Rochdale at Springfield Park.

In October 1978, Zambia became the first national team to play at Springfield Park. Coached by Brian Tiler who managed the Latics' Northern Premier League Championship side of 1975, they had just been eliminated from the World Cup Finals that year in a threeway play-off. They had beaten Algeria, Kenya, Morocco, Nigeria and Zaire - but they could not beat the Latics who won 2-1. On 17 February 1979 the match against Huddersfield Town at Springfield Park was the only English game played north of Leicester. The League's new boys turned out to be the area's lone football flag-bearers on what was an ice-age weekend. Conditions were by no means perfect, but 7,420 fans had a match to go to, as the Latics began the push for promotion.

Wigan boss Ian McNeill's recipe for beating the freeze was simple - about £150 of straw, plastic sheeting, some hot air on the worst ice-hit sections of Springfield Park and voluntary sweat and toil from a willing band of supporters. Despite the slippery surface, Wigan played some superbly controlled football at times to win the game 2-1, with skipper Noel Ward scoring both goals. By the Easter weekend, the promotion race was becoming a sprint. The question now was could Latics keep up the challenge and continue with the recent form that had made them the League's most consistent team? Easter was the crunch period, for three games over four days would surely answer the promotion question one way or another. Latics were in fourth place on goal difference, although Barnsley and Wimbledon were just behind them with four games in hand.

For 65 minutes in the match against Port Vale, Wigan played some atrocious football and were 3-0 down, and their last chances of promotion seemed to have slipped away. Then the unbelievable happened, Latics scored five goals in 19 minutes with Peter Houghton notching the club's first hat-trick in League football. By the time Latics played their last home game of the season, against Darlington, promotion should have been sewn up. After the most appalling start to the season, Wigan had become the most consistent team in the League, and at one stage even bettering Liverpool's record. Discounting the first five disastrous games and calculating the League form from mid-September, this record put Wigan four points clear at the top. Could anybody have really asked for more?

The League programme was however, still incomplete and while it looked exceedingly unlikely that promotion could still be achieved, the old adage of 'never over 'til the last games played', still rang true. The players themselves had certainly not given up. Success in the remaining four games could still give a season's total of 59 points - one above the target set by manager Ian McNeill.

Darlington came to Springfield Park deep in the mire of re-election worry, and after Gore had given the Latics a 17th minute lead, everyone expected that to be a signal for a Wigan charge, but Darlington had other ideas and clung on for a 2-2 draw. Latics then beat Scunthorpe United 1-0 at the Old Show Ground before losing 2-1 at Bournemouth. Wigan Athletic must have been one of the best supported teams in the Division, for even with nothing to play for, a good thousand supporters made the trip across the Pennines to Bradford City for the last match of the 1978-79 season. Micky Moore scored for Latics in the first minute, but if anyone thought this was going to be a memorable match then such thoughts were quickly dispelled as Bradford equalised and took control of the first-half. The second-half degenerated into a scrappy ending with both teams failing to add to their first-half goals.

After waiting so long for League football it had been a memorable season with Latics finishing in 6th position, only six points behind a promotion place.

The top of the League table read as follows:

	P.	W.	D.	L.	F.	A.	Pts.
Reading	46	26	13	7	76	35	65
Grimsby Town	46	26	9	11	82	49	61
Wimbledon	46	25	11	10	78	46	61
Barnsley	46	24	13	9	73	42	61
Aldershot	46	20	17	9	63	47	57
Wigan Athletic	46	21	13	12	63	48	55

In the season's Cup competitions, Latics had a dream start in the Football League Cup, holding Third Division Tranmere Rovers to a 1-1 draw at Prenton Park with Tommy Gore scoring Latics goal from fully 35 yards in the last minute of the game. Also in that game, Neil Davids became the first ever Wigan Football League player to receive a booking, but both Houghton and Corrigan were later joined cautioned. In the second leg at Springfield Park, two goals from Frank Corrigan gave Latics a 2-1 win and a place in round two away to Luton Town, where Latics played well but fell to two Brian Stein goals. In the FA Cup, Latics drew Bury at Springfield Park and were 2-0 down with just 28 minutes remaining. Gore pulled one back before Brownbill set up Houghton for the equaliser. The replay at Gigg Lane was all one-way traffic as Latics lost 4-1. On a bitterly cold night, the Latics players even struggled to keep their feet in the pre-match warm up!

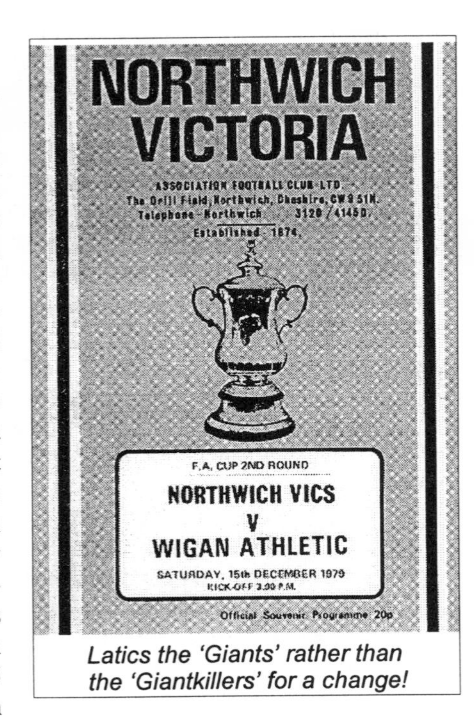

Latics the 'Giants' rather than the 'Giantkillers' for a change!

In 1979-80, early season injuries which included centre-half Noel Ward breaking his leg in the home defeat by Portsmouth, accounted for Latics poor start. However, on 29 September 1979, Latics signed Colin Methven from East Fife, and if ever £30,000 constituted a bargain, then the fee paid was surely the case. He made his full League debut for Latics against Doncaster Rovers at Belle Vue in October 1979 and went on to appear in 296 first team games, never missing a game at competitive level through injury.

Also that season, Methven became the first Latics player to be sent off in a Football League match. He was dismissed after fouling Bradford City's Don Hutchins after 70 minutes of Latics 2-1 defeat at the Valley Parade on 16 February 1980. After losing 3-2 at Newport County on 27 October 1979, the Latics went 12 League games without defeat before losing in that match in Bradford.

Joe Hinnigan was transferred to Sunderland that month, for a then record fee of £135,000. A 17-year-old named Mick Quinn broke into the Latics first team in April and scored on his debut against Halifax Town as Wigan won 3-1. During February it was announced that millionaire scrap dealer Freddie Pye and former England World Cup star Bobby Charlton were to join the Wigan Athletic Board of Directors. The move followed discussions between the flamboyant Pye, the new major shareholder in the club, and the Latics Chairman, Arthur Horrocks.

Despite their poor start to the season, the Latics bounced back to eventually finish 6th, the same position as in 1978-79. In fact, the statistics from the club's opening two League campaigns are interesting. The final figures are almost identical and as can be seen - though the number of goals scored and conceded are different - the goal difference of +15 remained the same.

	P.	W.	D.	L.	F.	A.	Pts.
1978-79	46	21	13	12	63	48	55
1979-80	46	21	13	12	76	61	55

Having lost 2-1 to Stockport County over two legs in the League Cup, the FA Cup brought the Latics memorable success. They reached the fourth round for the first time in their history thanks to victories over Blackpool (the replay at Springfield Park bringing Wigan their biggest crowd of the season, 14,589), Northwich Victoria and Chelsea (where a Tommy Gore goal won the day), to draw mighty Everton at Goodison Park.

Martin Hodge foils Everton 'keeper Corrigan in the FA Cup-tie.

Well over 100 coaches, trains and cars made the short trip and the attendance of 51,863 was the best of the day. This number was only bettered once throughout the whole season at Goodison, and that for the Mersey derby against Liverpool.

There had been a massive build-up and the match was tel-evised. The Latics gave as good as they got until the First Division side's greater class and exper-ience began to tell. Goals from McBride, Latchford and Kidd, who was later sent off, gave Everton a 3-0 win.

Nationally acclaimed as one of the 'giant-killers' of the country, no such name was in evidence during the 1980-81 season of Cup football. Latics went out of the League Cup in the second round, having won the home first round leg against Crewe Alexandra 2-1 and completing the tie with a 2-2 draw at Gresty Road, but only to lose 2-1 against Preston North End at Springfield Park after going down 1-0 at Deepdale in the first leg.

The FA Cup proved to be even worse with a 2-2 draw at home to Chesterfield, before the Saltergate club put paid to Latics chances by 2-0. During that season, Colin Methven was the club's only ever-present and it was he who was voted the club's Player of the Year.

The leading scorer was Mick Quinn who bagged 14 League goals and always impressed. He continued to be a prolific scorer throughout his long career, therefore it was quite surprising that he was allowed to join Stockport County on a free transfer.

When Latics entertained Bury on 20 September 1980, a goal in each half was enough to give them victory in front of Granada's television cameras as well as the Fourth Division's biggest crowd. Playing in goal for Bury was a certain Neville Southall who had opted for the Shakers instead of Wigan. The Latics later slammed Granada TV for comments made by presenter Elton Welsby about having to televise Fourth Division games and with regard to the quality of the performance.

In February 1981, manager Ian McNeill paid the price for a series of poor results when he was sacked following a 3-0 reverse at lowly Port Vale. Two of the club's directors, Graham Gorner and Brian Connolly, resigned over the sacking. Reserve team coach Fred Eyre took over as caretaker-manager (two games unbeaten - Mansfield Town, Home 2-0 and Bury, Away 0-0), before Larry Lloyd took over as player-manager in March. Despite these events, with one of the strongest squads Latics have ever had, they finished 11th in the Fourth Division, and continued to receive praise from all corners of the country for the way they had become a force in their short Football League history.

Larry Lloyd's new team started off by playing a remarkable nine pre-season friendlies before the 1981-82 campaign got underway. Hot-shot Micky Quinn scored 13 goals in these matches and was at that time valued at £500,000 by manager Lloyd. The 1981-82 season was one to remember as under the guidance of the manager, Latics achieved their first ambition - promotion to Division Three of the Football League.

The first game of the season saw the mighty Sheffield United visit Springfield Park with a large following from Bramall Lane adding to the excellent 8,001 crowd. Latics lost 1-0, however, that was to be their only home defeat of a superb season. One of the highlights was the return fixture at Bramall Lane, which attracted a massive crowd for the Fourth Division of 22,326.

Latics players celebrate after beating Chelsea in the 1981/82 League Cup.

However, the evening was soured, for Latics that is, with Keith Edwards scoring the winner for the Blades a minute from time. Latics largest attendance of the season at Springfield Park was to follow four games later for the visit of Blackpool. A crowd of 9,439 saw Latics win 2-1 with both goals scored by Les Bradd. The climax of the season however were the scenes of jubilation which saw Wigan beat Mansfield Town 3-0 with an Eamonn O'Keefe hat-trick, sending the 8,517 Latics fans wild with delight with promotion to the Third Division secured.

That season, as with all campaigns, was a hard slog from start to finish. The club's best run of games without defeat in the Football League is 21 and was established during this period. The run began on 25 October 1981 as Latics beat Scunthorpe United 2-1 at Springfield Park, and finished with a victory in the return fixture on 12 March 1982, as Latics thrashed the Irons 7-2 - the most goals the club has scored in a Football League fixture. The season also saw the club establish their best defensive record, for they only conceded 46 goals and were beaten in only seven matches. In the League Cup, Latics excelled going through to the fourth round. After victories over Stockport County and Aldershot, the Latics beat Chelsea 4-2 with goals from Wignall 2, Evans and Bradd. Facing a strong Aston Villa side at Springfield Park, the Latics lost 2-1 with Peter Withe scoring the winner, following a Colin Methven mistake.

Another award at the end of the 1981/82 season was that of 'Fourth Division Programme Of The Year'
The successful team: Larry Lloyd, Lynda Filligan (Junior Latics), Bill Hadley (Publicity Print Services), Helen Turner (Editor), Jimmy Hoy (Supp. Club), Colin Burke (Secretary), David Roberts (Commercial) and Jack Farrimond (Vice Pres.)

The FA Cup proved to be a disappointment, as in the previous season, with a first round exit after a replay at Hartlepool United. But all this paled into insignificance with promotion to the Third Division when Larry Lloyd was hailed a hero !

7 September 1981 saw the first meeting of the Junior Latics. It was a very special occasion with almost 300 children and parents packed into the Wigan Athletic Supporters Club. The guest list was like a Who's Who of Wigan Athletic Football Club, with Junior Latic's President Bobby Charlton, manager Larry Lloyd, Club Chairman Freddie Pye, Captain Colin Methven, members of the Board of Directors and members of the playing staff.

Scottish International Archie Gemmill made 13 appearances for Latics during the season.

Peter Houghton scores one of his record 64 League goals versus Brentford in the Latics first home game in the Third Division.

In a very disappointing first season in the Third Division, the Latics started off with the customary away fixture and defeat, as they lost 2-1 at Sincil Bank against Lincoln City. It was to be a mediocre campaign during which Latics lost 5-0 at Bristol Rovers, their record League defeat. Though they ended in 18th place, this did not deter the supporters of Wigan Athletic, as the final home attendance against neighbours Preston North End attracted 7,191 spectators.

Larry Lloyd in action against Southend United

Latics record signing Eamonn O'Keefe, was the club's leading goalscorer with 16 goals, of which 5 came from the penalty spot. It was interesting in this season of 1982-83 to see the likes of David Lowe, who was an apprentice player at the time, and also Steve Walsh who was an able debutant to the injured boss Larry Lloyd, both beginning to come through the ranks. Player-manager Lloyd was axed in April following a 2-0 defeat against Walsall, the club's fourth consecutive reversal; Bobby Charlton took over as caretaker-manager.

In fact, financial problems nearly caused the club to fold. Apparently Latics had run up an overdraft of £250,000 in gaining promotion. It was a season in which Latics Lifeline was launched in an attempt to raise money for the club.

Steve Johnson Joint leading goalscorer in the 1984/85 season.

Latics Cup exploits were to elude them this season with a second round exit at the hands of Manchester City in the League Cup after Stockport County had been defeated in round one, and the humilation of a first round defeat in the FA Cup by non-League Telford United which required a replay.

Under the threat of bankruptcy at the start of the 1983-84 season, the Latics improved their League position on the previous one, to finish 15th in the Third Division, as manager Harry McNally and a new Board got the ship back on an even keel. Brian Heathcote became the fourth Club Chairman in as many months following Pye, Muir and Barrington.

Relegation threatened briefly around Christmas, but for most of the season Wigan coasted in mid-table. Among those who lost to the Latics were Wimbledon and Sheffield United, beaten 3-2 and 3-0 respectively, as the Latics ran the show.

The local derby against Bolton Wanderers attracted 10,045 spectators to Springfield Park. It was Wigan's largest crowd of the season, but the Wanderers hung on for a 1-0 victory. A shortage of goals, in fact the worst in the Division, was a major problem although the £20,000 signing from Rochdale of Steve Johnson made a big impact.

Proven goalscorers Peter Houghton and Steve Taylor left for Preston North End and Stockport County respectively, whilst youngsters Tony Kelly and Mike Newell came on the scene.

Latics worst defeat this season was a 6-2 thrashing at Bradford City, and unfortunately their Cup exploits also proved to be uneventful as Latics lost to Bury in the first round of the Milk Cup but reached the third round of the FA Cup competition. After a goalless draw away, Bradford City were defeated 4-2 in the first round replay, then Whitby Town were beaten 1-0 at Springfield Park in the second round, before Wigan were drawn to play at First Division West Ham United. With a crowd of 16,000 looking on, Wigan went down to the only goal of the game, scored by Ray Stewart from the penalty spot.

Prior to the start of the 1984-85 season, Latics won the Lancashire Manx Cup, beating Blackburn Rovers 2-1 in the final at Springfield Park with goals from Barrow and Methven. Latics opening game of the season saw their usual first day defeat at Bristol City, before they recorded their first League victory in their next match by a single goal victory over Bradford City.

With such names as Newell, Kelly and Butler in the line-up, and with Paul Beesley and Paul Cook just beginning to break through into the first team, Wigan were beginning to look a formidable team. Bolton Wanderers produced the highest gate of the season with 8,871 watching the game at Springfield Park on Boxing Day. The Latics took the points thanks to an own goal from Bolton's Irish international centre-half, Gerry McElhinney.

The two major Cup competitions produced no real surprises. In the League Cup, Latics beat Wrexham 5-0 on aggregate in the first round before losing to then First Division side West Bromwich Albion. The Latics were held to a goalless draw at Springfield Park before going down 3-1 at the Hawthorns.

In the FA Cup, Latics started well, winning 2-0 at Wrexham in the first round to set up a second round tie against non-League Northwich Victoria at Springfield Park, a game Latics won 2-1. The third round almost produced one of the shocks of the season's competition. Latics visited Stamford Bridge, home of First Division Chelsea, on a Saturday that left a lot to be desired weather-wise, in a freezing sub-zero temperature in January. The Latics produced a magnificent performance to draw 2-2 with goals from Paul Jewell and Mike Newell, but then went down 5-0 at Springfield Park in the replay.

Tony Kelly scores from the 'spot' in the 3-3 home draw versus Cambridge United. (1984-85)

Mike Newell scores in the FA Cup-tie at Stamford Bridge.

Following a nine match League run without a win, manager Harry McNally resigned in March 1985 after being asked to let his assistant Roy Tunks and coach Alex Bruce take charge for a while. Steve Johnson, who ended the season as Latics leading scorer in the League left for Bristol City for £30,000 before new manager Bryan Hamilton took over. Results immediately began to improve and the season ended on a high note with Latics winning the Freight Rover Trophy at Wembley on a memorable day in June, beating Brentford 3-1.

The 1985-86 season started on an unusual high as Latics actually won their first game of the new season, 1-0 at Swansea with Graham Barrow scoring the goal. Following this, came impressive home wins over Brentford(4-0) and Darlington(5-1) to put the Latics third in a League that contained large clubs such as Derby County and Wolverhampton Wanderers.

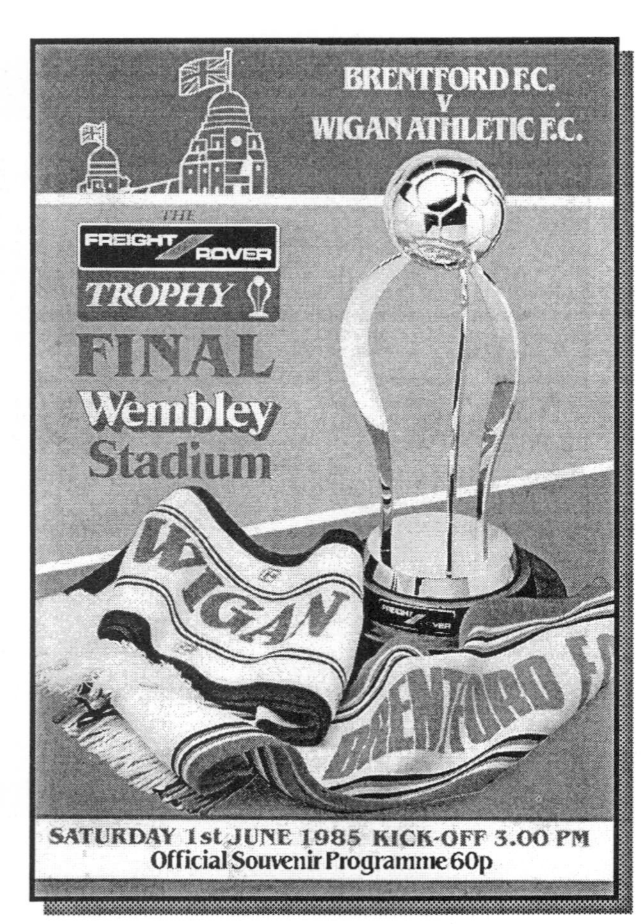

By mid-December, Latics were the only unbeaten home side in Division Three. However, their away form left a lot to be desired. Their only away points had come from that win at Swansea on the opening day of the season - and it ironically looked as if it would be expunged following the Swans likely sad demise - and four drawn games.

With the boardroom wrangling taking the limelight away from the football, a new Chairman, a certain Bill Kenyon announced that Wigan Athletic were having serious financial difficulties and that something urgently needed to be done. That certain something was the sale of players in an attempt to balance the books. The first player to leave was Mike Newell in early January, who signed for Luton Town for £85,000, that money being swallowed up by Latics' huge debts. Newell's replacement was young Warren Aspinall, who scored five times in just three games in January and ended the campaign as the club's record League goalscorer in a season. It therefore came as no surprise that Everton made a bid for Aspinall that would net Wigan somewhere in the region of £300,000. This bid was accepted, but on signing for the Goodison Park club, Aspinall was loaned back immediately to Latics for the remainder of the season. In April, Tony Kelly went to Stoke City.

What the Latics would have done for an unbeaten home record of 25 games, a record that was finally dented by derby rivals Bolton Wanderers who inflicted a 3-1 defeat on Latics on 29 March 1986. During the first League meeting between the clubs on New Years Day, one of the strangest sendings-off occurred, and it was Bolton midfielder Steve Thompson who suffered. The referee Ken Walmsley of Blackpool later admitted that when he sent Thompson off, he thought he had already booked him, but in fact it was Graham Barrow the Wigan number eight who had previously been cautioned!

On 15 April, Latics were desperately unlucky not to get three points at Walsall. Winning 3-2 with just minutes to go, the Saddlers nicked an injury time equaliser to keep Latics in fourth position.

Then came Plymouth Argyle, who had won nine games on the trot and from a mid-table position found themselves in third position after this great run. Latics ran out comfortable 3-0 winners. However, indifferent end of season form meant that Plymouth, Derby County and Reading were promoted. Honours had looked likely in the season for Bryan Hamilton's talented side, but as Latics lost against Bolton Wanderers in the Northern Area Final of the Freight Rover Trophy, they heard the same night that Derby County had won and so pipped them by a point for promotion to Division Two.

The club's Milk Cup hopes ended in round one with a 3-2 aggregate defeat by Port Vale. In the FA Cup, Wigan defeated Doncaster Rovers 4-1 in the first round and then came from behind to earn a 1-1 draw at Runcorn before winning the replay 4-0. In the third round Latics beat Bournemouth 3-0 before losing by the same scoreline to First Division Southampton at The Dell.

Prior to the start of the 1986-87 season, Latics were involved in the Isle of Man Festival. Playing in Group 'B', the Latics finished top of the group to qualify for the final where they beat Portsmouth 1-0 after extra-time with David Lowe grabbing the all-important goal.

1988: Latics visit Wembley again - for the Mercantile Credit Festival.

New manager Ray Mathias had an unenviable job following former manager Bryan Hamilton's departure to Leicester City, who took with him Steve Walsh. Kevin Langley went to Everton, Graham Barrow and Billy Stewart both went to Chester, and Colin Methven departed to Blackpool.

The club made wonderful progress after an incredibly bad start, when the first four League games were lost, for the shrewd signings of Bobby Campbell and Andy Holden soon transformed matters. Following the near miss of promotion the previous season, Latics were to be the nearly men yet again, finishing fourth and winning a record 10 League games away from Springfield Park.

This season saw the introduction of the play-offs, where Latics were paired against Swindon Town in the semi-final. After leading 2-0 inside the first fifteen minutes, with goals from Chris Thompson and David Lowe, suicidal defending allowed Swindon to score three goals in the last 18 minutes. In the return leg, luckless Latics hit the woodwork, but not the net and went out after holding the Robins to a goalless draw.

After defeating Wrexham and Tranmere Rovers, Latics went out of the Freight Rover Trophy at Bury on a penalty shoot-out. The Littlewoods Cup saw the Latics make a first round exit at the hands of Blackburn Rovers, losing 5-1 on aggregate. However, in the FA Cup, the Latics produced their most successful run ever, in the history of the club. Having proved themselves in the fourth round against First Division opposition in Norwich City, the Latics went into the fifth home tie with Hull City with every confidence, and so it proved as the Tigers were beaten 3-0. Facing the once mighty Leeds United at Springfield Park, Latics went down 2-0 but proved that they were more than capable of handling football at a higher level.

Following David Lowe's departure to Ipswich Town, Springfield Park also became a venue for Rugby League with Springfield Borough sharing the ground with Latics. The Latics led the 1987-88 League table after seven games but an increasing injury crisis (three broken legs in a season - Chris Thompson, Ainscow and Holden) meant that mid-season signings had to be made. Phil Hughes, Steve Senior, Dave Thompson, Alan Kennedy and Stan McEwan arrived. These signings coincided with a good run in which Latics won four games in eight hectic days over Christmas, ending up in a strong position in the League and earning the Latics a trip to Wembley for the Mercantile Credit Festival.

It was over the weekend of 16-17 April 1988 that Latics were involved in the Mercantile Credit Festival, though both of their games were played on the Saturday. Qualification for the tournament was based on the number of League points won in the first 15 League games after 1 November 1987.

Eight clubs came from Division One, four from Division Two and two each from the Third and Fourth Divisions. Latics 15 games after 1 November brought 10 wins, 3 draws and 2 defeats. The club finished 'second' in the Third Division table behind Sunderland. One of the Latics defeats came in the 'last' away game at Chester, and if Blackpool hadn't beaten Notts County, the team from Meadow Lane would have pipped Wigan at the post.

Playing twenty minutes each way, Wigan and Sunderland fought out a goalless draw before Latics won 2-1 on penalties, scored by Stan McEwan and Paul Cook. In the quarter-finals, Chris Thompson scored Latics goal in a 1-1 draw with Sheffield Wednesday, though on this occasion, Latics lost 3-2 in the penalty shoot-out with Bobby Campbell missing his attempt.

A disappointing end to the season saw the last four League games end in defeat which dropped Latics to 7th position and out of the play-off spots. In the Littlewoods Cup, a superb hat-trick by Irish international Bobby Campbell gave Latics a 5-4 first round aggregate victory over Bolton Wanderers after they had lost the first leg at Springfield Park 3-2. In the next round Latics went down 5-2 over two legs against Luton Town. In the FA Cup they won 2-0 at Altrincham before losing 3-1 to Wolverhampton Wanderers in the second round.

Following the transfers of Paul Cook to Norwich City and Paul Jewell to Bradford City in the summer of 1988, one might have guessed what sort of season lay in store for the Latics when new signing Colin Russell departed for a better deal with the now defunct Colne Dynamoes. In fact, Wigan Athletic looked probable relegation candidates from the Third Division for most of the season, when the Latics hovered heart-stoppingly close to the bottom four for much of the season. During the 1988-89 campaign, John Butler to Stoke City and Andy Holden to Oldham Athletic, were transferred and with results not going well, manager Ray Mathias was sacked in early March after refusing to step down. He was replaced by Chief Executive and former manager Bryan Hamilton, with Tom Cavanagh appointed as his assistant. Almost immediately, Don Page was bought from Runcorn for £20,000.

It was Hamilton who was responsible in turning the tide at Springfield Park and maintaining the club's Third Division status, for he convinced players Joe Parkinson and Alan Johnson to sign new contracts which offered benefits for the club in both the short and long term. The battle for safety was a test of nerve for the Latics, as they were one of six teams trying to avoid the two available relegation places in May. Thankfully, the Latics rallied and managed to stave off relegation by losing only one of their last twelve League games - winning six and drawing five - and finished 17th. The 1-1 draw against neighbours Preston North End attracted Latics' biggest gate of the season, with 5,671 turning up to see that game. The club's Cup enterprises were poor with two first round exits against Preston in the League Cup and Hartlepool United in the FA Cup.

In the Sherpa Van Trophy they fared a little better, for after losing their first game at home to Blackpool by 2-1, they won 2-0 at Rochdale to qualify for the knockout stages. In the first round, a Dave Thompson goal gave them a 1-0 victory at Prenton Park against a strong Tranmere Rovers side, but the Latics then lost by the only goal of the game against Crewe Alexandra in the Northern Area quarter-final.

Mark Hilditch scoring in the 5-0 Littlewood's Cup victory over Wrexham during the 1989/90 season.

Phil Daley, amongst a crowd of players scores one of his 40 League goals.

Jimmy Carberry, scores in the Leyland DAF January 1990 Match versus Doncaster Rovers.

Latics League form continued to slide in 1989-90 as the club ended the season in 18th position. After starting with a goalless draw at Blackpool, Latics did not win their first League game until their twelfth match when they beat Walsall 3-0 on 21 October. The club's leading goalscorer was Mark Hilditch with 10 goals, including a hat-trick in Latics 4-0 win over Mansfield Town on New Years Day. Another hat-trick hero in that 1989-90 season was Dave Thompson who scored all three in Latics 3-1 win at Shrewsbury Town.

In 1989, Steve Nugent became Latics youngest player.

Bolton Wanderers once again provided Latics with their highest League attendance, 6,850 witnessing Wigan's 2-0 victory. Also during the League campaign, Steve Nugent became the youngest player to appear in a Latics first team when at the age of 16 years 132 days he played in the 1-0 defeat at Leyton Orient on 16 September 1989.

The club's Cup record was better, with a convincing 5-0 aggregate win over Wrexham in the League Cup before bowing out to mighty Liverpool by an aggregate score of 8-2, all that after being 2-1 up in the first half at Anfield!

In the FA Cup, Latics beat Mansfield Town and Carlisle United before losing 2-0 at Watford in the third round. In the Leyland Daf Cup, a goal from Phil Daley was enough to give Latics victory over Bolton Wanderers in their first group match, though they lost by the same score at Gresty Road against a determined Crewe Alexandra side. Nevertheless, Latics qualified for the knockout stages and travelled to Deepdale where goals by Phil Daley and Neill Rimmer gave them victory over Preston North End. In the second round, a goal by Jimmy Carberry gave Latics a 1-1 draw at home to Doncaster Rovers but unfortunately they went out of the competition in extra-time.

Despite losing their opening game of the 1990-91 season, 2-0 at home to Mansfield Town, Latics made an improvement on their form of the previous couple of seasons to finish 10th. The leading scorer was Bryan Griffiths with 12 League goals, including one in Latics 6-1 win at Swansea City on 6 April 1990, the club's biggest win of the season.

In the League Cup, Latics made an early exit, losing to Barnsley in round one on penalties after both sides had won their away fixture 1-0. In the FA Cup, Wigan thrashed Carlisle United 5-0 in the first round with Rimmer and Griffith scoring two goals apiece and Ray Woods - who later signed for Coventry City for £150,000 - scoring the other.

Bryan Griffiths was on the mark again in the next round along with Don Page as Hartlepool United were beaten 2-0.

Phil Jones - who joined Latics from Everton in the 1990/91 season - was voted Player of The Year.

Drawn against First Division Coventry City in the third round, Latics battled hard to draw 1-1 at Highfield Road, before losing to a single goal in the replay at Springfield Park.

Latics qualified for the knockout stages of the Leyland Daf Cup with a 4-0 win over Chester City with Don Page grabbing a hat-trick, despite losing 2-1 at Bury. Latics who beat Rochdale 2-0 in the first round and Bury 2-0 in the second round, crashed out of the competition in round three, losing 3-0 to Tranmere Rovers. As in seasons gone by, Latics won the Lancashire Manx Cup prior to the start of the 1991-92 season, beating Preston North End 4-1 in the final.

Latics started the League programme in familiar style, losing 1-0 at Shrewsbury Town. After appearing in the number 4 shirt in this game, Peter Atherton joined Coventry City for £350,000, the club's record transfer fee received.

The club's leading scorer in the League was Gary Worthington with 15 goals, including two in each of the following three wins (Chester City Home 2-1; Preston North End Home 3-0; and Birmingham City Home 3-0).

It was in the last of these games that the club's highest attendance of the season was recorded when 5,950 witnessed Latics final home game. Latics ended the season in 15th place in the Third Division.

Latics disappointed in the Autoglass Trophy, failing to win either of their group games and so failed to qualify for the knockout stages. After beating Burnley 6-3 on aggregate in the first round of the League Cup, Latics lost 3-2 over two legs to Sheffield United in the next round. In the FA Cup, Latics beat Scarborough and Stockport County by the same 2-0 margin, before losing at Notts County in round three by the same score.

The 1992-93 season was without doubt, the most turbulent in the club's short Football League history and it ended in total disappointment, as the Latics were relegated for the first time since their election to the Football League in 1978. On the evidence of the first few matches, it appeared once again that Latics were going to have a difficult campaign. By the end of October, only three League wins (Rotherham United Away 3-2; Mansfield Town Home 2-0; and West Bromwich Albion Home 1-0) had been recorded although the previous season's leading scorer Bryan Griffiths had scored nine goals - one more than the last term's total! To be fair though, the club were not helped by long-term injuries to Joe Parkinson, Neill Rimmer and Gary Worthington, and choosing to plug the gaps with loan players caused even further disruption.

By the turn of the year the club were still in the bottom four and a home League defeat 2-1 by Chester on 23 March 1993 saw the departure of manager Bryan Hamilton by mutual consent. Dave Philpotts was asked again to step up from first team coach to caretaker-manager in the hope of achieving a miracle. After winning his first two games (Leyton Orient Away 2-1 and Hull City Home 2-0) hopes were raised but a run of eight League games without a win, completed a miserable season. Scoring only 43 goals in 46 League games was arguably the main factor behind relegation and was not helped by the club's habit of conceding late goals.

In the League Cup, Latics defeated Shrewsbury Town over two legs, on the away goals rule before losing to First Division Ipswich Town 6-2 on aggregate after drawing the first leg at Springfield Park. In the FA Cup, Latics had missed out on a money-spinning trip to champions-elect Manchester United, losing a second round replay at Bury 1-0. The only bright spot in that 1992-93 season was the club's form in the Autoglass Trophy, recording victories at Rotherham United in a penalty shoot-out and at Springfield Park over Huddersfield Town and Scunthorpe United. Latics beat Stockport County 2-1 in the first leg of the Northern Area Final with goals from Daley and Griffiths but went down 2-0 in the second leg at Edgeley Park.

The season was even more traumatic off the field than on. Latics Chairman Bill Kenyon strained relations with the Wigan faithful finally ended when he sold his Corporate Resources Ltd. The club's new Chairman, Stephen Gage, stated his aim to enhance the club's image but his refusal to identify the new major shareholders did little to improve public confidence or trust. Crewe Alexandra's assistant-manager Kenny Swain fought off around 50 challengers as Latics sought a successor to Dave Philpotts. If relegation was a disappointment, then Latics finishing 19th I the League's Third Division in 1993-94, and thus recording their lowest ever position in the Football League, must have run it pretty close.

Latics lost their opening game of the season 2-0 at home to Scunthorpe United and made an early exit from the League Cup, losing 4-2 on aggregate to Rotherham United. In those first few weeks of the season, Latics won away at Rochdale (2-1) and Northampton Town (2-0), but had to wait until 2 October for their first home success. The visitors to Springfield Park that day were Chester City who were beaten 6-3, Latics best win of the season. Making his Latics debut in that game, although not scoring, was former Crewe Alexandra player Andy Lyons. He went on to become the club's leading scorer with 11 goals in 33 League appearances.

The club disappointed too in the Autoglass Trophy, losing both its group matches to Stockport County (0-2) and Bury (1-3). In the FA Cup, Latics beat Leek Town 3-0 at Springfield Park after the two sides had drawn 2-2, and then defeated Scarborough 1-0 with Pat Gavin scoring the goal. In the third round, Latics travelled to Blundell Park and though they battled hard, went out of the competition, losing to Grimsby Town by the only goal of the game.

There was a slight improvement in the club's fortunes in 1994-95 despite the club not winning their first League match until the sixth game of the season when the Latics triumphed 2-1 at Hereford United. The club's top scorer was again Andy Lyons with 15 goals in 32 League appearances, including a hat-trick in the 4-1 win against Darlington at Springfield Park in November 1994. The two games against Doncaster Rovers brought a total of 13 goals. Latics lost 5-3 at Belle Vue but gained revenge with a 3-2 win at Springfield Park on the final day of the season.

This enabled the Latics to finish 14th in the table, though they would have ended the season in the top half if they hadn't lost four consecutive games in April, without scoring a goal ! There wasn't much to shout about in the various Cup competitions.

After defeating Crewe Alexandra 4-2 on aggregate in the first round of the League Cup, Latics were soundly beaten 8-0 over the two games with Premier League Aston Villa. After defeating Spennymoor United 4-0 in the first round of the FA Cup, Latics went out of the competition to another non-League club, Altrincham, in the second, losing 1-0 at Moss Lane. Despite losing their opening group game in the Autowindscreen Shield 1-0 at Rochdale, Latics beat Blackpool by the same score to qualify for the knockout stages. A 3-1 win at Rotherham United took the Latics into the Northern Area quarter-final where they lost 3-1 at home to Crewe Alexandra.

1995/96 - 'The Three Amigos': Doaz, Martinez and Seba

The summer of 1995 saw the Latics astound the football world with the signings of three Spaniards, Isidro Diaz, Roberto Martinez and Jesus Seba. The Three Amigo's as they became known were joined by Chris Lightfoot from Chester City, signed for £87,500, he became the club's record signing.

The club made an indifferent start to the 1995-96 season, losing 2-1 at Gillingham on the opening day of the campaign with Roberto Martinez scoring on his League debut, though winning home games against Scunthorpe United and Barnet. The Latics made an early exit from the League Cup, losing 7-2 on aggregate to Chester City.

September witnessed the tragic death of young Michael Millett. Rated as one of the club's brightest prospects to develop through the youth system, the former England Youth international died in a car crash a day before his 18th birthday.

A month later, manager Graham Barrow paid the ultimate price following Latics 6-2 home defeat by Mansfield Town, after he had been in charge for just thirteen months. Former Norwich City manager John Deehan was appointed in Barrow's place and immediately promised Latics would gain a play-off place !

In the FA Cup, Latics beat non-League Runcorn and Barrow but were defeated at Walsall in round three. Progress in the Autowindscreen Shield ended in the second round when Latics lost against eventual winners Rotherham United in a penalty shoot-out. A new record transfer deal of £100,000 saw former England Youth international Kevin Sharpe arrive at the club from Leeds United, while striker Graham Lancashire signed from Preston North End following a successful loan period. Unfortunately for the much - travelled striker, a serious knee injury ended his season in the first game following his transfer.

Michael Millett: Until his tragic death, was one of Latics brightest prospects

David Lowe rejoined Latics towards the end of the 1995/96 season, seen here scoring one of his 43 League goals.

Neill Rimmer - Latics longest serving player when he was released in 1996

Chris Lightfoot was allowed to join Crewe Alexandra after appearing in just 21 League and Cup games for the Latics, and former player David Lowe returned to the club after an eight year absence for £125,000 as Latics broke their record transfer fee for the third time in the season. Lowe scored three goals in as many games to take Latics into an automatic promotion spot, but unfortunately just one point in the last four games, including a 2-1 home defeat by Northampton Town in the final game of the season, saw Latics drop down to 10th position.

During the close season, John Deehan released six first team squad men including former skipper Neill Rimmer, the club's longest-serving player. The Latics manager also held a host of press conferences to announce the latest arrivals as part of his Springfield Park revolution. First up was the signing of Lee Butler from Barnsley.

The 30 year-old former Aston Villa goalkeeper arrived on a free transfer, replacing Simon Farnworth who was appointed as the club's physiotherapist. Another cross-Pennine swoop saw Charlie Bishop also make the journey from Oakwell in return for a fee of £40,000. The third signing was Coventry City utility man Steve Morgan. Hours later Deehan smashed the club transfer record when he paid Doncaster Rovers £150,000 for Graeme Jones.

No manager has spent as much as John Deehan in Wigan Athletic's history - and the stunning thing is he had at the time only been at Springfield Park for under a year! There is no doubt that Latics Chairman Dave Whelan will again provide financial backing, as he seeks all Latics supporters ultimate dream of top flight football in a new stadium at Robin Park.

THE SPRINGFIELD PARK STORY

20 January 1897 - The cutting of the first sod ceremony, the construction of Springfield Park begins.

Springfield Park first came into existence during the reign of Queen Victoria but it was not until the formation of Wigan County in 1897 that the ground first came to be used as a venue for Association Football.

Prior to that historic introduction, Springfield Park had been used as a sports arena, boasting a concrete bicycle track and a half-mile running track. Horse-trotting too was very popular at the ground with the horse-and-trotting negotiating the running track and stables on the town side of the ground. In addition, Springfield Park was also used for rugby and by the local police for their athletics meetings.

The first professional football match to be staged at Springfield Park took place on 1 September 1897 when Wigan County played Burton Swifts in a friendly match.

The home of five football clubs bearing the title Wigan, Wigan Town were the next team to play at the ground and in 1901-02 they shared Springfield Park with Wigan Rugby League Football Club, using the ground on alternate Saturdays.

During Wigan Borough's years at Springfield Park, the existing standing covers were erected, the first in the early 1920's at the Shevington End and the second on the Popular side late in that decade. Wigan Borough lasted twelve League games into the 1931-32 season when due to financial difficulties the club went into voluntary liquidation.

After prolonged negotiations, Wigan Athletic purchased Springfield Park the following year for the princely sum of £2,800 from the owners of Woodhouse Lane Dog Track. There was one very interesting clause in the agreement of the sale which read that the new owners must guarantee Springfield Park would never be used for greyhound racing.

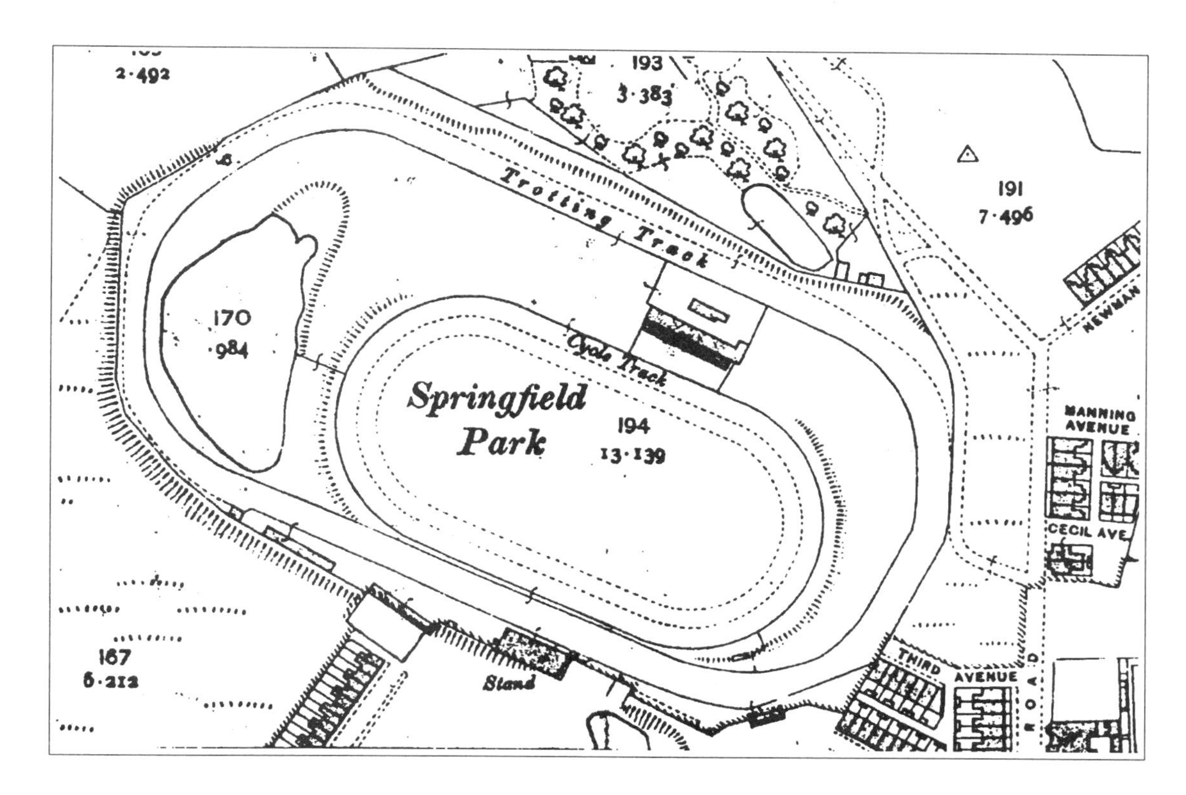

(Above) Springfield Park in the early days - from a map of 1900

(Below) Some years later, by which time the covered end had been added, together with a more substantial main stand

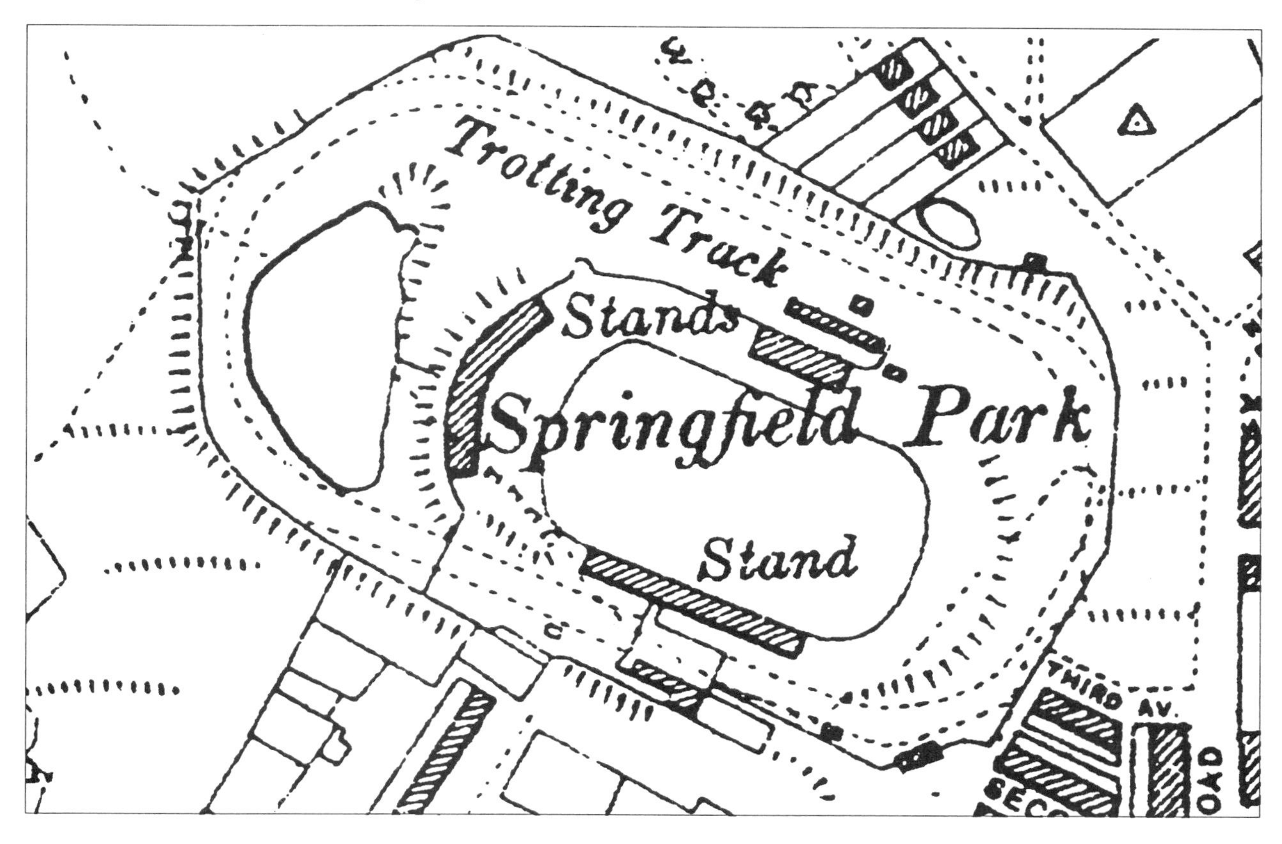

A view from the air, in pre-floodlight days... Note the side and end covers, but only part built.

This valuable acquisition consisted 14 acres of land, a wooden stand with seating for 2,000 spectators and shelter on the popular side. Though the ground was kept in reasonably good order throughout the war by the older directors, the old wooden stand needed major repairs and the popular side shelter re-roofing. The stand's seating capacity of 2,000 had a quarter of its seats upholstered. The grandstand was totally destroyed by fire early on Thursday morning 30 May 1953, when damage was estimated at £7,000. In addition two of the cup plinths won by Latics were left in the offices underneath the stand and were also destroyed, though fortunately, earlier that evening the Latics trophies had been taken away from the boardroom by the chairman to display elsewhere. The only item of property which was salvaged was the club's safe, which fireman got out of the offices on rollers.

In all probability the fire cost Latics their chance of Football League membership at the end of the season, for the flames engulfed not only the spectators facilities, but also the dressing rooms and baths and despite some enthusiastic fund raising by the club's supporters, it took nearly twelve months to raise sufficient money to build a replacement. The following season saw a record crowd of 27,526 watch Latics beat Hereford United 4-1 - a record that still stands today as the largest attendance ever recorded for a game between two non-League clubs excluding Wembley finals. However, the largest attendance recorded at Springfield Park is 30,611 when Wigan Borough entertained Sheffield Wednesday in 1929.

To assist the club financially, local builder and club chairman, Lesley Jackson brought around four hundred acres of land from the club and built houses on them. In the late 1950's this was an honourable move; however with the Taylor Report and safety regulations today, the idea prohibits access round the complete area of the ground.

The floodlights were first switched on, on Wednesday 19 October 1966 for a Northern Floodlit League match against Crewe Alexandra which Latics won 4-2, although they were not officially opened until five days later when a crowd of 10,119 saw Wigan play Manchester City.

In 1972 the club applied to build a greyhound track at Springfield Road in an attempt to alleviate their financial problems. The idea was rejected out of hand and the original condition remained as in the early bill of sale for Springfield.

Also in 1972, the club tried to erect a proper roof over the actual terracing, but this was taken down four years later, because it was much too close to the playing area and reduced the numbers of spectators who could see from that end. However, the club did manage to sell the steelwork to a local engineering firm for more than it cost them to build the cover in the first place! Once Latics were elected to the Football League in place of Southport in 1978, ground improvements had to be carried out, and were undertaken by the staff and numerous volunteers.

Another Ground view.
From a popular design programme cover of the period

To many Springfield Park would have made the perfect site for a modern multi-sports stadium, or alternatively the club could have shared Wigan Rugby League club's Central Park Stadium, but it now looks as if the club's move to Robin Park will be going ahead, with Latics aiming to be in their new home for the start of the 1997-98 season.

The future plans are for a playing surface which will be contained within a running track and for stands on two sides only, the ends being left empty.

The initial capacity will be in the region of 12,000 (all seated). Should the Latics reach the First Division and the club's attendances warrant an increase, the council have promised to build over the track and complete the stadium by erecting new stands behind the goals.

THIRTY MATCHES TO REMEMBER

No.	Team	Opponent	Date
1	Wigan Athletic 0	Port Vale Res. 2	27 Aug.1932
2	Carlisle United 1	Wigan Athletic 6	24 Nov.1934
3	Wigan Athletic 3	Torquay United 2	8 Dec.1934
4	Wigan Athletic 4	Hereford United 1	12 Dec.1953
5	Newcastle Utd. 2	Wigan Athletic 2	9 Jan. 1954
6	Wigan Athletic 2	Newcastle Utd. 3	13 Jan. 1954
7	Wigan Athletic 12	Stubshaw Cross 0	15 Sep.1954
8	Doncaster R. 2	Wigan Athletic 2	13 Nov.1965
9	Wigan Athletic 3	Doncaster R. 1	17 Nov.1965
10	Wigan Ath. 11	Darwen 1	4 Feb.1970
11	Macclesfield 1	Wigan Athletic 3	24 Oct.1970
12	Wigan Athletic 4	Stafford Rang. 1	28 Dec.1970
13	Manchester C. 1	Wigan Athletic 0	2 Jan.1971
14	Scarborough 2	Wigan Ath. 1 (aet)	28 Apr.1973
15	Wigan Athletic 2	Shrewsbury T. 1	25 Nov.1974
16	Wigan Athletic 1	Sheffield Wed. 0	17 Dec.1977
17	Birmingham C. 4	Wigan Athletic 0	7 Jan. 1978
18	Hereford Utd. 0	Wigan Athletic 0	19 Aug.1978
19	Wigan Athletic 5	Port Vale 3	13 Apr.1979
20	Chelsea 0	Wigan Athletic 1	14 Jan.1980
21	Everton 3	Wigan Athletic 0	31 Jan.1980
22	Wigan Athletic 4	Chelsea 2	11 Nov.1981
23	Wigan Athletic 1	Aston Villa 2	1 Dec.1981
24	Scunthorpe U.. 2	Wigan Athletic 7	12 Mar.1982
25	Brentford 1	Wigan Athletic 3	1 Jun.1985
26	Wigan Athletic 1	Norwich City 0	31 Jan.1987
27	Wigan Athletic 0	Leeds United 2	15 Mar.1987
28	Bolton Wand. 1	Wigan Athletic 3	25 Aug.1987
29	Wigan Athletic 2	Liverpool 5	19 Sep.1989
30	Coventry City 1	Wigan Athletic 1	5 Jan.1991

MATCH TO REMEMBER No.1

Wigan Athletic 0 Port Vale Reserves 2 : 27 August 1932

This was the first match ever played at Springfield Park by Wigan Athletic. The historic game took place on 27 August 1932, when, about a year after Wigan Borough folded, a team under the managership of former international centre-half Charlie Spencer took the field at Springfield Park against Port Vale Reserves.

Latics had been accepted into the Cheshire League, a competition they were to grace for many years. Sadly though, that first match ended in defeat, Port Vale winning 2-0. Port Vale Reserves were considered to be the best side in the Cheshire League at that time and against such strong opposition, Latics who a week previously had no team at all signed on, put up a performance that did the side every credit.

The two goals which decided the historic match were scored 15 minutes into the second half, both within the space of three minutes. First, a long cross was taken by McGrath who gave Wigan goalkeeper Abbott no chance with a powerful shot, then Nolan slipped clean through and scored an easy goal.

Wigan Athletic: Abbott, O'Dell, Callaghan, Allon, Spencer, Wake, Chambers, Smith, McCabe, Henderson, Murphy

Port Vale Reserves: B.Davies, Cope, Breeze, Millington, Bliss, Birks, Baker, R.G.Davies, Nolan, Beech, McGrath

Attendance 5,000

MATCH TO REMEMBER No.2

Carlisle United 1 Wigan Athletic 6: 24 November 1934

[4]—CUMBERLAND EVENING NEWS, SATURDAY, NOVEMBER 24, 1934.

INGLORIOUS EXIT FROM THE CUP

Carlisle United Humiliated by Lads fra' Wigan.

ARMES ON THE TARGET.

Demoralised Team Again Falls to Non-League Club.

A BITTERLY-DISAPPOINTED CROWD SAW A DEMORALISED CARLISLE UNITED AGAIN KNOCKED OUT OF THE CUP BY A NON-LEAGUE TEAM. WIGAN DEMONSTRATED THEIR SUPERIORITY TO THE TUNE OF SIX GOALS TO ONE.

Nearly three hundred spectators of Wigan Athletic accompanied the team to Brunton Park to see the Cheshire County League champions tackle the Third Division North club, Carlisle United.

Wigan took the lead after four minutes when Sammy Armes was put in possession and shot away unmarked. He cut in well, his shot being deflected off Wolf's body onto the bar and into the net.

The Latics went further ahead after ten minutes when Roberts evaded two tackles to shoot past Wolf. Carlisle should have pulled a goal back on the half-hour but Ranson completely missed his kick in front of an open goal. Two minutes later, Wigan went 3-0 up when Scott's shot was fisted out by Wolf straight to the winger who followed up to make no mistake. The Latics scored a fourth goal in the 34th minute when Roberts collected a fine ball by Armes and had the simplest of tasks in tapping the ball past the Carlisle 'keeper. In the final minute of the first-half, Robson added a fifth goal when his header hit the foot of the post before bouncing into the net.

Latics extended their lead two minutes into the second-half when Tuffnell crossed for Armes to race clear and shot past the advancing Wolf. The Carlisle goalkeeper decided to try and reduce the arrears himself when he dribbled the ball from his own goal to well inside the Wigan half, beating a couple of Latics players on the way!

As the game wore on, Carlisle got stronger and Elliott rattled the Wigan crossbar with a thunderous shot. The home side did eventually pull a goal back in the closing minutes when Ranson fired in a low shot, but even then the Latics protested as the ball appeared to pass outside the post. The referee ran to the Wigan goal and pointed to the net near the upright, apparently meaning that the ball had passed through it.

Carlisle United: Wolf, Robinson, Legge, Johnston, Parker, Allen, Ferguson, Slinger, Ranson, Stevenson, Elliott
Wigan Athletic: Caunce, Robinson, Talbot, Patterson, Watson, Tuffnell, Armes, Robson, Roberts, Felton, Scott

Attendance 6,692 Referee: W.Booth (Preston)

MATCHES TO REMEMBER No.3

Wigan Athletic 3 Torquay United 2: 8 December 1934

Within three minutes of the start of this F.A. Cup second round match, Latics were a goal down. Talbot missed his kick and Morgan rounded Caunce to put the visitors ahead. Three minutes later, Wigan equalised when Roberts cut in from the right, beat two opponents and shot hight into the roof of the net.

In the 35th minute, Roberts scored his and Wigan's second when he beat to the ball Langford in the Torquay goal, just as it seemed the 'keeper was about to collect it. The visitors by now were down to ten men with Rees off the field having treatment to a cut face. The left-half returned after half-time but only to play on the wing.

However, within four minutes of the restart, the Devon side were level when Caunce let a simple looking shot from Protheroe slip through his grasp. Langford made good saves from Roberts and Felton as Wigan pressed forward in search of the winning goal. It came courtesy of Scott, who after beating two defenders near the corner flag moved towards the Torquay and from the narrowest of angles, drove the ball high into the net.

Wigan Athletic: Caunce, Robinson, Talbot, Patterson, Watson, Tuffnell, Armes, Robson, Robson, Roberts, Felton, Scott

Torquay United: Langford, Gregg, Tapp, Jones, Welsh, Rees, Morgan, Beedall, Walters, Hutchinson, Protheroe.

Attendance 20,000

MATCH TO REMEMBER No.4

Wigan Athletic 4 Hereford United 1 : 12 December 1953

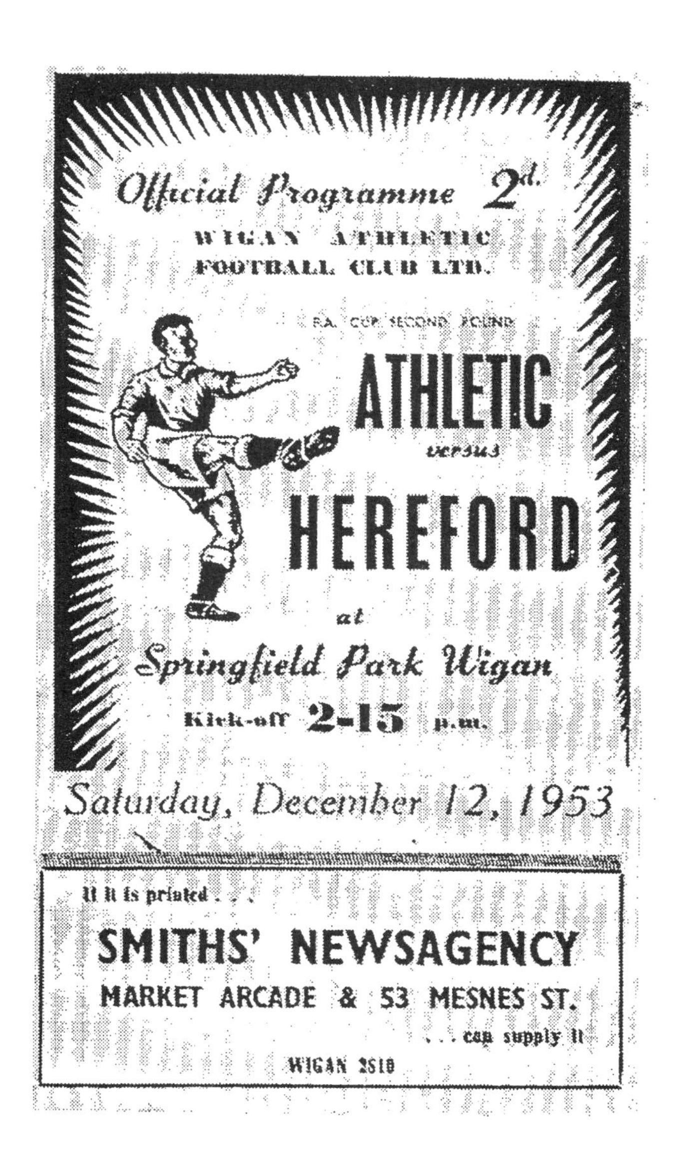

A record attendance of 27,500, the highest for a clash of two non-League clubs outside of a Wembley Final packed into Springfield Park for this F.A. Cup second round tie.

Wigan took the lead as early as the 3rd minute when Lyon scored with a rising 20 yard shot that left Lewis in the Hereford goal well beaten. Only nine minutes had gone when the Latics extended their lead through Livesey after Lomax had left the Wigan inside-right the simple task of tapping the ball into the empty net. The same two players combined for Wigan's third goal three minutes before half-time when Lomax cut inside, beat Thompson, and put Livesey in with a clear run on goal from which he made no mistake.

Shortly after half-time, John Lewis made a superb fingertip save from a powerful Hindle shot and then punched the ball off Lomax's head just when it seemed certain that the Wigan centre-forward would score.

It was all Wigan and it came as no surprise when the home side went further ahead when Hughes, the Hereford left-back, put the ball into his own net when under pressure from Lomax. Only two minutes remained when Jack Lewis the Hereford right-half scrambled the ball home from close range for a late consolation goal.

Wigan Athletic: Lomas, Lindsay, Parkinson, Lynn, Mycock, Banks, Butler, Livesey, Lomax, Lyon, Hindle
Hereford United: John Lewis, Layton, Hughes, Jack Lewis, Thompson, Johnson, Bowen, Farquhar, Mountford, O'Hara, Crowe

Attendance 27,500 Referee: R.H.Mann (Worcester)

MATCH TO REMEMBER No.5

Newcastle United 2 Wigan Athletic 2 : 9 January 1954

8 THE SUNDAY SUN, January 10, 1954.

NORTH'S TWO CUP HOPES ARE IN AWAY REPLAYS

Milburn special saved United humiliation

By Ken McKenzie

NEWCASTLE UN. ... 2 WIGAN ATHLETIC ... 2

The attendance of 52,222 was the third highest of the day in the F.A. Cup third round, and included 4,000 Wigan fans who travelled in three special trains, motor coaches and private cars. On arrival in Newcastle, the Wigan contingent made their way to the County Hotel where the Wigan Athletic team was staying. Players came to the windows to acknowledge the cheers of their supporters.

Both teams took to the field to a deafening reception. Newcastle began strongly and it came as no surprise when they took the lead after 27 minutes through Broadis. But it was a gift goal. Dave Mycock the Wigan centre-half, who up until then had had an outstanding game, was caught off balance and in trying to control the ball only succeeded in tapping it to the feet of Broadis who banged it into the net. In the next few minutes, Newcastle hit the post, shot wide or over and had shots charged down with Mycock always the main stumbling block.

Gradually the Latics forwards began to get into the game and came out for the second-half like a team possessed. They literally ran rings round United's defence until Jackie Lyon equalised in the 52nd minute. Lindsay carried the ball for 40 yards before passing to Livesey. The Wigan inside-forward pushed the ball between Scoular and Stokoe to Lomax, who quickly glanced it wide of Brennan for Lyon to score.

The Latics took the lead after 75 minutes when Hindle beat Batty and crossed for Livesey to race in and score with almost a duplicate of Wigan's first goal. The Wigan players were still congratulating themselves when Newcastle got back on level terms through Milburn. He raced right through the Wigan defence without anyone touching him, to fire home. From then until the final whistle, it was anyone's game with play swinging from end to end. Hindle did get the ball into the net again but was given offside. It was one of the most remarkable days in the history of the club.

Newcastle United: Simpson, Batty, McMichael, Scoular, Brennan, Stokoe, Walker, Broadis, Monkhouse, Milburn, Mitchell

Wigan Athletic: Lomas, Lindsay, Parkinson, Lynn, Mycock, Banks, Butler, Livesey, Lomax, Lyon, Hindle

Attendance 52,222 Referee: J.T.Williams (Woodthorpe, Notts)

MATCH TO REMEMBER No.6

Wigan Athletic 2 Newcastle United 3: 13 January 1954

The teams come out at Springfield Park

Following the incredible result in this F.A. Cup third round cup tie four days earlier, the Latics were in a confident mood for this return fixture at Springfield Park. The match however got off to an unsporting start when Stan Seymour, the Newcastle chairman, refused to let his team change in Wigan's makeshift dressing rooms, calling the facilities 'crude'.

His remark was very insensitive given that Latics supporters and directors had worked hard in their attempts to repair the damage caused by the great fire.

Perhaps the talking point of the match came eight minutes into the second-half, when Jackie Lyon 'scored' with a shot which practically everybody, but the referee, considered a goal! Simpson collected Lyon's shot high under the bar but its force compelled him to step back so that the ball he was clutching passed at least a foot over the line before he cleared it.

The first five minutes of the game were packed with thrills. Within seconds of Scoular winning the toss, he had fouled Hindle, and Latics free-kick had shaken the Newcastle defence. Broadis nearly got through, Milburn had a drive turned over the top for a corner, whilst Parkinson kicked off the line with Lomas beaten. Newcastle took the lead in the 12th minute when Keeble scored with a headlong dive which was well out of the reach of Lomas. There were chances at both ends before White doubled the visitors lead after 36 minutes. Gloom settled on the Wigan crowd, but this was lifted two minutes later when Livesey crossed for Lomax to score from close in.

Early in the second-half came the Lyon 'goal'. Indeed it happened again with Hindle the marksman, but with the same result. The Latics were now dictating the play, but when Milburn suddenly crossed a high ball from the right, Broadis scored Newcastle's third goal with a well taken header. There were just ten minutes to go when Lomax headed Wigan's second goal - what a roar! White then headed on to the Wigan crossbar. In the final minute, Lyon received the ball from a Livesey throw-in and curled his sharp-angled shot just behind the angle of the bar and post.

Wigan Athletic: Lomas, Lindsay, Parkinson, Lynn, Mycock, Banks, Butler, Livesey, Lomax, Lyon, Hindle

Newcastle United: Simpson, Cowell, McMichael, Scoular, Brennan, Casey, White, Broadis, Keeble, Milburn, Mitchell

Attendance 26,000 Referee: J.T.Williams (Woodthorpe, Notts)

MATCH TO REMEMBER No.7

Wigan Athletic 12 Stubshaw Cross 0: 15 September 1954

The display by Lee, the Stubshaw Cross goalkeeper, did not save his side from an inglorious and sound trouncing at Springfield Park in this Lancashire Combination Cup first round match.

The Latics took the lead after three minutes when Davies headed home a centre from Penk, and then from that point the match was already won. Corfield, Vincent and Davies netted eight goals between them and it was one-way traffic practically all through the match. The game was almost 20 minutes old when Lomas the Wigan 'keeper was brought into action. Even late in the second-half when Stubshaw Cross launched a series of desperate sorties, they either overran the ball, shot straight at Lomas or drove the ball yards wide.

After the interval lead of 5-0, with Wigan's goals being scored by Vincent 2, Corfield 2 and Davies, the Latics added another seven in the second-half, with Lee producing some really magnificent saves to keep the score down! Second-half scorers were Corfield 2, Hindle 2, Vincent, Penk and Livesey, who scored from the spot, after Penk had been tripped by Boardman.

Wigan Athletic: Lomas, Lindsay, Parkinson, Lynn, Wood, Banks, Penk, Corfield, Vincent, Davies, Hindle
Stubshaw Cross: Lee, Boardman, Barber, Billington, Vizard, Bamber, Smith, Grimshaw, Doyle, Arnold, Peet
Attendance 2,000 Referee: H.Taylor (Salford)

MATCH TO REMEMBER No.8

Doncaster Rovers 2 Wigan Athletic 2 : 13 November 1965

This was a match to remember for two reasons; the first that in the opening 45 minutes, Wigan played a brand of soccer far and away above the standard of the average non-League side; the second that after the interval, though handicapped by the absence of injured Stuart Houghton for the last half hour, they fought back from 2-1 down to snatch an equaliser.

Wigan took the lead in the 23rd minute when Walter Stanley's corner was headed in by the unmarked Harry Lyon. Although ten minutes before, he was pulled up for an offence, and denied a goal, which to this day remains a mystery. Four minutes after Wigan scored, they had the ball in the net for a third time as Stanley crashed the ball home from close range, only for Llewellyn to be deemed offside.

In the opening minutes of the second-half, both Lyon and Llewellyn missed open goals before Doncaster equalised through left-half Ricketts. Rovers went ahead in the 77th minute when Kelly took advantage of a misunderstanding between Craig and Halsall. Three minutes later, ten-men Wigan equalised, Dennis Crompton rising unchallened to guide Stanley's free-kick wide of Dawson. The final ten minutes were nerve-wracking for the Latics as Doncaster went all out for the winner but Wigan's depleted side held on bravely until the final whistle.

Doncaster Rovers: Dawson, Kelly, Nicholson, Wylie, Ripley, Ricketts, Robinson, Jeffrey, Sheffield, Durrant, Wilson
Wigan Athletic: Halsall, Wilkinson, S.Houghton, Crompton, Craig, Roberts, Ryan, Llewellyn, Lyon, Brown, Stanley

Attendance 10,005 Referee: H.Davey (Mansfield)

MATCH TO REMEMBER No.9

Wigan Athletic 3 Doncaster Rovers 1: 17 November 1965

In an incredible fairy-tale second-half, Harry Lyon scored a superb hat-trick, two of the goals coming from his head, the other with the foot he had feared was broken by a first-half tackle. Lyon was stretchered off in the 19th minute with an injury diagnosed by the club doctor as torn ankle ligaments. He was given two tots of whisky, a couple of tablets and 15 minutes later he was back on the field, his injured ankle heavily strapped.

After a goalless first-half, Latics took the lead in the 57th minute when Lyon rose to meet Wilkinson's expertly placed free-kick to head in off the underside of the bar. Doncaster almost levelled the scores when Alick Jeffrey headed against a post. Ten minutes from the end, Lyon and Llewellyn combined well to put Wigan 2-0 up. Llewellyn controlled another well-placed Wilkinson free-kick (with his hand the Doncaster players claimed), flicked it on to Lyon, and the centre-forward hooked a great shot over Potter's head - with his injured left foot.

With three minutes left, Ryan crossed for Lyon to rise at the far post and find the net with a beautifully judged header. Doncaster were a well beaten side and when centre-forward Ogden headed home Wilson's cross in the last minute, it was merely a consolation goal. Lyon was chaired off the field by cheering fans. Over 7,000 supporters roared their appreciation from the terraces and Bill Lievers, the Doncaser player-manager who was roundly booed throughout the game after some robust challenges, got involved in a skirmish with one over-excited Wigan fan.

Wigan Athletic:	D.Houghton, Wilkinson, Crompton, Craig, Roberts, Ryan, Llewellyn, Lyon, Brown, Stanley
Doncaster Rovers:	Potter, Kelly, Nicholson, Wylie, Ripley, Lievers, Robinson, Jeffrey, Ogden, Ricketts, Wilson
Attendance 7,113	Referee: H.Davey (Mansfield)

Lyon jumps to head home his first goal

MATCH TO REMEMBER No.10

Wigan Athletic 11 Darwen 1: 4 February 1970

Poor little Darwen reeled off the field after this Lancashire F.A. Challenge Trophy second round match, not knowing what had hit them. The Latics slammed in the goals with unashamed delight and they were running and shouting as hard when they were 10-0 up as when the scoresheet was blank.

Tony McLoughlin was letting Darwen know just how great it was to be back, after three months suspension, by scoring seven of the goals.

Despite the limitations of the opposition, Wigan showed a refreshing, aggressive approach from first to last, steamrolling through the Darwen defence either with cunningly placed centres from the wings or lightning through passes.

McLoughlin's goals came in the 13th, 18th, 23rd, 50th, 58th, 64th and 90th minutes and Jim Fleming (19th and 32nd), Mandy Hill (a 38th minute penalty) and Johnny Fielding (65th) weighed in with the rest. Centre-forward Bell snatched Darwen's consolation goal.

Wigan Athletic: Reeves, Turner, Sutherland, Gillibrand, Coutts, Ross, Hill, Fielding, McLoughlin, Fleming, Breen

Darwen: Wallace, D.Waddicor, Oldham, Cairns, Wright, M.Waddicor, Conway L.Waddicor, Bell, Barrett, Hutchinson

Attendance 742 Referee: N.Hayes (Bolton)

MATCHES TO REMEMBER No.11

Macclesfield Town 1 Wigan Athletic 3: 24 October 1970

Wigan Athletic were involved in what was one of the finest matches ever played in the Northern Premier League. The opposition was provided by the almost unbeatable Macclesfield Town, Winners of the League for the first two years of its existence and a force second to none on their own Moss Rose ground.

Macclesfield were top of the League at the time and with Wigan quickly emerging as the country's best non-League club, the match was billed as a possible classic. The match contained everything. Thrills, goals, cont-roversy and a missed penalty.

Macclesfield took the lead through the almost legendary Brian Fidler in the first-half and though Latics pressed hard, there was no further scoring by half-time. The second-half saw Latics storm forward, responding to the leadership of the magnificent Jim Fleming and goals from Fleming himself, Geoff Davies and an own goal by Macclesfield's Sievewright set the seal on a great Latics performance. The missed penalty came in the last minute of the game and was fluffed twice by Macclesfield's goalscorer, Fidler.

Latics had inflicted upon Macclesfield only their third defeat in 46 home Premier League games. The game marked the decline of Macclesfield and the re-emergence of Wigan Athletic.

Macclesfield: Cooke, Sievewright, Bennett, Beaumont, Collins, Roberts, Morris, B.Fidler, Young, Corfield, Lyon; Sub: D.Fidler

Wigan Athletic: Reeves, Morris, Sutherland, Turner, Couts, Gillibrand, Temple, Todd, Davies, Fleming, Breen; Sub: Milne

Attendance 4,253
Referee: D.Lumb (Cleethorpes)

Northern Premier League
Saturday, October 24th, 1970
Kick off 3 p.m.

Macclesfield v. Wigan Athletic

Macclesfield	Wigan Athletic
1. Cooke	1. Reeves
2. Berry	2. Morris
3. Sievewright	3. Sutherland
4. Beaumont	4. Milne
5. Collins	5. Coutts
6. Bennett	6. Gillibrand
7. Morris	7. Temple
8. Broadhead	8. Todd
9. Fidler (B)	9. Davies
10. Roberts	10. Fleming
11. Lyon	11. Breen
Sub.	Sub. Koo

Referee: D. Lumb (Cleethorpes)
Linesmen: B. Coxon (Lincolnshire) B. Davies (Sale)

MATCHES TO REMEMBER No.12

Wigan Athletic 4 Stafford Rangers 1: 28 December 1970

Stafford Rangers were lying second in the Northern Premier League while Wigan Athletic were sitting pretty on the top of the league table. A big crowd was expected as this was Wigan's last game before they met First Division Manchester City at Maine Road in the third round of the F.A.Cup, but just how many people attended was a revelation. A total of 8,170 went through the turnstiles and when you remember that it was for a league game between two non-League clubs, then it gives some idea of the interest shown by local fans at that time.

The game turned out to be one of the most exciting seen at Springfield Park for a long time. Wigan turned in a superb performance to beat Rangers 4-1. Gordon Milne's long-range effort was followed by a Jim Fleming penalty and although Stafford came back into the picture with a goal from Ray Williams, later to manage Northwich Victoria, further efforts from Graham Oates and Geoff Davies gave Latics a tremendous win and sent them off to Maine Road in good heart.

Wigan Athletic: Reeves, Morris, Sutherland, Milne, Coutts, Gillibrand, Temple, Todd, Davies, Fleming, Oates; Sub: Turner

Stafford Rangers: Quigley, Chadwick, Morgan, Sargent, Clayton, Machin, Bailey, S.Chapman, Williams, R.Chapman, Jones; Sub: Windsor

Attendance: 8,170

MATCH TO REMEMBER No. 13

Manchester City 1 Wigan Athletic 0: 2 January 1971

It was a real gala day for everyone connected with Wigan Athletic. The Wigan side held out the might of the First Division outfit until the 72nd minute when goalkeeper Dennis Reeves' boot split while he was taking a goal-kick. The ball went straight to Neil Young who switched it inside to Colin Bell and before the Wigan defence could move, the ball was in the back of the net. It was a tragedy for Wigan, and afterwards Dennis Reeves blamed himself for the defeat, but he needn't have bothered, for he like every other Wigan player had played the game of his life.

Indeed if it had not been for City goalkeeper Joe Corrigan, who denied Latics centre-forward Geoff Davies with two world class saves late in the game, then who knows what might have happened. But with the 'Match of the Day' cameras there to take it all in, Wigan revelled in the praise they received.

The City players trooped off at the end more than a little releived at not being knocked out of the F.A. Cup by a non-League side, and the magnificent standing ovation from every person on the ground showed just what they thought of Latics' efforts.

Manchester City: Corrigan, Book, Mann, Doyle, Booth, Oakes, Summerbee, Bell, Lee, Young, Jeffries; Sub: Carrodus

Wigan Athletic: Reeves, Turner, Sutherland, Milne, Coutts, Gillibrand, Temple, Todd, Davies, Fleming, Oates; Sub: Ledgard

Attendance 46,212   Referee: P.Partridge (Cockfield, Co.Durham)

(Below) Doug Coutt's head clears Colin Bell's shot

MATCH TO REMEMBER No. 14

Scarborough 2 Wigan Athletic 1 (aet): 28 April 1973

The Spirit that had taken Wigan Athletic to Wembley for this F.A. Challenge Trophy Final was only too willing, but the flesh - shattered by 70-odd games over a long, hard season - was for once too weak to respond.

Scarborough settled far more quickly than Wigan and cashed in on an early piece of dithering in the 11th minute to go a goal up. The ball ought to have been cleared on the right before it was scooped low into the centre and Reeves twice seemed to have it within his grasp only to lose it, with Leask eventually snapping up the chance to angle a low shot into the untenanted net.

Wigan's huge following, estimated to be about 17,000 strong, had to wait until 15 seconds from the end of normal time for their first real cheer. That came when Siddle nodded away Sutherland's header into a packed goalmouth and John Reeves drove it ferociously back through a 20 yard forest of legs and bodies and finally through Garrow's legs.

Before that, Wigan had appealed with justification for a penalty when Hewitt seemed to fist away Worswick's shot with both hands. In extra-time despite Kenny Morris' disabling cramp, Latics looked the stronger team but four minutes from the end despite vain appeals for offside, Thompson scored Scarborough's winner.

Scarborough: Garrow, Appleton, Shoulder, H.Dunn, Siddle, Fagan, Donoghue, Franks, Leask (sub: Barmby), Thompson, Hewitt.

Wigan Athletic: Reeves, Morris, Sutherland, Taylor, Jackson, Gillibrand, Clements, Oakes (sub: McCunnell), Rogers, King, Worswick.

Attendance 24,000 Referee: H.P.Hackney (Sheffield)

MATCH TO REMEMBER No. 15

Wigan Athletic 2 Shrewsbury Town 1: 25 November 1974

Brian Tiler's Latics, then in the Northern Premier League, had played out a memorable draw at Gay Meadow in the first F.A. Cup meeting between the two sides and indeed they were unfortunate not to win, for only a goal seven minutes into injury time earned Shrewsbury a replay after John King had given Latics the lead.

But if the first match was exciting, the replay was something special. The picture had looked black for Wigan when Shrewsbury's centre-forward Haywood gave the visitors an early lead. They held on to this lead despite some tremendous Latics pressure until late in the game. In a magnificent rally, two goals sent Springfield Park wild. Firstly Tommy Gore found the corner of the net with a blistering 30 yard drive and then, in the final minutes, Wigan substitute Albert Jackson slammed the ball into the roof of the net after a throw-in had evaded the Shrewsbury defence.

It was a marvellous night and Latics were rewarded with a home tie against Division Four leaders Mansfield Town in the second round. Latics drew that game 1-1 before finally bowing out of the F.A. Cup in the replay at Field Mill where they lost 3-1. One sad note in this match, was an injury to full-back Billy Sutherland, which virtually finished the career of one of the best defenders ever to wear Wigan Athletic's colours.

Wigan Athletic:	Reeves, Morris, Sutherland, Gore, Molyneux, Gillibrand, Garrett, Worswick, Rogers, King, Wright. (sub: Jackson)
Shrewsbury Town:	Mulhearn, King, Calloway, Durban, Kearney, Cochrane, Irvine, Tarbuck, Haywood, Bates, Morris. (sub: Turner)
Attendance 11,860	Referee: D.W. Civil (Birmingham)

MATCH TO REMEMBER No. 16

Wigan Athletic 1 Sheffield Wednesday 0: 17 December 1977

Just after twenty past four, the left boot of Maurice Whittle scored the kind of goal Wigan Athletic fans had been waiting for. The goal sent the biggest F.A. Cup crowd of the day wild with delight and put the Latics on the road to glory.

Only once in the match, in a startling opening 20 minutes, did Wednesday show they were a Third Division side. Wigan were clearly rocked by the lively pace of the match and it was only a matter of good fortune when Wylde hit the angle of the post and crossbar that kept the scoresheet blank. Wigan refused to panic and climbed back into the match. They scored what looked like a perfectly good goal after 30 minutes when Jeff Wright struck the crossbar and Micky Moore headed into the empty net. The referee judged that Chris Turner the Sheffield Wednesday goalkeeper had been fouled.

The deciding goal came when Walden fouled Worswick on the edge of the area in a position tailor-made for free-kick specialist Whittle. His left foot planted a shot through Wednesday's wall into the back of the net.

Wigan Athletic:	Brown, Morris, Hinnigan, Gore, Ward, Gillibrand, Whittle, Worswick, Moore, Wilkie, Wright.
Sheffield Wednesday:	Turner, Walden, Grant, Down, Cusack, Mullen, Wylde, Johnson, Tynan, Rushbury, Prendergast.
Attendance 13,871	Referee: N.Ashby (Nantwich)

MATCH TO REMEMBER No.17

Birmingham City 4 Wigan Athletic 0: 7 January 1978

This third round F.A. Cup tie was arguably the most important game ever played in the history of the Club. They lost it 4-0 but in doing so won a place in the Football League, for on the strength of their performance that day through their style of football, the behaviour of the fans, and the gentlemanly presence of the Club's officialdom, they gained the admiration and support of their First Division opposition. It was that support that swung the Midland Club behind Latics' application and earned them their League place.

Birmingham took the lead after five minutes when Keith Bertschin flicked the ball up for Trevor Francis to shoot past Brown. In the next twenty minutes or so, Brown found himself under considerable pressure and despite making some good saves was beaten for a second time when Francis returned the compliment by setting up Bertschin.

Goalmouth scrambles were the order of the day and both Ward and Hinnigan cleared off the line. The traffic wasn't all one way and Montgomery had to be on top form to save Moore's downward header. The second-half was only one minute old when Latics defence crumbled again as Francis headed home Hibbitt's corner. Though they were 3-0 down, Wigan's midfield began to take control and Wilkie almost reduced the arrears with a fine drive. With just minutes remaining a fine through ball by Styles gave Bertschin the chance to score Birmingham's fourth goal.

Wigan left the field to great applause, they had gone down in style. Sir Alf Ramsey, the City manager, visited the Latics dressing room after the match to congratulate the team.

Birmingham City: Montgomery, Calderwood, Styles, Towers, Howard, Gallagher, Connolly, Francis, Bertschin, Hibbitt, Dillon. (sub: Page)

Wigan Athletic: Brown, Morris, Hinnigan, Gore, Ward, Gillibrand, Whittle, Worswick, Moore, Wilkie, Wright. (sub: Smart)

Attendance 29,202 Referee: T.Mills (Barnsley)

MATCH TO REMEMBER No.18

Hereford United 0 Wigan Athletic 0: 19 August 1978

Over three thousand Wigan fans made the historic journey to Edgar Street for Latics' first-ever game in the Football League and the roar that greeted the team as Ian Gillibrand proudly led them out would have intimidated the greatest in the land.

Despite playing with a five man defence, the Latics looked like an all-out attacking side, with Corrigan commanding the midfield and Gore and Hinningan making effective overlapping attacks on the wings. After 18 minutes, Houghton rose to head home a Hinnigan free-kick but the Hereford defence were quickly out and the referee judged it offside. A second free-kick from Gore beat Hereford's defensive wall, forcing Hughes to make a brilliant point-blank save from Wilkie. Then a superb through ball from Gore split the Hereford defence once again - Corrigan raced with Hughes, only to be narrowly beaten.

For Hereford, Jones forced Brown in the Wigan goal to make a number of good saves, including a powerful header which Brown at full stretch, tapped over the bar. With just four minutes left, the home side almost took the lead when Spiring's free-kick left Jones completely unmarked in front of goal but he completely missed his kick. Jeff Wright nearly snatched a last minute winner with a long range shot that Hughes only just only got his fingers to.

Hereford United: Hughes, Roberts, Price, Cornes, Spiring, Marshall, W.Holmes, K.Holmes, Jones, Powell, Barton. (sub: Feeley)

Wigan Athletic: Brown, Gore, Hinningan, Davids, Ward, Gillibrand, Corrigan, Wright, Houghton, Wilkie, Purdie. (sub: Crompton)

Attendance 5,674 Referee: A.J.Hamill (Wolverhampton)

Action from Latics first League match.

MATCH TO REMEMBER No.19

Wigan Athletic 5 Port Vale 3: 13 April 1979

For the first hour of this game Wigan played atrociously, and their last chances of promotion seemed to have slipped away. Many supporters started to stream out of the ground in disgust, and at half-time discarded season tickets were found in the players' tunnel. Vale went one up when Bernie Wright dived to head past Brown, and increased their score to two just before half-time when Todd took advantage of a misunderstanding between Ward and Smart. In the 59th minute Todd scored a third for the visitors and a large black cloud gathered over Springfield Park.

Five minutes later, Brownbill replaced Ward and almost immediately freed Houghton to shoot past the diving Dance in the Port Vale goal. Six minutes later Houghton added a second when he chipped the ball over Dance from a virtually impossible angle.

There was an almighty roar in the seventy-forth minute, when Houghton completed his hat-trick, glancing the ball home from Wright's cross. The roar had hardly died down when the unbelievable happened. Hinnigan rose to head Purdie's corner to Brownbill who smashed it into the roof of the net to make it 4-3 to Wigan.

Moore made it five a few minutes from time when he chipped over the advancing Dance. The crowd went wild and Latics were given a standing ovation as they left the field - five incredible goals in 19 minutes!

Wigan Athletic: Brown, Smart, Hinnigan, Gore, Ward (sub Brownbill), Fretwell, Corrigan, Wright, Houghton, Moore, Purdie

Port Vale: Dance, Keenan, Griffiths, Beech, Delgado, Hawkins, N.Chamberlain, Farrell, Wright, Todd, Healey. (sub: M.Chamberlain)

Attendance 8,452 Referee: K.J.Butcher (Kendal)

MATCH TO REMEMBER No.20

Chelsea 0 Wigan Athletic 1: 14 January 1980

This was a memorable F.A. Cup third round victory at Stamford Bridge, the home of the Second Division leaders. It was obvious from the start that this young inexperienced Chelsea side would struggle to cope with a Wigan side snapping like terriers, but playing football way above their status on a bone-hard surface.

Wigan carried the game to Chelsea in the first-half and could have gone ahead in the first minute but finally sent their large following delirious six minutes before half-time when a cross from the right was collected by Tommy Gore on the edge of the penalty area. He found the net with a delightful chip over the stranded Borota.

The Latics faced a nerve-tingling rearguard action throughout most of the second-half as Chelsea went in search of the equaliser. The post came to Wigan's rescue when Fillery's shot beat Tunks before rebounding to safety. Wigan too had their chances even when they were under such pressure in the second-half, but were denied further goals by the pitch and their own understandable eagerness.

The final whistle went, and the players sped to the end of the ground where the Latics fans were housed - it was a case of magnificent performers saluting their magnificent supporters.

Chelsea: Borota, Locke, Sparrow, Hales, Pates, Chivers, Britton, Fillery, Langley, Walker, Harris

Wigan Athletic: Brown, Fretwell, Hinnigan, Gore, Methven, Davids, Corrigan, Wright, Houghton, Brownbill (sub: T.Quinn), Urquhart

Attendance 22,300 Referee: D.Lloyd (Fernhill Heath)

MATCH TO REMEMBER No.21

Everton 3 Wigan Athletic 0: 31 January 1980

Derek Brownbill almost scores for Latics.

Reaching the fourth round of the FA Cup for the first time in their history, this tie captured the imagination of the town. Thousands upon thousands made the short trip to Goodison and the staggering attendance of 51,863 was the biggest Cup crowd of the day. There had been a massive build up, and the match was televised and it really was an occasion to savour.

In the opening minutes, Peter Houghton put in a dazzling left-wing run and cross that Derek Brownbill just failed to convert. It was only just before half-time that winger Joe McBride put Everton in front with a shot that John Brown just failed to save. After half-time the match became more physical but the turning point came when Joe Hinnigan was injured and carried off on a stretcher. It transpired that a breakdown of communication from the Latics bench to the other side of the pitch resulted in substitute Tony Quinn getting on the field too quickly. Hinnigan could have carried on, but the damage had been done - Latics' poise was lost.

Bob Latchford added a second for Everton when he headed home a corner and when Brian Kidd blasted home a third the job was complete. But then the match, which had been simmering for some time, finally boiled over with an off the ball incident between Brian Kidd and Neil Davids. It left Davids flattened in the back of the net but it also resulted in Kidd getting sent to the dressing room. It was a sad end to what was a memorable match.

Everton : Hodge; Gidman, Bailey, Wright, Lyons, Eastoe, Hartford, Stanley, Latchford, Kidd, McBride: Sub: Ross:

Wigan Athletic: Brown; Fretwell, Hinnigan, Gore, Methven, Davids, Corrigan, Wright, Houghton, Brownbill, G.Urquhart: Sub: T.Quinn:

Attendance: 51,863: Referee: P.Willis (Durham)

MATCH TO REMEMBER No. 22

Wigan Athletic 4 Chelsea 2: 11 November 1981

Latics again overcame the discrepancy in status in a League Cup contest of traditional passion and romance. Much of the drama was squeezed into the thrilling first-half, which was punctuated by five goals. After nine minutes Lee wasted a good chance for the visitors, but four minutes later Bumstead put Chelsea ahead, although it took him three attempts to beat Tunks' spectacular attempts to save.

The Latics retort to such adversity could scarcely have been more impressive; three goals in 11 minutes, two of them credited to 18-year-old midfielder Mark Wignall. Wignall chipped his first-ever senior goal from 20 yards over Steve Francis, and the Chelsea goalkeeper was again helpless when the same player scored with an arrowing drive from five yards further out. Sandwiched in between these two goals was a mishit effort from Evans that rolled inside Francis' far post, after Sheldon, looking offside, had been allowed to cross.

The next twist came when Fillery's free-kick took a hugh deflection off the Wigan wall and left Tunks again cursing his luck. In the second-half, Sheldon got to the by-line and crossed for Bradd to score at the far post. Larry Lloyd Wigan's player-manager joyously led his side into the fourth round of the League Cup for the first time in the Club's history.

Wigan Athletic: Tunks, McMahon, Cribley, Wignall, Lloyd, Methven, Sheldon, Barrow, Bradd, Houghton, Evans

Chelsea: Francis, G.Wilkins (sub Droy), Hutchings, Britton, Pates, Chivers, Rhodes-Brown, Bumstead, Lee, Walker, Fillery

Attendance 12,063 Referee: K.V. Redfern (Whitley Bay)

MATCH TO REMEMBER No.23

Wigan Athletic 1 Aston Villa 2: 1 December 1981

Peter Houghton scores Latics goal.

A crowd of 15,362 roared the Latics to an early goal and a splendid fighting finish. They reserved their jeers and catcalls for the Football League champions who escaped with a streaky equaliser, a last minute goal, and dreary negative tactics.

The Latics took the lead in the 9th minute. Quinn glanced the ball through to Houghton who was in oceans of space, who curled his measured shot over and beyond Rimmer in the Villa goal and pandemonium ensued for several minutes. It was Houghton again a few minutes later who held off three Villa defenders with a 40 yard run and cross.

Tunks had to make his first real save after 37 minutes when Morley at last found the target with a fierce, low drive. Early in the second-half, Bremner shot wide from a good position and Tunks saved well from a Withe header. The equaliser came in and most unsatisfactory way. Cowans fed Shaw with a lovely through pass and Tunks dived at his feet, Shaw pushed the ball past him and dived spectacularly. There may have been contact with Tunks but Shaw made a meal of it and the boos continued long after Cowans had dispatched the penalty kick. The last quarter of an hour belonged to Wigan as the League champions resorted to time-wasting and passes to their goalkeeper. It was a rank injustice, and heart-breaking for Wigan when Methven's slip presented the ball to Evans and Withe put the ball past the gallant Tunks at the second attempt.

Wigan Athletic: Tunks, McMahon, Cribley, Wignall (sub: Wright), Bradd, Methven, Sheldon, Barrow, Quinn, Houghton, C.Evans

Aston Villa: Rimmer, Swain, Gibson, A.Evans, Williams, Deacy, Bremner, Shaw, Withe, Cowans, Morley

Attendance 15,362 Referee: D.Hutchinson (Harrogate)

MATCH TO REMEMBER No.24

Scunthorpe United 2 Wigan Athletic 7: 12 March 1982

In a match full of incident, Scunthorpe, with former England cricket captain Ian Botham in their ranks were overpowered right from the start.

The goal feast started after just three minutes. Les Bradd headed in Evans' corner, and by half-time, Latics had powered their way to a 3-0 lead. The team was given a thunderous ovation at the interval by Scunthorpe's fans as well as their own.

(Top) Les Bradd completes his hat-trick)
(Below) Colin Methven acknowledges his goal and Latics sixth.

Scunthorpe's hopes flickered temporarily after the break when Telfer pulled a goal back as the referee ignored the linesman's offside flag. But Wigan soon got to grips with the tricky, swirling wind and stepped up a gear to sail into a 5-1 lead. Telfer made it 5-2, before Latics added two further goals to complete their highest score in League football and their best away win.

Bradd scored three glorious goals, Houghton got a couple and Methven and Barrow chipped in with the other two. But perhaps the unluckiest man on the field was Eamonn O'Keefe who had an outstanding game, for he was denied two first-half goals by the posts and then in the second-half when Wigan were awarded a penalty, his firmly struck kick was saved by Neenan who blatantly moved before the ball was kicked.

Scunthorpe United: Neenan, Lambert, Pilling, Keeley, Dall, Oates, Arins, Telfer, Botham, Moss,Pointon

Wigan Athletic: Tunks, McMahon, Glenn, Wignall, Cribley, Methven, O'Keefe, Barrow, Bradd, Houghton, Evans

Attendance 2,599 Referee: M.Scott (Nottingham)

MATCH TO REMEMBER No,.25

Brentford 1 Wigan Athletic 3: 1 June 1985

Wigan Athletic completed a unique double for the town by winning the Freight Rover Trophy Final against Brentford with a display of style and skill that won the admiration of all. They emulated the town's Rugby League side who beat Hull 28-24 in exciting style a month earlier.

The teams come out at Wembley

Latics outnumbered off the field by fans who could virtually walk to Wembley Stadium, made up for that on the famous old turf with an almost faultless display.

Brentford, unbeaten for 13 games were seldom in the hunt as Latics always looked the more composed and determined side. Goalkeeper Roy Tunks did well in the 4th minute, saving well from the giant Booker, and in the early stages all the Latics defenders worked hard, but Wigan got on top and the first goal came in the 25th minute. Barry Knowles, only in the team because of an injury to John Butler, looped a ball to the right after a clearance from Tunks and Mike Newell took advantage of a mistake by Keith Millen to gain control before crashing a great shot into the net. Latics second goal came 12 minutes later when Graham Barrow beat Steve Wignall to the ball and back-heeled it for Tony Kelly to beat Brentford goalkeeper Gary Phillips with a well struck long shot. Both sides were playing attacking football, and there was a shock for the Latics soon after the restart when Robbie Cooke scored for Brentford with a super volley from a left-wing centre by Gary Roberts.

Latics hit back and Newell was unlucky to have a shot cleared off the line. From the corner which followed, David Lowe scored a spectacular third goal for Wigan with an overhead kick from a pass by Gary Bennett. From then on, try as Brentford might, they were not destined to become the first winners of the Freight Rover Trophy ... that honour belonged to Wigan Athletic.

Brentford: Phillips, Salman, Murray, Millen, Wignall, Hurlock, Kamara, Cooke, Booker (sub: Torrance) Cassels, Roberts. (sub: Bullivant)
Wigan Athletic: Tunks, Cribley, Knowles, Kelly, Walsh, Methven, Lowe, Barrow, Bennett, Newell, Langley. (subs: Aspinall and Jewell)

Attendance 39,897 Referee: T.Bune (Newbury)

MATCH TO REMEMBER No.26

Wigan Athletic 1 Norwich City 0: 31 January 1987

Latics marched proudly into the fifth round of the F.A. Cup with a staggering win over the First Division outfit who just didn't know what hit them. This was no lucky victory derived by dragging Norwich City down to Third Division level, it was achieved through careful planning and the determination of 11 men who performed like heroes. Records show that Paul Jewell grabbed the all important goal after 78 minutes in a tie lacking skill on a tricky surface, but packed to the brim with incident and excitement.

Bobby Campbell missed two good openings early on, then David Lowe headed wide from a free header, but even though Norwich were second best for most of the match, they had a ten-minute spell early in the second-half that gave Latics food for thought.

Just when it seemed as if the teams would be heading back to Carrow Road, a Hamilton cross was headed down by Campbell and there was Jewell nipping in to finish things off and put the Latics into the fifth round of the F.A. Cup for the first time in their history.

Wigan Athletic:	Tunks, Hamilton, Knowles, Cook, Cribley, Holden, Lowe, Thompson, Campbell, Jewell, Hilditch
Norwich City:	Gunn, Culverhouse, Spearing, Bruce, Phelan, Butterworth, Crook, Drinkell, Rosario, Biggins, Gordon
Attendance 8,095	Referee: M.Reed (Birmingham)

MATCH TO REMEMBER No.27

Wigan Athletic 0 Leeds United 2: 15 March 1987

A scoreline of 4-2 in Latics favour would not have been out of place. Leeds couldn't have complained about that, as Latics displaying all the skill and poise that got them within striking distance of Wembley proved once again what a talented side they were.

But in a game where the howling wind had the biggest say of all, they couldn't convert their undoubted superiority into goals. The Yorkshire side weathered all Wigan's pressure and carved out two openings of their own. Midway through the second-half Leeds pounced to send Latics on the slippery road to defeat in this F.A. Cup sixth round tie. John Stiles, son of Nobby, curled a shot round a bemused Latics defence and into the corner. Moments later Thompson squandered the easiest of chances to drag Latics level. Then after 74 minutes, Mickey Adams scored Leeds' second goal with a screaming 20-yarder past the stranded Tunks. The standing ovation afforded to Latics at the end of the game was their way of saying, 'thanks lads you've done us all proud'.

Wigan Athletic:	Tunks, Hamilton, Knowles, Hilditch, Cribley, Beesley, Lowe, Thompson, Campbell, Jewell (sub: Butler), Griffiths
Leeds United:	Day, Aspin, Adams, Stiles, Ashurst, Rennie, Ritchie, Sheridan, Pearson, Edwards, Swan
Attendance 12,497	Referee: B.Hill (Kettering)

MATCH TO REMEMBER No.28

Bolton Wanderers 1 Wigan Athletic 3: 25 August 1987

The Latics banished memories of their first leg disaster when they'd lost to Wanderers 3-2 at home with a blistering display when the chips were down.

It was the old warhorse Bobby Campbell - at just £25,000 he must rank as one of Latics finest ever buys - who led the charge and took the honours with an incredible half-hour hat-trick in a pulsating tie. Bolton took the lead in the 17th minute through striker John Thomas to put the home side into a 4-2 aggregate lead.

Eight minutes into the second-half, manager Ray Mathias made an inspired double substitution with Ian Griffiths and Mark Hilditch replacing an off-key Paul Cook and a limping Stuart Storer - who was later to play for Bolton.

After 61 minutes, Hilditch flicked the ball on and Campbell blasted a thundering drive in off the underside of the bar. Ten minutes later, Campbell rose high to power a free-kick into the bottom corner after Hilditch had been fouled. There was an explosive finish when Jewell rattled the Bolton bar and as the ball bounced down, Campbell raced in to score with a brave header.

Bolton Wanderers: Felgate, Scott, Crombie, S.Thompson, Came, Sutton, Henshaw, Joyce, Morgan, Thomas, Chandler. (sub: Neal)

Wigan Athletic: Tunks, Butler, Knowles, Hamilton, Cribley, Beesley, Storer (sub: Hilditch), Thompson, Campbell, Jewell, Cook. (sub: I.Griffiths)

Attendance 5,847 Referee: G.Courtney (Spennymoor)

MATCH TO REMEMBER No.29

Wigan Athletic 2 Liverpool 5 (at Anfield): 19 September 1989

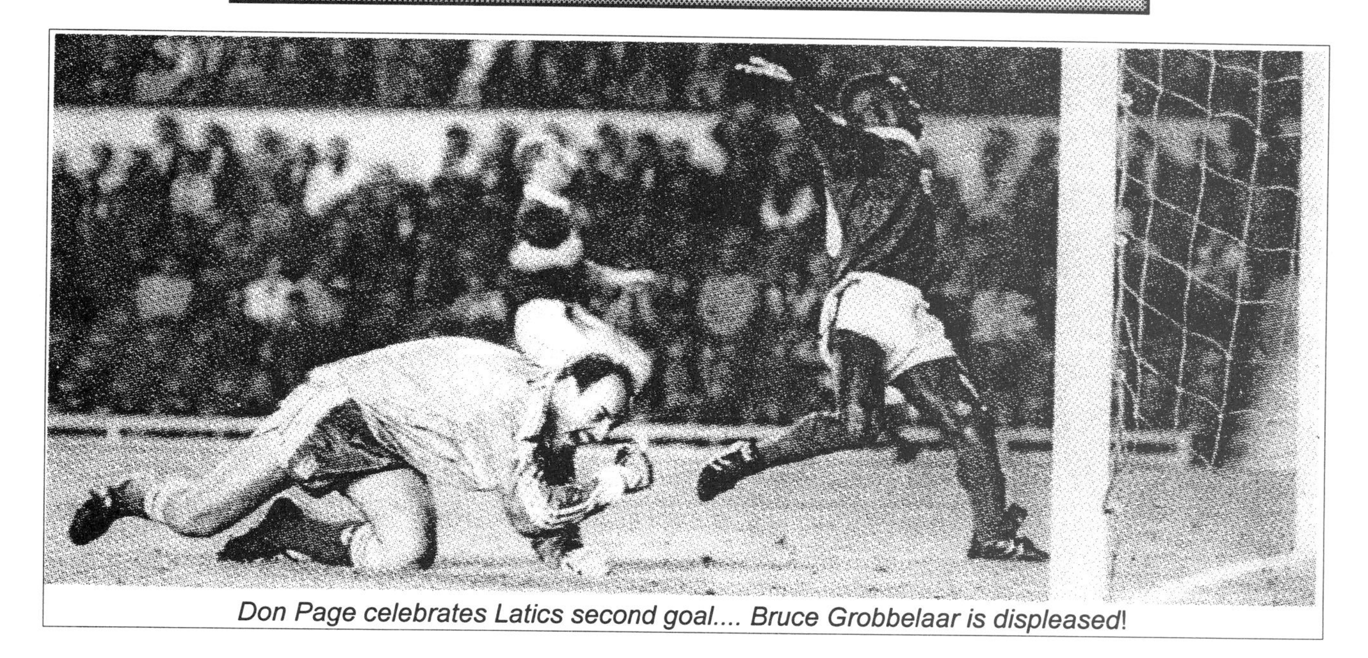

Don Page celebrates Latics second goal.... Bruce Grobbelaar is displeased!

For ten magical minutes of this absorbing Littlewoods Cup clash, Wigan's team of bargain basement buys had the multi-million pound megastars of Liverpool in total turmoil.

Liverpool went ahead in the 4th minute through Glenn Hysen. Then the tried and trusty left peg of little Bryan Griffiths pulled Latics level in the 17th minute with a superbly struck free-kick that goalkeeper Bruce Grobbelaar never saw. One of the greatest shocks in British soccer seemed on the cards when David Thompson turned on a sixpence to shoot Latics into an unbelievable 55th minute 2-1 lead.

From being 2-1 down and in the bad books of their fans, Liverpool's clinical style turned the tables at 3-2, as Ian Rush scored two goals from close range. Liverpool were rampant now and Latics party celebrations were broken up by a series of high speed attacks. Nigel Adkins was called upon to save a 70th minute penalty from John Barnes after Tankard had tripped Peter Beardsley. The striker tried to ram home the rebound but Adkins stayed his ground to complete a breathtaking double save. Liverpool's blushes were spared by Beardsley who gathered a through ball from Jan Molby to score the Red's fourth goal, then Barnes redeemed himself two minutes from the end of the game by heading home Liverpool's fifth goal. Wigan manager Bryan Hamilton gave 16-year-old Steve Nugent a baptism of fire as he replaced Don Page on a never to be forgotten night.

Wigan Athletic: Adkins, Atherton, Tankard, Rimmer, Patterson, Beesley, Thompson, Parkinson, Carberry (sub: Johnson), Page (sub: Nugent), Griffiths.
Liverpool: Grobbelaar, Hysen, Burrows, Nicol, Whealan, Hansen, Beardsley, Gillespie (sub: Venison), Rush, Barnes, Molby
Attendance 19,231 Referee: L.R. Dilkes (Mossley)

MATCH TO REMEMBER No.30

Coventry City 1 Wigan Athletic 1: 5 January 1991

Wigan 'keeper Tony Pennock, making his debut in this F.A. Cup third round tie, pulled off a series of fine saves in the early stages to keep his side in the game. The first-half remained goalless but two minutes into the second, the Latics should have taken the lead when Neill Rimmer found himself with only Ogrizovic to beat but failed to hit the target.

Coventry took the lead after 66 minutes when they were awarded a controversial free-kick; Micky Gynn evaded his marker after the deftest of touches from Cyrille Regis inside the box, had outfoxed Latics.

Darren Patterson, an 83rd minute substitute, equalised for Latics well into injury time. Winger Ray Woods who had a superb game and later joined Coventry, skipped out of his marker's tackle and fired over a cross that honed in on Patterson's head, with Radar-like efficiency. City 'keeper Stev Ogrizovic was beaten hands down and a replay was no more than Latics deserved. In the replay at Springfield Park, Latics went down 1-0 in front of a crowd of 7,429.

Coventry City: Ogrizovic, Borrows, Edwards, Billing, Kilcline, Peake, Gallager (sub: Drinkwell), Gynn, Regis, Emerson, Smith

Wigan Athletic: Pennock, Parkinson, Tankard, Atherton, Johnson, Langley, Woods, Rimmer, Fairclough (sub: Patterson), Page, B.Griffiths. (sub: Carberry)

Attendance 10,802

Referee: C.Trussell (Birkenhead)

LATICS MANAGERS

Charlie Spencer	(1932-37)
Jimmy Milne	(1946-47)
Bob Pryde	(1949-52)
Ted Goodier	(1952-54)
Walter Crook	(1954-55)
Ron Suart	(1955-56)
Billy Cooke	(1956)
Sam Barkas	(1957)
Trevor Hitchen	(1957-58)
Malcolm Barrass	(1958-59)
Jimmy Shirley	(1959)
Pat Murphy	(1959-60)
Allenby Chilton	(1960)
Johnny Ball	(1960-63)
Allan Brown	(1964-66)
Alf Craig	(1966-67)
Harry Leyland	(1967-68)
Allan Sanders	(1968)
Ian McNeill	(1968-70)
	(1976-81)
Gordon Milne	(1970-72)
Les Rigby	(1972-74)
Brian Tiler	(1974-76)
Larry Lloyd	(1981-83)
Harry McNally	(1983-85)
Bryan Hamilton	(1985-86)
	(1989-93)
Ray Mathias	(1986-89)
Dave Philpotts	(1993)
Kenny Swain	(1993-94)
Graham Barrow	(1994-95)
John Deehan	(1995 -)

CHARLIE SPENCER: 1932-1937

The first manager Wigan Athletic ever had, Charlie Spencer was appointed in August 1932. He only had two weeks to get a team together but after some frantic efforts and shrewd persuasion, he managed to form a side.

Charlie Spencer was more than just a good manager, he was a great character and a strict disciplinarian. One of the best known stories about him concerns the ritual which surrounded his arrival at the ground in the morning. At the time he lived in Blackpool and was one of the few people in the area to have a car. The players, all full-time professionals, had been told to report every morning at 10 o'clock and Charlie Spencer generally arrived about ten minutes later. The players used to lounge around the dressing rooms until they heard the familiar sound of their manager's car drawing up outside. That was the signal to move, for by the time Charlie walked into the dressing room the players were changed into their kit and ready for training!

When he left Wigan to join First Division Grimsby Town, he promised the Latics he would bring his new team to play them in a friendly. It was another six years before he brought his star-studded side to Springfield Park and they beat Latics 5-2. After managing Grimsby Town, he joined York City and in the early fifties, he wanted to rejoin Wigan and was on the short list for the managerial vacancy when Latics appointed Ted Goodier.

JIMMY MILNE: 1946-1947

One of the best uncapped wing-halves of the inter-war period, he was a regular in the Preston North End side up to the outbreak of war and made 272 League appearances for the Club. A very consistent player, who attacked well and was reliable in defence, he played in the 1937 F.A. Cup Final when North End lost to Sunderland, but missed the Lilywhites winning Final the following year due to injury.

Appointed Wigan's manager at the start of the 1946-47 season, the Club had a disastrous season under him, finishing bottom of the Cheshire League. Worse was to come because in a fight for re-election between Latics and Ashton United, Ashton took the honours 16-8 and Wigan had to make way for Winsford United. Meanwhile, Milne had departed to Morecambe before returning to Deepdale as trainer in the early 1950's.

He later managed North End and led them to the 1964 F.A. Cup Final where they lost 3-2 to West Ham United. He sold his son Gordon, a former Latic, to Liverpool's Bill Shankly, a former team-mate of his at Deepdale.

BOB PRYDE - 1949-1952

Player-manager Bob Pryde arrived at Springfield Park from Blackburn Rovers in the summer of 1949, after playing in 320 League games for the Ewood park club.

Making his Latics debut in a 2-2 draw at home to Barrow on the opening day of the 1949-50 season, he went on to play in 22 games as Wigan finished runners-up in the Lancashire Combination. The following season he decided not to play and Latics took the title on goal average from Nelson.

In January 1952, with Latics topping the Lancashire Combination table, the Scottish-born manager parted company with the Club.

TED GOODIER - 1952-1954

Ted Goodier was brought to Wigan Athletic by the then chairman, Sid Littler, at the start of the 1952-53 season and in the years that followed Latics trophy cabinet was almost permanently filled. A tall, fair-haired wing-half, he was no mean player and played for Oldham Athletic, Queen's Park Rangers, Watford, Crewe and Rochdale, helping the Spotland club to win the Lancashire Senior Cup in 1949.

When he came to Springfield Park, Ted Goodier kept just two players, left-back Harry Parkinson and inside-forward Jackie Lyon, but he proceeded to build up a tremendous line-up that was soon to rule the world of non-League football. Standing more than six feet tall, Ted Goodier was the strictest of disciplinarians. The players knew exactly where they stood and not one of them ever put a foot out of line for they had the highest respect for their boss.

In the famous season 1953-54, Latics won practically everything there was to win under Ted Goodier - the Lancashire Combination Championship, the Lancashire Junior Cup and the Makerfield Cup.

In fact one year earlier they had gone one better and also won the Lancashire Combination Cup. First Division Newcastle United were also given a real fright in the F.A. Cup by Ted Goodier's side.

Ted Goodier stayed with the Latics until October 1954 when a personal row with Sid Littler, the man who had brought him to Springfield Park, led to him being sacked. He wasn't out of a job for long though, taking over at Oldham Athletic soon after his surprise dismissal.

WALTER CROOK - 1954-1955

A popular wing-half with Blackburn Rovers, Walter Crook made 218 League appearances for the Ewood Park club before later playing 28 games for Bolton Wanderers.

Retiring from playing in 1948 he went into management with Accrington Stanley. However, the club's fortunes sunk to the lowest possible depths as the Peel Park club plunged into a financial crisis. He was in charge at Accrington for two seasons, resigning after the club had finished bottom of the Third Division(North) in 1953-54.

Ted Goodier was replaced at Springfield Park by Walter. In his only season in charge at Wigan, the Latics finished third in the Lancashire Combination after goalscoring legend Billy Lomax moved to Nelson on Christmas Eve.

Walter Crook went on to manage Ajax of Amsterdam who turned professional in 1954. He had great success in Holland and helped establish Ajax as the renowned club of today.

RON SUART - 1955-1956

Ron Stuart made 280 appearances for Blackpool and Blackburn Rovers, mostly at full-back, although his favourite position was centre-half. He became player-manager at Wigan Athletic in September 1955, making his debut in a 6-0 win against Bacup Borough at Springfield Park on 8 October. He played in 34 first team games for Latics that season as the Club finished 5th in the Lancashire Combination.

Suart left Springfield Park at the end of the season to manage Scunthorpe United, steering them into Division Two as Northern Section champions in 1957-58, before leaving to manager Blackpool. After finishing 8th in his first season at Bloomfield Road, Blackpool and Stuart had to fight a constant battle against relegation and after the inevitable happened in 1967, the manager was dismissed.

Shortly after he worked in various capacities at Stamford Bridge. Initially he was assistant to Tommy Docherty, and succeeded Dave Sexton as manager in 1974. At the end of his first season, Chelsea were relegated and he became general manager.

BILLY COOKE - 1956

Arriving at Springfield Park in the summer of 1956, Billy Cooke managed the Latics for just three months at the beginning of the 1956-57 season.

The Club's biggest win during this period was a 7-0 first round Lanc. Combination Cup win over Lomax F.C. Surprisingly after a run of eight games without defeat, Cooke parted company with the Club and was replaced on a temporary basis by team captain Angus McLean.

SAM BARKAS - 1957

A brilliant left-back who cost Manchester City £5,000 when signed from Third Division Bradford City in 1934, he was one of four brothers who played football at League level. He was an important member of City's 1936-37 League Championship winning team. Barkas was still fit enough at the age of 38 to captain City to the Second Division championship of 1946-47.

There is no doubt that he would have won more than his five England caps but for the presence of Arsenal's Eddie Hapgood on the international scene.

He left Maine Road to become manager of Workington in 1947, and took over the reins of Wigan Athletic in 1957, where he led the side to fourth place in the Lancashire Combination before leaving just before the end of the season to be replaced by Trevor Hitchen. He then returned as talent scout to his beloved Maine Road where his achievements for the club are commemorated by a bar named after him in City's main stand.

TREVOR HITCHEN - 1957-1958

A former 'Bevin Boy', Trevor Hitchen worked down the pits during the Second World War. He became one of Southport's finest servants, making 241 League appearances and scoring 34 goals for the Haig Avenue club. Initially, he had joined Southport as a centre-forward but developed into a utility player.

Replacing Sam Barkas at Springfield Park towards the end of the 1956-57 season, he only stayed a short while before joining Southport as manager. He was at Haig Avenue for only half a season, later being involved with Formby F.C. for many years.

MALCOLM BARRASS - 1958-1959

Following in the footsteps of his father, Matt, who played League football for Blackpool, Sheffield Wednesday and Manchester City, he signed professional forms for Bolton Wanderers in November 1944. Honours soon came his way when he was chosen to play for England in the Victory International against Wales at the Hawthorns in October 1945.

He became a versatile player, once scoring four goals from the centre-forward position against Manchester City. But it was at centre-half that he won his three full England caps.

After twelve years at Burnden Park in which he played in 357 League and Cap games for the Wanderers, he ended his playing career at Sheffield United.

He became player-manager of Wigan Athletic in the summer of 1958 and made his debut against Skelmersdale United in a goalless draw on 23 August 1958. He played in 25 first team games for the Latics before resigning on New Years Day 1959. He ended his career in football with a two-and-a-half year spell at Southern League Nuneaton Borough before settling in the Bury area.

JIMMY SHIRLEY - 1959

The youngest player to appear in Charlie Spencer's side, he made 167 League appearances for the Latics, playing his last game in May 1952.

He was player-manager at Morecambe for just twelve months before travelling difficulties forced him to quit the job and return to Wigan in 1959 for a short spell as manager. He lifted the Latics from the lower reaches of the Lancashire Combination in his one season in charge and got them to the final of the Lancashire Junior Cup where they lost 4-1 to Chorley at Ewood Park before relinquishing the manager's chair. He continued to play an active part in the affairs of the Club and could lay claim to having helped with the pools, the social club and almost anything else he was asked to do!

PAT MURPHY - 1959-1960

Replacing Jimmy Shirley at the end of the 1958-59 season, Pat Murphy set about restoring the Club to its former glories after a disastrous season in which they finished 18th in the Lancashire Combination. Pat signed a number of players including former Nottingham Forest and Doncaster Rovers centre-forward Peter Higham who ended the season as the club's top scorer with 20 goals in his 29 League appearances. Latics ended the campaign as runners-up, a marked improvement on the previous season's fortunes.

In spite of this achievement, Murphy was sacked at the end of the season. Perhaps the friendly match in February 1960 when Latics chartered a plane to fly to Scotland to play Stirling Albion where they lost 5-1 went against him; the trip home was disastrous as the plane broke down and the Wigan party were forced to hitch home on separate flights as they became available!

ALLENBY CHILTON - 1960

A key figure in Manchester United's post-war teams, he made 353 appearances for the Reds before joining Grimsby Town on a free transfer. At Old Trafford he won an F.A. Cup winners' medal when United beat Blackpool in the 1948 Final and four years later he received a League Championship medal.

He was rated by Sir Matt Busby as his best-ever centre-half. The Mariners were in dire trouble when Allenby Chilton arrived as player-manager in March 1955 and though they won a few matches, they were unable to avoid relegation. However, within a year, he had transformed the club into Third Division (North) champions.

He retired from playing just after the start of the 1956-57 season and became a publican in York. The pull of the game was too great for him and he was appointed Wigan manager at the end of the 1959-60 season, Latics twelfth manager in ten years.

The popular Chilton was sacked on 15 December 1960, after Latics had been beaten 3-1 at home by New Brighton, only their fifth defeat in 27 games!

JOHNNY BALL - 1960-1963

Signed by Wigan in 1947 after he had left the armed services, his greatest asset was his tremendous speed, not only off the mark, but he was also able to keep up a terrific pace over long distances.

He stayed at Springfield Park just over twelve months, but to those who saw him play, it was obvious that Johnny Ball was destined for bigger things. Sure enough, in 1948, Manchester United offered Latics £2,000 for his services. He never lost his affection for Wigan, his home-town club, and was destined to return a few years later, after an illustrious Football League career.

He only stayed at Old Trafford for twelve months before moving to another First Division club in Bolton Wanderers. He enjoyed several excellent seasons at Burnden Park, many of those as club captain.

His First Division days over, Ball returned to Latics as team manager. But Wigan were struggling at the time in the Cheshire League and despite Ball's efforts, the team could not turn in the performances that the critical Wigan public expected of them and after a brief stay, Johnny Ball parted company with the Club.

ALLAN BROWN - 1964-66

Appointed player-manager in 1964, Allan Brown began the formation of one of the most attractive Wigan teams for many years.

A well-known former Scottish inside-forward, he began signing players immediately - Les Campbell, Ralph Gubbins, Roy Wilkinson, Bert Llewellyn and John Ryan, men who proved to be great favourites with the fans. The team superbly drilled and organised by Brown, won the Cheshire League under his guidance and no-one will forget the part that Brown the player had in the set-up. Cool, thoughtful and a fanatic for physical fitness, he made a tremendous impact at Springfield Park.

His success with Wigan Athletic soon had League clubs sniffing around and just 18 months after joining the Latics, he left to join Luton Town, one of his former clubs. After Luton Town, Allan Brown managed Torquay United and Blackpool but there were many of the qualities Brown brought to the game as a player-manager that seemed to elude him when he hung up his boots to concentrate solely on management.

ALF CRAIG - 1966-1967

Alf Craig joined the Latics in December 1964 and made his debut in a goalless draw at Bangor City. He went on to appear in 35 first team matches that season, eventually appearing in 203 games for the club.

In October 1966 he took over from Allan Brown as the Latics player-manager, but despite the Club finishing as runners-up in the Cheshire League, it was not a role he enjoyed and he was replaced by Harry Leyland at the end of the season.

HARRY LEYLAND - 1967-1968

Goalkeeper Harry Leyland made 381 League appearances for Everton, Blackburn Rovers and Tranmere before taking charge as manager at Wigan at the beginning of the 1967-68 season.

In a mixed campaign in which Wigan eventually finished 8th, Harry Leyland was dismissed in February 1968 after the Latics had gone seven matches that month undefeated!

ALLAN SANDERS - 1968

Replacing Harry Leyland as Latics manager during the 1967-68 season, Allan Sanders lasted just 32 days in the post.

However, during that time, he signed five new players, including Ian Gillibrand, who went on to play for Latics for over ten years.

IAN McNEILL - 1968-1970 & 1976-1981

A former Southend, Leicester City, Brighton and Aberdeen player, Ian McNeill was twice the manager of Wigan Athletic. He first took charge in May 1968 after having great success at Ross County. He had under three months to prepare a team for the newly formed Northern Premier League, and in his first season the Club finished as runners-up to Macclesfield and also runners-up to Southport in the Northern Floodlit League Cup.

The following season he was surprisingly sacked six weeks after the epic F.A. Cup encounter with Port Vale.

Following a spell at Salisbury and also back at Ross County, he rejoined the Latics in April 1976 following the resignation of Brian Tiler. After a disappointing 1976-77 season, the Latics gained League admission at the end of the following campaign.

Appointed full-time manager, he took Wigan to the creditable position of 6th in the first two seasons. However, following a heavy 3-0 defeat at lowly Port Vale the following season, he was sacked for a second time, on 18 February 1981.

GORDON MILNE - 1970-1972

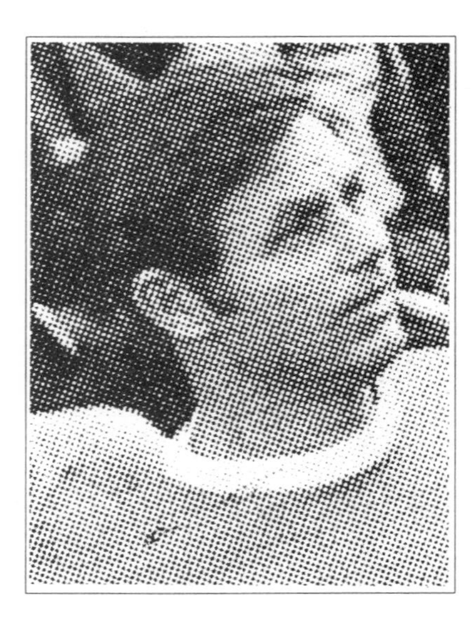

Gordon Milne joined the Latics in 1970 and followed in his father's footsteps, for Jimmy Milne was boss at Springfield Park for a short time when Latics were in the Cheshire League just after the war.

Beginning his career with Preston North End in 1958, he made 81 appearances for the Lilywhites before joining Liverpool. At Anfield he played in that magnificent side of the mid-sixties and won two League Championship medals, an F.A. Cup winners' medal and 14 England caps.

On leaving Liverpool, he joined Blackpool and it was from there that he joined Wigan to take up his first managerial post early in 1970. Although he guided the Latics to runners-up spot in his first season as manager of the Northern Premier League side, it is for his exploits as player-manager in the famous 1970-71 season that Gordon Milne will be remembered by Latics fans.

He guided the Club to the third round of the F.A. Cup, beating Peterborough United along the way, before Wigan were finally put out by First Division Manchester City. The Northern Premier League Championship came to Springfield Park at the end of the that season and the following year Third Division Halifax Town were put out of the F.A. Cup by Latics.

While he was at Springfield Park he was appointed manager of the England Youth team. It was obvious he would move on to better things and in 1972 he joined First Division Coventry City, and later took charge at Leicester City and of Turkish side Besiktas.

LES RIGBY - 1972-1974

Part-time manager of Wigan Athletic, Les Rigby's other job was that of Physical Education Lecturer at Wigan Technical College.

As a player, he had spells with Blackburn Rovers and Preston North End, but then National Service intervened. He started in non-League management with Lytham in the Lancashire Combination and then went on to Fleetwood and Rossendale United before joining Wigan in 1972. His first season at Springfield Park saw the Latics win through to the final of the F.A. Challenge Trophy at Wembley. He resigned as Latics manager in early March 1974 when the Wigan Board insisted on a full-time manager to run the Club and Les didn't want to leave his Physical Education job.

BRIAN TILER - 1974-1976

Brian Tiler started his League career with his home-town club of Rotherham United in July 1962 and scored 27 goals in 212 League appearances before joining Aston Villa in December 1968. Playing more of a defensive midfield role at Villa Park, he played in 107 League games before ending his League career with Carlisle United.

He joined Wigan Athletic as player-manager in July 1974 and made his Northern Premier League debut the following month in a 2-0 defeat at Northwich Victoria. Though he only played in 11 League games that season, the defeat at Northwich was one of only seven that term as Tiler's side took the League title by 4 points from Runcorn, gaining a record number of points in doing so.

The Club also did their traditional giant-killing in the F.A. Cup disposing of Shrewsbury Town after a replay. The following season, Latics finished 6th, the first time out of the top three in the Northern Premier League, and manager Tiler left the Club in 1976 to manage American side Portland Timbers.

One of his first jobs after taking over at Springfield Park had been to ensure that the Latics Youth side that Les Rigby had built up did not disintegrate. On the contrary, the side went from strength to strength, winning the Lancashire Youth Cup and having a tremendous run in the F.A. Cup Youth Cup competition.

In October 1978, Zambia, coached by Brian Tiler, became the first national team to play at Springfield Park. Sadly, Brian Tiler was killed in a car crash in 1990.

LARRY LLOYD - 1981-1983

A dominant figure in the centre of defence, Larry Lloyd's spells at both Liverpool and Nottingham Forest coincided with some vintage years for the clubs. Signed from Bristol Rovers for £50,000 in April 1969, he played in 150 League games for Liverpool and scored one of the goals in the Reds' UEFA Cup Final win over Borussia Moenchengladbach in 1973. He appeared in two European successes for Forest and won League Championship medals at both Anfield and the City ground.

Winning four full caps for England, he joined Wigan Athletic as player-manager in March 1981 and made his debut in a 1-0 defeat at home to Rochdale. Playing in 36 League games the following season, he led the Latics to third place in Division Four and promotion for the first time in the Club's history. However, following the Club's disappointing showing in 1982-83, he was sacked on 4 April 1983.

HARRY McNALLY - 1983-1985

Harry McNally never appeared in the Football League and spent most of his playing career with Skelmersdale United where he was also a coach in his latter days there. He was then appointed manager of non-League Altrincham and later Southport before joining Wigan Athletic as their chief scout, but later progressing to assistant-manager.

He was appointed Latics manager in June 1983 and after two seasons of struggling, he resigned in March 1985, after being asked to let his assistant Roy Tunks and coach Alex Bruce take charge for a while.

Three months later he took charge at Chester City and led them to runners-up spot in the Fourth Division in his first season and to 8th in the Third Division in 1988-89. Though attendances dropped off alarmingly following the loss of their Sealand Road ground, McNally kept the Club in the Third Division and was rewarded with a four year contract. However, after a poor start to the 1992-93 season, he was sacked.

BRYAN HAMILTON
1985-1986 & 1989-1993

A terrier-like midfield player in his days with Linfield, Ipswich Town, Everton, Swindon and Tranmere Rovers, he won 50 caps for Northern Ireland, who he currently manages.

He joined Tranmere Rovers as their player-manager in October 1980 and though he played his final game for them in November 1983, he remained in charge at the Prenton Park club until February 1985, when the likeable Irishman was sacked.

He joined Wigan Athletic later that year and led the Club to success in the Freight Rover Trophy Final in June 1985. One year on, after Latics had finished the season in 4th place in the Third Division, he joined Leicester City. In his first season in charge, the Filberts were relegated and when they were struggling the following season,he was sacked.

He returned to Springfield Park in March 1988 in a rather ambiguous role and only took full charge of team affairs a year later. Struggling with low crowds and little success on the pitch, Hamilton still managed to keep the Latics in the Third Division for four seasons, which was no mean achievement.

He lost his job in March 1993 as the Club struggled to get away from the foot of Division Two. The Latics did reach the Northern Final of the Autoglass Trophy in Hamilton's last season, but lost to Stockport County and so missed out on another trip to Wembley.

RAY MATHIAS - 1986-1989

Only Harold Bell had made more appearances for Tranmere Rovers than Ray Mathias, who played in 636 games in over 21 years at Prenton Park. He was assistant-manager to Bryan Hamilton at Tranmere, and followed him to Wigan Athletic before taking over as Latics manager in June 1986.

After a dreadful start, he led the Latics to their most successful season to date with an F.A. Cup run to the sixth round, where they lost 2-0 to Leeds United, and to fourth place in the League - thus gaining a play-off place. After a poor season with the Latics in 1988-89 he returned to Tranmere Rovers as coach.

DAVE PHILPOTTS - 1993

His playing career consisted of spell with Coventry City, Tranmere Rovers and also three-and-a-half years in American football before returning for a second spell with Tranmere where he finished his playing career when a back injury forced him to retire in 1984.

Dave Philpotts was appointed Latics coach in the summer of 1986 but later moved to assistant-manager before becoming manager in 1993.

KENNY SWAIN - 1993-1994

Birkenhead-born Kenny Swain started his career as a midfield player with Chelsea, scoring 26 goals in 119 League appearances for the Stamford Bridge club. In December 1978 he joined Aston Villa and moved to right-back. He won League Championship and European Cup winners' medals whilst at Villa Park before signing for Nottingham Forest in October 1982.

He later played for Portsmouth, West Bromwich Albion and Crewe Alexandra, appearing in 625 League games for his six clubs. He became Latics manager in 1993 but after the Club finished 19th in the Third Division, in his only season in charge, he was dismissed.

GRAHAM BARROW - 1994-1995

Joining Latics from Altrincham in 1981, Graham Barrow played in 212 League and Cup games for Latics before signing for Chester City in July 1986. A long-time friend of Harry McNally, whom Barrow played under at Altrincham, Wigan and Chester, he was employed at the Sealand Road club as player-coach before becoming assistant-manager in 1988. After Chester had made a poor start to the 1992-93 season, McNally was sacked and replaced by Barrow.

Things did not improve much after he took over and at the end of his first season in charge, which was also Chester's first in their new Deva Stadium, they were relegated. In 1993-94 they finished runners-up to Shrewsbury Town to win immediate promotion. He became Latics manager in September 1994 and sparked a dramatic improvement in the Club's fortunes. The Latics' revival under Graham Barrow was so emphatic that there was a period during the 1994-95 season when the air was thick with the talk of a possible play-off place. After starting the 1995-96 season with a squad containing a good balance of youth and experience, Graham Barrow was surprisingly sacked in October 1995 following Latics 6-2 home defeat by Mansfield Town.

JOHN DEEHAN - 1995 to date

Birmingham-born John Deehan enjoyed a lengthy playing career, making 379 League appearances and scoring 121 goals. He began with Aston Villa before playing with West Bromwich Albion, Norwich City, Ipswich, Manchester City and Barnsley. He won League Cup winners' medals with Aston Villa in 1977 and Norwich City in 1985.

He was also capped by the England Under-21 side on seven occasions. He worked as a coach with Manchester City, Barnsley and Norwich City before becoming manager at Carrow Road in January 1994. He took charge of the Canaries following the departure of Mike Walker, but Norwich were at the time adopting a policy of selling their best players, so he resigned in November 1995.

He took over at Springfield Park following the departure of Graham Barrow early in the 1995-96 season and almost took the Latics to promotion via the play-offs in his first season, the Club losing their last match at home to Northampton Town.

The Club made a good start to the 1996/97 season under the popular Deehan, and many Latics fans believe he is the manager who will bring the good times back to Springfield Park.

NAME	Born		Joined		Left		Pos	Appearances		Goals	
								League	Cup	Lge.	Cup
ADEKOLA David	Lagos, Nigeria	19 May 1968	Bury	94-95	Hereford U.	94-95	F	4	0(1)	0	0
ADKINS Nigel H.	Birkenhead	11 Mar 1965	Tranmere R.	86-87	Released	92-93	G	155	24	0	0
AINSCOW Andrew P.	Orrell	1 Oct 1968	Apprentice	87-88	Rotherham U.	89-90	F	14(8)	0(2)	4	0
APPLETON Stephen	Liverpool	27 Jul 1973	Y.T.	90-91	Released	92-93	CD	31(17)	4(2)	1	0
ASPINALL Warren G.	Wigan	13 Sep 1967	Apprentice	94-95	Everton	86-87	F	39(12)	3(4)	22	2
ASPINALL Wayne	Wigan	10 Dec 1964	Atherton	83-84	Released	84-85	FB	8	0	0	0
ATHERTON Peter	Orrell	6 Apr 1970	Y.T.	87-88	Coventry C.	91-92	CD	145(4)	15	1	0
BAILEY Neil	Billinge	26 Sep 1958	Newport C.	83-84	Stockport C.	86-87	LM	31(10)	7(2)	2	0
BARNWELL-EDINBORO Jamie	Hull	26 Dec 1975	Coventry C.(L)	95-96			F	2(8)	0	1	0
BARACLOUGH Ian R.	Leicester	4 Dec 1970	Leicester C.	89-90	Grimsby T.	90-91	F	8(1)	0	2	0
BARROW Graham	Chorley	13 Jun 1954	Altrincham	81-82	Chester C.	86-87	M	173(6)	24	36	3
BEESLEY Paul	Liverpool	21 Jul 1965	Marine	84-85	Leyton O.	89-90	CD	153(2)	19	3	0
BENJAMIN Ian T.	Nottingham	11 Dec 1961	Brentford	94-95	Kettering T.	95-96	F	14(9)	0(1)	7	0
BENNETT Gary M.	Liverpool	20 Sep 1962	Kirkby T.	84-85	Chester C.	85-86	F	10(10)	0	3	0
BIGGINS Wayne	Sheffield	20 Nov 1961	Stoke C.	95-96	*		F	15(1)	0	2	0
BLACK Anthony	Barrow	20 Nov 1961	Bamber Bridge	94-95	*		F	17(11)	2	2	2
BOUGHEY Darren J.	Stoke	15 Jul 1969	Stoke C.	90-91	Exeter C.	90-91	RW	2	0	2	0
BRADD Leslie J.	Buxton	6 Nov 1947	Stockport C.	81-82	Bristol R.	82-83	CF	57(6)	12	25	2
BROLLY Richard			U.S.A.	92-93	Released	92-93					
BROWN John C.	Bradford	30 Dec 1947	Stockport C.	78-79	Macclesfield	81-82	G	93	19	0	0
BROWNBILL Derek A.	Liverpool	4 Feb 1954	Port Vale	78-79	Released	79-80	M	32(16)	4(1)	8	1
BRUCE Alexander R.	Dundee	23 Dec 1952	Preston N.E.	83-84	Retired	84-85	F	35(8)	6(1)	7	2
BUCKLEY Glen	Wigan	31 Aug 1960	Preston N.E.	79-80	U.S.A	79-80	F	1	0	0	0
BUTLER John E.	Liverpool	7 Feb 1962	Prescot Cables Stokc C.	81-82 95-96	Stoke C. *	88-89	RB	270(7)	41(1)	16	2
CAMPBELL David	Eglinton	2 Jun 1965	Burnley	94-95	Cambridge U.	94-95	M	7	4	0	0
CAMPBELL Robert M.	Belfast	13 Sep 1956	Bradford C.	86-87	Released	87-88	F	61(8)	11	27	9
CARBERRY James	Liverpool	13 Oct 1969	Everton	89-90	Released	91-92	W	30(35)	5(2)	6	0
CARRAGHER Matthew	Liverpool	14 Jan 1976	Trainee	93-94	*		FB	91(10)	14(1)	0	3
COLLINS David D.	Dublin	30 Oct 1971	Liverpool	91-92			M	9	0	0	0
COMSTIVE Paul T.	Southport	25 Nov 1961	Rochdale	83-84	Wrexham	84-85	M	35	9	2	0
CONNELLY Dean	Glasgow	6 Jan 1970	Barnsley	91-92	Released	93-94	M	27(5)	3	3	0
COOK Paul A.	Liverpool	22 Feb 1967	Juniors	84-85	Norwich C.	88-89	M	77(6)	10	14	0
COOPER Steven	Birmingham	22 Jun 1964	Tranmere R.(L)	92-93			F	4	0	0	0
CORRIGAN Frank J.	Liverpool	13 Nov 1952	Northwich V.	78-79	Stafford R.	80-81	M	113(3)	15	12	3
CRIBLEY Alexander	Liverpool	1 Apr 1957	Liverpool	80-81	Retired	87-88	CD	268(3)	44(1)	16	1
CROMPTON Alan	Manchester	6 Mar 1958	Blackburn R.	78-79	Released	79-80	M	7(7)	2	0	0
CROMPTON Jonathan D.	Orrell	25 Jan 1970	Y.T.	89-90	Altrincham	89-90	G	1	0(1)	0	0
CURTIS John	Poulton-le-Fylde	2 Sep 1954	Blackburn R.	78-79	Released	80-81	FB	32	1	0	0
DALEY Phillip	Liverpool	12 Apr 1967	Newton	89-90	Lincoln City	93-94	F	152(9)	20(1)	40	1
DAVIDS Neil G.	Bingley	22 Sep 1955	Swansea C.	78-79	Released	81-82	CD	66(2)	11	1	0
DIAMOND Anthony J.	Rochdale	23 Aug 1968	Blackburn R.	88-89	Blackpool	89-90	F	6	0	2	0
DIAZ Isidoro	Valencia (Spain)	15 May 1972	CF Balaguer	95-96	*		F	31(5)	6	10	2
DOOLAN John	Liverpool	10 Nov 1968	Knowsley U.	91-92	Released	95-96	M	29(9)	5	1	0
DOWE Julian	Manchester	9 Sep 1975	Trainee	94-95	Released	94-95	M	0	0(2)	0	0
DUFFY Christopher	Manchester	31 Oct 1873	Trainee	93-94	Northwich Vic.	94-95	M	15(16)	3(1)	1	1
EDWARDSON Barry J.	Hindley	4 Nov 1972	Y.T.	91-92	Released	91-92	M	0(1)	0	0	0
ENTWISTLE Wayne P.	Bury	6 Aug 1958	Bury	88-89	Altrincham	89-90	F	24(5)	1	6	0
EVANS Clive A.	Birkenhead	1 May 1957	Tranmere R.	81-82	Crewe A.	82-83	FB	29(3)	7	2	1
FAIRCLOUGH David	Liverpool	5 Jan 1957	Tranmere R.	90-91	Released	90-91	F	4(3)	3	1	0
FALLON Shaun	Widnes	10 Sep 1970	Y.T.	88-89	Released	89-90	LB	2(1)	0	0	0
FARNWORTH Simon	Chorley	28 Oct 1963	Preston N.E.	93-94	*		G	126	16	0	0
FARRELL Andrew	Colchester	7 Oct 1965	Burnley	94-95	Released	95-96	WD	51(4)	7(1)	1	0
FELGATE David W.	Blaenau Ffestinog	4 Mar 1960	Chester C.	95-96	Released	95-96	G	3	2	0	0
FRETWELL David	Normanton	18 Feb 1952	Bradford C.	78-79	Northwich Vic.	80-81	CD	111(1)	14	0	0

NAME	Born		Joined		Left		Pos	Appearances		Goals	
								League	Cup	Lge.	Cup
FURLONG Carl D.	Liverpool	18 Oct 1976	Trainee	93-94	Released	95-96	F	1(2)	0(1)	1	0
GARDNER Paul A	Southport	22 Sep 1957	Preston N.E.	84-85	Released	84-85	RB	5	0	0	0
GARNETT Shaun	Wallasey	22 Nov 1969	Tranmere R.(L)	92-93			CD	13	0	1	0
GAVIN Patrick	Hammersmith	5 Jun 1967	Northampton T.	93-94	Released	94-95	F	37(5)	9(1)	8	3
GAY Geoffrey	Romford	4 Feb 1957	Southport	78-79	Released	78-79	M	1	0	0	0
GEMMILL Archibald	Paisley	24 Mar 1947	Jacksonville USA	82-83	Derby C.	82-83	M	11	2	0	0
GILLESPIE Keith	Larne	18 Feb 1975	Manchester U.(L)	93-94			F	8	0	4	0
GILLIBRAND Ian V.	Blackburn	24 Nov 1948	Arsenal	78-79	Coaching Staff	78-79	D	7	3	0	0
GLENN David A.	Wigan	30 Nov 1962	Apprentice	80-81	Blackburn R.	83-84	RB	68(4)	7	4	0
GORE Thomas J.	Liverpool	26 Nov 1953	Tranmere R.	78-79	Bury	80-81	M	102	17	14	8
GRAY Paul R.	Portsmouth	28 Jan 1970	Luton T.(L)	91-92			F	2(3)	2(1)	0	0
GREENALL Colin A.	Billinge	30 Dec 1963	Lincoln C.	95-96	*		CD	37	3	2	0
GREW Mark S.	Bilston	15 Feb 1958	W.B.A.(L)	78-79	Leicester C.		G	4	0	0	0
GRIFFITHS Bryan K.	St. Helens	26 Jan 1965	St. Helens T.	88-89	Blackpool	93-94	LW	176(13)	25(6)	44	8
GRIFFITHS Ian J.	Birkenhead	17 Apr 1960	Port Vale	85-86	Wrexham	91-92	LW	79(14)	13(1)	7	1
HAMILTON David	South Shields	7 Nov 1960	Cardiff C.	86-87	Chester C.	89-90	M	97(6)	14	7	1
HARFORD Paul	Kent	21 Oct 1974	Blackburn R.(L)	94-95			F	3	0	0	0
HART Nigel	Golborne	1 Oct 1958	Apprentice	78-79	Leicester C.	79-80	CD	1	0	0	0
HEMMING Christopher	Newcastle-Upon-Tyne	13 Apr 1966	Stoke C.	88-89	Hereford U.	89-90	CD	4	0	0	0
HILDERSLEY Ronald	Kirkcaldy	6 Apr 1965	Blackburn R.	90-91	Halifax T.	91-92	M	4	1	0	0
HILDITCH Mark W.	Royton	20 Aug 1960	Tranmere R.	86-87	Rochdale	90-91	F	89(14)	14(1)	26	3
HINNIGAN Joseph P.	Liverpool	3 Dec 1955	South Liverpool	78-79	Sunderland	79-80	FB	66	12	10	1
HOLDEN Andrew I.	Flint	14 Sep 1962	Chester C.	86-87	Oldham A.	88-89	CD	48(1)	10	4	0
HOLLIS Steven	Liverpool	22 Aug 1972	Liverpool	93-94	Released	93-94	M	0(1)	0	0	0
HOUGHTON Peter	Liverpool	30 Nov 1954	South Liverpool	78-79	Preston N.E.	79-80	F	169(16)	33(1)	62	6
HOUSTON Graham	Gibraltar	24 Feb 1960	Burnley	86-87	Carlisle U.	87-88	W	16(1)	4	4	0
HUGHES Philip	Manchester	16 Jun 1953	Bury	87-88	Rochdale	91-92	G	99	7	0	0
HUTCHINSON Robert	Glasgow	7 Dec 1956	Hibernian	80-81	Tranmere R.	81-82	M	34(1)	6	3	1
JAKUB Yanek	Falkirk	7 Dec 1956	Chester City	94-95	P.N.E. (Youth Dev.)	94-95	M	16	4	0	0
JEWELL Paul	Liverpool	28 Sep 1964	Liverpool	84-85	Bradford C.	88-89	F	117(20)	15	35	5
JOHNSON Alan K.	Wigan	19 Feb 1971	Y.T.	88-89	Lincoln C.	94-95	CD	163(17)	21(4)	13	2
JOHNSON Gavin	Stowmarket	10 Oct 1970	Ipswich T.	95-96	*		CD	27	0	3	0
JOHNSON Stephen A.	Liverpool	23 Jun 1957	Rochdale	83-84	Bristol C.	84-85	F	50(1)	7	18	4
JONES Philip A.	Liverpool	1 Dec 1969	Everton	90-91	Released	92-93	RB	84(4)	10	2	1
KELLY Anthony G.	Prescot	1 Jan 1964	Prescot Cables	83-84	Stoke C.	85-86					
			Peterborough U.	95-96	Altrincham	95-96	M	100(3)	15	15	3
KENNEDY Alan P.	Sunderland	31 Aug 1954	Sweden	87-88	Colne Dynamos	87-88	LB	22	0	0	0
KENNEDY Michael	Salford	9 Apr 1961	Chesterfield	93-94	Released	93-94	M	15(2)	1	1	0
KETTLE Brian	Prescot	22 Apr 1956	Houston USA	80-81	Formby	80-81	FB	14	0	1	0
KILFORD Ian	Bristol	6 Oct 1973	Nottingham F.	93-94	*		M	60(8)	7(2)	11	1
KILNER John I.	Bolton	3 Oct 1959	South Africa	83-84	Released	83-84	G	4	1	0	0
KIRWAN Paul			Liverpool		Released	92-93	F	0	1(2)	0	0
KNOWLES Barry J.	Wigan	25 Apr 1959	Barrow	84-85	Released	87-88	LB	124(3)	21	3	1
LANCASHIRE Graham	Blackpool	19 Oct 1972	Preston N.E.(L)	95-96	*		F	5	0	3	0
LANGLEY Kevin J.	St. Helens	24 May 1964	Apprentice	81-82	Everton	86-87					
			Birmingham C.	90-91	Released	93-94	M	307(10)	48(1)	12	2
LEONARD Mark A.	St. Helens	27 Sep 1962	Chester C.	94-95	Released	95-96	F	60(3)	8	12	2
LIGHTFOOT Christopher I.	Warrington	1 Apr 1970	Chester C.	95-96	Crewe A.	95-96	CD	11(2)	4	1	0
LLOYD Laurence V.	Bristol	6 Oct 1948	Nottingham F.	80-81	Dismissed	82-83	CD	52	5	2	2
LODGE Paul	Liverpool	13 Feb 1961	Everton (L)	82-83	Rotherham(L)	82-83	M	5	0	1	0
LOWE David A.	Liverpool	30 Aug 1965	Apprentice	82-83	Ipswich T.	87-88					
			Leicester C.	95-96	*		RW	186(9)	24(2)	43	2
LOWEY John A.	Manchester	7 Mar 1958	Blackburn R.	86-87	Chesterfield T.(L)	86-87	M	1(2)	0	0	0
LYONS Andrew	Blackpool	19 Oct 1966	Crewe A.	93-94	Partick Thistle	95-96	F	78(6)	11(1)	27	1
McADAM Steven	Portadown	2 Apr 1960	Bransley	80-81	Released	81-82	FB	26	2	0	0

NAME	Born	Joined	Left	Pos	Appearances		Goals	
					League	Cup	Lge.	Cup
McEWAN Stanley	Wishaw 8 Jun 1957	Hull C. 87-88	Hartlepool U. 89-90	CD	26(3)	1(1)	4	0
McGARVEY Scott	Glasgow 22 Apr 1963	Oldham A.(L) 89-90		F	3	0	0	0
McIVOR Ronald	Edinburgh 23 Mar 1951	East Fife 79-80	Released 79-80	FR	3	0	1	0
McKEARNEY David	Crosby 20 Jue 1968	Crewe A. 93-940	Chorley 94-95	F	45(4)	7(1)	9	1
McMAHON John J.	Manchester 7 Dec 1949	Crewe A. 81-82	Tranmere R. 83-84	RB	71	13	5	0
McMULLEN David	Debby 13 Jun 1960	Cumbernauld U. 79-80	Northwich Vic. 80-81	M	20(7)	3	1	0
MAKIN Christopher	Manchester 8 May 1973	Oldham A.(L) 94-95		CD	1	0	2	0
MARTINEZ Roberto	Balaguer (Spain) 13 Jul 1973	CF Balaguer 95-96	*	M	42	6	8	4
METHVEN Colin J.	India 10 Dec 1955	East Fife 79-80	Blackpool 86-87	CD	295(1)	44	21	7
MILLER David B.	Burnley 8 Jan 1964	Stockport C.	Released 95-96	CD	34(3)	4	3	0
MILLETT Michael	Wigan 22 Sep 1977	Trainee 94-95	Deceased 95-96	CD	1(2)	0	0	0
MITCHELL James R.	Liverpool 13 Jun 1967	Apprentice 84-85	Southport 85-86	FB	2	0	0	0
MOORE Michael	Chorley 20 Jul 1952	Port Vale 78-79	Released 79-80	F	57(7)	2	12	1
MORTON Neil	Congleton 21 Dec 1968	Chester C. 93-94	Altrincham 93-94	W	41(7)	7(1)	5	1
MUTCH Andrew T.	Liverpool 28 Dec 1968	Swindon T.(L) 95-96		F	7	0	1	0
NEWELL Michael C.	Liverpool 27 Jan 1965	Crewe A. 83-84	Luton T. 85-86	F	64(8)	14	25	7
NUGEN Stephen	Orell 7 May 1973	Y.T. 89-90	Released 92-93	M	7(6)	0(2)	0	0
OGDEN Neil	Billinge 29 Nov 1975	Trainee 93-94	Northwich V. 95-96	FB	10(3)	0(2)	0	0
O'KEEFE Eamonn	Manchester 13 Mar 1953	Everton 81-82	Port Vale 83-84	F	56(2)	3	25	1
OLIVER James	Fern 13 Jan 1958	Montrose 80-81	Scotland 80-81	M	1(1)	0	0	0
ORMSBY Brendan T.C.	Birmingham 1 Oct 1960	Scarborough 94-95	Released 94-95	CD	2	0	0	0
PAGE Donald R.	Manchester 18 Jan 1964	Runcorn 88-89	Rotherham U. 91-92	F	62(12)	10	15	4
PALADINO Guiseppe	Prescot 21 Aug 1965	St. Helens T. 90-91	Altrincham 90-91	G	7	0	0	0
PARKINSON Joseph S.	Eccles 11 Jun 1971	Y.T. 88-89	Bournemouth 92-93	M	115(4)	20	6	1
PATTERSON Darren J.	Belfast 15 Oct 1969	W.B.A. 89-90	Crystal P. 92-93	CD	69(28)	12(5)	6	4
PATTERSON Ian D.	Chatham 4 Apr 1973	Burnley 93-94	Stalybridge C.	CD	2(2)	0	0	0
PENDER John P.	Luton 19 Nov 1963	Burnley 95-96	*	CD	41(1)	4	1	0
PENNCOCK Anthony	Swansea 10 Apr 1971	Stockport C. 90-91	Released 93-94	G	10	3	0	0
PILLING Andrew J.	Wigan 30 Jun 1969	Preston N.E. 87-88	Released 92-93	M	131(25)	11(3)	20	1
POWELL Gary	Hoylake 2 Apr 1969	Everton 90-91	Bury 92-93	F	57(27)	11(2)	17	3
PURDIE Ian	Motherwell 7 Mar 1953	Motherwell 78-79	Portsmouth 79-80	W	54(1)	7	12	0
QUINN Anthony M.	Liverpool 24 July 1959	Everton 79-80	Witton Albion 80-81	F	36(7)	4(10	14	0
QUINN Michael	Liverpool 2 May 1962	Derby C.(App) 79-80	Stockport C. 82-83	F	56(13)	9	19	2
RAMAGE Craig D.	Derby 30 Mar 1970	Derby C.(L) 88-89		M	10	0	2	0
REDFERN David	Sheffield 8 Nov 1962	Rochdale(L) 87-88	Stockport C. 88-89	G	3	1	0	0
REDSHAW Raymond	Salford 23 Dec 1958	Horwich RMI 84-85	Northwich Vic. 84-85	F	2(2)	0(1)	0	0
RENNIE Paul	Nantwich 26 Oct 1971	Stoke C. 93-94	Released 94-95	FB	36(4)	9(1)	3	1
RIMMER Neill	Liverpool 13 Nov 1967	Ipswich T. 88-89	Released 95-96	M	185(6)	24	10	3
ROBERTSON John	Liverpool 8 Jan 1974	Trainee 92-93	Lincoln C. 95-96	CD	108(4)	20(1)	4	0
RODWELL Anthony	Southport 26 Aug 1962	Scarborough (L) 94-95		F	5	0	1	0
ROGERS John C.	Liverpool 16 Sep 1950	Altrincham 82-83	Altrincham 82-83	F	4(2)	2	2	0
ROGERSON Lee A.	Darwen 21 Mar 1967	Clitheroe 89-90	Released 90-91	F	1(3)	0(1)	0	0
RUSSELL Colin	Liverpool 21 Jan 1961	Scarborough 88-89	Colne Dynamo 88-89	F	8	2	3	0
SCHOFIELD Mark A.	Wigan 10 Oct 1966	Apprentice 83-84	Released 86-87	D	1(1)	0	0	0
SEBA Jesus	Zaragoza (Spain) 11 Apr 1974	Real Zaragoza 95-96	*	F	8(11)	2(2)	3	0
SEDDON Ian	Prestbury 14 Oct 1950	Rochdale 78-79	Released 78-79	M	1	1	0	0
SENIOR Stephen	Sheffield 15 May 1963	Northampton T. 87-88	Preston N.E. 90-91	RB	107(2)	11	3	1
SHARP Kevin	Ontario, Canada 19 Sep 1974	Leed U. 95-96	*	M	20	1	6	0
SHARRATT Christopher M.	West Kirby 13 Aug 1970	Stalybridge C. 91-92	Released 92-93	F	11(13)	1(2)	3	0
SHAW Mark W.	St. Helens 15 Oct 1964	Juniors 82-83	Released 82-83	M	3	0	0	0
SHEARER David J.	Inverness 16 Oct 1958	Middlesbrough (L)79-80		F	11	0	9	0
SHELDON Kevin J.	Stoke 14 Jun 1956	Stoke C. 81-82	Crewe A. 83-84	W	29	10	1	0
SHYNE Christopher	Rochdale 10 Dec 1950	Rochdale 79-80	Released 79-80	G	10	1	0	0
SKIPPER Peter D.	Hull 11 Apr 1958	Wrexham 91-92	Reelased 93-94	CD	88(3)	6	4	1

NAME	Born		Joined		Left		Pos	Appearances		Goals	
								League	Cup	Lge.	Cup
SMART Kevin G.	Newcastle	14 Oct 1958	Plymouth A.	78-79	Released	79-80	RB	48(1)	5	1	0
SMITH Barry J.	Wigan	21 Sep 1969	Y.T.	87-88	Released	87-88	M	0(1)	0(1)	0	0
SMYTH John M.	Dublin	28 Apr 1970	Burnley	91-92	Released	91-92	RB	2(6)	0(2)	0	0
STATHAM Mark	Barnsley	11 Nov 1975	Nottingham F.	94-95	*		G	1(1)	0	0	0
STEEL James W.	Dumfried	4 Dec 1959	Oldham A.(L)	82-83			F	2	0	2	0
STEWART William I.	Liverpool	1 Jan 1965	Liverpool	84-85	Chester C.	86-87	G	14	0	0	0
STORER Stuart J.	Rugby	16 Jan 1967	Everton (L)	87-88			RW	9(3)	4	0	0
STRONG Greg	Bolton	5 Sep 1975	Trainee	93-94	Bolton W.	94-95	CD	28(7)	6	3	0
TAIT Paul	Newcastle	24 Oct 1974	Everton	94-95	Northwich V.	95-96	F	1(4)	0	0	0
TANKARD Allen J.	Fleet	21 May 1969	Southampton	88-89	Port Vale	93-94	LB	205(4)	28	4	1
TAYLOR Brian J.	Gateshead	2 Jul 1949	Preston N.E.(L)	81-82			FB	7(1)	0	0	0
TAYLOR Colin D.	Liverpool	25 Dec 1971	W/hampton W.(L)	91-92			F	7	0	2	0
TAYLOR Steven J.	Royston	18 Oct 1955	Burnley	83-84	Stockport C.	83-84	F	29(1)	6	7	3
THOMPSON Christopher D.	Walsall	24 Jan 1960	Blackburn R.	86-87	Blackpool	88-89	M	67(7)	11	12	4
THOMPSON David S.	Manchester	27 May 1962	Notts C.	86-87	Preston N.E.	90-91	RW	107(1)	8(1)	16	2
THORNE Peter	Manchester	21 Jun 1973	Blackburn R.(L)	93-94			F	10(1)	0	0	0
TIERNEY Lawrence	Leith	4 Apr 1959	Hibernian	80-81	Released	80-81	M	4(3)	2	0	0
TUNKS Roy W.	Worthing	21 Jan 1951	Preston N.E.	81-82	Hartlepool U.	88-89	G	245	39	0	0
URQUHART George S.	Glasgow	22 Apr 1950	Ross C.	79-80	Released	80-81	M	63(5)	6	6	0
URQUHART William M.	Inverness	22 Nov 1956	Rangers	80-81	Inverness	80-81	F	5(5)	2	2	0
VAUGHAN Daniel	Liverpool	18 Feb 1972	Crewe A.	93-94	Released	93-94	FB	2(2)	1	0	0
WALSH Steven	Preston	3 Nov 1964	Juniors	82-83	Leicester C.	86-87	CD	123(3)	12	4	0
WARD Anthony	Warrington	4 Apr 1970	Everton	89-90	Chorley	89-90	W	8(3)	2	2	0
WARD Noel G.	Derry (NI)	8 Dec 1952	Aberdeen	78-79	Retired	81-82	CD	47(1)	6	4	0
WARD Robert A.	West Bromwich	4 Aug 1953	Blackpool	80-81	Released	81-82	G	46	1	0	0
WEST Paul	Birmingham	22 Jun 1970	Bradford C.	93-94	Released	93-94	FB	2(1)	1	0	0
WESTON James J.	Whiston	16 Sep 1955	Torquay U.	81-82	Morecambe	82-83	M	63(3)	7	2	0
WHITEHEAD Alan	Bury	20 Nov 1956	York C.(L)	86-87			CD	2	0	0	0
WHITNEY Jonathan D.	Nantwich	23 Dec 1970	Huddersfield (L)				FB	12	0	0	0
WHITTLE Maurice	Wigan	5 Jul 1948	Barrow	79-80	Barrow	80-81	LB	21	4	1	0
WHITWORTH Neil A.	Wigan	12 Apr 1972	Y.T.	89-90	Manchester U.	90-91	CD	1(1)	0	0	0
WIDDRINGTON Thomas	Newcaslte	1 Oct 1971	Southampton (L)	91-92			M	5(1)	2	0	0
WIGNALL Mark	Preston	6 Dec 1962	Apprentice	80-81	Released	81-82	M	34	6	0	2
WILKIE John C.	Dundee	1 Jul 1947	Elgin C.	78-79	Released	79-80	F	3(1)	3	0	0
WILLIAMS John W.	Liverpool	3 Oct 1960	Bournemouth (L)	91-92			CD	4	0	0	0
WILLIAMS Philip J.	Swansea	7 Feb 1963	Crewe A.	82-83	Crewe A.	83-84	M	1(2)	3	0	0
WILSON Andrew	Wigan	7 Jan 1965	Skelmersdale U.	87-88	Released		M	1(1)	0	0	0
WILSON Ian W.	Aberdeen	27 Mar 1958	Out of contract		Released		M	5	0(1)	0	0
WOODS Raymond G.	Birkenhead	7 Jun 1965	Colne Dynamoes Coventry C.(L)	88-89 92-93	Coventry C.	90-91	RW	37(4)	6	3	1
WORSWICK Michael A.	Preston	14 Mar 1945	Chorley	78-79	Chorley	78-79	W	0(1)	0	0	0
WORTHINGTON Gary L.	Cleathorpes	10 Nov 1966	Wrexham	90-91	Released	92-93	F	51(12)	9(2)	20	4
WRIGHT Jeffrey K.	Alston	23 Jun 1952	Netherfield	78-79	Barrow	81-82	M	139(4)	20	19	1
WRIGHT Mark A.	Manchester	29 Jan 1970	Huddersfield T.	93-94	Chorley	93-94		13(1)	5	1	0
YOUNG David J.	Birkenhead	27 Apr 1962	Mossley	82-83	Released	82-83	M	3	0	0	0

KEY

* Still with club (start of 1996/97 season).

(L) indicates player on loan (joined as and/or returned).

POS Refers to player's normal playing position, F – forward, G – goalkeeper, CD – central defenders, FB – full back, M – midfield, W – wing, CF – central defender, WD – winger/defender (L – left, R – right).

Blank in 'Left' column indicates player retired or transferred to (unknown) non-League club. Several players had joined the club prior to the first Football League season, however, their first season with the club has been shown as 1978/79. Statistics correct to start of 1996/97 season.

FIFTY LATICS STARS

Sammy Armes
Peter Atherton
Kenny Banks
Graham Barrow
Paul Beesley
Les Bradd
John Bramwell
John Butler
Bobby Campbell
Duncan Colquhoun
Frank Corrigan
Alf Craig
Alex Cribley
Simon Farnworth
Teddy Felton
Jimmy Fleming
Ian Gillibrand
Tommy Gore
Bryan Griffiths
Mark Hilditch
Joe Hinnigan
Derek Houghton
Peter Houghton
Paul Jewell
Alan Johnson
Tony Kelly
Kevin Langley
Berk Llewellyn
Billy Lomax
David Lowe
Harry Lyon
Roberto Martinez
Colin Methven
Dave Mycock
Mike Newell
Eamonn O'Keefe
Harry Parkinson
Mick Quinn
Dennis Reeves
Jack Roberts
Teddy Robinson
Harry Sharratt
Jimmy Shirley
Billy Sutherland
Sid Tuffnell
Roy Tunks
Steve Walsh
Maurice Whittle
Harold Woolley
Jeff Wright

SAMMY ARMES

Signed by Charlie Spencer from Blackpool, right-winger Sammy Armes was a great controller and crosser of the ball and it was he who provided much of the ammunition for the side's two principal goalscorers Felton and Scott.

However, he also scored his fair share of goals and in 1934-35, he netted 16 in the Cheshire League. That season, Latics were drawn away to Carlisle United in the F.A. Cup first round and staggered the football world by winning 6-1. One humorous side to the match was as Wigan supporters were leaving the Carlisle ground; one remembered that Sammy Armes who had scored a couple of goals in the match, once played for the opponents and the next thing, written in big chalk letters across the main gate, appeared 'Carlisle want Sammy Armes back!'

During the 1935-36 season, Sammy moved to Leeds, where he appeared in 47 League games, scoring 20 goals.

PETER ATHERTON

Coming through the Latics junior ranks, he made his League debut at Blackpool on 24 October 1987 in a goalless draw just prior to turning professional. After playing in 15 games that season he then claimed a regular place in the Wigan side and apart from one appearance as a substitute, he did not miss a match.

Twice voted Wigan's Player of the Year, he obviously impressed the then Coventry City manager Terry Butcher in the Latic's two F.A. Cup ties against the Highfield Road club for he joined the Sky Blues in the opening week of the 1991-92 season for £300,000. He appeared in 149 League games for Wigan, scoring just one goai, against Sheffield United at Bramall Lane on 22 October 1989. Quickly establishing himself at the heart of the Coventry defence he won England Under-21 honours and was voted the club's Player of the Year at the end of the 1992-93 season.

Reading the game extremely well, he played in 114 League matches for Coventry before joining another Premier League club, Sheffield Wednesday, for £800,000 in June 1994.

An unsung hero of the Owls defence, he has now played in almost 350 League games for his three clubs and is currently captain of the Hillsborough team.

KENNY BANKS

Like many of Latics players, Kenny Banks represented the town whilst a schoolboy, but it was not until he left school that League clubs started to take notice of the well-built youngster who could kick well with either foot. Both Bolton and Southport were keen to sign him, but it was the Haig Avenue club who finally got his signature. Impressing the fans in pre-season games prior to the 1947-48 season, he was signed as a professional, much to the annoyance of Aston Villa who were also keen to sign him.

Insisting on keeping his job, he only played as a part-time professional with Southport but after three years he was placed on the transfer list for £1,000. Kenny Banks' allegiance had always been to his home-town club, and when manager Ted Goodier found him a position at a local factory he was more than happy to sign for Latics.

A sound but seldom spectacular player, he made his debut in a 3-0 win against Accrington Stanley Reserves on the opening day of the 1952-53 season. Complimenting the talents of Lynn and Mycock, he went on to play 260 first team games as Latics won the Lancashire Combination for three consecutive seasons.

After his playing career, he stayed with the Latics to become one of the Club's greatest ever servants, working as a trainer, coach, physiotherapist and temporary manager!

GRAHAM BARROW

Signed from Altrincham in July 1981, Graham helped the club to promotion in his first season at Springfield Park, scoring 12 goals from midfield.

He was voted Latic's Man of the Match in the Freight Rover Trophy Final at Wembley on 1 June 1985, when they beat Brentford 3-1. He played his last game for the Club at Burnden Park on 9 May 1986 as Latics went down 2-1 to Bolton Wanderers in the Freight Rover Trophy Northern Area Final. In his five seasons at Springfield Park, he had played in 212 League and Cup games, plus another six as substitute and scored an astonishing 44 goals.

He signed for Chester City for a tribunal fixed fee of £6,000 in July 1986 and played in over 200 games for the Blues. Employed as player-coach, he became assistant-manager in 1988 and took over from Harry McNally as manager after the Club had made a poor start to the 1992-93 season.

He became Wigan manager in September 1994 but was surprisingly dismissed in October 1995.

PAUL BEESLEY

Paul Beesley joined the Latics from Marine and took a long time to get established. But once he had staked his claim for a regular shirt, he developed into a very classy proposition. He made his debut at Reading on 3 October 1984, but only appeared once more that season.

Always comfortable and confident on the ball, he learnt his centre-half trade from the likes of Colin Methven, Alex Cribley, Steve Walsh and Andy Holden, and matured into a powerful and clever reader of the game.

After 177 full games with the Latics, he moved to fellow Third Division side Leyton Orient in a £175,000 deal in October 1989. Though he only played 32 League games in his first season at Brisbane Road, the Orient players voted him their Player of the Year. At the end of that season, he moved to Bramall Lane in a £300,000 deal which in turn brought in some extra cash for Wigan. He made 168 League appearances for the Blades before signing for rivals Leeds United.

LES BRADD

One of the most popular players to wear the number nine shirt since the Club's election to the Football League, Les Bradd started his career with Notts County for whom he scored 125 League goals in his 398 matches.

After leaving Meadow Lane, he spent three seasons at Stockport County before attracting the attention of Latics player-manager Larry Lloyd, who was looking for an experienced striker to spearhead the Club's attack. Bradd made his Latics debut in the opening match of the 1981-82 season at Bradford City, scoring a goal in a 3-3 draw. Forming an effective partnership with Peter Houghton, he ended that season with 19 League goals, including a hat-trick in the 7-2 away win over Scunthorpe United, and was voted the Club's Player of the Year.

However, the following season, injuries were to restrict his appearances and following the departure of Lloyd, Bradd retired from the game at the end of the season. He returned to Notts County and after a couple of years running their weekly lottery, he became the Club's Commercial Manager. In 1994 he crossed the River Trent to take up a similar position with Nottingham Forest.

JOHN BRAMWELL

Signed by Pat Murphy, the recruitment of Ashton-in-Makerfield born John Bramwell proved to be a great success. After a short spell in Latics reserve side, he was introduced to the first team who were at that time challenging for honours in the Lancashire Combination. He made his debut in the 1-1 draw at home to Blackpool 'B' on 9 April 1955.

The powerfully built and tall Bramwell soon became a great favourite with the Springfield Park fans and his exceptional ability both in the air and on the ground soon had the big Clubs snooping around. It was obvious from the outset that Latics would have difficulty hanging on to Bramwell and after 109 first team appearances he was snapped up by First Division Everton for £3,500.

The Goodison Park club converted Bramwell into a left-back and he had great success there for a number of seasons, making 52 League appearances before moving on to Luton Town where he played in a further 187 Leagues games.

JOHN BUTLER

Recommended to the Latics by his club, Prescot Cables of the Northern Counties League, John Butler arrived at Springfield Park in January 1981 when the ground was covered in snow and ice. He had only trained for half-an-hour when a message was passed to the Wigan secretary, *'Get a contract ready. This boy's a natural'.* Impressing with his speed, control and ability to use both feet, he made his Latics debut against Bradford City on 7 September 1982, scoring in Wigan's 3-2 win.

John had played in 245 League games for Wigan when he was transferred to Stoke City at Christmas 1988 for £75,000. After 262 League appearances for the Potters he returned to Springfield Park for a second spell in August 1995. At the Victoria Ground he won a Second Division Championship medal and an Autoglass Trophy medal.

One of the most versatile players ever to wear the colours of Wigan Athletic, he had the distinction of having played in every position on the field, including goalkeeper. His goalkeeping consisted a 7 minute spell against Bury in a Freight Rover Trophy match at Gigg Lane when Roy Tunks was injured.

He played in 40 League and Cup games for Wigan in 1995-96 and though he was switched to play at left-back on a number of occasions, he coped like a true professional. He has now (end 1995-96) appeared in 341 first team games for Latics, scoring 18 goals.

BOBBY CAMPBELL

Bobby Campbell arrived at Bradford City in December 1979 from Australia on trial, but was soon offered a full-time contract. He made his debut for the Valley Parade club on 12 January 1980, scoring City's goal in a 1-1 draw against Peterborough United.

Though there was no doubt about his ability to score goals - he topped the list in each of his five full seasons with the club - but there were doubts about his temperament, for Halifax had sacked him for 'persistent misconduct'.

He joined Derby County in August 1983 for £70,000 but never really settled at the Baseball Ground and was soon back with Bradford. The club's leading aggregate scorer with 121 League goals, he won two caps for Northern Ireland before signing for Wigan Athletic in October 1986.

Bobby made his debut for Latics on 5 October that year, scoring the Wigan goal in a 3-1 defeat at Swindon Town. He ended the season as the club's top scorer with 20 League and Cup goals in his 43 appearances. The following season he hit a magnificent hat-trick at Burnden Park as Wigan came from behind to beat Bolton Wanderers 5-4 over two legs in a first round League Cup tie. Again he ended the season as top scorer with 16 goals but retired after scoring 36 goals in 83 games.

DUNCAN COLQUHOUN

Duncan Colquhoun was on trial with Hibernian when he was told that Wigan Athletic were interested in him. He came down to Springfield Park and was offered a month's trial. The likeable Scot refused the terms and was on his way out of the ground when he met the club's giant centre-half, a player by the name of Hancock, with whom he had been at Millwall. He asked what was going on and when Colquhoun told him, Hancock went in to see manager Charlie Spencer. What was said remains a mystery, but Charlie Spencer came out of his office and offered Duncan Colquhoun an acceptable contract.

He stayed with the Latics for a few seasons, scoring the club's first hat-trick in the F.A. Cup in a 7-0 win over Lytham St. Annes before the club's financial difficulties forced them to sell him to Bristol City. He then moved on to Southport and later Bradford City in 1939.

During the war, Colquhoun guested for a number of clubs including Blackpool, Rochdale and Partick Thistle.

After the hostilities ended, he returned to Springfield Park as trainer-coach to the team that won the Lancashire Combination. He was also manager of Wigan for a short time, taking over the reins in early 1970 before the arrival of Gordon Milne. In fact during his years at Springfield Park, Duncan Colquhoun had been player, coach, trainer, scout, manager and physiotherapist!

FRANK CORRIGAN

After winning selection for the Liverpool Schools XI, Frank Corrigan played in the very demanding local leagues for two years before eventually signing for Blackpool at the age of 18. After twelve months at Bloomfield Road in the reserve side, he joined Walsall for a short three month stay, before moving on and playing for two years with Burton Albion.

Anxious to return to the area, he joined Bangor City but again he failed to settle and moved on to Northwich Victoria. The much-travelled midfielder moved to Wigan Athletic and eventually into League football. Making his debut in a 2-1 win against Gainsborough Trinity in March 1978, it took him a little while to produce his form at Wigan, but he eventually silenced his critics by turning in a succession of top-class performances. His strong running, his almost artistic left foot, and his will-to-win attitude were shining examples for his team-mates to follow.

After 142 first team appearances for the Latics, the popular Corrigan moved on again, this time to Stafford Rangers.

ALF CRAIG

A powerfully built man, Alf Craig was signed from Blackpool where he had enjoyed a very successful playing career and that success was to continue at Springfield Park.

Making his debut in a goalless draw at Bangor City on 12 December 1964, he soon became a big favourite with the Latics fans, who admired his no-nonsense style and his authority on the field. He was noted for his fearsome tackling and his heading ability was second to none. This robust player was to make a major contribution to the success of Allan Brown's well disciplined and organised team.

There is always one incident which stands out when the name of Alf Craig is mentioned and that is the famous "no goal" incident against Tranmere Rovers in 1966. The setting was a first round F.A. Cup replay at Springfield Park. The League side were winning by the only goal of the game when in the dying seconds, Alf fired in a terrific shot that almost broke the back of the net but the referee's whistle had already gone for the end of the match!

Alf Craig eventually took over from Allan Brown as player-manager but did not particularly enjoy the role and left to join Netherfield as a player the following season.

ALEX CRIBLEY

A tough, skilful player with a footballing brain, it is hard to believe that he ever had the time to become a professional footballer. His school in Liverpool had a great Rugby Union tradition and he played in the First XV until leaving school to go to University. He also played soccer for his Youth Club and was spotted by Liverpool who signed him when he was 16.

After several appearances in the full Liverpool Youth side, he signed as a full-time professional. He played in the Central League side, but as there was no sign of him breaking into the first team, he decided to accept Ian McNeill's offer and signed for Wigan Athletic in November 1980.

He made his debut for the Latics at Bournemouth that month and went on to appear in 30 League games in that 1980-81 season.

A great utility player who could play in several positions, he went on to appear in 271 League games for Latics, scoring 16 goals before injury ended his career in 1988. He later became the club's physiotherapist and coach.

SIMON FARNWORTH

Completing his apprenticeship with Bolton Wanderers, he made his League debut for the Trotters against Wimbledon on the opening day of the 1983-84 campaign. He kept clean sheets in his opening two games and held his place until suffering an injury playing against Rotherham United the following February.

Within a few weeks Simon was back in the side and he maintained an ever-present record the following season. He held his place in the Bolton side for the best part of three years before going on loan to Stockport and Tranmere. He played in 113 League games for the Wanderers before signing for Bury.

Simon played in 105 League games for the Gigg Lane side before joining Preston North End during the summer of 1990. For most of his three years at Deepdale he was the number one choice and played in 81 League games for the Lilywhites.

Wigan signed him for £7,500 during the 1993 close season and he made his debut against Scunthorpe United on the opening day of the new season. He played in 126 League games for the Latics, when at the end of the 1995-96 campaign he became the club's physiotherapist.

TEDDY FELTON

Inside-left Teddy Felton was signed from Gateshead in 1933. A very powerful runner, he was tricky and possessed a terrific shot.

Forming a brilliant left-wing partnership with George Scott, Felton top-scored in 1933-34, his first season at Springfield Park, with 36 goals in League and Cup matches, including four in a 5-1 Cheshire League Cup victory over Northwich Victoria. The following season he scored 33 goals including both Latics goals in their 3-2 Lancashire Junior Cup Final defeat against Fleetwood.

Midway through the 1935-36 season, Felton was transferred to Huddersfield Town. He had appeared in 113 Cheshire League games for the Latics and scored 75 goals.

JIM FLEMING

Jim Fleming was signed from Hearts, having seen service with Aberdeen and Dunfermline, in Ian McNeill's first spell as manager with the club. Equally at home in midfield or attack, he is best remembered for the striking partnership he struck up with Geoff Davies in Gordon Milne's magnificent team.

At the start of the 1970-71 season, Davies and Fleming were literally taking it in turns to score hat-tricks, such was their fine understanding of each others' play. Gordon Milne rated Jim Fleming *"a tremendous player"*, and certainly Fleming's vast experience picked up in top-class Scottish football stood him in good stead in the Northern Premier League.

He turned in some memorable performances for the Latics, with the Peterborough United F.A. Cup-tie at Springfield Park in 1970 standing out the most. He had already made the first goal with an inch-perfect cross for Geoff Davies to score, but it was in the dying seconds of the game that all his years of experience and class finally made their mark. Latics were awarded a penalty in the last minute of the game with the scores level at 1-1. As he stepped up to take the kick, his coolness shone through as he struck the ball home.

After a couple more seasons with Wigan, Jim was released when the directors came to the conclusion that a knee injury he had picked up would probably finish his career. Fleming proved them wrong and went back to join Ian McNeill at Ross County.

IAN GILLIBRAND

On leaving school, Ian Gillibrand signed for Arsenal as an apprentice professional. During his time at Highbury, he played in Arsenal's F.A. Youth Cup winning side in 1966 and gained several trophies in successful youth and junior team competitions. By 1968 'Gilly' was playing as a professional in the Gunners' London Combination side but, after a two month loan period at Blackburn and one month at Mansfield, he was unable to make the big breakthrough into League football.

Bertie Mee, then Arsenal's manager, recommended Ian to Allan Sanders, Wigan Athletic's manager. Making his debut for the Latics against Rhyl on 24 April 1968, the popular Blackburn-born player appeared in 661 first team games for the club in their non-League days. Voted the club's Player of the Year in 1968-69 and 1970-71, he did astound Latics supporters with a rare but spectacular goal against Accrington Stanley in a Lancashire Junior Cup game before a mere 1,500 spectators.

Captain of Latics first ever Football League side, he made just seven appearances in the Fourth Division before becoming heavily involved in the coaching side at Springfield Park.

One of the most loyal, effective and honest players ever to pull on a Wigan Athletic shirt, he sadly died a few years ago at a tragically early age.

TOMMY GORE

Tommy Gore joined Liverpool on schoolboy forms when 15 and stayed at Anfield for four years. The highlight of his days at the club was playing in an F.A. Youth Cup Final, when the Merseysiders were beaten by Aston Villa.

When Ron Yeats moved to Tranmere, Tommy Gore went with him and spent eighteen months at Prenton Park on full-time terms but thing did not work out as he hoped. Somewhat disenchanted, he joined Wigan on loan, but eventually decided to sign.

A busy player, he brought the crowd to its feet on a number of occasions to greet one of his goalscoring right foot thunderbolts. Tommy Gore had a wonderful first year in the Football League, having won the club's Player of the Year competition in 1977-78.

He is one of only three players to have played in over 100 consecutive League games following his debut at Hereford United on the opening day of the 1978-79 season.

BRYAN GRIFFITHS

Signed from non-League St. Helens Town, he made his debut for the Latics against Northampton Town on 5 November 1988.

Bryan Griffiths had the knack of scoring important goals and had a cool head when it came to the pressure finish, especially from the spot. Perhaps his sweetest goal was the free-kick which left Bruce Grobbelaar standing at Anfield in the Rumbelows Cup.

The one criticism that Wigan fans levelled at him, was his lack of consistency, but one thing no one will take away from him was his ability and determination to come back and prove critics wrong.

Though one of the smallest players on the park, Bryan scored his fair share of goals, with 58 in 233 first team appearances. For a winger that is an excellent strike rate and many strikers would be more than happy to swap their figures for these. At the end of the 1992-93 season, he refused terms and joined Blackpool.

MARK HILDITCH

Signed initially as a central striker in September 1986, Royton born Mark Hilditch went on to play in a variety of different positions during his four seasons at Springfield Park, wearing nine different numbered shirts!

A former Rochdale player, he scored 40 goals in 184 appearances for the Spotland club before moving on to Tranmere Rovers in July 1983.

It was Ray Mathias who brought Hilditch to Springfield Park at the start of the 1986-87 season when he made his debut in a 2-1 defeat at home to Newport County. His first goal for the club came four days later in a 5-1 thrashing of Walsall.

In his first season at the club, he made 32 appearances as Wigan Athletic made the play-offs following. During that season he also helped Latics reach the sixth round of the F.A. Cup, beating First Division Norwich City on the way.

Injuries restricted Mark's appearances over the next couple of seasons to 48 League games, at time playing alternative matches in midfield or attack and at one stage at right-back.

Never a prolific scorer, 'Marco Van' scored a goal in every three games for the club before financial restrictions forced the club not to renew his contract. He returned to Spotland before later joining Northern Premier League Mossley as Assistant Manager.

JOE HINNIGAN

Hailing from the Kirkby area, he represented Kirkby Schools at Junior, Under 14 and Under 15 levels and was with Everton on amateur forms for over a year. That period was followed by a six month spell with Aston Villa, but he was released by the Midlanders and joined South Liverpool.

After some impressive performances, Wigan Athletic stepped in and signed him for £1,200. He made his debut for the Latics on 6 September 1975 in a 1-0 win at Worksop Town. However, after a season things turned a little sour for the full-back and he asked to be transfer listed. The story had a happy ending for after a discussion with Wigan manager Ian McNeill, Hinningan was selected to play in the Lancashire Junior Cup Final at Chorley and scored the only goal of the game. After playing in 153 first team games in Wigan's non-League days, he made his Football League debut for the club on the opening day of the 1978-79 season. He also wrote himself into Latics history when he scored the club's first Football League goal in a 3-2 defeat at home to Newport County. After making 66 League appearances for the club he moved to Sunderland, later playing for Preston North End, Gillingham, Wrexham and Chester City, making in all 367 League appearances for his six clubs.

DEREK HOUGHTON

Joining the Latics from Golborne Juniors, Derek Houghton served the club well for ten seasons. Making his first team debut in the opening games of the 1958-59 season in a goalless draw at Skelmersdale United, he went on to appear in 46 first team games during that campaign.

A versatile player, he turned out in a number of different positions for the club, notably centre-half, left-half and both full-back roles. He played in 511 first team games for Latics scoring 37 goals. In 1963-64 he scored seven goals in his 42 appearances, including a spell of six games in which he scored four goals as Latics were undefeated.

He left Springfield Park in April 1968 and joined Altrincham in exchange for Norman Sykes.

PETER HOUGHTON

One of the players who made a smooth transition from non-League football when Wigan were first elected to the Football League, Peter Houghton still holds the club record for most goals in that competition with 62.

Born in Liverpool, he was a member of the Liverpool Schools F.A. Squad which won the English School's Trophy. He first attracted attention when with South Liverpool in the Northern Premier League, often playing for them on a Saturday after doing a night shift at Ford's Hailwood plant. Not only did he play, but despite the fact that he was often in a struggling team, he banged in plenty of goals and in 1977 was signed by the Latics who were near the top of the same league.

In his time at Springfield Park, he endeared himself to the Wigan fans with his powerful running and several memorable goals. In the Club's first season in the League, despite being dogged by injuries, he was the leading scorer with 14 goals including a hat-trick against Port Vale. He was also the club's top scorer in the 1979-80 season with 16 goals and scored another hat-trick against Tranmere Rovers at Prenton Park. During the club's promotion winning season of 1981-82 he formed a formidable partnership with Les Bradd, scoring 17 League and Cup goals.

He left Wigan in 1983, and joined Preston North End, playing in 52 League games and scoring 16 goals. After being released he teamed up with Harry McNally at Chester at the start of the 1985-86 season and became club captain. At the end of the 1987-88 season he was released and played for Runcorn before retiring from the game.

PAUL JEWELL

Born in Liverpool, Paul Jewell was an apprentice at Anfield, but was snapped up by Wigan Athletic, making his debut for the Latics in a 3-3 draw against Rotherham United on 22 December 1984.

His best season for the club was 1986-87 when he scored 15 League and Cup goals, including the goal that knocked First Division Norwich City out of the F.A. Cup. The following season, he hit his only hat-trick for the club in a 4-0 win over Aldershot at Springfield Park, and missed a penalty! A regular for four years, he had scored 35 goals in his 137 League appearances when Bradford City signed him for £80,000 at the beginning of the 1988-89 season.

However, as the season unfolded he was unable to maintain a regular first team place, but the arrival of free-scoring Jimmy Quinn improved his selection chances and in seven seasons at Valley Parade, the likeable Liverpudlian has played in 251 League games for the Yorkshire side, scoring 53 goals.

ALAN JOHNSON

A former apprentice at the club, he made his debut along with Joe Parkinson in a 1-0 win at Mansfield Town on 14 January 1989. His first League goal came towards the end of that season in a 1-0 home victory against Bury, which ensured the Club's Division Three status. Over the next four seasons, the Wigan-born centre-half was to become a virtual ever-present in the Latics defence, making a total of 218 first team appearances for the club.

However, after failing to agree a new contract at the start of the 1993-94 season, he signed a week to week contract, playing the last game in February 1995 at Lincoln City. Two days later he actually signed for the Red Imps with a transfer tribunal only setting the fee at £65,000. Since moving to Sincil Bank, Johnson has played in a number of defensive positions and made over 50 League appearances.

TONY KELLY

Liverpool fan Tony Kelly started his apprentice ship at Anfield in September 1982, however, after failing to make the grade he joined Derby County. After leaving the Baseball Ground, he signed for Prescot Cables before being spotted by Latics boss Harry McNally. He made his debut at right-back in the 1-0 home defeat by Walsall on 26 November 1983.

After moving to a midfield position, he became a regular in the Wigan side that challenged for promotion from Division Three and won the Freight Rover Trophy in 1984. He played in 127 League and Cup games for Latics, scoring 22 goals, including one at Wembley.

He joined Stoke City for £80,000 but only played 45 games for the Potters before moving to West Bromwich Albion. Unable to settle at the Hawthorns, he had loan spells at Chester and Colchester before former Latics boss Ian McNeill took him to Shrewsbury. He became captain at Gay Meadow and played in 120 games before joining Bolton Wanderers.

At Burnden Park, when he was on song, he gave the team a different dimension. He reached a creative peak during Wanderers' F.A. Cup run off 1993-94 but after appearing in 102 League games he lost form and was dropped.

There followed spells at Port Vale and Peterborough United before he rejoined the Latics for the start of the 1995-96 season, but sadly things did not work out for him and he joined Altrincham.

KEVIN LANGLEY

It was while working as a 17 year-old painter and decorator that Kevin Langley wrote to Wigan Athletic asking for a trial. After a handful of youth games, he impressed so much that manager Ian McNeill offered him an apprenticeship. However, it was under Larry Lloyd that he got his first chance of first team football playing at Stockport County in the League Cup on 14 September 1981. The following Saturday he made his League debut in the 3-1 home win over Northampton.

He had played in 160 League games for Latics when he joined Everton in July 1986 for £120,000. He made his debut for the Toffees in the opening game of the following season, scoring two goals in his first four games. However, by March 1987 he was on his way to Manchester City but could not settle at Maine Road and was even loaned out to Chester City. In March 1988 he joined Birmingham City and played in 76 League games for the St. Andrews club before returning to Springfield Park in September 1990.

His first game back saw him inspire the Latics to a 2-1 win over neighbours Bolton Wanderers. Giving the club a further four years service, Kevin Langley holds the Latics Football League appearance record, having played in 317 games.

BERT LLEWELLYN

Golborne-born Bert Llewellyn started his career with Everton in 1956 and made his League debut for the Goodison Park club against Blackpool on 22 August, scoring in a 3-2 defeat. He also scored in his next game three days later in a 2-2 draw with Bolton Wanderers.

After only 11 first team appearances in two seasons Llewellyn joined Crewe Alexandra and scored 51 goals in his 96 League games before signing for Port Vale in November 1960. He continued to score with great regularity and after 88 League appearances, in which he netted 42 goals, he left to play one game for Northampton before ending his League career with Walsall.

He joined Wigan Athletic in the summer of 1965 and scored two goals on his Cheshire League debut as Latics beat Buxton 4-3. He had a remarkable first season at Springfield Park, scoring 57 goals in 57 first team appearances, including hat-tricks, at home, against Rhyl (4-0), New Brighton (7-0), Frickley Colliery (7-0) and Bognor City (4-2). He also netted four goals in three games that season - Chester Reserves (Home 7-1), Stafford Rangers (Away 6-1) and Tranmere Rovers Reserves (Home 4-0).

In 1966-67 his goal tally was 50, including all five in a 5-1 win over Stockport County Reserves at Springfield Park and five in a 6-0 win over Bradford City in the Northern Floodlit League. He ended the 1967-68 season, his last at Springfield Park as top scorer with 33 goals, to end his Wigan career with 140 goals in 185 appearances!

BILLY LOMAX

Joining Lancashire Combination side Netherfield, Billy Lomax made a sensational debut, scoring four goals. He bagged 14 goals for Netherfield in just seven matches before entering League football with Carlisle United. He stayed at Brunton Park until 1946, when he joined Macclesfield Town. In his two and half seasons with the Silkmen, he scored 90 goals.

Billy Lomax joined the Latics during the 1949-50 season and made his debut against Barrow Reserves on 20 August 1949, scoring both goals in a 2-2 draw, and ending the campaign with 42.

The following season he netted 54 times, including four against Atherton Colls. and Earlestown, plus hat-tricks against Prescot Cables and Stubshaw Cross. He had scored 11 goals in the 1951-52 season when he was transferred to Nelson.

It was in his second spell at Springfield Park that Billy Lomax hit the goalscoring heights. Signed by Ted Goodier at the start of the 1952-53 season he scored 35, whilst the following season he was joint top scorer with Jack Livesey and Jackie Lyon as each player accrued 40!

In October 1953 he hit five in Wigan's 8-3 win against Hyde United at Ewan Fields to become the first man in Latics history to score 150 first team goals; He then scored four a week later,as Latics beat Prescot Cables 9-0.

His career with Wigan Athletic ended in 1954 and he left Springfield Park failing by only 14 to register a double century of goals for Latics first team.

DAVID LOWE

Coming from a family with a typical Northern passion for the game, David Lowe's early football was restricted to school and local league level. His teacher recommended him to his friend, Harry McNally, and the youngster was immediately selected for Latics Youth team. After a week's training with the first team in which he kept scoring goals, he was offered an apprenticeship.

However, injuries to first team regulars forced Larry Lloyd to take a calculated risk and play him in the League against Reading on 23 October 1982. Though his inexperience showed, the Latics boss made the decision to carry on playing him. He scored his first goal for the club in a 3-2 win over Sheffield United at Springfield Park.

After 221 League and Cup appearances for Wigan, he joined Ipswich Town in 1987 and played in 134 League games for the Portman Road club before signing for Leicester City. A former England Under-21 international, he rejoined the Latics in March 1996 in a then record £125,000 deal.

HARRY LYON

Probably the greatest goalscorer ever to wear the Latics shirt, he holds the club record for the most goals in a season - 67 - a figure that will never be beaten. Signed from Burscough by manager Allan Brown in 1962, he began to hit the net straight away.

Equally deadly with both feet and head, Harry Lyon was a big, bustling centre-forward in the old mould who would if necessary 'run through a brick wall' to score a goal. But of all the 273 goals he did score for Wigan there are three that stand out in the memory.

It was on 17 November 1965 when Latics entertained Doncaster Rovers in an F.A. Cup first round replay after coming away from Belle Vue with a magnificent draw. Things did not look too good for Wigan when Lyon was injured just before half-time, and he had to be carried from the field on a stretcher with what appeared to be a severe leg injury. After half-time however, he reappeared on the touchline swathed in bandages. The cheers as he proceeded to score a glorious hat-trick could be heard for miles around as Latics won 3-1 and Harry Lyon became a Springfield Park immortal.

He stayed at Wigan through the reign of Allan Brown, and when Ian McNeill arrived for his first spell as manager, he was switched to centre-half for a time. In fact, in his later years, Harry played in nearly every position for the team, even in goal when needed! Released at the end of the 1969-70 season, he joined Chorley, but never really settled at Victory Park and in the early part of the 1970's, the career of a superb goalscorer came to an end.

ROBERTO MARTINEZ

Signed from Spanish Second Division side FC Balageur, Roberto Martinez was one of a trio of Spanish players to join Wigan Athletic in the summer of 1995.

Making his Latics debut against Gillingham on the opening day of the 1995-96 season, he scored Wigan's goal in a 2-1 defeat at the Priestfield Stadium. Playmaker Martinez was able to leave opponents spellbound with a string of match-winning performances.

His team contribution was vast, earning him a place in the P.F.A. Third Division team. He was also voted the Wigan Athletic Shareholders and Supporters Association Player of the Year and received his award prior to the kick-off in Latics last home match of that season. He ended the 1995-96 season as the club's joint top-scorer with 12 goals in his 50 appearances.

COLIN METHVEN

The former holder of the Latics record for the most Football League appearances with 296, Colin Methven began his career with East Fife, making his League debut for the Bayview club against Stranraer at the end of the 1974-75 season. Yet surprisingly, he never had any ambition to be a professional football, merely wishing to play as much as possible, and it was only when East Fife converted his professional contract into a proper contract that he thought he had a chance of making a career in football.

He remained an ever-present in all League and Cup games for the Scottish club until signing for Wigan in September 1979 for £30,000. He made his full League debut for the Latics against Doncaster Rovers in the Fourth Division game at Belle Vue the following month. Never missing a game at competitive level, the rugged Scot's performances rightly earned him the title of 'Mr Consistency', for he was superb in the air and solid on the ground.

As captain of Wigan Athletic, he became a firm favourite with the Springfield Park faithful, who elected him Player of the Year in 1979-80 and 1984-85. But perhaps his greatest honour came in 1981-82 when his fellow professionals voted him into the Fourth Division Select XI. Leaving Wigan in July 1986, he played in 173 League games for Blackpool before ending his League career with Walsall.

DAVE MYCOCK

Centre-half Dave Mycock is rated by many of the older Latics fans as the best centre-half ever to wear the colours of Wigan Athletic.

He played most of his career in the Third Division (North) with Bradford Park Avenue and Halifax Town, where he scored 17 goals in 170 League appearances before Ted Goodier signed him from the Shaymen in 1953.

Making his Latics debut in a 3-0 win against Accrington Stanley Reserves on 23 August, Dave was a member of the famous Wigan team of the 1950's. A solid, commanding figure and a folk-hero to the Wigan fans of that era, he played the last of his 108 first team games for the club on 7 May 1955 against the same opposition as he faced in his first match, before joining Darwen.

MIKE NEWELL

Formerly a Liverpool junior, he was not offered terms at Anfield and made his Football League debut whilst on trial with Crewe Alexandra. Failing to impress Crewe manager Dario Gradi, he moved on to Wigan Athletic and played his first game against Rotherham United on 31 December 1983.

Winning a regular place in the 1984-85 season, he did not become a consistent scorer until the following season when he netted 16 goals in 24 League games, although he had scored one of the goals in Wigan's 3-1 Freight Rover Trophy success over Brentford at Wembley in 1985.

After scoring a total of 35 goals in 92 first team appearances, he signed for First Division Luton Town in January 1986. In 1986-87 he was an ever-present and ended the season as the club's joint top scorer with 12 goals. Soon after he was signed by Second Division Leicester City, and in two seasons at Filbert Street he hardly missed a match, ending the 1988-89 season as top scorer.

In the summer of 1989 he returned to his native city when he signed for Everton for £1,100,000. A lack of goals resulted in him losing his place and in November 1991 he joined Blackburn Rovers. Scoring on his debut, he became a great favourite with the Ewood Park fans and scored the only goal from the penalty spot in their play-off win against Leicester City. He became an important member of Rovers' Championship winning team, and appeared in over 100 League games before joining Birmingham City in the summer of 1996.

EAMONN O'KEEFE

Eamonn O'Keefe took a strange route to success, moving from Stalybridge Celtic to Plymouth Argyle, then to Hyde United. Next came a spell in Saudi Arabia before he returned to England to sign for Mossley. He made his debut for Mossley against Wigan Athletic in the 1977-78 season and was a regular in their side until signing for Everton in July 1979.

The £25,000 fee paid for him was the second highest ever paid for a non-League player at the time.

He made his debut for the Goodison Park club against Bolton Wanderers at Burnden Park on Boxing Day 1979. Capped by the Republic of Ireland, he won the first of his five caps in 1981 against Wales. He went on to appear in 51 League and Cup games for the Toffees, scoring 8 goals, before signing for Wigan Athletic in January 1982 for a then record fee of £65,000.

His first game for the Latics saw him score one of the goals in a 3-2 win at Northampton Town. Though not a prolific goalscorer, he hit all three in Latics 3-0 win over Crewe Alexandra and the 3-1 win against Mansfield Town, both in the same season. In 1982-83 he scored another hat-trick in the 4-0 home win over Southend United but at the end of that season, in which he was the club's top scorer, he left to join Port Vale. He had played in 61 first team games for the Latics, scoring 25 goals. He later moved on to Blackpool and Chester City.

HARRY PARKINSON

One of the most popular players ever to turn out in Latic's colours, he played for Chorley Schoolboys before signing for Wigan Athletic in 1946, claiming it to be the proudest day of his life. He played ten full seasons as a full-back for Latics and still holds the club record for consecutive appearances in the first team - a staggering 212. A tigerish full-back of a very successful era, when he played in the same Wigan team as Kenny Banks, Billy Lomax and Dave Mycock, he appeared in 456 first team games for the club.

When he finally hung up his boots, after playing his last game against South Liverpool on 2 May 1957, he took over as Youth Team Coach and held the post for twelve years until he finally called it a day in 1974.

MICK QUINN

An old-fashioned striker who scored at the rate of at least one in every two matches nearly everywhere he has played, he first came into League football with Wigan

Athletic in 1979 after being freed by Derby County, following an apprenticeship which started in July 1978. He had to wait until the end of the season for his Football League debut, scoring the first goal for the Latics in a 3-1 win over Halifax Town on 12 April 1980. He became a regular goalscorer in his second season at Springfield Park, finishing as top marksman with 14 goals in the League, but after a disappointing 1981-82 campaign when he secured just four goals in his 29 appearances, he was released and joined Stockport County.

An immediate success at Edgeley Park, he ended his first season with 24 League goals and was the first County player to top 20 in a season for fifteen years. He scored 15 goals from 24 games the following season before he was snapped up by Oldham Athletic. Leading scorer at Boundary Park, he soon joined Portsmouth, but left Fratton Park when his contract expired to sign for Newcastle United, the fee being decided by the Transfer Tribunal.

He made a sensational start to his Newcastle career, netting four goals on his debut against Leeds United. By the end of that 1989-90 season, he had scored 32 League goals to become the Magpies highest goalscorer since Hughie Gallagher hit 36 in 1926-27. Loaned to Coventry City in November 1992, his start at Highfield Road was even more dramatic than that with Newcastle. After getting two on his debut, he hit ten goals in his first six starts including a brace in a 5-1 thrashing of Liverpool. The transfer was needless to say, made permanent.

DENNIS REEVES

Signed from Wrexham in the late 1960's, he quickly established himself in the first team. He was a firm favourite with the Latics fans, who admired his solid, dependable performances.

Never spectacular, Dennis, a painter and decorator by trade, was perhaps one of the most efficient 'keepers to wear the Wigan Athletic colours. He had appeared frequently in the Wrexham first team before joining the Latics and earlier in his career had played for Chester.

After signing for Latics, Dennis played in a number of successful teams and gave many memorable performances, not least against Manchester City in 1971 when he pulled off some tremendous saves before ironically his boot split while taking a goal-kick and the ball fell to a City player who set up the winning goal for Colin Bell.

Another performance remembered by Latic fans came in the F.A. Challenge Trophy semi-final replay against Stafford Rangers at Boundary Park, Oldham in 1973. His ability helped Latics win 1-0 and Dennis played against Scarborough at Wembley in what must have been one of the highlights of his career.

JACK ROBERTS

In 1934-35 centre-forward Jack Roberts' haul of 66 goals set a club scoring record that was to stand for thirty years until Harry Lyon equalled it in season 1964-65. Latics won the Cheshire League that season, scoring 153 goals of which Jack Roberts' contribution was 46.

A former amateur international, Jack was a big, strong forward, and a powerful runner with a ball, whilst his heading ability was particularly good. Yet halfway through the following season, he was rather surprisingly allowed to join Port Vale in exchange for JRM Wilson. Sadly, a few years later, Jack Roberts was seriously injured and had to have a leg amputated.

TEDDY ROBINSON

One of the best full-backs ever to wear the colours of Wigan Athletic, the Hindley-born youngster played for numerous school and junior sides before joining Southport. Affectionately known as "Lamiker" he spent two seasons at Haig Avenue before being snapped up by Latics manager Charlie Spencer. A regular member of the Latics side from 1932 to 1936, Teddy Robinson was in the mould of the old style full-back - stocky, hard and fiercely competitive.

The nickname "Lamiker" is a mystery. He apparently picked it up on joining Southport and it stuck with him throughout his career. Despite his hard, tough reputation, he was never sent off, and during the first couple of seasons of Latics existence he formed a great full-back partnership with Bob McLoughlin.

After retiring from the game, he took to running a pig farm at Hindley but after the war he joined the Fire Service.

HARRY SHARRATT

Signing for Wigan in 1948, Harry Sharratt kept his amateur status throughout his career. Making his Latics debut against Bootle in a 6-1 F.A. Cup qualifying round victory. Wigan were just one of many clubs who tried to persuade him to turn professional. The popular goalkeeper resisted the temptation because he wanted to remain a schoolteacher and also play for England at amateur level. He fulfilled both ambitions. He stayed with the Latics, "on and off", for about three seasons, making 86 first team appearances, but in the meantime he had spells with the then top amateur club in the north-east of England, Bishop Auckland. It was while playing for 'The Bishops' that he was capped for England.

A good all-round goalkeeper, it was difficult to point to a weakness. Never spectacular, he was strong on crosses, always alert for the long range shot, quite agile, and even the stronger challenges dished out to goalkeepers by forwards in those days never put him off.

The club that got nearest to signing Harry Sharratt on full-time professional forms was Sheffield Wednesday for whom he had trials. But in the end, not even the illustrious Owls could tempt him away from fulfilling his ambition to pull on an England shirt.

JIMMY SHIRLEY

Jimmy Shirley was a right-half when Latics signed him from school in 1939 for a short spell. He was the youngest player to play in the famous side managed by Charlie Spencer, but his first spell with Latics did not last long before his impressive form took him to Stockport County as a full-time professional.

His spell there did not last long either, because, almost as soon as he signed, war broke out. During the hostilities, the former Wigan Schools' Town Team skipper captained the Services' International side. At the end of the war he joined Rochdale for the short time before returning to Springfield Park, and he played for Wigan until Ted Goodier came to the club to take over the managers' post.

Goodier arrived at Wigan to find that Sid Littler had placed the whole team on the transfer list! Given the opportunity to become Goodier's assistant-manager, he turned it down and opted for the player-manager's job at Morecambe.

He stayed there for just twelve months before travelling difficulties forced him to quit the job and he returned to Latics in 1959 for a short spell as manager. He lifted them from the lower reaches of the league in his one season and got them to the final of the Junior Cup before relinquishing the manager's chair.

An interesting fact about Jim Shirley is that he was probably one of the first Wigan lads ever to be selected for England Schoolboy trials. When he got there, however, the coaches told him he was too old to be selected. He had passed the age limit by the massive total of ... 24 hours!

BILLY SUTHERLAND

Signed from Glasgow Rangers, Billy Sutherland came to Springfield Park with a number of games for the Ibrox club behind him. Immediately settling into the left-back position, he became a firm favourite with the fans, for although he was an excellent defensive full-back he liked to move forward in attack. He possessed a terrific shot and scored many memorable goals during his career at Springfield Park.

Two of his never-to-be forgotten efforts came in F.A. Cup-ties at Springfield Park. The first was against Third Division Port Vale in 1969, when he sent 13,000 Latics fans wild with delight with a thundering free-kick from nearly 30 yards; and the second came against Rhyl when he scored with a tremendous volley from 25 yards to put Latics into the first round proper. Billy also had the distinction of scoring Wigan Athletic's first-ever goal in the Northern Premier League in a 2-0 win at Scarborough in 1968.

He remained at Springfield Park through the reigns of Ian McNeill, Gordon Milne, Les Rigby and Brian Tiler before an injury in an F.A. Cup replay versus Shrewsbury Town in 1975 virtually ended his playing days. He left at the end of that season after picking up his second Northern Premier League Championship medal.

SID TUFFNELL

Left-half Sid Tuffnell holds the distinction of probably being the smallest man ever to play for Wigan Athletic. Standing just five feet tall, he was a battler and possessed no little skill. Signed by Charlie Spencer from Sheffield United, older fans will remember his harassing play, always snapping at the heels of the opposition players, and in his four years with the Latics he became a great favourite with the fans.

Part of a famous Wigan half-back line of Patterson, Hancock and Tuffnell, he made 108 league appearances for Latics scoring nine goals. When his playing days were over he returned to live in the Sheffield area but never forgot the club with whom he had enjoyed so many good times. When Wigan Athletic played Sheffield Wednesday at Hillsborough, he met the Latics coach and along with Duncan Colquhoun and Jack Farrimond, talked about the good old days.

ROY TUNKS

Born in West Germany while his father was serving there in the armed forces, Roy first made his mark as a centre-forward, being the hot-shot of the school team and then being made captain of Worthing Boys. He was invited along for a trial for the county team and when the goalkeeper did not turn up, volunteered to take his place ... little knowing what the future held for him.

Roy Tunks joined Rotherham United and made the first of 138 League appearances for the Millmoor club a few days after his 17th birthday. During his time with the Yorkshire club he became dissatisfied and had trials with Newcastle United, Ipswich Town, and York City. Eventually, in November 1974, he arrived at Preston North End and kept goal in 277 League games for the Lilywhites before joining Wigan Athletic in November 1981.

He made his debut for the Springfield Park club against Hereford United in a 1-1 draw and went on to play in 31 League games. In 1982-83 he was an ever-present and went on to appear in 302 League and Cup games for the Latics before having a short spell with Hartlepool United and later returning to Preston North End.

Roy Tunks is also the oldest player to turn out in a Latics team in the Football League. He was approaching his 37th birthday when he last turned out for Wigan in a goalless draw at Blackpool on 24 October 1987.

STEVE WALSH

Steve Walsh joined Wigan as an apprentice and signed full terms in September 1982. Making his first team debut against Manchester City in a Football League Cup second round second leg tie on 27 October 1982, he went on to make 32 League and Cup appearances that season which was the club's first in the Third Division.

He soon established himself in the Latics back four and enjoyed a very successful two seasons, playing in a further 83 League games. The next season was a frustrating one for both club and player with Walsh making only 13 League appearances but gaining a Freight Rover Trophy Winner's medal.

Former Wigan manager Bryan Hamilton paid £100,000 to take Walsh to Leicester City in June 1986 but he had a hard time as the club were relegated. Appointed club captain, he is a great favourite with the fans and in the Summer of 1996 led the Filberts into the Premier League via the play-offs. By the start of the following season the Preston-born centre-half had made over 250 League and Cup appearances for the Filbert Street club.

MAURICE WHITTLE

Starting his career with Blackburn Rovers, his chances of first team football were limited and so he moved on to Oldham Athletic. It was there that the Wigan-born full-back's career took off, making 312 League appearances and scoring 39 goals.

On leaving Boundary Park, he went to America to join the Fort Lauderdale Strikers where he came face to face with some legendary players, notably Pele.

His first spell at Springfield Park came in 1977 and coincided with the club's historic F.A. Cup run. It was Maurice Whittle whose strike from a direct free-kick in the second round gave the Latics a 1-0 victory over Sheffield Wednesday who were then in the Third Division and managed by Jack Charlton. That win meant a third round tie against Birmingham City and national exposure which led to Wigan joining the Football League in 1978.

Contracted to return to the US, he spent part of the English season playing for non-League Barrow and Stafford Rangers before jumping at the chance to return to League football to fill the spot left by the departure of Joe Hinnigan to Sunderland. He played in 21 League games for Latics, scoring his only goal in a 2-2 draw at Torquay United.

HAROLD WOOLLEY

One of the best goalkeepers Latics ever had, Harold Woolley played in 108 first team matches in his three years at Springfield Park. It was he who performed heroically between the sticks when Latics won the Lancashire Combination in their first season in the competition. They got off to a pretty poor start through as did Woolley, for he let in five goals as Latics lost their first match in the Lancashire Combination 5-1 at home to Fleetwood!

However, the team soon picked themselves up and Harold, a local pitman who lived near to Springfield Park, became a great favourite with the Wigan crowd. He took defeat very badly, and on one occasion Latics lost a cup-tie at Marine 3-1 with Woolley feeling the second goal was partly his fault.

After the game he was seen by a Latics fan squatting on his haunches on his doorstep. When the fan asked him what was wrong, Woolley said, *"I should have caught the ball, shouldn't I"*, *"Never mind"* said the supporter, *"It couldn't be helped"*. *"Couldn't be helped"* snapped Woolley, *"If Jimmy Shirley had left it to me, I could have taken the ***** lace out of the thing, never mind caught it"*.

JEFF WRIGHT

Born in the small market town of Alston in Cumbria, he gained representative honours as a schoolboy with the East Cumbria Under-15 and Under-17 teams. After leaving school, he started work as a trainee office manager at the local foundry works but continued to play football in the local amateur leagues.

Eventually signing for Tow Law Town, he had only made 15 appearances when he joined Netherfield. In the next two and a half seasons he played in over 120 games before being brought to Springfield Park by Les Rigby in February 1974. During his time with the Latics, he was a member of Brian Tiler's Northern Premier League Championship side and was an ever-present in the club's first season in the Football League.

In the eyes of most Wigan supporters, Jeff always played the role of 'hero' or 'villain' but even the most critical Latics fans acknowledged that he possessed a range of skills not commonplace at Fourth Division level. Playing in 143 League games for the Latics, much of his quietly efficient work was often overlooked.

STATISTICAL SECTION

The various lists and tables are either self-explanatory or appropriate notes have been given. In all cases these records and statistics apply to the end of the 1995/96 season.

Seasonal Statistics (pages 130 to 191):
Abbreviated details have been given for seasons 1932/33 to 1978/79 (non-League days) inclusive. The boxes provide the 'home' and 'away' results (Wigan Athletic score first) of every League match, but not in chronological order, with a summary below. Total appearances and goalscorers in League matches follow, with substitute appearances shown in brackets. Abbreviated details are given for all major Cup matches, consisting of the round number, opposition, venue, result and goalscorers.

Full details have been given for seasons 1978/79 to 1995/96 (Football League days) inclusive. Statistic tables provide the following details: First column League match number or Cup round - typically thus: 2R = 2nd round. 1Rr = 1st round replay. 2R1 = 2nd round 1st leg. NQF = Northern Section quarter-final (SF = Semi Final, F = Final). Pre = prelminary. Second column shows the date. Third Column shows the opposition (Wigan Athletic 'home' matches in upper case - capitals). Fourth column the result (Wigan score first). Fifth column match attendance. Sixth column goalscorers; number in brackets indicates number of goals scored by that player, O.G. indicates an 'own goal', (pen) is a goal scored from a penalty. The Sixth column provides details of each line-up, with every player's position/shirt number. Where a player has been substituted, '12' replaced the player marked with an asterisk (*), '13' or '14' replaced the player marked with a hash (#). Unused substitutes have not been included. A summary is given below of total Football League only appearances, substitute appearances and goals scored.

WIGAN ATHLETIC F.C.
- RECORDS -

NON-LEAGUE FINAL POSITIONS: 1932-33 to 1977-78

Season	P.	W.	D.	L.	F.	A.	W.	D.	L.	F.	A.	Pts	Lg.Pos.
CHESHIRE LEAGUE													
1932-33	42	14	3	4	90	24	7	8	6	31	30	53	5th
1933-34	42	21	0	0	68	9	9	6	6	43	37	66	lst
1934-35	42	19	2	0	106	20	8	7	6	47	39	63	lst
1935-36	42	20	0	1	91	18	11	6	4	45	28	68	lst
1936-37	42	15	3	3	59	24	4	3	14	35	49	44	8th
1937-38	42	15	2	4	67	25	4	2	15	27	64	42	llth
1938-39	42	15	3	3	69	26	6	2	13	34	58	47	7th
1945-46	38	11	4	4	60	41	1	2	16	28	75	30	19th
1946-47	42	7	3	11	43	47	2	4	15	23	67	25	22nd
LANCASHIRE COMBINATION													
1947-48	42	16	3	2	42	16	9	6	6	30	21	59	lst
1948-49	42	13	5	3	45	23	6	4	11	28	45	47	6th
1949-50	42	13	5	3	46	18	11	3	7	33	29	56	2nd
1950-51	42	13	3	5	52	25	14	4	3	46	18	61	lst
1951-52	42	12	5	4	44	27	9	4	8	29	30	51	4th
1952-53	42	16	5	0	73	16	11	8	2	51	29	67	lst
1953-54	40	15	3	2	65	21	16	1	3	45	27	66	lst
1954-55	42	13	5	3	54	21	8	5	8	39	35	52	3rd
1955-56	38	12	2	5	48	26	6	8	5	34	30	46	6th
1956-57	38	10	2	7	40	22	7	1	11	33	39	37	10th
1957-58	42	14	5	2	60	25	7	6	8	35	35	53	4th
1958-59	42	11	3	7	45	36	1	4	16	15	48	31	18th
1959-60	42	15	1	5	66	25	12	5	4	35	26	60	2nd
1960-61	42	15	3	3	59	20	10	5	6	49	36	58	3rd
CHESHIRE LEAGUE													
1961-62	42	15	3	3	54	19	9	4	8	32	32	55	5th
1962-63	42	15	4	2	41	15	7	2	12	30	39	50	7th
1963-64	42	11	2	8	66	42	7	5	9	28	40	43	12th
1964-65	42	18	0	3	76	20	14	3	4	45	26	67	lst
1965-66	42	17	4	0	79	14	15	4	2	54	26	72	2nd
1966-67	42	16	4	1	65	20	10	4	7	36	41	60	2nd
1967-68	42	11	6	4	37	21	7	6	8	25	27	48	8th
NORTHERN PREMIER LEAGUE													
1968-69	38	11	5	3	34	20	7	7	5	25	21	48	2nd
1969-70	38	13	6	0	33	11	7	6	6	23	21	52	2nd
1970-71	42	15	5	1	52	14	12	8	1	39	18	67	lst
1971-72	46	14	6	3	30	16	13	4	6	40	27	64	3rd
1972-73	46	16	6	1	48	11	7	8	8	23	27	60	3rd
1973-74	46	18	3	2	63	15	10	5	8	33	24	64	2nd
1974-75	46	20	1	2	58	14	13	5	5	36	24	72	lst
1975-76	46	13	5	5	47	18	8	10	5	34	24	57	6th
1976-77	44	9	8	5	37	23	5	7	10	25	31	43	14th
1977-78	46	13	7	3	37	17	12	8	3	46	28	65	2nd

NON-LEAGUE OPPOSITION

Wigan Athletic have played 77 clubs in non-League football in three competitions (ie: Cheshire League, Lancashire Combination and Northern Premier League). Below is Latic's League record against each club.

	P.	W.	D.	L.	F.	A.	W.	D.	L	F.	A.
Accrington.Stanley Res.	20	5	1	4	26	14	4	2	4	20	18
Altrincham	50	11	6	8	42	30	6	9	10	29	55
Ashington	2	0	1	0	2	2	1	0	0	2	1
Ashton National	14	5	1	1	25	10	3	2	2	11	11
Ashton United	26	9	2	2	33	15	5	4	4	19	19
Bacup Borough	16	5	2	1	17	6	2	3	3	15	17
Bangor City	40	16	2	2	49	17	3	8	9	25	30
Barrow	12	6	0	0	21	5	4	1	1	14	
Barrow Res	16	5	1	2	20	11	1	5	2	13	13
Blackpool 'B'	8	1	2	1	12	6	1	1	2	4	8
Bolton Wanderers 'B'	4	2	0	0	7	3	2	0	0	3	0
Bootle	8	3	1	0	7	1	2	1	1	4	4
Boston United	20	5	3	2	16	7	1	5	4	10	14
Bradford.(Park Avenue)	8	4	0	0	10	1	0	3	1	2	3
Burscough	14	3	2	2	13	9	0	1	6	7	15
Buxton	42	16	4	1	79	24	8	3	10	32	37
Chester Reserves	32	12	3	1	59	15	7	4	5	36	32
Chorley	34	9	2	6	29	26	9	4	4	36	28
Clitheroe	16	7	0	1	21	8	7	0	1	20	10
Congleton Town	24	11	0	1	56	11	4	3	5	17	20
Crewe Alexandra Res.	18	6	2	1	19	8	3	1	5	21	27
Crompton Recs.	2	0	1	0	1	1	0	1	0	0	0
Darwen	28	8	4	2	33	10	8	2	4	27	21
Droylsden	12	3	1	2	15	13	2	1	3	9	12
Earlestown	8	3	0	1	15	6	4	0	0	16	1
Ellesmere Port Town	18	4	5	0	20	11	5	3	1	19	13
Fleetwood	44	11	5	6	41	25	8	6	8	36	31
Frickley Athletic	18	7	0	2	32	11	4	1	4	11	16
Gainsborough.Trinity	20	7	3	0	20	6	2	6	2	11	12
Gateshead	12	6	0	0	13	1	3	1	2	6	4
Goole Town	20	6	3	1	26	11	6	2	2	12	7
Great Harwood	18	5	4	0	18	3	4	3	2	20	15
Horwich RMI	24	9	2	1	31	11	6	1	5	20	22
Hurst	18	6	0	3	37	14	4	1	4	21	18
Hyde United	36	15	1	2	54	18	8	4	6	32	37
Kirkby Town	4	1	1	0	4	3	2	0	0	6	2

	P.	W.	D.	L.	F.	A.	W.	D.	L	F.	A.
Lancaster City	44	13	5	4	47	21	10	9	3	44	25
Leyland Motors	4	2	0	0	6	2	0	2	0	1	1
Lytham St Annes	4	2	0	0	3	0	1	0	1	7	9
Macclesfield Town	50	11	7	7	43	26	8	8	9	39	48
Manchester.North End	14	6	1	0	33	8	2	2	3	13	14
Marine	28	10	2	2	42	18	7	3	4	21	17
Matlock Town	18	6	2	1	19	6	5	1	3	18	16
Morecambe	48	16	8	0	44	13	10	5	9	34	30
Mossley	44	14	3	5	68	31	11	3	8	40	36
Nantwich Town	12	6	0	0	20	1	4	2	0	19	8
Nelson	28	6	4	4	24	17	9	2	3	29	19
Netherfield	48	21	2	1	67	17	9	2	13	30	37
New Brighton	34	10	5	2	46	15	7	8	2	29	23
Northwich Victoria	52	20	1	5	76	30	7	6	13	32	46
Oldham Athletic Res.	24	9	3	0	34	8	4	1	7	15	20
Oswestry Town	14	6	0	1	21	4	6	0	1	12	8
Port Vale Reserves	16	6	1	1	18	6	1	3	4	11	20
Prescot Cables	30	8	3	4	35	19	3	3	9	20	30
Rhyl	22	8	1	2	39	14	3	3	5	18	20
Rochdale Reserves	16	5	2	1	21	9	4	2	2	15	9
Rossendale United	26	9	1	3	46	22	7	4	2	29	23
Runcorn	52	19	3	4	71	38	10	4	12	50	54
Sandbach Ramblers	4	2	0	0	11	1	2	0	0	8	3
Sankeys(Wellington)	8	3	1	0	8	1	1	2	1	6	8
Scarborough	20	5	3	2	15	12	3	3	4	12	15
Skelmersdale United	20	6	2	2	27	9	4	2	4	14	16
South Liverpool	38	12	3	4	41	15	9	7	3	36	24
Southport Reserves	26	11	2	0	43	15	6	2	5	17	17
South Shields	12	4	1	1	11	7	4	1	1	8	4
Stafford Rangers	32	9	3	4	38	15	6	3	7	25	27
Stalybridge Celtic	30	12	1	2	48	16	8	3	4	30	30
St Helens Town	4	2	0	0	10	4	0	1	1	1	3
Stockport.County Res	22	9	1	1	30	10	3	3	5	18	29
Tranmere.Rovers Res	32	11	3	2	49	15	5	1	10	25	34
Wellington Town	6	3	0	0	9	3	0	0	3	4	10
Whitchurch	2	1	0	0	6	1	0	1	0	1	1
Winsford United	28	11	2	1	55	11	9	1	4	28	14
Witton Albion	32	9	3	4	41	21	3	2	11	13	47
Workington	2	1	0	0	4	1	1	0	0	4	1
Worksop Town	10	5	0	0	15	1	2	3	0	7	5
Wrexham Reserves	18	7	1	1	24	8	6	0	3	17	12

FOOTBALL LEAGUE FINAL POSITIONS: 1978-79 to 1995-96

Season	P.	W.	D.	L.	F.	A.	W.	D.	L.	F.	A.	Pts	Lg.Pos.
FOOTBALL LEAGUE DIVISION FOUR													
1978-79	46	14	5	4	40	24	7	8	8	23	24	55	6th
1979-80	46	13	5	5	42	26	8	8	7	34	35	55	6th
1980-81	46	13	4	6	29	16	5	7	11	22	39	47	llth
1981-82	46	17	5	1	47	18	9	8	6	33	28	91	3rd
FOOTBALL LEAGUE DIVISION THREE													
1982-83	46	10	4	9	35	33	5	5	13	25	39	54	18th
1983-84	46	11	5	7	26	18	5	8	10	20	38	61	15th
1984-85	46	12	6	5	36	22	3	8	12	24	42	59	16th
1985-86	46	17	4	2	54	17	6	10	7	28	31	86	4th
1986-87	46	15	5	3	47	25	10	5	8	36	34	85	4th
1978-88	46	11	8	4	36	23	9	4	10	34	38	72	7th
1988-89	46	9	5	9	28	22	5	9	9	27	31	56	17th
1989-90	46	10	6	7	29	22	3	8	12	19	42	53	18th
1990-91	46	14	3	6	40	20	6	6	11	31	34	69	10th
1991-92	46	11	6	6	33	21	4	8	11	25	43	59	15th
FOOTBALL LEAGUE DIVISION TWO (Formerly Division Three)													
1992-93	46	6	6	11	26	34	4	5	14	17	38	41	23rd
FOOTBALL LEAGUE DIVISION THREE													
1993-94	42	6	7	8	33	33	5	5	11	18	37	45	19th
1994-95	42	7	6	8	28	30	7	4	10	25	30	52	14th
1995-96	46	15	3	5	36	21	5	7	11	26	35	70	10th

FOOTBALL LEAGUE OPPOSITION

Wigan Athletic have played 69 clubs in the Football League (197879 to 1995-96 incl.) Below is Latic's record against each club. Some clubs have changed their names (e.g. Leyton Orient became Orient and then Leyton Orient again). In all cases the current name used by each club also cover all games under previous names.

	P.	W.	D.	L.	F.	A.	W.	D.	L.	F.	A.
Aldershot	12	6	0	0	13	4	2	0	4	7	9
Barnet	4	1	0	1	2	2	0	1	1	1	6
Barnsley	2	0	1	0	2	2	0	1	0	0	0
Birmingham City	6	2	1	0	5	1	0	3	0	3	3
Blackpool	14	4	3	0	12	6	2	2	3	6	11
Bolton Wanderers	18	4	2	3	10	10	3	2	4	11	12
Bournemouth	24	5	2	5	13	11	4	3	5	12	15
Bradford City	20	6	0	4	19	12	1	4	5	16	24
Brentford	18	5	4	0	15	7	3	1	5	10	16
Brighton & Hove Albion	4	0	1	1	4	5	0	0	2	0	2
Bristol City	12	1	3	2	9	9	1	0	5	3	12
Bristol Rovers	16	5	1	2	14	10	1	1	6	8	21
Burnley	6	2	1	0	4	1	2	0	1	3	4
Bury	24	7	1	4	15	13	3	6	3	21	20
Cambridge United	6	1	1	1	6	5	1	1	1	5	5
Cardiff City	10	3	2	0	7	2	0	2	3	6	12
Carlisle United	6	1	0	2	2	4	1	0	2	3	5
Chester City	18	7	1	1	20	9	3	2	4	7	8
Chesterfield	14	2	2	3	9	10	1	3	3	6	9
Colchester United	8	2	0	2	6	4	2	0	2	7	9
Crewe Alexandra	14	5	2	0	10	2	2	1	4	8	12
Darlington	20	6	1	3	25	11	2	4	4	11	14
Derby County	4	2	0	0	4	1	0	1	1	2	3
Doncaster Rovers	22	6	3	2	17	10	3	4	4	22	24
Exeter City	14	5	1	1	14	5	3	2	2	11	6
Fulham	18	3	2	4	10	11	1	3	5	8	16
Gillingham	20	4	3	3	17	14	3	2	5	9	16
Grimsby Town	6	1	0	2	2	4	1	0	2	6	7
Halifax Town	8	4	0	0	10	2	2	2	0	3	1
Hartlepool United	16	3	4	1	11	10	1	3	4	9	13
Hereford United	14	2	4	1	9	8	1	3	3	6	12

	P.	W.	D.	L.	F.	A.	W.	D.	L.	F.	A.
Huddersfield Town	16	3	1	4	9	11	0	3	5	5	15
Hull City	10	2	2	1	6	4	1	2	2	4	5
Leyton Orient	16	3	1	4	10	9	1	5	2	7	9
Lincoln City	18	5	1	3	11	9	3	1	5	6	12
Mansfield Town	22	7	1	3	22	15	5	1	5	18	16
Middlesbrough	2	0	0	1	0	2	0	1	0	0	0
Millwall	6	1	1	1	3	2	0	0	3	1	8
Newport County	14	1	2	4	5	8	2	1	4	13	16
Northampton Town	20	4	4	2	15	10	3	6	1	14	10
Notts County	10	3	1	1	7	4	0	3	2	6	9
Oxford United	4	0	0	2	0	3	0	1	1	0	2
Peterborough United	8	3	1	0	11	2	2	2	0	5	1
Plymouth Argyle	12	3	1	2	8	4	1	1	4	4	8
Portsmouth	6	1	0	2	3	3	0	2	1	1	2
Port Vale	18	7	0	2	18	11	1	4	4	9	14
Preston North End	24	5	3	4	16	11	3	3	6	15	23
Reading	18	5	4	0	16	6	2	0	7	8	17
Rochdale	14	3	3	1	11	3	4	1	2	9	6
Rotherham United	16	6	1	1	14	7	3	3	2	13	16
Scarborough	6	1	1	1	4	3	1	1	1	2	4
Scunthorpe United	16	5	2	1	12	6	3	2	3	17	14
Sheffield United	8	2	0	2	7	5	0	1	3	3	7
Shrewsbury Town	8	0	3	1	5	8	1	2	1	3	2
Southend United	10	4	0	1	12	2	2	0	3	6	7
Stockport County	12	4	0	2	11	8	4	1	1	8	7
Stoke City	6	2	1	0	6	1	0	0	3	1	7
Sunderland	2	0	1	0	2	2	0	0	1	1	4
Swansea City	14	4	0	3	15	9	3	1	3	12	12
Swindon Town	2	1	0	0	3	2	0	0	1	1	3
Torquay United	16	4	2	2	11	8	1	6	1	6	7
Tranmere Rovers	10	0	3	2	2	5	2	2	1	7	6
Walsall	20	6	1	3	21	10	3	4	3	12	16
West Brom Albion	4	1	0	1	1	1	0	1	1	2	6
Wimbledon	6	2	0	1	5	4	0	1	2	3	5
Wolverhampton Wanderers	4	1	1	0	6	4	0	1	1	3	4
Wrexham	2	1	0	0	3	1	0	1	0	1	1
Wycombe Wanderers	2	0	1	0	1	1	1	0	0	1	0
York City	16	4	2	2	14	13	2	2	4	7	13

APPEARANCES, GOALS AND ATTENDANCES
(UPTO, AND INCLUDING, 1995/96 SEASON)

TOP TWENTY - APPEARANCES AND GOALS

(includes all matches except friendlies)

TOTAL APPEARANCES

1.	I.Gillibrand	621
2.	D.Houghton	511
3.	H.Parkinson	456
4.	B.Sutherland	410
5.	K.Langley	393
6.	J.Wright	384
7.	H.Lyon	379
8.	T.Gore	366
9.	D.Reeves	357
10.	C.Methven	354
11.	K.Morris	352
12.	M.Worswick	339
13.	J.Butler	337
14.	A.Cribley	329
15.	R.Tunks	302
16.	K.Banks	260
17.	A.Tankard	257
18.	J.Shirley	246
18.	A.Halsall	246
20.	J.Rogers	243

TOTAL GOALS

1.	H.Lyon	264
2.	B.Lomax	179
3.	B.Llewellyn	140
4.	J.Lyon	119
5.	J.Rogers	111
6.	M.Worswick	106
7.	G.Scott	101
8.	E.T.Felton	96
9.	H.Thomas	90
10.	R.Smith	88
11.	P.Houghton	87
12.	J.Livesey	81
13.	G.Davies	74
14.	P.Higham	70
15.	F.Taberner	67
16.	J.Roberts	66
17.	J.Robson	64
18.	B.Griffiths	58
19.	J.Fleming	56
20.	P.Daley	55
20.	K.Twidle	55

TOP TWENTY - APPEARANCES
League Competitions
(including as substitute)

Cheshire League

1.	D.Houghton	249
2.	T.Robinson	237
3.	H.Lyon	222
4.	A.Halsall	150
5.	D.Colquhoun	127
5.	R.Wilkinson	127
7.	A.Craig	126
8.	D.Crompton	121
9.	G.Scott	120
9.	W.McLauchlan	120
11.	B.Llewellyn	115
12.	E.T.Felton	113
13.	D.Roberts	110
14.	F.Briars	109
14.	J.Patterson	109
16.	S.Tuffnell	108
17.	J.Robson	103
18.	H.Thomas	81
19.	L.Caunce	79
20.	W.O'Loughlin	77

Lancashire Combination

1.	H.Parkinson	342
2.	K.Banks	170
3.	B.Lomax	169
4.	J.Shirley	161
5.	J.Lyon	151
6.	A.Lomas	148
7.	E.Cunliffe	144
7.	C.Tolley	144
9.	J.Lindsay	104
10.	T.Hindle	103
11.	D.Houghton	99
11.	R.Smith	99
13.	J.Prescott	98
14.	J.Pollard	95
15.	S.Lynn	88
16.	H.Woolley	85
17.	J.Bramwell	83
18.	F.Taberner	82
19.	P.Taylor	80
20.	K.Twidle	78

Northern Premier League

1.	I.Gillibrand	384
2.	M.Worswick	248
3.	D.Reeves	233
4.	B.Sutherland	228
5.	K.Morris	219
6.	T.Gore	185
7.	J.Wright	175
8.	J.Rogers	163
9.	J.Hinnigan	120
10.	A.Jackson	108
11.	D.Coutts	102
11.	J.Garrett	102
13.	G.Oates	100
14.	N.Ward	86
15.	J.Wilkie	83
16.	J.Fleming	76
16.	G.Davies	76
18.	M.Taylor	75
19.	W.Molyneux	74
20.	G.Milne	73

Football League

1.	K.Langley	317
2.	C.Methven	296
3.	J.Butler	277
4.	A.Cribley	271
5.	R.Tunks	245
6.	A.Tankard	209
7.	D.Lowe	195
8.	N.Rimmer	191
9.	B.Griffiths	189
10.	P.Houghton	185
11.	A.Johnson	180
12.	G.Barrow	179
13.	P.Daley	161
14.	A.Pilling	156
15.	N.Adkins	155
15.	P.Beesley	155
17.	P.Atherton	149
18.	J.Wright	143
19.	P.Jewell	137
20.	B.Knowles	127

TOP TWENTY - GOALS

Cheshire League

1.	H.Lyon	174
2.	B.Llewellyn	96
3.	G.Scott	79
4.	H.Thomas	77
5.	E.T.Felton	75
6.	J.Roberts	54
7.	J.Robson	44
8.	G.Wallbanks	40
9.	W.Chambers	39
10.	D.Colquhoun	38
11.	C.Davenport	33
12.	P.Higham	26
13.	C.Wilson	22
14.	G.Cansfield	21
15.	G.Morgans	20
15.	S.Armes	20
17.	W.O'Loughlin	17
18.	R.Barker	16
18.	R.Murdoch	16
20.	T.Graham	14
20.	W.Grange	14

Lancashire Combination

1.	B.Lomax	131
2.	J.Lyon	83
3.	R.Smith	54
4.	J.Livesey	53
5.	F.Taberner	45
6.	K.Twidle	42
7.	J.Prescott	36
8.	T.Hindle	32
9.	W.Bootle	31
10.	W.McLean	26
11.	P.Taylor	24
11.	H.Davis	24
13.	E.Cunliffe	23
13.	W.Hazelden	23
15.	J.Lindsay	21
15.	J.Vincent	21
17.	E.Corfield	20
17.	P.Higham	20
19.	R.Barker	13
20.	F.Miller	12

Northern Premier League

1.	J.Rogers	77
2.	M.Worswick	73
3.	G.Davies	52
4.	W.McLoughlin	34
4.	J.Fleming	34
6.	J.Wilkie	33
7.	G.Oates	30
8.	A.Jackson	27
8.	T.Gore	27
8.	J.Wright	27
11.	J.Garrett	25
12.	T.Marsden	17
13.	P.Clements	15
14.	A.Ryan	13
15.	B.Sutherland	11
15.	J.Fletcher	11
15.	M.Moore	11
18.	P.Houghton	9
18.	R.Todd	9
20.	D.Temple	8

Football League

1.	P.Houghton	62
2.	B.Griffiths	44
3.	D.Lowe	43
4.	P.Daley	40
5.	G.Barrow	36
6.	P.Jewell	35
7.	A.Lyons	27
7.	B.Campbell	27
9.	M.Hilditch	26
10.	L.Bradd	25
10.	M.Newell	25
10.	E.O'Keefe	25
13.	W.Aspinall	22
14.	C.Methven	21
15.	A.Pilling	20
15.	G.Worthington	20
17.	M.Quinn	19
17.	J.Wright	19
19.	S.Johnson	18
20.	G.Powell	17

TOP TWENTY - CUP COMPETITIONS

APPEARANCES

(including as substitute)

F.A.Cup

1.	H.Parkinson	36
2.	I.Gillibrand	34
3.	K.Morris	28
4.	K.Langley	27
5.	T.Robinson	26
6.	D.Reeves	25
6.	B.Sutherland	25
8.	J.Butler	24
8.	A.Cribley	24
10.	B.Lomax	23
10.	C.Methven	23
12.	D.Houghton	22
13.	R.Tunks	21
14.	H.Lyon	19
15.	J.Shirley	18
16.	D.Lowe	16
17.	P.Houghton	14
17.	A.Johnson	14
19.	G.Barrow	13
19.	J.Lyon	13

League Cup

1.	K.Langley	21
1.	C.Methven	21
1.	J.Butler	21
1.	A.Cribley	21
5.	P.Houghton	20
6.	R.Tunks	18
7.	A.Tankard	15
8.	N.Rimmer	14
9.	B.Griffiths	13
9.	P.Beesley	13
11.	G.Barrow	11
11.	J.Parkinson	11
13.	J.Robertson	10
13.	J.Wright	10
15.	T.Gore	9
15.	A.Johnson	9
15.	P.Daley	9
15.	J.Brown	9
19.	P.Atherton	8
19.	D.Lowe	8
19.	D.Patterson	8

GOALS

F.A.Cup

1.	H.Lyon	20
2.	B.Lomax	13
3.	E.T.Felton	7
3.	R.Finan	7
3.	T.McLoughlin	7
6.	G.Scott	6
6.	B.Sutherland	6
6.	B.Griffiths	6
6.	M.Newell	6
6.	T.Gore	6
11.	D.Colquhoun	5
11.	J.Fleming	5
11.	P.Jewell	5
11.	C.Methven	5
11.	B.Campbell	5
16.	S.Armes	4
16.	H.Thomas	4
16.	F.Taberner	4
16.	M.Worswick	4
16.	D.Temple	4
16.	B.Llewellyn	4
16.	J.Lyon	4
16.	R.Smith	4
16.	D.Lowe	4
16.	W.Hazelden	4

League Cup

1.	T.Gore	4
1.	B.Campbell	4
3.	P.Houghton	3
3.	D.Patterson	3
3.	C.Methven	3
3.	G.Barrow	3
3.	S.Johnson	3
3.	P.Gavin	3
3.	G.Worthington	3
10.	F.Corrigan	2
10.	L.Lloyd	2
10.	M.Wignall	2
10.	L.Bradd	2
10.	T.Kelly	2
10.	D.Page	2
10.	D.Thompson	2
10.	B.Griffiths	2

23 players have each scored one goal

ATTENDANCES

(Average and highest League attendances from 1947-48 to 1995-96)

Season	Average	Highest
	Lancashire Combination	
1947-48	4,507	7,300 v Bacup Borough
1948-49	4,063	9,000 v Prescot Cables
1949-50	4,947	8,000 v Barrow Reserves
1950-51	4,668	11,000 v Nelson
1951-52	3,420	8,000 v Nelson
1952-53	5,689	11,000 v Prescot Cables
1953-54	4,691	7,000 v Horwich RMI
1954-55	3,523	8,000 v Horwich RMI
1955-56	3,738	10,000 v Horwich RMI
1956-57	2,182	4,109 v Burscough
1957-58	2,570	4,911 v Lancaster City
1958-59	2,219	3,457 v Lancaster City
1959-60	2,688	6,611 v Chorley
1960-61	2,024	5,300 v Chorley
	Cheshire League	
1961-62	2,443	4,589 v Hyde United
1962-63	1,809	3,782 v Winsford United
1963-64	1,567	3,216 v Runcorn
1964-65	2,704	5,207 v Macclesfield
1965-66	2,216	3,747 v Altrincham
1966-67	2,434	5,374 v Altrincham
1967-68	1,801	3,100 v Mossley
	Northern Premier League	
1968-69	3,393	6,721 v Ashington
1969-70	2,516	4,567 v Macclesfield
1970-71	4,178	5,438 v Runcorn
1971-72	2,539	4,389 v Stafford Rangers
1972-73	2,128	4,964 v Boston United
1973-74	2,372	4,723 v Stafford Rangers
1974-75	2,932	4,408 v Runcorn
1975-76	1,462	2,379 v Runcorn
1976-77	1,107	1,760 v Northwich Vic
1977-78	1,334	2,608 v Stafford Rangers
	Football League	
1978-79	6,701	9,427 v Barnsley
1979-80	5,902	8,198 v Portsmouth
1980-81	4,208	6,029 v Rochdale
1981-82	5,839	9,021 v Bournemouth
1982-83	4,439	7,724 v Huddersfield.T.
1983-84	3,898	10,045 v Bolton Wanderers
1984-85	3,264	8,871 v Bolton Wanderers
1985-86	4,310	9,485 v Plymouth Argyle
1986-87	3,396	6,857 v Blackpool
1987-88	3,737	6,949 v Sunderland
1988-89	3,134	5,671 v Preston.N.E.
1989-90	2,772	6,850 v Bolton Wanderers
1990-91	2,881	4,728 v Preston.N.E.
1991-92	2,847	5,956 v Birmingham City
1992-93	2,593	5,408 v Bolton Wanderers
1993-94	1,897	3,741 v Preston.N.E.
1994-95	1,748	3,618 v Preston.N.E.
1995-96	2,856	5,567 v Preston.N.E.

EVER-PRESENTS

(Football League Latics players who have been ever-presents - in any one season.)

1978-79 Tommy Gore, Ian Purdie, Jeff Wright
1979-80 Dave Fretwell, Tommy Gore, Jeff Wright
1980-81 Colin Methven
1981-82 Colin Methven
1982-83 Roy Tunks
1985-86 David Lowe
1990-91 Peter Atherton Allan Tankard
1991-92 Nigel Adkins
1993-94 Simon Farnworth

(Top) Dave Fretwell (1979/80), (Above) Colin Methven (1980/81 and 1981/82) and (Above left) Nigel Adkins (1991/92).

(Right) Paul Jewell scores the first of his hat-trick v. Aldershot in 1988.

HAT-TRICKS HEROES

Football League:

Peter Houghton	v Port Vale (H)	13 April 1979
David Shearer	v Port Vale (H)	26 March 1980
Mick Quinn	v Doncaster.R. (H)	8 October 1980
Peter Houghton	v Tranmere.R. (A)	29 March 1981
Les Bradd	v Scunthorpe.U. (A)	12 March 1982
Eamonn O'Keefe	v Crewe Alex (H)	10 April 1982
Eamonn O'Keefe	v Mansfield.T. (H)	8 May 1982
Peter Houghton	v Doncaster.R. (A)	28 September 1982
Eamonn O'Keefe	v Southend.U. (H)	9 October 1982
Mike Newell	v Darlington (H)	14 September 1985
Warren Aspinall	v Wolverhampton.W. (H)	3 May 1986
Chris Thompson	v Walsall (H)	16 September 1986
David Lowe	v Mansfield.T. (A)	21 December 1986
Paul Jewell	v Aldershot (H)	1 March 1988
Mark Hilditch	v Mansfield.T. (H)	1 January 1990
David Thompson	v Shrewsbury.T. (A)	20 March 1990
Andy Lyons	v Darlington (H)	19 November 1994
League Cup		
Bobby Campbell	v Bolton.W. (A)	25 August 1987

David Thompson scored three at Shrewsbury in March 1990

LEADING GOALSCORERS

(Football League seasonal leading goalscorers)

		Lge.	FAC	Lge.Cup	Others	Total
1978-79	Peter Houghton	13	1	0	0	14
1979-80	Peter Houghton	15	0	1	0	16
1980-81	Mick Quinn	14	0	0	0	14
1981-82	Les Bradd	19	0	1	0	20
1982-83	Eamonn O'Keefe	15	0	1	0	16
1983-84	Steve Taylor	7	3	0	0	10
1984-85	Steve Johnson	11	1	3	1	16
	Mike Newell	9	3	1	3	16
1985-86	Warren Aspinall	21	2	0	4	27
1986-87	Bobby Campbell	16	4	0	0	20
	David Lowe	17	2	0	1	20
1987-88	Bobby Campbell	11	1	4	0	16
1988-89	Bryan Griffiths	8	0	0	1	9
1989-90	Mark Hilditch	8	1	1	0	10
1990-91	Don Page	12	1	1	3	17
	Bryan Griffiths	12	3	0	2	17
1991-92	Gary Worthington	15	1	2	0	18
1992-93	Bryan Griffiths	13	1	0	3	17
1993-94	Andy Lyons	11	0	0	0	11
1994-95	Andy Lyons	15	0	0	0	15
1995-96	Roberto Martinez	9	3	1	0	13

OTHER MATCHES

TESTIMONIALS AND BENEFITS

Most of the matches detailed below were played as a reward for long and distinguished service to Wigan Athletic.FC, although in some instances they were tributes to players whose careers had been brought to an early end.

Duncan Colquhoun Benefit 6 April 1949
v All Star XI 3-5 (Goals: E.Cunliffe; Fryer; Bootle;)

(Team) Woolley; Tolley; Parkinson; R.Cunliffe; Howcroft; Finch; Munro; Taylor; E.Cunliffe; Fryer; Bootle;

Jimmy Shirley Benefit 16 April 1952
v All Star XI 1-0 (Goal: J.Lyon;)

(Team) Lea; Tolley; Parkinson; Parkin; Parkes; S.Lyon; Langford; Bourne; Vollmer; J.Lyon; Bootle;

Harry Parkinson Benefit 23 April 1956
v All Star XI 2-4 (Goal: Leaver 2;)

(Team) Appleton; Ball (Bolton.W) Parkinson; Hopwood; Binns (Blackburn.R); Bramwell; Sudworth; Butler (Lancaster); Leaver (Blackburn.R); Gleadall (Bury); Simm (Bradford.C)

Harry Lyon and Derek Houghton Benefit 17 May 1967
v All Star XI 4-4 (Goals: Llewellyn; Lace; Hayes; Roberts)

(Team) Halsall; D.Houghton; Wilkinson; Lace; Craig; Roberts; Ryan; Llewellyn; Lyon; Hayes; Grundy:

Dennis Reeves and Ken Morris Benefit 6 May 1974
v Wrexham 1-1 (Goal: Rogers)

(Team) Reeves; Bruck(Coventry.C); Sutherland; Melling; Morris; Gillibrand; Garrett; Worswick; Rogers; King; Wright;

Micky Worswick Benefit 4 May 1978
v Everton 4-8 (Goals: Moore 2; Bruce 2;)

(Team) Brown; Gore; Hinnigan; Prescott; Ward; Baxter(PNE); Elwiss(PNE); Burns (Blackpool); Bruce(PNE); Moore; Worswick;

John Brown Testimonial 11 May 1982
v Bolton Wanderers 1-0 (Goal: Houghton)

(Team) Brown; McMahon; Glenn; Cribley; Davids; Methven; O'Keefe; Barrow; Butler; Houghton; Wignall;

Noel Ward Testimonial 17 May 1982
v Chelsea 0-0

(Team) Brown; McMahon; Weston; Cribley; Wignall; Methven; Sheldon; Barrow; Bradd; Houghton; Evans;

John Rogers and John King Testimonial 19 May 1982
v Altrincham 3-2 (Goals: Sheldon 2; Barrow;)

(Team) Brown; Langley; Weston; Wright; McAdam; Cribley; Sheldon; Barrow; Quinn; Houghton; Evans;

Bob Ward Benefit 15 March 1983
v West Bromwich Albion 1-2 (Goal: Bradd;)

(Team) Tunks; McMahon; Weston; Fazackerley(Blackburn.R); Bradd; Chandler(Bolton.W); Morgan(ex-Man.U); Bruce(PNE); Charlton; Houghton; Williams;

Kenny Banks and Duncan Colquhoun Benefit 14 May 1984
v Larry Lloyds XI 5-2 (Goals: Rogers 3; Johnson 2[1 pen])

(Team) Tunks; Cribley; Comstive; Gillibrand; Methven; King; Worswick; Barrow; Johnson; Bruce; Rogers;

Bryan Hamilton Testimonial 27 July 1985
v Everton 1-4 (Goal: Bennett;)

(Team) Tunks; Cribley; Knowles(Bennett); Kelly; Walsh; Methven; Lowe(Aspinall); Barrow; Newell(Cook); Langley; Griffiths (Hamilton);

Alex Cribley Testimonial 6 May 1990 v Everton 2-3 (Goals: Carberry; Griffiths[pen])

(Team) Adkins; Cribley(Rogerson); Tankard; Parkinson; Atherton; Johnson(Whitworth); Senior(Carberry); Rimmer; Daley(Patterson); Page; Griffiths;

FRIENDLY LATICS

This section contains all the results of known Latics first team friendlies since the Second World War. It does not include testimonial matches (see previous page), where the beneficiary was associated with Wigan Athletic F.C.

1949-50

1 May	v Grimsby Town	(Home) 3-5

1950-51

7 May	v Blackburn Rovers	(Home) 1-1

1951-52

21 April	v St Mirren	(Home) 2-1 (Aban.)

1952-53

11 October	v Congleton Town	(Home) 4-2

1953-54

29 September	v Ashton United	(Away) 3-4
10 October	v Hyde United	(Away) 8-3
28 December	v Stockport County	(Away) 1-5
10 March	v Hereford United	(Away) 0-2

1954-55

23 April	v Ellesmere P. Town	(Home) 0-1

1957-58

4 January	v Brentford	(Home) 1-2

1958-59

20 September	v Macclesfield	(Away) 1-6
22 April	v Southport	(Home) 1-1
27 April	v Everton	(Home) 2-5

1959-60

27 February	v Stirling Albion	(Away) 1-5

1962-63

23 August	v Prescot Cables	(Away) 4-0

1963-64

17 August	v Southport	(Away) 2-10
19 August	v Southport	(Home) 3-1

1964-65

15 August	v Bury	(Home) 2-0

1965-66

7 August	v Chorley	(Home) 2-2
14 August	v Burnley	(Home) 2-0

1966-67

10 August	v Bury	(Home) 1-1
13 August	v Bolton Wanderers	(Home) 1-2
2 January	v Southport	(Home) 0-3
3 May	v Blackburn Rovers	(Home) 3-3

1967-68

5 August	v Nuneaton Borough	(Home) 2-1
12 August	v Burnley	(Home) 3-0
14 August	v Nuneaton Borough	(Away) 0-2
1 January	v Port Vale	(Home) 3-3

1968-69

31 July	v Bury	(Home) 3-0
3 August	v Raith Rovers	(Home) 4-4
7 May	v Airdrieonians	(Home) 0-3

1969-70

30 July	v Cambridge United	(Home) 0-2
2 August	v Cambridge United	(Away) 2-0
5 August	v Wrexham	(Home) 0-2
23 March	v Kharkov, USSR	(Home) 2-3

1970-71

3 August	v Stirling Albion	(Home) 5-2
5 August	v Bradford City	(Home) 3-1
8 August	v Southport	(Home) 2-0
26 April	v Hibernian	(Home) 1-1

1971-72

31 July	v Nantwich Town	(Away) 6-3
2 August	v Stockport County	(Home) 3-1
4 August	v Southport	(Home) 0-1
7 August	v Lincoln City	(Away) 0-0

1972-73

29 July	v Wrexham	(Home) 0-2
2 August	v Southport	(Home) 2-0

1973-74

28 July	v Yeovil Town	(Home) 1-1
1 August	v Kettering Town	(Home) 0-0
4 August	v Yeovil Town	(Away) 2-3
29 April	v Barnsley	(Home) 1-2

1974-75

5 August	v Coventry City	(Home) 2-0
10 August	v Chesterfield	(Away) 1-0
12 August	v Rotherham United	(Home) 4-1
29 November	v Moscow Torpedo	(Home) 2-3
8 May	v York City	(Home) 2-1

1975-76

2 August	v Rotherham United	(Home) 1-1
11 August	v Stockport County	(Home) 1-3

1976-77

7 August	v Clyde	(Home) 2-1
11 August	v Winsford United	(Away) 2-1
16 August	v Prescot Town	(Home) 5-0

1977-78

6 August	v Stranraer	(Away) 1-1
13 August	v Nuneaton Borough	(Away) 2-1
19 September	v Manchester City	(Home) 1-2

1978-79

11 October	v Zambian National Side	(Home) 2-1
6 November	v Dundee	(Home) 2-2

1979-80

28 July	v Cliftonville	(Home) 2-0
30 July	v Arbroath	(Away) 0-3
1 August	v Montrose	(Away) 1-1
2 August	v East Fife	(Away) 0-2
17 October	v Tulsa Roughnecks	(Home) 4-3

1980-81

26 July	v Runcorn	(Away) 3-1
30 July	v Macclesfield	(Away) 3-0
2 August	v East Fife	(Home) 2-1
6 August	v CWKS Legia	(Home) 0-3

1981-82

1 August	v Bangor City	(Home) 6-1
5 August	v New Mills	(Away) 3-0
8 August	v Swansea City	(Home) 2-3
10 August	v Yeovil Town	(Away) 3-2
12 August	v Bristol Rovers	(Away) 1-1
13 August	v Frome Town	(Away) 2-0
18 August	v Walsall	(Home) 0-0
20 August	v Sheffield Wed.	(Home) 4-1
22 August	v Liverpool Res.	(Home) 1-2
16 January	v Chorley	(Away) 3-0

1982-83

9 August	v East Fife	(Home) 2-0
11 August	v Swansea City	(Home) 1-4
14 August	v Republic of China	(Home) 1-1
17 August	v Stoke City	(Home) 0-1
20 August	v Everton	(Home) 1-6

1983-84

6 August	v Kettering Town	(Away) 1-1
9 August	v Stafford Rangers	(Away) 2-1

1984-85

28 July	v Queen of the South	(Away) 2-1
30 July	v Kilmarnock	(Away) 3-2
1 August	v Ayr United	(Away) 1-3
8 August	v Chester	(Away) 1-0

1988-89

27 July	v St Helens Town	(Away) 4-0

1989-90

21 February	v Moscow Torpedo	(Home) 0-0

1990-91

31 July	v Dynamo Brest	(Away) 1-2
2 August	v Brest Select XI	(Away) 1-4
19 December	v Dynamo Brest	(Home) 3-1

1992-93

21 July	v Runcorn	(Away) 0-1
5 August	v Newry Town	(Away) 7-1
6 August	v Bangor	(Away) 1-2

1993-94

20 July	v Skelmersdale Utd.	(Away) 4-1
7 August	v Aston Villa	(Home) 0-1

1994-95

2 August	v Sheffield Wed.	(Home) 2-2
6 August	v Hamilton Acad.	(Away) 1-6

1995-96

20 July	v Morecambe	(Away) 2-2
22 July	v Lancaster City	(Away) 1-2
5 August	v Dumbarton	(Away) 2-1

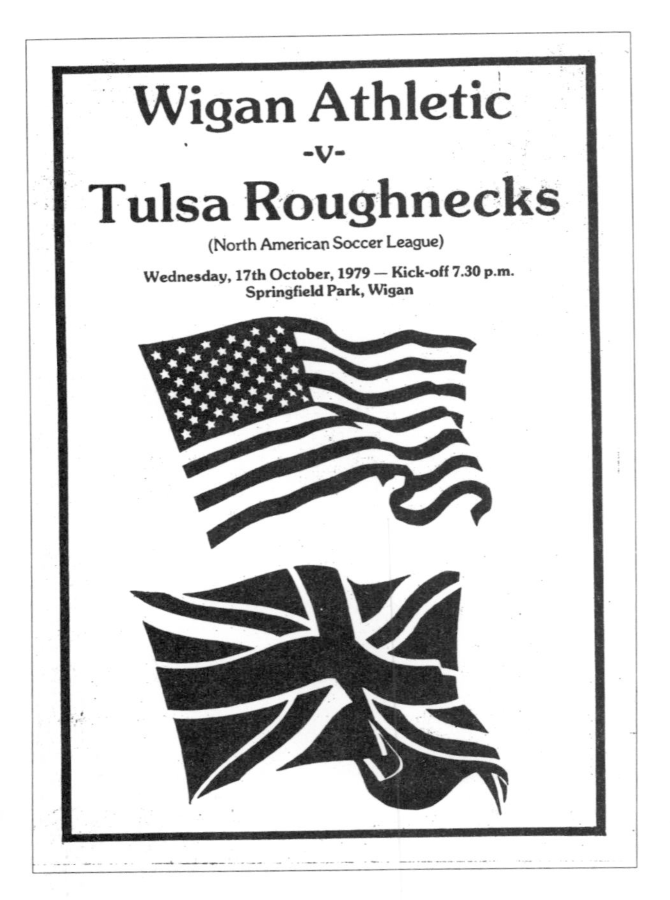
Wigan Athletic
-v-
Tulsa Roughnecks
(North American Soccer League)

Wednesday, 17th October, 1979 — Kick-off 7.30 p.m.
Springfield Park, Wigan

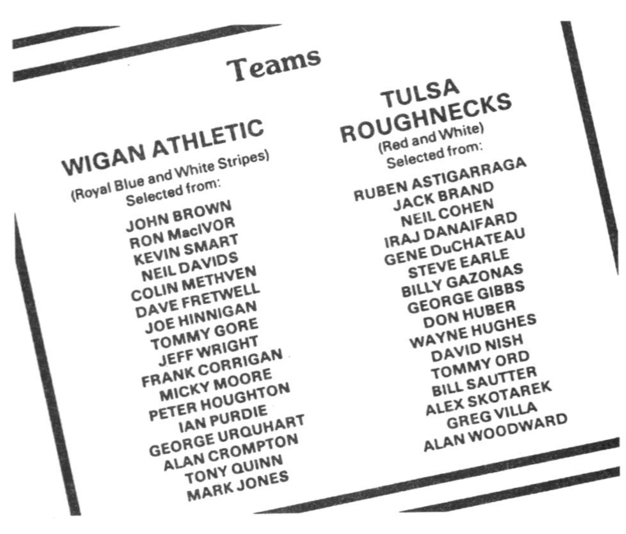
Teams

WIGAN ATHLETIC	TULSA ROUGHNECKS
(Royal Blue and White Stripes) Selected from:	(Red and White) Selected from:
JOHN BROWN	RUBEN ASTIGARRAGA
RON MacIVOR	JACK BRAND
KEVIN SMART	NEIL COHEN
NEIL DAVIDS	IRAJ DANAIFARD
COLIN METHVEN	GENE DuCHATEAU
DAVE FRETWELL	STEVE EARLE
JOE HINNIGAN	BILLY GAZONAS
TOMMY GORE	GEORGE GIBBS
JEFF WRIGHT	DON HUBER
FRANK CORRIGAN	WAYNE HUGHES
MICKY MOORE	DAVID NISH
PETER HOUGHTON	TOMMY ORD
IAN PURDIE	BILL SAUTTER
GEORGE URQUHART	ALEX SKOTAREK
ALAN CROMPTON	GREG VILLA
TONY QUINN	ALAN WOODWARD
MARK JONES	

(Above) The programme line-ups for the match

(Left) Friendly opposition from abroad in 1979.

(Below) Mick Quinn scores one of his 13 pre-season goals - 1981/82 season.

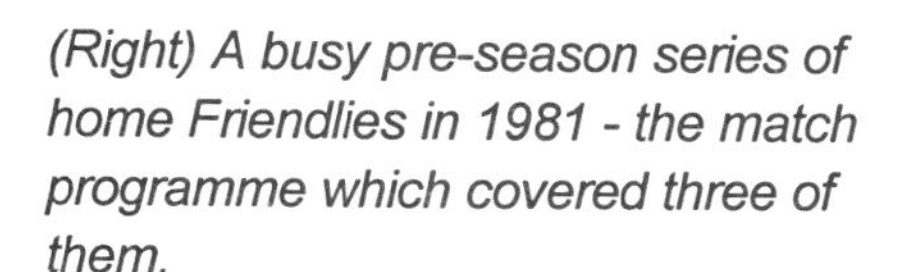

(Right) A busy pre-season series of home Friendlies in 1981 - the match programme which covered three of them.

Pre-Season Football at
Springfield Park
August 1981

WIGAN ATHLETIC
WELCOMES

Tuesday 18th August
WALSALL
KICK-OFF 7.30 p.m.

Thursday 20th August
SHEFFIELD WEDNESDAY
KICK-OFF 7.30 p.m.

Saturday 22nd August
A LIVERPOOL XI
KICK-OFF 3 p.m.

OFFICIAL PROGRAMME 20p.

SPONSORED BY
BARTON
& COOPER
LIMITED

LIVERPOOL
FOOTBALL CLUB

(Below) Action from the February 1990 Friendly with Moscow Torpedo. Jimmy Carberry evades the attentions of Sergei Zhukov and Valentin Kovach.

ISLE OF MAN FESTIVAL

1985-86

29 July	v Blackburn Rovers	0-1
31 July	v Leicester City	2-0
1 August	v Newcastle United	1-4

1986-87

28 July	v Bohemians	4-1
30 July	v Heart of Midlothian	1-1
31 July	v Stoke City	1-0
2 August	v Portsmouth (Final)	1-0

1987-88

26 July	v Hibernian	6-3
28 July	v Stoke City	0-2
29 July	v Isle of Man XI	5-2

1992-93

26 July	v Isle of Man XI	3-0
29 July	v Stoke City	0-2
31 July	v Huddersfield Town	0-4

MANX LANCASHIRE CUP

(Later known as the Marsden Cup from 1983-84 when the club first entered)

1983-84

13 August	v Bury (Home)	1-2
16 August	v Bolton Wanderers. (Home)	0-0
20 August	v Rochdale (Away)	3-2

1984-85

11 August	v Rochdale (Home)	3-1
14 August	v Blackpool (Away)	0-0
18 August	v Burnley (Away)	2-1
21 August	v Blackburn Rovers (Home) (Final)	2-1

1985-86

5 August	v Blackburn Rovers (Away)	2-2
7 August	v Preston North End (Home)	2-1
10 August	v Blackpool (Away)	1-1

1986-87

9 August	v Burnley (Home)	1-1
13 August	v Preston North End (Away)	2-0
16 August	v Bolton Wanderers (Away)	4-3
19 August	v Bury (Away) (Final)	0-1

1987-88

3 August	v Bury (Away)	3-0
5 August	v Preston North End (Home)	1-1
7 August	v Rochdale (Home)	4-0
11 August	v Blackburn Rovers (Away) (Final) Lost on penalties.	2-2

1988-89

6 August	v Rochdale (Away)	0-1
11 August	v Bolton Wand. (at Oldham)	0-1
13 August	v Bury (Away)	1-1

1989-90

5 August	v Blackburn Rovers (Home)	0-3
8 August	v Bolton Wanderers (Home)	1-0
12 August	v Burnley (Away)	2-0

1990-91

11 August	v Bolton Wanderers (Home)	0-0
14 August	v Burnley (Away)	1-3
18 August	v Blackpool (Home)	3-2

1991-92

3 August	v Blackpool (Home)	1-1
7 August	v Rochdale (Away)	3-2
10 August	v Bolton Wanderers (Away)	1-0
13 August	v Preston North End (Home) (Final)	4-1

1993-94

24 July	v Bury (Away)	1-1
27 July	v Preston North End (Home)	2-1
31 July	v Manchester United (Home)	0-2

1994-95

23 July	v Preston North End (Home)	2-1
26 July	v Southport (Away)	2-3
30 July	v Blackpool (Away)	0-2

1995-96

25 July	v Burnley (Away)	3-0
29 July	v Southport (Home)	4-2
8 August	v Blackpool (Away) (Final) Lost on penalties	2-2

FINAL LEAGUE TABLES: 1932/33-1952/53

Cheshire League 1932/33

Macclesfield	42	29	5	8	121	64	63
Poer Vale Reserves	42	26	5	11	112	57	57
Manchester North End	42	24	7	11	124	78	55
Hurst	42	25	4	13	129	98	54
Wigan Athletic	42	21	11	10	121	54	53
Ashton National	42	23	7	12	130	83	53
Congleton Town	42	22	6	14	105	103	50
Hyde United	42	22	5	15	105	93	49
Crewe Alexandra Res.	42	19	8	15	110	77	46
Stalybridge Celtic	42	19	8	15	132	100	46
Chester Resreves	42	21	2	19	118	109	44
Altrincham	42	17	9	16	108	95	43
Mossley	42	19	4	19	96	101	42
Tranmere Rovers Res.	42	18	5	19	108	118	41
Northwich Victoria	42	17	6	19	100	123	40
Buxton	42	16	5	21	81	92	37
Runcorn	42	15	6	21	88	109	36
Nantwich	42	12	7	23	84	133	31
Witton Albion	42	9	7	26	71	119	25
Winsford United	42	8	6	28	65	143	22
Sandbach Ramblers	42	6	7	29	63	146	19
Whitchurch	42	6	6	30	70	146	15

Cheshire League 1933/34

Wigan Athletic	42	30	8	6	111	46	66
Macclesfield	42	29	3	10	142	71	61
Witton Albion.	42	21	9	12	85	75	51
Stockport County Res.	42	23	3	16	104	77	49
Prescot Cables	42	21	7	14	93	78	49
Altrincham	42	19	9	14	99	72	47
Tranmere Rovers Res.	42	22	3	17	110	95	47
Manchester North End	42	21	4	17	132	105	46
Stalybridge Celtic	42	18	9	15	100	84	45
Ashton National	42	21	3	18	89	85	45
Hyde United	42	19	6	17	99	84	44
Mossley	42	15	12	15	91	87	42
Runcorn	42	19	2	21	91	104	40
Chester Reserves	42	16	7	19	84	97	39
Buxton	42	14	11	17	81	95	39
Hurst	42	17	3	22	103	111	37
Nantwich	42	15	4	23	77	112	34
Crewe Alexandra Res	42	16	2	24	71	I11	34
Congleton Town	42	11	8	23	84	97	30
Northwich Victoria	42	14	2	28	63	87	30
Winsford United	42	11	6	25	70	118	28
Sandbach Ramblers	42	8	5	29	57	142	71

Cheshire League 1934/35

Wigan Athletic	42	27	9	6	153	59	63
Altrincham	42	26	11	5	118	57	63
Stalybridge Celtic	42	28	7	7	136	74	63
Port Vale Reserves	42	23	6	13	113	69	52
Hyde United	42	21	6	15	89	73	48
Stockport County Res.	42	21	5	16	94	88	47
Chester Reserves	42	22	2	18	116	98	46
Macclesfield	42	19	7	16	137	83	45
Buxton	42	19	5	18	95	95	43
Manchester North End	42	15	9	18	112	110	39
Congleton Town	42	17	5	20	93	113	39
Mossley	42	17	5	20	97	119	39
Ashton National	42	15	7	20	68	86	37
Witton Albion	42	16	5	21	60	106	37
Hurst	42	13	10	19	82	101	36
Northwich Victoria	42	14	7	21	83	95	35
Prescot Cables	42	13	9	20	70	100	35
Winsford United	42	12	9	21	68	104	33
Tranmere Rovers Res.	42	14	4	24	82	110	32
Runcorn	42	14	3	25	95	147	31
Nan twich	42	11	9	22	71	121	31
Crewe Alexandra Res.	42	12	6	24	72	105	30

Cheshire League 1935/36

Wigan Athletic	42	31	6	5	136	46	68
Altrincham	42	22	11	9	88	51	55
Stockport County Res.	42	23	8	11	103	57	54
Chester Reserves	42	22	9	11	104	85	53
Stalybridge Celtic	42	23	6	13	112	64	52
Runcorn	42	21	8	13	129	88	50
Northwich Victoria	42	20	10	12	98	74	50
Crewe Alexandra Res.	42	21	6	15	113	84	48
Macclesfield	42	21	4	17	105	106	46
Port Vale Reserves	42	17	10	15	69	72	44
Buxton	42	18	7	17	95	90	43
Hurst	42	16	10	16	89	106	42
Tranmere Rovers Res.	42	16	9	17	113	120	41
Manchester North End	42	17	6	19	94	107	40
Hyde United	42	17	5	20	107	108	39
Mossley	42	16	4	22	90	113	36
Congleton Town	42	15	4	23	95	114	34
Prescot Cables	42	15	4	23	59	94	34
Nantwich	42	13	7	22	74	115	33
Woitton Albion	42	11	5	26	58	96	27
Ashton National	42	7	8	27	64	114	22
Winsford United	42	4	5	33	44	135	13

Cheshire League 1936/37

Runcorn	42	30	6	6	156	60	66
Stockport County Res.	42	23	11	8	105	55	57
Northwich Victoria	42	27	3	12	92	52	57
Witton Albion	42	24	8	10	107	56	56
Port Vale Res.	42	22	8	12	97	91	52
Buxton	42	22	6	14	107	89	50
Ashton National	42	18	9	15	97	96	45
Wigan Athletic	42	19	6	17	94	73	44
Stalybridge Celtic	42	19	6	17	96	81	44
Rhyl	42	17	9	16	75	71	43
Crewe Alexandra Res.	42	18	5	19	77	88	41
Chester Reserves	42	14	9	19	79	93	37
Altrincham	42	14	8	20	91	94	36
Winsford United	42	14	8	20	75	94	36
Congleton Town	42	15	6	21	83	104	31
Tranmere Rovers Res.	42	15	6	21	74	100	36
Mossley	42	11	13	18	84	108	35
Macclesfield	42	14	6	22	74	96	34
Hyde United	42	13	7	22	97	114	33
Nantwich	42	11	6	25	78	146	28
Hurst	42	9	5	28	76	125	23

Cheshire League 1937/38

Tranmere Rovers Res.	42	30	6	6	148	45	66
Runcorn	42	30	3	9	123	54	63
Stockport County Res.	42	29	4	9	104	48	62
Hyde United	42	24	8	10	105	67	56
Crewe Alexandra Res	42	21	11	10	99	61	53
Witton Albion	42	20	7	15	104	68	47
Mossley	42	19	9	14	86	76	47
Northwich Victoria	42	19	6	17	86	79	44
Altrincham	42	17	le	15	77	80	44
Stalybridge Celtic	42	18	6	18	96	86	42
Wigan Athletic	42	19	4	19	95	89	42
Port Vale Reserves	42	16	7	19	77	76	39
Chester Reserves	42	17	4	21	84	92	38
Manchester North End	42	15	2	22	112	131	38
Macclesfield	42	14	10	18	96	115	38
Congleton Town	42	16	6	20	74	122	38
Ashton National	42	16	5	21	78	92	37
Buxton	42	14	5	23	87	108	33
Winsford United	42	12	6	24	71	98	30
Rhyl	42	11	7	24	74	117	29
Nantwich	42	8	4	30	59	140	20
Hurst	42	7	4	31	63	145	18

Cheshire League 1938/39

Runcorn	42	28	6	8	134	60	62
Tranmere Rovers Res.	42	29	2	11	136	63	60
Ashton National	42	25	7	10	131	90	57
Crewe Alexandra Res.	42	26	4	12	132	74	56
Wellington Town	42	23	8	11	108	68	54
Chester Reserves	42	22	8	12	111	74	52
Wigan Athletic	42	21	5	16	104	84	47
Northwich Victoria	42	20	7	15	88	87	47
Witton Albion	42	17	9	16	94	78	43
HydeUnited	42	20	3	19	84	91	43
Congleton Town	42	16	10	16	80	89	42
Mossley	42	14	12	16	77	78	40
Port Vale Reserves	42	18	4	20	84	86	40
Hurst	42	15	10	17	86	113	40
Stockport County Res.	42	18	3	21	86	90	39
Buxton	42	12	11	19	71	93	35
Macclesfield	42	14	7	21	55	90	35
Stalybridge Celtic	42	13	8	21	87	108	34
Rhyl	42	12	9	21	94	117	33
Altrincham	42	9	7	26	72	119	25
Winsford United	42	8	6	28	57	134	22
Manchester North End	42	7	4	31	57	142	18

Cheshire League 1945/46

Wellington Town	38	29	1	8	150	53	59
Droylsden	38	24	3	11	126	65	51
Buxton	38	21	8	9	131	72	50
Witton AJbion	38	21	4	13	98	69	46
Chester Res	38	20	4	14	118	86	44
Stalybridge Celtic	38	19	6	13	102	99	44
South Liverpool	38	19	5	14	99	94	43
Hyde Utd	38	17	8	13	83	66	42
Runcom	38	17	6	15	97	98	40
Hurst	38	17	6	15	95	108	40
Northwich Victoria	38	16	4	18	79	102	36
Stockport County Res	38	15	4	19	79	107	34
Oldham Athletic Res	38	13	6	19	87	116	32
Crewe Alexandra Res	38	11	9	18	74	104	31
Rhyi	38	11	8	19	96	116	30
Wrexham Res	38	12	6	20	54	76	30
Wigan Athletic	38	12	6	20	68	117	30
Port Vale Res	38	11	5	22	73	91	27
Tranmere Rovers Res	38	12	2	24	76	115	26
Mossiey	38	11	3	24	85	136	25

Cheshire League 1946/47

Wellington Town	42	25	7	10	113	69	57
Buxton	42	24	8	10	117	79	56
South Liverpool	42	23	9	10	92	62	55
Port Vale Res	42	24	6	12	100	58	54
Northwich Victoria	42	21	11	10	95	69	53
Stalybridge Celtic	42	24	5	13	108	89	53
Witton AJbion	42	20	7	15	96	84	47
Droyisden	42	22	1	19	108	101	45
Mossiey	42	17	10	15	94	90	44
Altrincham	42	17	8	17	85	83	42
Hyde Utd	42	19	3	20	108	100	41
Runcorn	42	13	13	16	80	89	39
Wrexham Res	42	17	4	21	81	80	38
Rhyl	42	16	6	20	96	106	38
Macclesfield	42	16	6	20	77	89	38
Chester Res	42	16	4	22	70	91	36
Congleton Town	42	15	5	22	83	100	35
Tranmere Rovers Res	42	14	7	21	70	89	35
Stockport County Res	42	14	7	21	79	104	35
Crewe Alexandra Res	42	13	6	23	90	120	32
Ashton	42	8	10	24	65	107	26
Wigan Athletic	42	9	7	26	66	114	25

Lancashire Combination Div.1 1947/48

Wigan Athletic	42	25	9	8	72	37	59
Nelson	42	24	9	9	84	62	57
Barrow Reserves	42	24	7	11	88	55	55
Morecambe	42	24	6	12	98	59	54
Fleetwood	42	23	7	12	73	52	53
Marine	42	23	6	13	103	64	52
Netherfield	42	23	6	13	83	58	52
Lancaster City	42	21	7	14	80	69	49
Bacup Borough	42	20	6	16	96	67	46
Oldham Reserves	42	19	8	15	76	71	46
Chorley	42	19	7	16	89	74	45
Prescot Cables	42	19	6	17	87	80	44
Rochdale Reserves	42	14	8	20	79	76	36
Bangor City	42	14	8	20	62	77	36
Rossendale United	42	11	12	19	80	90	34
Darwen	42	12	9	21	60	91	33
Accrington Stanley Res.	42	12	7	23	71	106	31
Clitheroe	42	13	5	24	70	110	31
New Brighton Reserves	42	11	8	23	56	85	30
Leyland Motors	42	11	7	24	73	115	29
Horwich	42	10	7	25	58	104	27
Southport Reserves	42	9	7	26	57	93	25

Lancashire Combination Div.1 1948/49

Netherfield	42	26	10	6	112	46	62
Chorley	42	23	12	7	72	55	58
Morecambe	42	22	6	14	80	60	50
Nelson	42	20	9	13	87	68	49
Darwen	42	21	7	14	81	65	49
Wigan Athletic	42	19	9	14	73	68	47
Bangor City	42	18	10	14	75	71	46
Prescot Cables	42	19	7	16	89	72	45
Lancaster City	42	15	14	13	58	50	43
Rochdale Reserves	42	17	10	15	75	71	44
Fleetwood	42	17	8	17	81	66	42
Rossendale United	42	17	8	17	85	78	42
Barrow Reserves	42	16	10	16	73	69	42
Oldham Ath. Reserves	42	13	15	14	80	71	41
Ashton United	42	14	13	15	73	79	41
Southport Reserves	42	17	7	8	60	69	41
Marine	42	14	10	18	73	83	38
Clitheroe	42	13	9	20	74	99	35
Accrington Stanley Res.	42	14	6	22	69	86	34
New Brighton Reserves	42	9	13	20	53	82	31
Leyland Motors	42	7	9	26	49	94	23
Bacup Borough	42	7	9	26	49	119	20

Lancashire Combination Div. 1 1949/50

Nelson	42	30	4	8	125	63	64
Wigan Athletic	42	24	8	10	79	47	56
Prescot Cables	42	22	12	8	102	64	56
Chorley	42	20	9	13	71	67	49
Ashton United	42	20	7	15	90	62	47
Rochdale Reserves	42	19	8	15	87	79	46
Bangor City	42	18	9	15	96	70	45
Fleetwood	42	18	9	15	76	67	45
Morecambe	42	17	11	14	62	55	45
Netherfield	42	20	5	17	88	83	45
Accrington Stanley Res	42	16	10	16	64	75	42
Southport Reserves	42	14	13	15	67	67	41
Oldham Ath. Reserves	42	15	10	17	77	72	40
Lancaster City	42	14	10	18	67	74	38
Barrow Reserves	42	14	10	18	63	81	38
Bootle	42	14	9	19	61	71	37
Darwen	42	13	11	18	55	66	37
Rossendale United	42	13	8	21	73	85	34
Clitheroe	42	13	8	21	66	90	34
New Brighton Reserves	42	13	6	23	63	102	32
Marine	42	11	9	22	74	104	31
Horwich R,M.I.	42	8	6	28	52	114	22

Lancashire Combination Div. 1 1950/51

Wigan Athletic	42	27	7	8	98	43	61
Nelson	42	29	3	10	120	64	61
Netherfield	42	26	7	9	107	57	59
Fleetwood	42	21	10	11	100	70	52
Rochdale Reserves	42	20	10	12	87	69	50
Bootle	42	22	5	15	89	61	49
Southport Reserves	42	19	8	15	98	81	46
Chorley	42	17	10	15	91	93	44
Oldham Ath. Reserves .	42	16	11	15	88	78	43
Barrow Reserves	42	17	9	16	68	63	43
Lancaster City	42	17	9	16	75	99	43
Ashton United	42	16	9	17	85	88	41
New Brighton Reserves	42	15	8	19	53	56	38
Darwen	42	12	12	19	62	79	36
Morecambe	42	12	12	18	56	73	36
Clitheroe	42	15	6	21	69	90	36
Eariestown	42	16	3	23	91	115	35
Blackpool 'B'	42	13	8	21	69	87	34
Rossendale United	42	13	7	22	63	102	33
Marine	42	11	8	23	68	87	36
Prescot Cables	42	10	10	22	57	89	30
Accrington Stanley Res., . .	42	7	10	25	44	104	24

Lancashire Combination Div.1 1951/52

Nelson	42	30	3	9	139	59	63
Lancaste City	42	24	7	11	89	69	55
Netherfeid	42	22	10	10	108	63	54
Wigan Athletic	42	21	9	12	73	57	51
Mlorecambe	42	21	7	14	74	72	49
Ashton United	42	21	6	15	96	87	48
Rochdale Reserves	42	20	6	16	104	79	46
Barrow Reserves	42	19	8	15	73	66	46
Fleetwood	42	20	5	17	94	87	45
Bootle Athletic	42	17	8	17	73	73	42
Chorley	42	16	10	16	66	72	42
Horwich R.M.I	42	17	7	18	99	97	41
New Brighton	42	16	8	18	73	85	40
Blackpool 'B'	42	18	4	20	72	88	40
Marine	42	13	12	17	77	85	38
Darwen	42	16	5	21	60	83	37
Oldham Ath. Reserves .	42	13	9	20	87	91	35
Clitheroe	42	13	9	20	59	79	35
Southport Reserves	42	12	10	20	70	76	34
Rossendale United	42	13	5	24	77	95	31
St. Helens Town	42	12	5	25	86	119	29
Earlestown	42	6	11	25	68	135	23

Lancashire Combination Div. 1952/53

Wigan Athletic	42	27	13	2	24	45	67
Prescot Cables	42	25	5	12	83	46	55
Darwen	42	19	11	12	88	65	49
Marine	42	19	11	12	91	72	49
Nelson	42	20	8	14	86	72	48
Lancaster City	42	21	6	15	81	72	48
Horwich R.M.1	42	17	13	12	109	105	47
Ashton United	42	18	9	15	105	85	45
Nethertield	42	20	4	18	82	81	44
Southport Reserves	42	17	8	17	78	80	42
Morecambe	42	16	9	17	60	61	41
Boottle Athletic	42	16	8	18	64	64	40
Oldham Ath. Reserve	42	16	7	19	84	89	39
Rossendale United	42	16	7	19	84	92	39
Fleetwood	42	16	7	19	76	105	39
Chorley	42	16	5	21	81	87	37
New Brighton	42	14	9	19	61	70	37
Accringion Stanley Res.,	42	13	11	18	64	78	37
Rochdale Reserves	42	11	9	22	61	76	31
Barrow Reserves	42	10	11	21	57	80	31
Clitheroe	42	11	9	22	69	115	31
Blackpool 'B'	42	11	6	25	49	97	28

SEASONAL STATISTICS: 1932/33 - 1995/96.

SEASON 1932-33
Cheshire League:

	Home	Away
Altrincham	6-0	0-1
Ashton National	2-4	1-0
Buxton	6-1	1-3
Chester Reserves	6-0	2-3
Congleton Town	6-2	1-3
Crewe Alexandra Reserves	0-0	0-0
Hurst	0-1	5-1
Hyde United	6-0	1-3
Macclesfield Town	1-2	1-4
Manchester North End	3-3	1-1
Mossley	7-2	0-0
Nantwich Town	7-0	2-1
Northwich Victoria	9-0	3-2
Port Vale Reserves	0-2	0-0
Runcorn	4-3	1-1
Sandbach Ramblers	5-0	3-2
Stalybridge Celtic	2-2	2-2
Tranmere Rovers Reserves	5-1	2-1
Whitchurch	6-1	1-1
Winsford United	5-0	3-0
Witton Albion	4-0	1-1

P.	W.	D.	L.	F.	A.	W.	D.	L.	F.	A.	Pts	Pos.
42	14	3	4	90	24	7	8	6	31	30	53	5th

League Appearances:
Abbott 32; Allan 41; Callaghan 40; Chambers 37; Davies 10; Henderson 8; Hughes 38; Jamieson 15; Jones 31; McCabe 42; Murphy 40; O'Dell 37; Smith 7; Spencer 39; Swift 4; Thomas 1; Wake 39; Williams 1;

League Scorers:
Unknown, but William Chambers was top scorer with 39.

Other Matches:
Cheshire Cup:

Ist Rd	Chester Res.	Away	2-2	McCabe 2;
Replay	Chester Res.	Home	7-0	Chambers 4; Jones 2; Hughes;
2nd Rd	Runcorn	Home	6-2	Chambers 4; Jones, Swift
3rd Rd	Ashton National	Home	5-2	McCabe 2; Chambers;Hughes; Murphy;
S-F	Manchester N.E.	Home	1-3	Hughes;

Seasons Honours: None

SEASON 1933-34
Cheshire League:

	Home	Away
Altrincham	3-0	1-1
Ashton National	4-1	3-0
Buxton	1-0	2-1
Chester Reserves	1-0	3-0
Congleton Town	1-0	0-0
Crewe Alexandra Reserves	2-0	5-3
Hurst	3-1	1-0
Hyde United	5-1	0-4
Macclesfield Town	7-0	3-3
Manchester North End	5-1	3-4
Mossley	4-1	2-5
Nantwich Town	4-0	1-1
Northwich Victoria	1-0	2-1
Prescot Cables	3-0	2-2
Runcorn	3-1	2-1
Sandbach Ramblers	6-1	5-1
Stalybridge Celtic	5-0	1-1
Stockport County Reserves	2-1	1-0
Tranmere Rovers Reserves	3-0	2-3
Winsford United	3-0	2-3
Witton Albion	2-1	2-3

P.	W.	D.	L.	F.	A.	W.	D.	L.	F.	A.	Pts	Pos.
42	21	0	0	68	9	9	6	6	43	37	66	Ist

League Appearances:
Anderton 10;Bentham 5;Caunce 41;Cherry 8;Cowper 37; Doyle 7; Felton 41;Glidden 8;Harrison 9;Hitchen 8;H.Jones 1; W.Jones 17;Kavanagh 25;O'Dell 39;O'Donnell 8;O'Rourke 3; Prosser 3;Quinn 2; Robinson 41;Robson 34;Scott 42;Snaith 31; Spencer 1;Talbot 24; Wallbanks 17;

League Scorers:
Felton 27(4 pens);Scott 24(2 pens);Cowper 13;Snaith 13;W.Jones 12 Glidden 5;Wallbanks 5;Bentham 3;Hitchen 3; Kavanagh 1;O'Dell 1; O'Donnell 1;O'Rourke 1;Quinn 1; Own Goals 1;(Total 111)

Other Results:
F.A.Cup:

Prelim Rd	Great Harwood	Home	1-1	og;
Replay	Great Harwood	Away	4-1	Cowper 2;Kavanagh; Felton;
Ist Qual	Horwich RMI	Away	3-0	W.Jones 2;Cowper;
2nd Qual	Lytham	Home	3-0	Felton;Harrison;Cowper
3rd Qual	Dick Kerrs	Home	2-1	O'Rourke 2;
4th Qual	Altrincham	Away	1-3	W.Jones

Cheshire League Cup:

Ist Rd	Northwich Vic.	Home	5-1	Felton 4;Scott;
2nd Rd	Runcorn	Away	2-4	Harvey;Scott;

Lancashire Junior Cup:

Ist Rd	Skelmersdale U.	Home	4-2	Cowper;Felton;W.Jones; Scott;
2nd Rd	Morecambe	Away	4-1	Scott 2;Thomas;og;
3rd Rd	Great Harwood	Home	5-1	Scott 2; Cowper; Felton; Spencer
S-F	Lancaster City	Home	0-0	
Replay	Lancaster City	Away	3-4	Felton; Prosser;Scott;

Champions v Runners-Up;
Macclesfield Town Home 1-2 Cowper

Seasons Honours: Cheshire League Champions

Season 1933-34

The First known Team Group of Wigan Athletic: Cheshire League Champions

Season 1935-36

Winners: Lancashire Junior Cup, Cheshire League, & Cheshire League Challenge Cup
Plus Finalists Lancashire Senior Cup.

SEASON 1934-35
Cheshire League:

	Home	Away
Altrincham	2-2	1-1
Ashton National	5-0	1-1
Buxton	9-0	0-1
Chester Reserves	10-1	2-2
Congleton Town	2-0	3-2
Crewe Alexandra Reserves	3-0	5-0
Hurst	1-0	1-4
Hyde United	2-1	5-1
Macclesfield Town	2-1	4-4
Manchester 14orth End	6-1	3-3
Mossley	8-2	0-1
Nantwich Town	1-0	4-1
Northwich Victoria	9-2	1-1
Port Vale Reserves	4-0	2-2
Prescot Cables	2-2	2-0
Runcorn	5-0	4-0
Stalybridge Celtic	9-3	2-5
Stockport County Reserves	3-1	3-1
Tranmere Rovers Reserves	6-2	2-6
Winsford United	6-2	2-1
Witton Albion	11-0	0-2

P.	W.	D.	L.	F.	A.	W.	D.	L.	F.	A.	Pts	Pos
42	19	2	0	106	20	8	7	6	47	39	63	Ist

League Appearances:
Ambler 5;Armes 39;Carr 3;Caunce 38;Connaughton 1;Felton 42;Job 2; H.Jones 3;Parsons 4;Patterson 39;Roberts 42; Robinson 33;Robson 35; Rutter 13;Scott 40;A.C.Swift 1; R.Swift 2;Talbot 37;Tuffnell 40; Waine 2;Watson 40;White 1;

League Scorers:
Roberts 46(1 pen);Scott 30;Felton 26;Robson 23;Armes 16;Watson 8 (7 pens);Tuffnell 4;(Total 153)

Other Results:

F.A.Cup.

Ist Qual	Nelson	Home	3-1	Scott 2;Felton;
2nd Qual	Morecambe	Away	5-0	Roberts 4;Scott;
3rd Qual	Dick Kerrs	Home	5-1	Armes 2;Felton 2; Watson(pen);
4th Qual	Northwich Vic.	Home	4-0	Roberts2;Robson2;
Ist Rd	Carlisle United	Away	6-1	Armes 2;Roberts2; Robson; Scott;
2nd Rd	Torquay United	Home	3-2	Roberts 2;Scott;
3rd Rd	Millwall	Home	1-4	Roberts;

Lancashire Junior Cup:

2nd Rd	Chorley	Away	5-1	Armes 2; Roberts 2; Felton;
3rd Rd	Rossendale United	Home	2-0	Robson;Scott;
S-F	Lancaster City	Home	6-2	Roberts 3;Scott 2; Robson;
Final	Fleetwood (At Preston)		2-3	Felton 2;

Lancashire Senior Cup:

Ist Rd	Accrington Stanley	Away	3-1	Roberts 2;Armes;
2nd Rd	Liverpool Reserves	Away	2-3	Armes 2;

Champions v Runners-Up:

Altrincham	Home	3-2	Roberts 2;Robson;

Seasons Honours:
Cheshire League Champions; Lancashire Junior Cup runners-up

SEASON 1935-36
Cheshire League:

	Home	Away
Altrincham	3-0	1-1
Ashton National	6-2	2-2
Buxton	5-1	2-1
Chester Reserves	1-2	2-2
Congleton Terrace	4-1	3-1
Crewe Alexandra Reserves	3-0	4-1
Hurst	8-0	7-2
Hyde United	4-2	5-1
Macclesfield Town	6-0	2-1
Manchester North End	4-0	1-0
Mossley	5-0	2-1
Nantwich Town	2-1	2-2
Northwich Victoria	5-1	2-2
Port Vale Reserves	5-1	2-1
Prescot Cables	4-0	0-1
Runcorn	6-3	4-5
Stalybridge Celtic	4-1	1-0
Stockport County Reserves	3-0	1-1
Tranmere Rovers Reserves	5-0	1-2
Winsford United	4-0	0-1
Witton Albion	4-3	1-0

P.	W.	D.	L.	F.	A.	W.	D.	L.	F.	A.	Pts	Pos
42	20	0	1	91	18	11	6	4	45	28	68	Ist

League Appearances:
Armes 8;Burke II;Colquhoun 34;Farrimond 1;Felton 30; Forshaw 1; Gregson 1;Hall 3;Hancock 42;Heywood 1; McLauchlan 40;Nuttall 1; Patterson 41;Ramsdale 1;Roberts 15; Robinson 42;Robson 34;Scott 38 Tuffnell 41;Urmston 2; Watson 8;Wilson 25;
League Scorers:
Scott 25(2 pens);Felton 22;Wilson 22;Robson 21;Colquhoun 9; Roberts 8;Burke 5;Tuffnell 5(1 pen);Armes 4;Hancock 4; McLauchlan 4(pens);Watson 3(1 pen);Patterson 2;Heywood1; Own Goals 1; (Total 136)

Other Results:

F.A.Cup

4th Qual	Chorley	Away	4-1	Colquhoun;Felton;Scott Robson;
Ist Rd	Rotherham United	Home	1-2	Felton;

Cheshire League Cup:

Ist Rd	Prescot Cables	Home	5-0	Roberts;Robson 2; Scott 2;
2nd Rd	Northwich Victoria	Home	2-0	Colquhoun;Robson;
3rd Rd	Chester Reserves	Home	1-0	Robson;
S-F	Macclesfield Town	Away	2-1	Burke;Wilson;
Final	Crewe Alex Res	Home	4-1	Colquhoun 2;Robson; Wilson;

Lancashire Senior Cup:

Ist Rd	Bury	Home	2-1	Felton;Roberts;
2nd Rd	Darwen	Away	5-1	Colquhoun; Felton; Roberts;Robson 2;
S-F	Manchester Utd Res	Away	2-0	Robson;Wilson;
Final	Blackpool Reserves	Away	2-6	Robson;Wilson;

Lancashire Junior Cup:

2nd Rd	Darwen	Away	0-0	
Replay	Darwen	Home	6-2	Colquhoun;Felton; Robson 2; Wilson; Scott;
3rd Rd	Rossendale United	Home	5-0	Felton 2;Robson 2; Wilson;
S-F	Clitheroe	Away	4-1	McLauchlan(pen);Scott; Wilson 2;
Final	South Liverpoo l (At Preston)		1-1	Robson;
Replay	South Liverpoo l (At Anfield)		3-0	Scott;Watson(pen); Wilson;

Seasons Honours:
Cheshire League Champions; Cheshire League Cup winners; Lancashire Junior Cup winners

SEASON 1936-37
Cheshire League:

	Home	Away
Altrincham	1-0	1-5
Ashton National	2-2	1-3
Buxton	3-3	2-3
Chester Reserves	3-1	4-0
Congleton Town	5-0	1-2
Crewe Alexandra Reserves	2-0	2-3
Hurst	4-1	0-0
Hyde United	4-2	1-0
Macclesfield Town	1-0	3-4
Manchester North End	6-2	1-2
Mossley	3-0	3-3
Nantwich Town	4-0	5-2
Northwich Victoria	3-0	1-4
Port Vale Reserves	1-1	1-2
Rhyl Athletic	5-2	2-3
Runcorn	2-4	0-4
Stalybridge Celtic	3-1	2-2
Stockport County Reserves	0-1	2-3
Tranmere Rovers Reserves	3-0	1-2
Winsford United	2-3	2-0
Witton Albion	2-1	0-2

P.	W.	D.	L.	F.	A.	W.	D.	L.	F.	A.	Pts	Pos.
42	18	3	3	59	24	4	3	14	35	49	44	8th

League Appearances:
Atkin 41;Baldwin 1;Barkas 10;Beaton 3;Boardman; 2;Colquhoun 38; Connaughton 1;Cottam 9;Crompton 3; Fishwick 5;Garfoot 1;Hickson 1; Humpish 35;Hurst 3; Johnson 1; Jones 19;Laidman 16;Lomas 6;Lowe 8; Marshall 1; McDermott 3;McLauchlan 42;Orritt 1;Patterson 29; Pennington 8;Ramsdale 3;Robinson 37;Sharratt 1;Shaw 4; Smith 3; Thomas 6;Tuffnell 27;Turner 35;Wallbanks 40; Watson ll;Wilson 6;Winstanley 2;
League Scorers:
Wallbanks 40(3 pens);Humpish 10;Atkins 9;Colquhoun 8; Thomas 7; Lowe 5;Barkas 3;Laidman 3;Pennington 2; Boardman 1;Hurst l;Johnson 1;Jones 1;Lomas 1; McLauchlan 1; Wilson 1;(Total 94)

Other Results:

F.A. Cup:

4th Qual	Darwen	Home	3-0	Colquhoun; Tufnell; Wallbanks;
Ist Rd	Burton Town	Away	1-5	Wallbanks;

Cheshire League Cup:

Ist Rd	Cheshire Reserves	Home	3-1	Atkins; Humpish; Wallbanks;
2nd Rd	Winsford United	Away	1-2	McLauchlan

Lancashire Junior Cup:

2nd Rd	Fleetwood	Away	0-2

Champions v Runners-Up (1935-36)

Altrincham	Home	3-0	Atkins; Colquhoun; Wallbanks;

Northern Midweek League:

Group A:	Home	Away
Blackpool	2-1	2-3
Burnley	4-1	2-1
Liverpool	5-3	1-3
Oldham Athletic	2-1	2-0
Preston North End	4-2	2-1
Southport	3-0	2-0
Group B:		
Blackpool	0-4	2-6
Burnley	2-0	4-5
Liverpool	1-3	0-1
Oldham Athletic	0-2	3-4
Preston North End	1-1	1-2
Southport	4-0	5-0

Seasons Honours: None

SEASON 1937-38
Cheshire League:

	Home	Away
Altrincham	2-3	1-1
Ashton National	1-0	1-0
Buxton	6-4	0-0
Chester Reserves	4-1	1-2
Congleton Town	12-1	0-3
Crewe Alexandra Reserves	2-4	0-4
Hurst	9-1	3-2
Hyde United	5-1	0-2
Macclesfield Town	4-2	1-3
Manchester North End	2-1	2-4
Mossley	1-1	1-4
Nantwich Town	2-0	5-1
Northwich Victoria	0-2	1-2
Port Vale Reserves	1-0	0-3
Rhyl Athletic	2-0	1-4
Runcorn	1-2	4-6
Stalybridge Celtic	3-0	1-4
Stockport County Reserves	2-0	1-8
Tranmere Rovers Reserves	1-1	1-4
Winsford United	5-0	2-1
Witton Albion	2-1	1-6

P.	W.	D.	L.	F.	A.	W.	D.	L.	F.	A.	Pts	Pos.
42	15	2	4	67	25	4	2	15	27	64	42	11th

League Appearances:
Birchall 3;Bullivant 10;Colquhoun 13;Connaughton 4;Cunliffe 2; Dawber 1;Farrimond 5;Foster 31;Goulder 3;Graham 35; Grange 36;Green 2;Hancock 35;Hart 1;Hitchen 1;Hooton 28;Hughes 19;Littler 6;McLauchlan 34;Melling 6;Mockett 2; Naylor 24;Norris 1;Pearson 12; Pennington 3;Pitcairn 25; Rhead 1;Robinson 38;Robson 7;Rutter 1; Shirley 8;Smith 1;Thomas 34;Townley 13;White 2;Winstanley 4;
League Scorers:
Thomas 30(2 pens);Graham 14;Grange 14(1 pen);Hughes 12(3 pens); Townley 7;Colquhoun 6;Pearson 3;Rhead 3; Birchall 2;Robson 2; Hooton 1;(Total 94)

Other Results:

F.A.Cup:

Ist Qual	Lytham St Annes	Home	7-0	Oakes;Thomas(2);Grange; Colquhoun(3);
2nd Qual	Chorley	Away	1-0	Grange;
3rd Qual	Leyland Motors	Home	3-0	Graham;Hughes;Thomas;
4th Qual	Northwich Victoria	Away	1-0	Grange;
Ist Rd	South Liverpool	Home	1-4	Thomas

Cheshire League Cup:

Ist Rd	Chester Reserves	Home	3-1	Thomas;Hughes(pen); Pennington;
2nd Rd	Winsford United	Away	0-2	

Lancashire Junior Cup:

2nd Rd	Bacup Borough	Away	0-1

Northern Midweek League:

Play-Off(1936-37) Blackpool Away 1-5 Graham;

League:	Home	Away
Blackburn Rovers	2-1	4-5
Blackpool	3-0	1-1
Burnley	1-4	1-2
Liverpool	1-3	2-5
Oldham Athletic	1-1	0-1
Preston North End	0-2	0-2
Southport	7-2	7-2

Seasons Honours: None

SEASON 1938-39
Cheshire League:

	Home	Away
Altrincham	1-0	2-1
Ashton National	5-1	2-5
Buxton	4-0	0-4
Chester Reserves	1-1	2-4
Congleton Town	3-0	1-1
Crewe Alexandra Reserves	2-1	2-7
Hurst	6-1	1-2
Hyde United	0-3	3-2
Macclesfield Town	3-0	0-2
Manchester North End	7-0	2-0*
Mossley	0-2	1-0
Northwich Victoria	5-2	0-2
Port Vale Reserves	3-1	4-5
Rhyl Athletic	8-1	3-3
Runcorn	2-4	0-3
Stalybridge Celtic	4-0	2-4
Stockport County Reserves	4-3	3-4
Tranmere Rovers Reserves	4-1	2-1
Wellington Town	3-1	3-4
Winsford United	1-1	1-0
Witton Albion	3-3	0-4

*Played at Wigan

P.	W.	D.	L.	F.	A.	W.	D.	L.	F.	A.	Pts	Pos.
42	15	3	3	69	26	6	2	13	34	58	47	7th

League Appearances:
Allen 5;Appleton 32;Birchall 1;Briscoe 8;Bullivant 9;Cansfield 33 Gill 9;Greenwood 4;Guest 1;C.Hartill 1;H.Hartill 33;Hitchen 11;Hooton 29;Lawrence 5;Littler 32;Lowery 14; McLauchlan 4;Melling 16; Milligan 26;O'Neill 2;Parle 26;Part 1;Pearson 3; Radcliffe 2;Robinson 39;Rollinson 4;Scott 4;Shirley 4;Sutton 9;Thomas 40;Townley 6;Whittaker 42;Wood 2;Wright 4;

League Scorers:
Thomas 40(8 pens);Cansfield 21(1 pen);Appleton 10;H.Hartill 10; Parle 6;Townley 3;Part 2;Bullivant 1;C.Hartill 1;Hitchen 1; Hooton 1;Lawrence 1;O'Neill 1;Robson 1;Whittaker 1;Wood 1; Wright 1 Own Goals 1;(Total 103)

Other Results:

F.A.Cup:

Ist Qual	Breightmet United	Home	3-0	Cansfield 2(1 pen); Townley;
2nd Qual	Skelmersdale United	Home	1-1	Part
Replay	Skelmersdale United	Away	2-1	Appleton; Cansfield;
3rd Qual	Chorley	Home	3-3	Appleton; H.Hartill; Whittaker;
Replay	Chorley	Away	1-5	Parle;

Cheshire League Cup:

Ist Rd	Chester Reserves	Home	1-0	O'Neill;
2nd Rd	Witton Albion	Away	4-2	Cansfield 2; Hooton; Thomas;
3rd Rd	Ashton National	Home	6-2	Thomas 4;Cansfield; Melling;
S-F	Port Vale Reserves	Away	1-2	Thomas;

Lancashire Junior Cup:

2nd Rd	Fleetwood	Home	3-2	Cansfield 2; H.Hartill;
3rd Rd	Rossendale United	Away	3-1	Cansfield; Thomas; Appleton;
S-F	Chorley	Home	3-1	Appleton; Cansfield; Thomas
Final	South Liverpool	(Anfield)	0-3	

Seasons Honours:
Lancashire Junior Cup runners-up

SEASON 1945-46
Cheshire League:

	Home	Away
Buxton	3-3	0-5
Chester Reserves	4-1	4-9
Crewe Alexandra Reserves	2-2	1-5
Droylsden	1-4	0-6
Hurst	4-5	2-3
Hyde United	3-3	1-2
Mossley	7-2	2-4
Northwich Victoria	4-1	2-3
Oldham Athletic Reserves	3-3	0-3
Port Vale Reserves	2-0	1-1
Rhyl Athletic	5-3	1-1
Runcorn	4-3	3-8
South Liverpool	3-1	2-6
Stalybridge Celtic	3-4	5-2*
Stockport County Reserves	4-2	1-4
Tranmere Rovers Reserves	3-0	0-1
Wellington Town	3-1	0-3
Witton Albion	0-2	1-6
Wrexham Reserves	2-1	2-3

*Abandoned after 78 minutes but result stood.

P.	W.	D.	L.	F.	A.	W.	D.	L.	F.	A.	Pts	Pos.
38	11	4	4	60	41	1	2	16	28	75	30	19th

League Appearances:
Allen 36;Almond 3;Angus 3;Aspinall 5;Barker 14;Berry 1; Brewster 7 Broadhurst 2;Brocklehurst 1;Casey 1;Cleworth 9; Colquhoun 25; Corcoran 1;Cunliffe 30;Doyle 7;Eastham 21; Eddleston 1;Evans 1; Garfoot 1;Green 16;Haigh 20;Hampson ll;Hankin 6;Hanna 13;Hickson 4;Hilton 9;Hooper 6;Hooton 8; Hughes 2;Johnson 3;A.Jones 1;J.Jones 1;Lightfoot 1;Littler 17;Marsh 4;Milligan 6;Murray 4;Napier 5; Neary 6;Painter 4; Pearce 1;Prescott 1;Rainford 2;Ratcliffe 1;Roberts 16; Robinson 2;Shirley 1;Smart 1;Smith 3;Taylor 16; Teers 22;Thomas 1;Tootill 3;Unsworth 13;Waite 1;Walsh 1;Wiggans 1 Wilson 2;Woodcock 2;Woods 1;
(Excludes game at Droylsden)

League Scorers:
Barker 16(3 pens);Colquhoun 14;Hampson 12(1 pen);Roberts 10; Hilton 5;Cunliffe 4;Taylor 4;Eastham 3;Haigh 2(1 pen); Hooper 2;Teers 2;Tootill 2;Aspinall 1;Brewster 1;Casey 1; Doyle l;Evans 1;Hankin 1;Napier l(pen);Wiggans 1;Woodcock 1;Own Goals 3; (Total 88)

Other results:

F.A.Cup:

2nd Qual	Chorley	Away	2-5	Hampson 2;

Lancashire Junior Cup:

Ist Rd	Barrow	Home	1-2	Marsh(pen);

Seasons Honours:
None

SEASON 1946-47
Cheshire League:

	Home	Away
Altrincham	1-2	2-2
Buxton	4-4	1-5
Chester Reserves	3-2	1-1
Congleton Town	2-4	1-3
Crewe Alexandra Reserves	3-1	2-5
Droylsden	2-3	0-1
Hurst	3-4	1-4
Hyde United	1-2	0-8
Macclesfield Town	1-1	2-1
Mossley	6-1	1-2
Northwich Victoria	3-6	1-3
Port Vale Reserves	2-1	1-6
Rhyl Athletic	0-1	1-1
Runcorn	3-2	2-3
South Liverpool	0-4	2-4
Stalybridge Celtic	1-2	0-4
Stockport County Reserves	2-0	3-3
Tranmere Rovers Reserves	2-2	1-0
Wellington Town	3-1	1-3
Witton Albion	1-3	0-7
Wrexham Reserves	0-1	0-1

P.	W.	D.	L.	F.	A.	W.	D.	L.	F.	A.	Pts	Pos.
42	7	3	11	43	47	2	4	15	23	67	25	22nd

League Appearances:
Adams ll;Allen 26;Almond 1;Arnold 1;Aspinall 3;Barker 6; Bartley 8 Beesley 2;Birchall 2;Booth 9;Colquhoun 17;Conser 4; Curless 2; Darley 13;Dickinson 5;Eastham 7;Ellis 2;Evans 1; Fearnley 2; Freeman 2;Geddes 1;Green 37;Grimes 1;Hagan 1; Heyes 8;A.Hilton 26;J.B.Hilton 4;Hughes 7;Isherwood 2; Lewis 6;Martin 3;McMillan 7;Milne 36;Mutch 5;Oakes 10; O'Neill 5;Parry 1;Peters 1;Porter;23;Rhead 1;Rimmer 25; Roberts 15;Robinson 5;Shirley 24;J.Taylor 12 P.Taylor 28; Turner 17;Watkins 1;Whitter 7;Wilson 8;Winstanley 1; Woodcock 9;Yarker 1;

League Scorers:
Roberts 10(1 pen);A.Hilton 8;P.Taylor 8(3 pens);Oakes 6(2 pens'); Shirley 4;Lewis 3;Rimmer 3;Robinson 3;J.Taylor 3; Eastham 2; Martin 2;Barker l;Bartley 1;Birchall 1;Booth 1; Colquhoun 1; Curless 1;Fearnley 1;J.B.Hilton l;Hughes 1;Milne 1;O'Neill 1; Parry 1;Turner 1;Woodcock 1; (Total 66)

Other Results:

F.A.Cup:

Prelim Rd	Crossen	Home	3-2	Roberts; Robinson; J.Taylor;
Ist Rd	Morecambe	Away	3-0	Barker 3;
2nd Rd	Darwen	Home	1-2	Holmes;

Cheshire League C up:

Ist Rd	Rhyl Athletic	Home	4-1	Colquhoun;A.Hilton; Rimmer; Roberts(pen);
2nd Rd	Droylsden	Away	3-0	Booth;Freeman;P.Taylor
S-F	Stalybridge Celtic	Home	0-1	

Lancashire Junior -Cup:

Prelim Rd	Earlestown	Home	5-1	Colquhoun;Green 2; P.Taylor 2;
Ist -Rd	-Chorley	Away	2-3	Roberts;P.Taylor;

Seasons Honours: None

SEASON 1947-48
Lancashire Combination:

	Home	Away
Accrington Stanley Reserves	1-0	5-1
Bacup Borough	2-2	1-1
Bangor City	3-0	3-0
Barrow Reserves	2-0	2-3
Chorley	2-1	1-1
Clitheroe	1-2	2-0
Darwen	2-0	3-1
Fleetwood	1-5	0-1
Horwich RMI	1-0	1-0
Lancaster City	3-2	2-0
Leyland Motors	2-0	0-0
Marine	2-0	0-0
Morecambe	0-0	1-1
Nelson	3-0	0-2
Netherfield	1-0	0-2
New Brighton Reserves	3-0	2-1
Oldham Athletic Reserves	4-0	2-0
Prescot Cab.'Les	2-0	1-3
Rochdale Reserves	3-2	1-1
Rossendale United	1-1	3-1
Southport Reserves	3-1	0-2

P.	W.	D.	L.	F.	A.	W.	D.	L.	F.	A.	Pts	Pos.
42	16	3	2	42	16	9	6	6	30	21	59	1st

League Appearances:
Aspley 4;Ball 18;D.Banks 1;Barker 23;Brown 28;Brunton 1; Colquhoun 3;Cooper 2;Cunliffe 26;Finch 38;A.Green 6; J.Green 3;Gregson 2; Heslop 4;Hinton 7;Howcroft 36; Howshall 1;Knowles 1;Lea 3;Mason 1; Miller 39;McGurk 6; North 19;Oakes 4;Parkinson 41;Pilling 13;Reid 2;Shirley 33; Smith 7;Taylor 39;Unsworth 1;Urmston 8;Wilson 2; Woolley 37;Wright 3;

League Scorers:
Taylor 15(3 pens);Barker 13;Miller 12;Shirley '7;Brown 6; Cunliffe 3;McGurk 3;North 3;Oakes 3;Aspley 1;Colquhoun 1; Gregson 1; Howcroft 1;Urmston 1;Own Goals 2;(Total 72)

Other Results:

F.A. Cup:

Prelim Rd	Formby	Home	4-0	Gregson 2;Taylor 2;
Ist Qual	Earlestown	Away	1-0	Oakes;
2nd Qual	Rhyl Athletic	Home	2-1	Brown;North;
3rd Qual	Prescot Cables	Home	3-0	Barker 3;
4th Qual	Marine	Away	1-3	Miller

Lancashire Combination Cup:

2nd Rd	Marine	Home	7-3	Cunliffe 2(2 pens); North 2; Urmston 2; Taylor;
3rd Rd	Prescot Cables	Home	1-1	Taylor;
Replay	Prescot Cables	Away	1-4	Miller;

Lancashire Junior Cup:

Prelim Rd	Prescot Cables	Away	0-3

Seasons Honours:
Lancashire Combination Champions

Season 1947/48

(Back): Colquhoun (Trainer), Howcroft, Finch, Ball, Woolley, Parkinson, Cunliffe, Shirley.
(Front): Brown, Taylor, Barker, North, Miller.

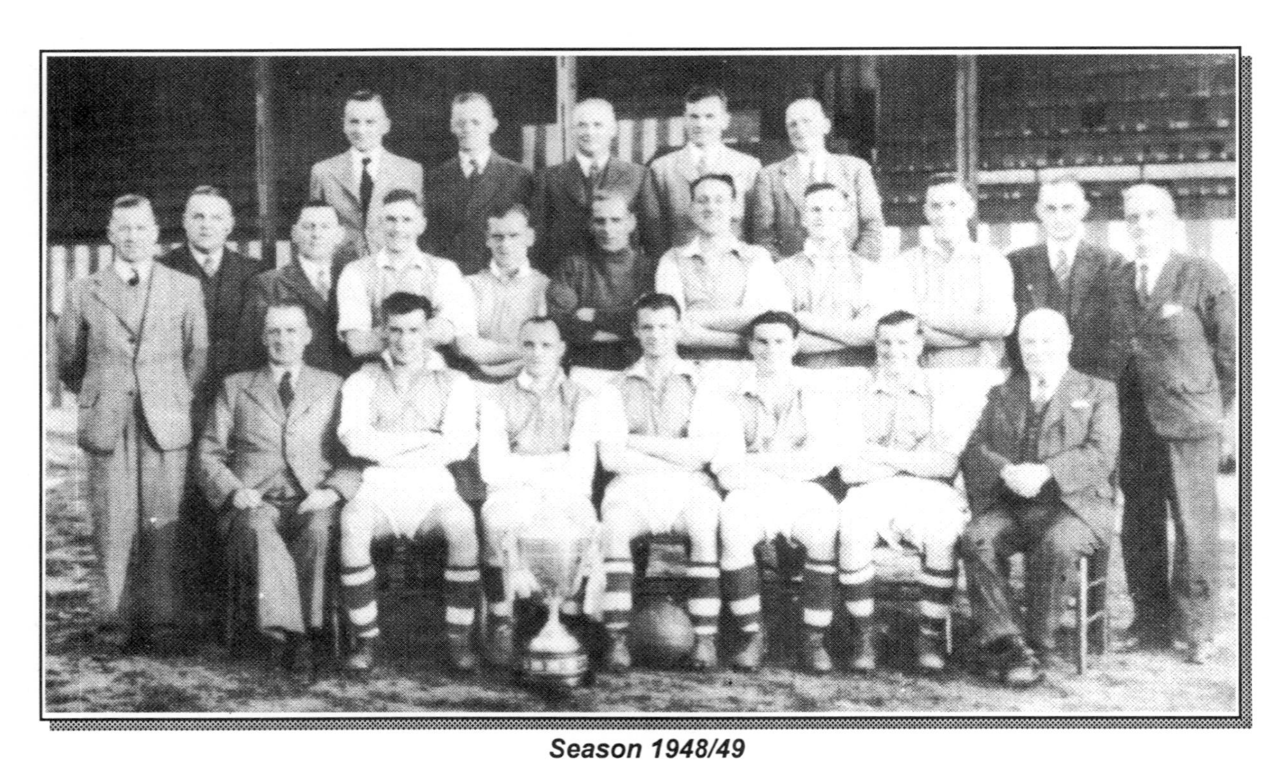

Season 1948/49

(Back): Smith, Farrimond, Wilson, Daniels, Smallshaw. (Middle): Colquhoun (Train.), Glover, Vose, Pilling, Finch, Woolley, Shirley, Cunliffe, Parkinson, McBride, McNamara.
(Front): Swalwell, Smith, Brown, Howcroft, McGurk, Miller, Roberts.

SEASON 1948-49
Lancashire Combination:

	Home	Away
Accrington Stanley Reserves	0-2	1-4
Ashton United	1-1	1-2
Bacup Borough	2-0	3-4
Bangor City	1-0	0-1
Barrow Reserves	0-2	2-2
Chorley	2-1	3-1
Clitheroe	5-2	2-1
Darwen	0-1	1-1
Fleetwood	2-0	4-3
Lancaster City	1-0	0-5
Leyland Motors	4-2	1-1
Marine	2-2	1-0
Morecambe	0-0	0-1
Nelson	4-4	0-4
Netherfield	2-0	0-6
New Brighton Reserves	5-1	0-0
Oldham Athletic Reserves	1-0	0-2
Prescot Cables	4-1	0-1
Rochdale Reserves	1-1	1-2
Rossendale United	3-1	6-3
Southport Reserves	5-2	2-1

P.	W.	D.	L.	F.	A.	W.	D.	L.	F.	A.	Pts	Pos.
42	13	5	3	45	23	6	4	11	28	45	47	6th

League Appearances:
Benyon 2;Booth 19;Boydell 1;Brown 25;Brunton 1;Coates 9; Colquhoun 1;E.Cunliffe 36;R.Cunliffe 17;Day 1;Finch 39;Fryer 29;Higham 2; Howcroft 27;Jones 2;Kirkman 1;Lowe 12; Melling 1;McGurk 4;North 15;Parkinson 42;Pilling 1;Robinson 12; Sharrock 8;Shirley 37;Smith 12;Styles 2;Taylor 37;Tolley 24; Vickers 4;Woolley 39:

League Scorers:
E.Cunliffe 23(3 pens);Fryer 10;Taylor 9;North 6;Robinson 6; Smith 3(all pens);Booth 2;Brown 2;Shirley 2;Finch 1;Howcroft 1; Lowe 1;McGurk 1;Sharrock 1;Tolley 1;Vickers 1;
Own Goals 3;(Total 73)

Other Results:

F.A. Cup:

Prelim Rd	Skelmersdale United	Home	2-1	Robinson 2;
Ist Qual	Prescot Cables	Home	1-2	North;

Lancashire Combination Cup.

Ist Rd	Horwich RMI	Home	4-1	Booth;Finch;Fryer;Taylor;
2nd Rd	Leyland Motors	Home	4-1	Cunliffe 2;Fryer:Taylor;
3rd Rd	Bootle	Away	1-0	Cunliffe;
S-F	Bangor City	Away	0-0	
Replay	Bangor City	Home	0-1	

Lancashire Junior Cup:

Prelim Rd	Atherton Collieries	Home	2-1	Fryer;Shirley;
Ist Rd	Belle Vue	Home	2-0	Fryer;Styles;
2nd Rd	Morecambe	Away	1-2	Cunliffe;

Seasons Honours: None

SEASON 1949-50
Lancashire Combination:

	Home	Away
Accrington Stanley Reserves	2-2	2-3
Ashton United	3-2	1-0
Bangor City	2-0	2-4
Barrow Reserves	2-2	3-0
Bootle	0-0	1-0
Chorley	3-1	4-2
Clitheroe	2-0	3-2
Darwen	2-0	1-0
Fleetwood	1-2	1-2
Horwich RMI	1-0	2-3
Lancaster City	3-0	1-1
Marine	4-0	0-1
Morecambe	1-0	3-3
Nelson	0-1	1-0
Netherfield	7-0	0-2
New Brighton Reserves	4-1	1-0
Oldham Athletic Reserves	0-0	1-0
Prescot Cables	1-1	1-3
Rochdale Reserves	2-3	2-1
Rossendale United	4-2	3-2
Southport Reserves	2-1	0-0

P.	W.	D.	L.	F.	A.	W.	D.	L.	F.	A.	Pts	Pos.
42	13	5	3	46	18	11	3	7	33	29	56	2nd

League Appearances:
Bretherton 4;Cunliffe 42;Finan 28;Higham 2;Hurst 2;Joynt 2; Kitchen 4;Laing 9;Lea 3;Lomax 42;McGilloway 5;Melling 3;;Moss 5; Parkinson 42;Pollard 37;Pryde 22;Rothwell 29;H.Sharratt 26; J.Sharratt 2;Shirley 31;Smith 3; J.Taylor 30;P.Taylor 4;Tolley 42; Vickers 10; Whiteside 24; Woolley 9;

League Scorers:
Lomax 33(1 pen);Finan II(I pen);Rothwell 9(1 pen);Cunliffe 5; Pollard 5;J.Taylor 4;Tolley 3(1 pen);Laing 2;Pryde 2(1 pen); Bretherton 1;Shirley 1;P.Taylor 1;Own Goals 2; (Total 79)

Other Results:

F.A.Cuip:

Extra Prelim	UGB(ST Helens)	Home	2-0	Pollard;Pryde;
Prelim Rd	South Liverpool	Away	1-0	Finan;
Ist Qual	Burscough	Away	5-1	Finan 2;Lomax;Rothwell Pryde(pen);
2nd Qual	Bootle	Home	6-1	Finan;Lomax;Pryde(pen) Rothwell;P.Taylor;og;
3rd Qual	Rhyl Athletic	Away	0-2	

Lancashire Combination Cup:

2nd Rd	St Helens Town	Away	1-1		Lomax;
Replay	St Helens Town	Home	2-1		Pollard;Rothwell;
3rd Rd	Earlestown	Home	3-0		Finan;Lomax;J.Taylor;
4th Rd	New Brighton Res	Away	1-1		J.Taylor
Replay	New Brighton Res	Home	4-2	AET	Lomax 2;Rothwell;Tolley;
S-F	Nelson	Home	1-1		Finan;
Replay	Nelson	Away	2-5		Finan 2(1 pen);

Lancashire Junior Cup:

Ist Rd	Accrington.S.Res	Home	4-1	Lomax 2;Pollard;Vickers;
2nd Rd	Nelson	Home	2-3	Lomax;J.Taylor;

Seasons Honours:
Lancashire Combination runners-up.

Season 1949/50
(Left to Right): Smith, Parkinson, Tolley, Woolley, Pryde (P/Manager), Cunliffe, Lomax, Laing, Finan, Pollard, Taylor.

Season 1952/53
(Back): Mycock, McGeachie, Williams, Lomas, Parkinson, Banks.
(Front): Corr, Lindsay, Shepherd, Hindle, Graham.

SEASON 1950-51
Lancashire Combination:

	Home	Away
Accrington Stanley Reserves	5-0	2-1
Ashton United	2-1	2-1
Barrow Reserves	1-3	1-1
Blackpool'B'	2-2	1-0
Bootle	2-0	2-1
Chorley	2-3	7-1
Clitheroe	2-1	2-1
Darwen	2-0	1-1
Earlestown	2-3	6-0
Fleetwood	1-1	1-1
Lancaster City	0-1	3-0
Marine	3-2	5-0
Morecambe	7-2	3-0
Nelson	2-3	3-2
Netherfield	3-1	2-4
New Brighton Reserves	0-0	0-0
Oldham Athletic Reserves	5-1	0-1
Prescot Cables	2-0	2-1
Rochdale Reserves	3-1	2-0
Rossendale United	2-0	1-0
Southport Reserves	4-0	0-2

P.	W.	D.	L.	F.	A.	W.	D.	L.	F.	A.	Pts	Pos.
42	13	3	5	52	25	14	4	3	46	18	61	Ist

League Appearances:
Bootle 39;Brown 4;Buchan 33;Cunliffe 39;Finan 3;Kitchen 2; Langford 1;Lea 4;Lewis 1;Lomax 40;Lyon 29;Mason 2; Norcross 1; Owen 24;Owens 7;Parkinson 36;Pollard 40; Rothwell Il;H.Sharratt 32;Shirley 41;Street 3;J.Taylor 9;Tolley 39; A.Wilson 3;G.Wilson 8;

League Scorers:
Lomax 36;Bootle 20(2 pens);Pollard 10;Lyon 6;Owen 6;Tolley 5(all pens);Rothwell 4;G.Wilson 4;Cunliffe 3;Finan 1;Taylor 1;Own Goals 2;(Total 98)

Other Results:

F.A.Cup:

Prelim Rd	South Liverpool	Away	0-0	
Replay	South Liverpool	Home	3-2	Lomax 2;Pollard;
Ist Qual	Flint Town United	Home	1-1	Cunliffe;
Replay	Flint Town United	Away	3-1	Finan 2;Rothwell;
2nd Qual	Crompton Recs	Home	1-0	Finan;
3rd Qual	Burscough Rangers	Away	2-0	Lomax;Taylor;
4th Qual	Rhyl Athletic	Away	0-0	
Replay	Rhyl Athletic	Home	2-3	Lomax 2;

Lancashire Combination Cup:

Ist Rd	Atherton Collieries	Home	8-0	Lomax 4;Bootle;Pollard Rothwell;Tolley(pen);
2nd Rd	Earlestown	Away	3-0	Owen 2;Lyon;
3rd Rd	Stubshaw Cross	Home	3-0	Lomax 3;
4th Rd	Netherfield	Home	3-0	Owen 2;Lomax;
S-F	Horwich RMI	Home	2-2	Lomax;og;
Replay	Horwich RMI	Away	3-0	Lomax 2;Cunliffe;
Final	Nelson	Away	0-3	

Lancashire Junior Cup:

Ist Rd	Prescot Cables	Home	7-0	Lomax3;G.Wilson2;Rothwell(pen);og;
2nd Rd	Rossendale United	Home	1-2	Bootle;

Seasons Honours: Lancashire Combination Champions
Lancashire Combination Cup runners-up

SEASON 1951-52
Lancashire Combination:

	Home	Away
Ashton United	4-0	3-1
Barrow Reserves	3-2	1-3
Blackpool 'B'	0-3	1-4
Bootle	4-1	0-2
Chorley	0-2	1-1
Clitheroe	1-0	2-0
Darwen	2-2	0-2
Earlestown	3-2	3-1
Fleetwood	4-1	1-0
Horwich RMI	1-1	2-1
Lancaster City	0-0	0-0
Marine	5-0	1-2
Morecambe	1-0	2-3
Nelson	1-0	0-3
Netherfield	0-3	0-0
New Brighton	1-1	2-2
Oldham Athletic Reserves	2-1	2-1
Rochdale Reserves	3-1	4-1
Rossendale United	2-3	3-1
Southport Reserves	1-1	1-0
St Helens Town	6-3	0-2

P.	W.	D.	L.	F.	A.	W.	D.	L.	F.	A.	Pts	Pos.
42	12	5	4	44	27	9	4	8	29	30	51	4th

League Appearances:
Abram 2;Bentham 1;Bootle 37;Bourne 9;Buchan 35;Butler 3; Crampton 5;Eastham 7;Eaves 15;Gannon 1;Green 1;Grieves 7; Hogg 28;Johnston 2;Kitchen 2;Langford 10;Lea 4;Lomax 18; Lunn Il;J.Lyon 32;S.Lyon 22;May 2;Parkes 13;Parkin 12; Parkinson 32;Peel 1;Peet 3;Pollard 18;Price 1;Rudd 3;Sharratt 5; Shirley 19;Tolley 39;Vollmer 10; Williams 1;A.Wilson 5; G.Wilson 23;Woodward 22;Young 1;

League Scorers:
J.Lyon 13;Lomax 12;Bootle Il;Langford 7(1 pen);Eaves 5; Johnston 4 Pollard 4;Tolley 4(2 pens);Crampton 3;Woodward 3; Vollmer 2;Bourne 1;Butler 1;S.Lyon 1;A.Wilson;
Own Goals 1;(Total 73)

Other Results:

F.A.Cup:

4th Qual	Witton Albion	Home	2-2	Bootle;J.Lyon;
Replay	Witton Albion	Away	3-3 (AET)	Eaves;J.Lyon;Tolley(pen);
2nd Replay	Witton Albion	Home	1-3	Eaves;

Lancashire Combination Cup:

2nd Rd	Stubshaw Cross	Home	1-0	J.Lyon;
3rd Rd	St Helens Town	Home	4-1	Tolley 2(2 pens); S.Lyon;Parkin;
4th Rd	Prescot Cables	Home	2-0	Bootle;J.Lyon;
S-F	Darwen	Home	3-0	Bootle;Eaves;J.Lyon;
Final	Fleetwood	Home	1-1	Langford
Replay	Fleetwood	Away	2-1	Eaves;J.Lyon;

Lancashire Junior Cup:

2nd Rd	Horwich RMI	Home	2-0	J.Lyon;A.Wilson;
3rd Rd	Chorley	Home	4-0	J.Lyon;Tolley(pen); Vollmer;Woodward;
S-F	Bootle	Home	1-0	Tolley(pen);
Final	Lancaster City	(Preston)	2-2	Bootle;Eaves;
Replay	Lancaster City	(Blackpool)	1-2	Langford;

Seasons Honours: Lancashire Combination Cup winners
Lancashire Junior Cup runners-up

FINAL LEAGUE TABLES: 1953/54 - 1967/68

Lancashire Combination Div.1 1953/54							
Wigan Athletic	40	31	4	5	110	48	66
Netherfield	40	20	11	9	104	73	51
Nelson	40	21	6	13	91	68	48
Howrich R. M. I	40	21	5	14	95	65	47
Darwen	40	15	9	13	80	49	45
Marine	40	17	6	17	70	77	40
South Liverpool	40	15	9	16	77	73	39
Oldham Ath. Reserves .	40	17	5	18	77	81	39
Lancaster City	40	16	7	17	79	84	39
Southport Reserves	40	16	7	17	56	67	39
Accrington Stanley Res..	40	17	3	20	91	88	37
Bolton Wand. 'B'	40	16	5	19	62	71	37
Rossendale United	40	14	8	18	87	89	36
Ashton United	40	17	2	21	74	85	36
Rochdale Reserves	40	14	8	18	61	8C	36
Barrow Reserves	40	15	6	19	57	79	36
Fleetwood	40	14	7	19	78	88	35
Chorley	40	12	10	18	51	60	34
Morecambe	40	14	6	20	58	83	34
New Brighton	40	13	7	20	70	94	33
Prescot Cables	40	13	7	20	63	89	33

Lancashire Combination Div.1 1954/55							
Accrington Stanley Res.	42	29	10	3	110	46	68
Rossendale United	42	24	6	12	123	84	54
Wigan Athletic	42	21	10	11	93	56	52
Burscough	42	22	8	12	75	49	52
Oldham Ath. Reserves .	42	21	10	11	98	74	52
Blackpool 'B'	42	22	5	15	101	59	49
Fleetwood	42	19	11	12	73	69	49
Horwich R.M.1	42	20	8	14	81	62	48
Morecambe	42	18	8	16	68	65	44
Marine	42	19	*5*	18	91	84	43
Netherfield	42	20	3	19	92	94	43
Darwen	42	15	13	14	64	79	43
Chorley	42	17	7	18	78	91	41
Lancaster City	42	16	9	17	68	84	41
Barrow Reserves	42	14	9	19	87	90	37
Nelson	42	14	8	20	82	84	36
Ashton United	42	13	9	20	75	107	35
Southport Reserves	42	12	9	21	74	79	33
Bolton Wand. 'B'	42	12	8	22	62	68	32
South Liverpool	42	12	8	22	67	105	32
Rochdale Reserves. .	42	8	9	25	58	92	25
New Brighton	42	6	3	33	48	147	15

Lancashire Combination Div.1 19555/56							
Burscough	38	26	7	5	96	37	59
Horwich R. M. 1	38	24	9	5	104	49	57
Accrington Stanley Res., . .	38	20	10	8	87	56	50
Netherfield	38	21	7	10	95	55	49
Lancaster City	38	19	11	8	83	59	49
Wigan Athletic	38	18	10	10	80	56	46
New Brighton	38	18	8	12	78	57	44
Prescot Cables	38	19	6	13	104	93	44
Chorley	38	17	5	16	78	68	39
Marine	38	14	8	16	71	83	36
Southport Reserves	38	13	9	16	54	60	35
Ashton United	38	14	7	17	62	75	35
Darwen	38	13	8	17	66	85	34
Fleetwood	38	12	8	18	65	79	32
Nelson	38	12	8	18	60	89	32
Morecambe	38	12	5	21	62	94	29
Bacup Borough	38	10	9	19	58	76	29
South Liverpool	38	12	3	23	69	98	27
Rossendale United	38	8	9	21	61	89	25
St. Helens Town	38	3	3	32	34	110	9

Lancashire Combination Div.1 1956/57							
Prescot Cables	38	26	5	7	23	52	57
New Brighton	38	25	4	9	94	50	54
Morecambe	38	20	7	11	81	53	47
Horwich R.M.1	38	22	3	13	93	70	47
Burscough	38	19	7	12	86	58	45
Accrington Stanley Res.,	38	15	8	12	82	61	44
Ashton United	38	19	5	14	89	74	43
Chorley	38	15	8	15	74	74	38
Netherfield	38	15	8	15	73	73	38
Wigan Athletic	38	17	3	15	73	61	37
Lancaster City	38	14	8	16	71	91	36
Bacup Borough	38	12	11	15	80	88	35
Nelson	38	15	5	18	53	59	35
Skelmersdale United	38	14	6	18	67	82	34
South Liverpool	38	14	5	19	71	82	33
Fleetwood	38	13	7	18	56	70	33
Marine	38	12	8	18	62	84	32
Southport Reserves	38	12	7	19	62	88	31
Darwen	38	11	5	22	62	88	27
Droylsden	38	4	6	28	59	153	14

Lancashire Combination Div.1 1957/58							
Horwich R. M. I	42	28	7	7	109	47	63
Prescot Cables . .	42	26	9	7	117	49	61
New Brighton	42	23	8	11	85	61	54
Wigan Athletic	42	21	11	10	95	60	53
Accrington Stantey	42	23	6	13	92	71	52
Netherfield	42	20	9	13	87	70	49
Morecambe	42	18	12	12	66	50	48
Rossendale United	42	19	10	13	104	88	48
Chorley	42	20	7	15	123	85	47
Marine	42	17	7	18	74	103	41
Nelson	42	17	6	19	65	71	40
Ashton United	42	17	5	20	96	108	39
Lancaster City	42	15	7	20	74	93	37
Southport Reserves	42	16	5	21	69	102	37
Burscough	42	14	8	20	80	79	36
South Liverpool	42	16	6	21	94	102	36
Skelmersdale United	42	15	6	21	77	92	36
Darwen	42	14	6	22	71	104	34
Droylsden	42	13	7	22	75	99	33
Bacup Borough	42	12	8	22	88	115	32
Fleetwood	42	11	10	21	57	82	32
Crompton's Recs	42	5	6	31	51	118	16

Lancashire Combination Div.1 1958/59							
New Brighton	42	29	6	7	127	53	64
Prescot Cables	42	27	6	9	111	57	60
Horwich R.M.1	42	25	9	8	95	57	59
Skelmersdale United	42	22	10	10	107	69	54
Morecambe	42	22	9	11	77	44	53
Chorley	42	22	7	13	109	82	51
Netherfield	42	22	5	15	91	73	49
Bacup Borough	42	19	10	13	104	88	48
Nelson	42	19	9	14	82	74	47
Fleetwood	42	20	4	18	72	87	44
Marine	42	16	8	18	80	97	40
Burscough	42	15	9	18	60	69	39
South Liverpool	42	16	6	20	81	94	38
Darwen	42	16	6	20	75	93	38
Lancaster City	42	13	12	17	69	95	38
Rossendale United	42	16	5	21	88	89	37
Oldham Ath. Reserves .	42	13	8	21	80	98	34
Wigan Athletic	42	12	7	23	60	84	31
Ashton United	42	12	6	24	69	103	30
Southport Reserves	42	10	8	24	70	104	28
Clitheroe	42	11	3	28	71	105	25
Droylsden	42	6	5	31	43	106	17

Lancashire Combination Div. 1959/60							
Chorley	42	31	5	6	133	48	67
Wigan Athletic	42	27	6	9	101	51	60
New Brighton	42	28	4	10	103	54	60
Morecambe	42	28	2	12	103	54	58
Rossendale United	42	21	7	14	116	95	49
Burscough	42	20	8	14	94	73	48
Nelson	42	22	4	16	78	68	48
Netherfield	42	20	7	15	88	70	47
Marine	42	19	6	17	92	98	44
Horwich R. M. I	42	17	8	17	82	76	42
Prescot Cables	42	16	9	17	74	68	41
Oldham Ath. Reserves .	42	16	7	19	64	66	39
Ashton United	42	13	12	17	61	86	38
Fleetwood	42	16	5	21	63	71	37
Bacup Borough	42	11	12	19	71	99	34
Earlestown	42	13	7	22	79	113	33
Lancaster City	42	12	9	21	73	107	33
Lytham St. Annes	42	10	12	20	60	88	32
Skelmersdale United	42	13	6	23	59	97	32
Darwen	42	10	11	21	57	86	31
Southport Reserves	42	9	10	23	57	92	28
South Liverpool	42	7	9	26	54	102	23

Lancashire Combination Div.1 1960/61							
Chorley	42	31	7	4	125	33	69
Nelson	42	29	7	6	106	47	65
Wigan Athletic	42	25	8	9	108	56	58
Burscough	42	25	8	9	76	49	58
Netherfield	42	24	8	10	123	71	56
Morecambe	42	23	5	14	96	76	51
Lancaster City	42	17	14	11	75	53	48
Prescot Cables	42	20	7	15	70	78	47
New Brighton	42	20	6	16	80	65	46
Marine	42	17	10	15	79	75	44
Clitheroe	42	17	7	1.8	84	88	41
Ashton United	42	18	5	19	78	88	41
Horwich R.M.1	42	14	7	21	75	94	35
Lytham St. Annes	42	13	8	21	69	85	34
Skelmersdale Utd	42	12	9	21	71	85	33
Rossendale United	42	13	7	22	92	139	33
Oldhan Ath. Reserves .	42	13	6	23	71	84	32
Earlestown	42	12	8	22	74	103	32
Bacup Borough	42	11	9	22	76	96	31
Fleetwood	42	12	5	25	82	110	29
Droylsden	42	10	5	27	73	132	25
Darwen	42	7	2	33	45	121	16

Cheshire League 1961/62							
Ellesmere P. Town	42	25	13	4	103	52	63
Macclesfield	42	25	10	7	109	61	60
Runcorn	42	27	3	12	108	60	57
Northwich Victoria	42	25	5	12	103	56	55
Wigan Athletic	42	24	7	11	86	61	56
Hyde United	42	24	4	14	81	65	52
Buxton	42	21	6	15	98	79	48
Mossley	42	20	7	15	87	78	47
Stalybridge Celtic	42	17	7	18	79	74	41
Bangor City	42	15	11	16	86	86	41
Altrincham	42	15	10	17	58	64	40
Sankeys (Wellington)	42	16	7	19	76	74	39
Stafford Rangers	42	12	13	17	72	84	37
Rhyl	42	12	11	19	52	63	35
Congleton Town	42	12	11	19	57	78	35
Wrexham Reserves	42	12	11	19	53	79	35
OswestryTown	42	13	8	21	76	103	34
Winsford Utd	42	12	8	22	73	100	32
Chester Reserves	42	11	10	21	66	106	32
Tranmere Rovers Res.	42	10	9	23	73	111	29
Frickley Colliery	42	10	9	23	65	108	29
Witton Albion	42	11	6	25	70	99	28

Cheshire League 1962/63							
Runcor	42	26	13	3	95	43	65
Buxton	42	24	7	11	104	71	55
Tranmere Rovers Res.	42	19	15	8	88	57	53
Stalybridge Celtic	42	22	9	11	98	71	53
Macclesfield	42	20	12	10	87	59	52
Ellesmere Port Town	42	19	14	9	78	57	52
Wigan Athletic	42	22	6	14	70	54	50
Altrincham	42	19	8	15	90	68	46
Northwich Victoria	42	15	15	12	77	68	45
Winsford Utd	42	16	11	15	69	73	43
Frickley Colliery	42	16	11	15	66	79	43
Hyde Utd	42	14	14	14	81	74	42
Bangor City	42	13	16	13	71	68	42
Witton Albion	42	16	10	16	84	86	42
Wrexham Reserves	42	18	4	20	72	86	40
Congleton Town	42	16	7	19	73	80	39
Rhyl	42	12	10	20	64	86	34
Sankeys (Wellington)	42	10	13	19	64	76	33
Mossley	42	10	9	23	55	81	29
Stafford Rangers	42	9	10	23	50	90	28
Chester Reserves	42	7	7	28	62	105	21
Oswestry Town	42	6	5	31	53	119	17

Cheshire League 1963/64							
Macclesfield	42	30	9	3	112	38	69
Sankey's(Wellington)	42	23	10	9	98	57	56
Altrincham	42	22	8	12	94	68	52
Bangor City	42	21	9	12	75	55	51
Witton Albion	42	22	7	13	67	64	51
Tranmere Rovers Res	42	19	10	13	108	71	48
Runcorn	42	19	10	13	81	71	48
Ellesmere Port Town	42	20	8	14	77	78	48
Buxton	42	18	11	13	92	77	47
Hyde Utd	42	18	11	13	64	60	47
Frickley Colliery	42	18	9	15	65	57	45
Wigan Athletic	42	18	7	17	94	82	43
Mossley	42	16	7	19	66	77	39
Rhyl	42	13	12	17	73	88	38
OswestryTown	42	13	10	19	85	94	36
Stafford Rangers	42	15	6	21	66	89	36
Chester Reserves	42	15	5	22	70	82	35
Stalybridge Celtic	42	14	6	22	66	80	34
Northwich Victoria	42	13	6	23	64	87	32
Winsford United	42	9	11	22	61	98	29
Congleton Town	42	4	13	25	43	95	21
Wrexham Reserves	42	7	5	30	58	113	19

Cheshire League 1964/65							
Wigan Athletic	42	32	3	7	121	46	67
Macclesfield	42	28	6	8	115	45	62
Runcom	42	27	5	10	121	60	59
Bangor City	42	25	4	13	94	58	54
Tranmere Rovers Res	42	22	6	14	93	70	50
Hyde United	42	22	6	14	96	76	50
Frickley Colliery	42	21	8	13	79	74	50
Altrincham	42	18	12	12	74	55	48
Stalybridge Celtic	42	17	11	14	78	74	45
Ellesmere Port Town	42	19	6	17	79	60	44
Northwich Victoria	42	18	6	18	100	87	42
Rhyl	42	17	6	19	69	79	40
Oswestry Town	42	17	5	20	100	100	39
Mossley	42	13	12	17	57	62	38
Buxton	42	15	7	20	77	99	37
Witton Albion	42	14	8	20	79	90	36
Winsford United	42	15	5	22	66	96	35
Wrexham Reserves	42	13	9	20	58	99	35
Sankey's(Wellington)	42	10	13	19	70	87	35
Chester Reserves	42	11	8	23	65	99	30
Stafford Rangers	42	6	5	31	44	120	17
Congleton Town	42	3	7	32	46	145	13

Cheshire League 1965/66							
Altrincham	42	33	7	2	132	49	73
Wigan Athletic	42	32	8	2	133	40	72
Macciesffield	42	26	8	8	102	48	60
Bangor City	42	24	6	12	91	67	54
Runcorn	42	22	7	13	105	77	51
Stalybridge Celtic	42	21	8	13	98	84	50
Northwich Victoria	42	20	6	16	93	77	46
Hyde Utd	42	16	11	15	74	72	43
Ellesmere Port Town	42	16	10	16	97	80	42
Stockport County Res	42	14	13	15	61	65	41
New Brighton	42	17	6	19	76	86	40
Buxton	42	15	8	19	74	82	38
Tranmere Rovers Res	42	13	11	18	85	88	37
Frickley Colliery	42	13	11	18	76	102	37
Mossley	42	13	10	19	66	72	36
Oswestry Town	42	15	6	21	78	102	36
Witton Albion	42	14	7	21	93	107	35
Wrexham Reserves	42	15	5	22	92	107	35
Stafford Rangers	42	9	10	23	60	109	28
Rhyl	42	8	10	24	57	104	26
Chester Reserves	42	9	7	26	52	116	25
Winsford United	42	6	7	29	55	127	19

Cheshire League 1966/67							
Altrincham	42	31	5	6	123	45	67
Wigan Athletic	42	26	8	8	101	61	60
Northwich Victoria	42	22	13	7	91	55	57
Hyde United	42	24	8	10	101	56	56
Macclesfield	42	24	8	10	78	47	56
Witton Albion	42	21	9	12	74	56	51
Bangor City	42	20	8	14	90	77	48
Frickley Colliery	42	18	10	14	71	69	46
Runcorn	42	16	11	15	75	75	43
New Brighton	42	16	7	19	69	73	39
Mossley	42	15	9	18	66	71	38
Chester Reserves	42	13	12	17	72	71	38
Oswestry Town	42	15	8	19	64	89	38
Ellesmere Port Town	42	11	15	16	61	70	37
Stafford Rangers	42	12	12	18	59	66	36
Buxton	42	13	10	19	69	78	36
Tranmere Rovers Res.	42	14	8	20	66	84	36
Stockport County Res.	42	12	9	21	58	76	33
Rhyl	42	11	9	22	59	86	31
Stalybridge Celtic	42	11	8	23	52	85	30
Wrexham Reserves	42	11	3	28	66	114	25
Winsford United	42	8	6	28	46	107	22

Cheshire League 1967/68							
Macclesfield Town	42	28	10	4	96	39	66
Altrincham	42	28	7	7	108	64	63
Bangor City	42	24	9	9	99	61	57
Witton Albion	42	21	12	9	90	65	54
Mossley	42	20	13	9	90	62	53
Tranmere Rovers Res.	42	22	6	14	71	50	50
Northwich Victoria	42	22	6	14	82	64	50
Wigan Athletic	42	18	12	12	62	48	48
Stafford Rangers	42	18	11	13	88	58	47
Hyde United	42	17	12	13	97	74	46
New Brighton	42	16	10	16	60	69	42
Ellesmere Port Town	42	15	11	16	68	67	41
Runcorn	42	16	8	18	69	95	40
Wrexham Reserves	42	16	8	18	72	77	40
Buxton	42	14	8	20	71	86	36
Rhyl	42	12	10	20	83	78	34
Winsford United	42	13	7	22	50	82	33
Oswestry Town	42	13	6	23	63	106	32
Frickley Colliery	42	10	10	22	61	83	30
Stockport County Res)	42	10	7	25	55	92	27
Stalybridge Celtic	42	6	14	22	54	93	26
Chester Reserves	42	2	5	35	48	134	9

SEASON 1952-53
Lancashire Combination:

	Home	Away
Accrington Stanley Reserves	7-1	3-0
Ashton United	4-1	1-1
Barrow Reserves	2-1	2-2
Blackpool'B'	9-0	1-1
Bootle	1-0	1-1
Chorley	2-1	4-2
Clitheroe	4-0	6-3
Darwen	2-2	4-2
Fleetwood	1-1	5-1
Horwich RMI	2-0	4-4
Lancaster City	6-1	3-3
Marine	3-0	2-1
Morecambe	2-2	3-0
Nelson	1-1	2-1
Netherfield	4-2	1-0
New Brighton	6-0	1-1
Oldham Athletic Reserves	4-0	0-1
Prescot Cables	1-0	0-1
Rochdale Reserves	1-1	4-1
Rossendale United	8-0	2-2
Southport Reserves	3-2	2-1

P.	W.	D.	L.	F.	A.	W.	D.	L.	F.	A.	Pts	Pts.
42	16	5	0	73	16	11	8	2	51	29	67	Ist

League Appearances:
Banks 40;Campbell 5;Corr 34;Cunliffe 1;Gannon 2;Graham II; Hindle 41;Hughes 2;Isherwood 1;Ketley 6;Langford 3;Lindsay 40; Livesey 30; Lomas 41;Lomax 26;Lyon 31;McGeachie 13; Mycock 35;Parkes 4; Parkinson 39;Shepherd II:Williams 35; (Excludes game at Barrow Reserves)
League Scorers:
Lyon 29;Lomax 21;Livesey 21(6 pens);Lindsay 15;Corr II; Williams II;Hindle10;Banks 2;Mycock 2;Graham 1:Shepherd 1; (Total 124)

Other Results:

F.A.Cup:

4th Qual	Netherfield	Home	2-3	Corr;Lindsay;

Lancashire Combination Cup:

2nd Rd	Crompton Recs	Home	4-1	Ketley; Lindsay;Mycock;McGeachie;
3rd Rd	Prescot Cables	Home	5-1	Corr 2;Lyon 2; Williams;
4th Rd	Earlestown	Home	6-0	Livesey 3;Lomax 2; Williams;
S-F	Horwich RMI	Home	1-0	Lyon;
Final	Fleetwood	Away	3-1	Hindle;Livesey;Lomax;

Lancashire Junior Cup:

Ist Rd	Earlestown	Home	5-1	Williams 2;Corr;Lomax; Lindsay;
2nd Rd	Padiham	Home	9-1	Livesey 4;Corr 2;Banks;Hindle;Lomax;
3rd Rd	Clitheroe	Home	3-0	Livesey;LOmax;Lyon;
S-F	South Liverpool	Home	2-1	Lomax 2;
Final	Lancaster City	(Blackburn)	I - I	Livesey;
Replay	Lancaster City(	Blackburn)	2-1	Livesey(pen);Lomax;

Makerfield Cup:

Crompton Recs	Home	5-1	Lindsay 2;Graham 2; Williams;

Seasons Honours:
Lancashire Combination Champions; Lancashire Combination Cup winners
Lancashire Junior Cup winners; Makerfield Cup winners

SEASON 1953-54
Lancashire Combination:

	Home	Away
Accrington Stanley Reserves	5-1	3-1
Ashton United	3-2	0-2
Barrow Reserves	5-0	1-0
Bolton Wanderers 'B'	4-1	1-0
Chorley	1-1	3-2
Darwen	1-1	2-1
Fleetwood	5-1	2-2
Horwich RMI	2-1	3-1
Lancaster City	5-0	2-0
Marine	3-2	2-1
Morecambe	3-1	2-1
Nelson	1-2	6-1
Netherfield	3-0	2-1
New Brighton	4-0	3-2
Oldham Athletic Reserves	4-0	3-0
Prescot Cables	9-0	1-4
Rochdale Reserves	2-0	3-1
Rossendale United	0-5	1-4*
South Liverpool	2-2*	2-1
Southport Reserves	3-1	3-2

*Both played on Ist May (2nd team at home,3rd team away Ist Team rested for the Lancashire Junior Cup Final replay)

P.	W.	D.	L.	F.	A.	W.	D.	L.	F.	A.	Pts	Pos.
40	15	3	2	65	21	16	1	3	45	27	66	Ist

League Appearances:
Abram 1;Ashcroft 1;Aspinall 1;Baird 10;Banks 36;Bramwell 1;Brewer 1;Brooks 1;Butler 32;Colquhoun 1;Davies 1;Edwards 1; Ellwood 1;Grindrod 1;Hepplestall 1;Hindle 31;Hogan 4;Hyde 5; Isherwood 1;Langham 7;Larkin 2;Lee 1;Lindsay 32;Livesey 31; Lomas 37;Lomax 28;Lynn 36;Lyon 32;Mansley 5;Mason 1; Morris 1;Mycock 34;Newbury 3; Parkinson 30;Penk II; Prytherch 1;Slinger 1;Sudworth 1;A.Wilson 5; Wood 1; (Excludes game at Fletwood)
League Scorers:
Livesey 27(8 pens);Lomax 23;Lyon 22;Hindle 10;Butler 6; Lindsay 6; Banks 4;Lynn 2;Ashcroft 1;Brooks 1;Davies 1; Edwards 1;Mansley 1; Mycock 1;Penk 1;Wilson 1;
Own Goals 2; (Total 110)

Other Results:

F. A. Cuip:

4th Qual	Burscough	Home	2-1	Lomax;Mycock;
Ist Rd	Scarborough	Home	4-0	Lomax 2;Hindle;Livesey
2nd Rd	Hereford United	Home	4-1	Livesey 2;Lyon;og;
3rd Rd	Newcastle United	Away	2-2	Livesey;Lyon;
Replay	Newcastle United	Home	2-3	Lomax 2;

Lancashire Combination Cup:

2nd Rd	Earlestown	Home	5-2	Livesey 2;Banks;Lomax; Lyon;
3rd Rd	Prescot Cables	Away	2-0	Lindsay;Mycock;
4th Rd	South Liverpool	Home	4-1	Lindsay 2;Butler;Lyon;
S-F	Horwich RMI	Home	1-1	Lomax
Replay	Horwich RMI	Away	2-3	Lindsay;Lyon;

Lancashire Junior Cup:

2nd Rd	Earlestown	Home	10-1	Lomax 3;Hindle 2;;Lyon 2;Penk 2; Butler;
3rd Rd	Netherfield	Home	5-1	Lyon 3;Livesey;Penk;
S-F	Nelson	Home	3-0	Lindsay 2;Lyon;
Final	Horwich RMI (at Blackburn)		2-2	Lyon;Penk;
Replay	Horwich RMI (atChorley)		2-1	Hindle(pen);Lyon;

Makerfield Cup:

Crompton Recs	Home	7-0	Livesey 3;Hindle 2; Lomax;Lyon;

Seasons Honours:
Lancashire Combination Champions
Lancashire Junior Cup winners; Makerfield Cup winners

Season 1953/54

(Back):Colquhoun (Trainer), Parkinson, Lomas, Lindsay, Banks, Lyon, Lynn.
(Front): Butler, Liversey, Mycock, Lomax, Hindle.

Season 1955/56

(Back): Colquhoun (Train.), Greenhalgh, Parkinson, Hitchen, Appleton, Banks, Suart, Littler (Chairman). (Front): Wharton, Beattie, A.McLean, Davis, B.McLean

SEASON 1954-55
Lancashire Combination:

	Home	Away
Accrington Stanley Reserves	1-2	1-1
Ashton United	0-2	3-1
Barrow Reserves	5-1	1-1
Blackpool 'B'	1-1	1-3
Bolton Wanderers 'B'	3-2	2-0
Burscough	4-1	1-2
Chorley	4-1	2-1
Darwen	0-0	0-3
Fleetwood	0-2	1-1
Horwich RMI	2-0	0-3
Lancaster City	3-1	0-2
Marine	2-2	2-2
Morecambe	0-0	1-0
Nelson	0-0	9-4
Netherfield	2-1	1-2
New Brighton	4-2	4-1
Oldham Athletic Reserves	4-1	2-3
Rochdale Reserves	6-0	0-0
Rossendale United	4-0	3-2
South Liverpool	5-0	4-1
Southport Reserves	4-2	1-2

P.	W.	D.	L.	F.	A.	W.	D.	L.	F.	A.	Pts	Pos.
42	13	5	3	54	21	8	5	8	39	35	52	3rd

League Appearances:
K-Banks 39;Bramwell 4;Burnett 14;Corfield 26;Davis II;Gillott 5; Grainger 7;Hindle 31;Hopwood 9;Hudson 13;Lindsay 16; Livesey 4; Lomas 42;Lomax 15;Lynn 33;Lyon 27;Mycock 6; Newbury 24;Parkes 12;A.Parkinson 3;H.Parkinson 36;Penk 38; Smith 1;Vincent 23;Walsh 8: A.Wilson 5;

League Scorers:
Vincent 21;Corfield 14;Lyon 13;Hindle 12(1 pen);Burnett 6;Lomax 6;Livesey 5;Penk 5(1 pen);Hopwood 4;Banks 2;Davis 1; Lyon 1;Walsh 1; Own Goals 2;(Total 93)

Other Results:

F.A.Cup:

4th Qual	Farsley Celtic	Home	3-1	Hindle;Lomax;Vincent;
Ist Rd	Barnsley	Away	2-3	Hindle;Penk;

Lancashire Combination Cup:

2nd Rd	Stubshaw Cross	Home	12-0	Corfield 4;Vincent 3; Hindle 2; Davis;Penk; Lindsay(pen);
3rd Rd	Rochdale Reserves	Away	2-0	Lyon 2;
4th Rd	Prescot Cables	Home	1-0	Vincent;
S-F	Blackpool 'B'	Home	2-1	Corfield;Vincent;
Final	Accrington.S. Res	Away	2-2	Hindle;Vincent;
Replay	Accrington.S. Res	Home	0-2	

Makerfield Cup:

	Crompton Recs	Home	3-0	Corfield;Livesey; Vincent:

Lancashire Junior Cup:

Ist Rd	Clitheroe	Home	6-0	Lyon 3;Corfield 2(1 pen);Penk;
2nd Rd	Burscough	Home	3-1	Hindle 2(1 pen)Burnett
3rd Rd	Horwich RMI	Away	3-1	Corfield 2;Vincent;
S-F	Lancaster City	Home	0-3	

Liverpool Non-League Senior Cup:

2nd Rd	St Helens Town	Home	6-0	Livesey 3;Lyon;Vincent o.g.
S-F	Marine	Home	3-2	Davis 2;Vincent;
Final	South Liverpool	Away	3-3	Lyon;Vincent;og;
Replay	South Liverpool	Home	3-2	Banks;Davis;Vincent;

Ashton United Floodlit Competition:

Droylsden	Neutral	5-1	Hindle 3;Banks;Vincent
Macclesfield.T.	Neutral	4-1	Corfield 3;Hindle;
Hyde United	Neutral	1-6	Vincent;

Seasons Honours:; Liverpool Non-League Senior Cup winners
Makerfield Cup winners; Lancashire Combination Cup runners-up

SEASON 1955-56
Lancashire Combination:

	Home	Away
Accrington Stanley Reserves	0-4	1-1
Ashton United	0-2	1-0
Bacup Borough	6-0	0-0
Burscough	2-2	2-3
Chorley	2-3	1-4
Darwen	7-1	4-0
Fleetwood	2-0	0-3
Horwich RMI	0-0	1-4
Lancaster City	1-2	2-2
Marine	3-2	3-1
Morecambe	2-1	3-1
Nelson	2-1	0-0
Netherfield	3-1	0-1
New Brighton	1-0	4-4
Prescot Cables	2-3	3-3
Rossendale United	4-1	0-0
St Helens Town	4-1	1-1
South Liverpool	2-1	4-2
Southport Reserves	3-1	4-0

P.	W.	D.	L.	F.	A.	W.	D.	L.	F.	A.	Pts	Pos.
38	12	2	5	46	26	6	8	5	34	30	46	6th

League Appearances:
Alker 2;Appleton 10;Bailey 7;K.Banks 31;Beattie 19;Bramwell 7; Darcy 4;Davis 28;Graham 13;Greenhalgh 30;Hitchen 20;Hopwood 19; Hudson 5;Kenyon 5;Lomas 28;Lynn 9;A.McLean 26;W.McLean 33;Newbury14; Parkinson 28;Penk 6;Richardson 3;Scott 5;Smith 22;Suart 23; Sudworth 3;Vincent 7;Wharton 11;

League Scorers:
Davis 24(3 pens);Smith 17;W.McLean 14;Beattie 5;Greenhalgh 5; A.McLean 4;Graham 2;Kenyon 2;Vincent 2;Banks 1;Darcy 1; Hopwood 1; Penk 1;Richardson (Total 80)

Other Results:

F.A.Cup:

4th Qual	Ashton United	Away	0-5	

Lancashire Combination Cup:

Ist Rd	Earlestown	Home	7-0	W.McLean 3;Wharton 2; Hopwood; Smith
2nd Rd	Crompton Recs	Away	2-2	Davis(pen);og;
Replay	Crompton Recs	Home	2-2	Hitchen;Smith;
2nd Replay	Crompton Recs	Home	4-1	Hitchen 2;W.McLean; Smith;
3rd Rd	Prescot Cables	Home	9-2	W.McLean 3;Smith 3; Greenhalgh 2;Darcy;
S-F	Lytham	Home	0-0	
Replay	Lytham	Away	4-2	Smith 4;
Final Ist Leg	Netherfield	Home	3-2	Davis;Hitchen;Smith;
Final 2nd Leg	Netherfield	Away	1-3	Davis;

Makerfield Cup:

	Crompton Recs	Home	2-2	Beattie;W.McLean;

Lancashire Junior Cup:

Ist Rd	Horwich RMI	Home	4-0	W.McLean 3;Davis;
2nd Rd	Formby	Home	4-2	Greenhalgh 3;Smith;
3rd Rd	Marine	Home	2-0	Graham;Smith;
S-F	Prescot Cables	Home	1-0	Greenhalgh;
Final	Nelson	(at Blackburn)	3-1	Smith 2;Darcy;

Liverpool Non-League Senior Cup:

Ist Rd	Skelmersdale United	Home	4-1	Banks;Beattie;Vincent; Penk(pen);
2nd Rd	Burscough	Away	0-3	

Seasons Honours: Lancashire Junior Cup winners Makerfield Cup(shared)
Lancashire Combination Cup runners up

SEASON 1956-57
Lancashire Combination:

	Home	Away
Accrington Stanley Reserves	0-2	1-3
Ashton United	2-2	3-1
Bacup Borough	2-0	1-3
Burscough	1-0	1-2
Chorley	4-0	3-1
Darwen	0-1	1-4
Droylsden	4-1	5-3
Fleetwood	0-1	2-3
Horwich RMI	9-1	2-3
Lancaster City	4-2	3-0
Marine	2-3	1-0
Morecambe	2-0	0-1
Nelson	3-0	2-1
Netherfield	5-2	0-3
New Brighton	0-0	0-1
Prescot Cables	0-4	2-5
Skelmersdale United	0-1	3-0
South Liverpool	0-1	2-2
Southport Reserves	2-1	1-3

P.	W.	D.	L.	F.	A.	W.	D.	L.	F.	A.	Pts	Pos.
38	10	2	7	40	22	7	1	11	33	39	37	10th

League Appearances:
Bagwell 8;B.Banks 19;K.Banks 30;Billington 5;Birchall 1; Birkett 10;Bramwell 37;Brocklehurst 3;Darcy 8;Davis 3; Fairhurst 1;Forde 1;Holton 5;Hopwood 20;Hudson 18;Lachlan 15; Ledwith 3;Lindsay 16; Lydon 4;Lynn 8;A.McLean 21; W.McLean 31;Parkin 37;A.Prkinson 1; H.Perkinson 16;Peet 9; Porter 4;Pritchard 2;Rigby 6;Smith 28; Speakman 32;Taylor 13; Waller 3;
League Scorers:
Smith 19;K.Banks 12(1 pen);W.McLean 12(2 pens);Speakman 12(2 pens); B.Banks 7;Darcy 2(1 pen);A.McLean 2(1 pen); Bagwell 1; Billington 1;Birchall 1;Lachlan 1;Lynn 1;Pritchard 1; Own Goals 1; (Total 73)

Other Results:
F.A.Cup:

4th Qual	Netherfield	Home	2-2	Smith 2;
Replay	Netherfield	Away	3-3 (AET)	Brocklehurst; W.McLean;Speakman;
2nd Rep.	Netherfield	Home	2-0	A.McLean(pen);Smith;
Ist Rd	Goole Town	Home	1-2	A.McLean(pen);

Lancashire Combination Cup:

Ist Rd	Lomax	Home	7-0	Bramwell 2;Speakman 2; B.Banks;Smith;W.McLean
2nd Rd	Darwen	Home	2-2	Doray;Smith;
Replay	Darwen	Away	2-3	A.McLean;Speakman;

Makerfield Cup:

	Crompton Recs	Home	1-1	Speakman;
Replay	Crompton Recs	Away	2-3	Billington;Smith;

Lancashire Junior Cup:

Ist Rd	Burscough	Home	1-4	og;

Liverpool Non-League Senior Cup:

Ist Rd	New Brighton	Home	3-3	A.McLean 2(1 pen); W.McLean;
Replay	New Brighton	Away	0-4	

Seasons Honours: None

SEASON 1957-58
Lancashire Combination:

	Home	Away
Accrington Stanley Reserves	5-0	1-3
Ashton United	1-0	0-2
Bacup Borough	0-1	2-1
Burscough	1-2	1-4
Chorley	3-2	1-1
Crompton Recs	1-1	0-0
Darwen	3-1	3-1
Droylsden	2-1	0-2
Fleetwood	3-3	1-3
Horwich RMI	3-2	0-1
Lancaster City	3-2	3-0
Marine	3-0	2-2
Morecambe	1-0	1-0
Nelson	4-2	2-0
Netherfield	5-2	5-0
New Brighton	2-3	2-4
Prescot Cables	1-1	0-0
Rossendale United	4-0	2-2
Skelmersdale United	2-2	3-6
South Liverpool	5-0	5-2
Southport Reserves	8-1	1-1

P.	W.	D.	L.	F.	A.	W.	D.	L.	F.	A.	Pts	Pos.
42	14	5	2	60	25	7	6	8	35	35	53	4th

League Appearances:
Arkwright 42;Baird 15;B.Banks 27;K.Banks 3;Birchall 15; Bramwell 34;Buckle 20;Forde 14;Forsyth 17;Harrison 24; Hitchen 37;Jarvis 16 McCaig 7;McLaren 16;Newbury 14; Perkins 2;Prescott 40;Rigby 1; Rowlands 20;Smith 41; Shepherd 13;Waller 3;Whitfield 15;Whyte 26;
League Scorers:
Prescott 22;Smith 18;Buckle II;Harrison 11(6 pens); Hitchen 7;McLaren 7;Birchall 6;Jarvis 5;Bramwell 2; McCaig 1;Mewbury I(pen); Own Goals 4;(Total 95)

Other Results:
F.A.Cup:

4th Qual	Chorley	Away	2-1	B.Banks;Smith;
Ist Rd	Southport	Away	2-1	B.Banks;Buckle;
2nd Rd	Mansfield Town	Home	1-1	Hitchen;
Replay	Mansfield Town	Away	1-3	Buckle;

Lancashire Combination Cup:

Ist Rd	Darwen	Home	7-1	Smith 4;Hitchen 2; Harrison;
2nd Rd	Prescot Cables	Away	1-2	Smith;

Makerfield Cup:

	Crompton Recs	Home	10-1	Hitchen 3;Smith 3; Harrison 2;McLaren2;

Lancashire Junior Cup:

Ist Rd	Earlestown	Home	5-0	Buckle 2(1 pen); Smith 2;Prescott;
2nd Rd	Burscough	Home	0-0	
Replay	Burscough	Away	2-3	Harrison;og;

Liverpool Non-League Senior Cup:

Ist Rd	St Helens Town	Home	6-2	Prescott 3;Birchall; McLaren;Rigby(pen);
2nd Rd	Burscough	Home	2-1	Hitchen;Prescott;
Final	New Brighton	(at Anfield)	3-3	Prescott 2;Newbury(pen Smith;
Replay 1st Lg	New Brighton	Home	1-1	
Replay 2nd Lg	New Brighton	Away	0-0	

Seasons Honours: Makerfield Cup winners Liverpool Non¯League Senior Cup(shared) Lancashire Junior Cup runners-up.

Season 1956/57
(Back): Taylor, Banks, Bramwell, Parkin, Peet, Lynn, Parkinson, B.McLean, Cook (Manager).
(Front): Holton, Speakman, A.McLean, Smith, D'arcy, Colquhoun (Trainer)

Season 1957/58
(Back): Forsyth, Rowland, Arkwright, K.Banks, Bramwell, Whyte.
(Front): Harrison, Hitchen, Smith, B.Banks, McCaig.

Season 1958/59
(Back): Baker, Barrass, Houghton, Kirwen, Shepherd, Ryan.
(Front): Holt, Prescott, Smith, Birchall, Banks.

Season 1959/60
A season of near-misses. No Championship or Cups won, but runners-up in four major competitions!

SEASON 1958-59
Lancashire Combination:

	Home	Away
Ashton United	2-1	1-4
Bacup Borough	3-1	2-4
Burscough	1-1	0-1
Chorley	0-2	1-3
Clitheroe	3-2	0-3
Darwen	3-1	1-4
Droylsden	4-2	0-0
Fleetwood	0-3	0-1
Horwich RMI	2-3	1-0
Lancaster City	3-0	1-2
Marine	2-3	1-5
Morecambe	1-0	1-4
Nelson	2-1	0-0
Netherfield	4-0	0-1
New Brighton	0-0	2-2
Oldham Athletic Reserves	5-2	1-4
Prescot Cables	2-4	2-3
Rossendale United	2-5	0-2
Skelmersdale United	2-3	0-0
South Liverpool	2-0	1-2
Southport Reserves	2-2	0-3

P.	W.	D.	L.	F.	A.	W.	D.	L.	F.	A.	Pts	Pos.
42	11	3	7	45	36	1	4	16	15	48	31	18th

League Appearances:
Alker 19;Baird 5;Baker 34;B.Banks 30;K.Banks 1;Barrass 20; Bennett 18;Berrington 2;Birchall 17;Clough 14;Coulson 1; Cranwell 1; Crompton 1;Cunningham 12;Foster 8;Hibbert 1; Holt 12;Houghton 36; Jarvis 5;Kirwen 5;Knowles 2;Leaver 14; Leishing 4;Lynn 2;McMamara 3;Murphy 5;Peet 10;Perkins 3; Prescott 30;Quigley 10;Rigby 1; Roberts 1;Robinson 2; Roper 5;Ryan 15;Sedgewick 6;Sharples 1; Shepherd 36; G.Smith 8;R.Smith 7;Sudworth 1;Taberner 17;Twidle 13; Waller 9;Wring 4;(Excludes game at Rossendale United)

League Scorers:
Prescott 10;Twidle 8;Quigley 7(1 pen);Taberner 6;Barrass 5(2 pens Alker 4;Leaver 4;Birchall 3;Holt 2;McNamara 2;B.Banks 1; Berrington 1;Cunningham 1;Foster 1;Roberts 1;Shepherd 1; Waller 1; Own Goals 2;(Total 60).

Other Results:
F.A. Cup.

4th Qual	Rhyl	Away	0-1	
Lancashire Combination Cuip:				
Ist Rd	Earlestown	Home	3-0	Holt;Prescott;R.Smith;
2nd Rd	Chorley	Away	0-3	
Lancashire Junior Cup:				
Ist Rd	Crompton Recs	Home	2-2	Berrington;Leaver(pen)
Replay	Crompton Recs	Away	7-2	Taberner 6;B.Banks;
2nd Rd	Prescot Cables	Away	1-1	Twidle;
Replay	Prescot Cables	Home	1-0	B.Banks;
3rd Rd	Horwich RMI	Home	3-1	Prescott 2;Taberner:
S-F	Lytham	Home	5-1	Twidle 2;Taberner;Foster;Leaver;
Final	Chorley (at Ewood Park)		1-4	Twidle;
Liverpool Non-League Senior Cup:				
Ist Rd	Burscough	Home	3-1	Prescott 2;R.Smith;
2nd Rd	Skelmersdale United	Away	0-2	

Seasons Honours: Lancashire Junior Cup runners-up.

SEASON 1959-60
Lancashire Combination:

	Home	Away
Ashton United	5-0	1-1
Bacup Borough	5-1	2-0
Burscough	4-1	1-1
Chorley	1-4	1-4
Darwen	5-0	2-1
Earlestown	4-1	4-0
Fleetwood	1-3	1-0
Horwich RMI	3-2	3-2
Lancaster City	0-2	2-2
Lytham St Annes	2-0	1-4
Marine	4-0	1-0
Morecambe	3-0	2-0
Nelson	1-2	2-0
Netherfield	3-0	1-4
New Brighton	5-2	2-1
Oldham Athletic Reserves	0-0	2-2
Prescot Cables	1-3	1-2
Rossendale United	6-4	2-1
Skelmersdale United	8-0	1-0
South Liverpool	2-0	1-1
Southport Reserves	3-0	2-0

P.	W.	D.	L.	F.	A.	W.	D.	L.	F.	A.	Pts	Pos.
42	15	1	5	66	25	12	5	4	35	26	60	2nd

League Appearances:
Baker 13;Barton 1;Brierley 2;Brown 38;Connor 35;Corfield 23; Cunliffe 1;Egerton 6;Farrell 3;Fielding 14;Gizzi 1;Harding 3; Herron 34;Higham 29;Hitchen 1;Houghton 35;Howard 22; Jones 20;Lydon 3;McDermott 36;Mitton 1;Murphy 4;Newton 1; Porter 3;Ratcliffe 1;Richardson 34;Riley 2;Savage 4;Simm 4; Taberner 29;Turner 7;Twidle 34;Vizard 10;Waller 8;
League Scorers:
Higham 20;Twidle 20;Taberner 18;McDermott ll;Corfield 6; Turner 6; Fielding 5(1 pen);Vizard 5;Waller 3;Connor 2;Brown 1; Lydon 1; Riley 1;Own Goals 2;(Total 101)

Other Results:
F.A.Cup:

4th Qual	Rhyl	Home	1-1	Higham;
Replay	Rhyl	Away	1-3	AET Higham;
Lancashire Combination Cup):				
Ist Rd	Crompton Recs	Home	6-1	Higham 2;McDermott 2; Corfield; Turner;
2nd Rd	Marine	Home	1-1	Fielding;
Replay	Marine	Away	6-1	Higham 2;Houghton(pen) Fielding;Lydon;Twidle;
3rd Rd	Morecambe	Home	2-2	Fielding;Higham;
Replay	Morecambe	Away	1-0	McDermott;
S-F	Chorley	Home	2-0	Houghton;McDermott;
Final	Nelson	Away	0-1	
Lancashire Junior Cup:				
Ist Rd	Earlestown	Home	8-0	Higham 3;Taberner 2;Twidle 2;og;
2nd Rd	South Liverpool	Home	4-1	McDermott 2;Taberner; og;
3rd Rd	Marine	Home	3-3	Taberner 2;McDermott;
S-F	Fleetwood	Home	2-0	Higham;Houghton(pen);
Final	Chorley (at Ewood Park)		2-1	Herron;Taberner;
Liverpool Non-League Senior Cup:				
Ist Rd	Wigan Rovers	Home	4-1	Higham 3;McDermott;
2nd Rd	Prescot Cables	Home	6-0	Higham 2;Connor; McDermott;Twidle;og;
Final	New Brighton (at Anfield)		0-2	

Seasons Honours: Lancashire Combination runners-up
Lancashire Junior Cup winners; Lancashire Combination Cup runners-up;
Liverpool Non-League Senior Cup runners-up.

Season 1960/61

(Back): Hayes, D.Houghton, Connor, Richardson, Rooke, Ball, Birkett (Trainer)
(Front): Turner, Prescott, Taberner, Twidle, Fielding.

Season 1961/62

(Back): Ball (Manager), Tucker, Prescott, Richardson, Higgins, Houghton, Connor, Birkett (Trainer).
(Front): O'Loughlin, Lambert, Williams, Booth, Shaw.

SEASON 1960-61
Lancashire Combination:

	Home	Away
Ashton United	6-1	2-2
Bacup Borough	3-1	4-4
Burscough	0-2	1-2
Chorley	1-4	1-0
Clitheroe	4-1	3-0
Darwen	4-0	4-0
Droylsden	2-2	4-0
Earlestown	6-0	3-0
Fleetwood	3-0	4-3
Horwich RMI	5-1	1-0
Lancaster City	0-0	2-2
Lytham St Annes	1-0	6-5
Marine	4-2	0-2
Morecambe	3-2	1-2
Nelson	0-0	2-1
Netherfield	2-1	2-4
New Brighton	1-3	1-1
Oldham Athletic Reserves	2-0	2-3
Prescot Cables	1-0	3-1
Rossendale United	6-0	3-3
Skelmersdale United	5-0	0-1

P.	W.	D.	L.	F.	A.	W.	D.	L.	F.	A.	Pts	Pos.
42	15	3	3	59	20	10	5	6	49	36	58	3rd

League Appearances:
Ball 5;Bamforth 6;Barber 21;Birkett 1;Connor 20;Crank 3;Crompton 12; Fairclough 4;Fielding 5;Hall 6;Hazelden 26;Herron 31;Heyes 31; Houghton 28;Hughes 1;Jones 21;Lydon 10;McDermott 2;Mosby 1; Newton 14;Prescott 28;Richardson 29;Rooke 6;Roper 20;Shaw 24;Taberner 36 Taylor 2;Turner 10;Twidle 31;Waller 9;Webb 19;

League Scorers:
Hazelden 23;Taberner 21;Twidle 14(2 pens);Webb 7;Lydon 5;Newton 5 Prescott 4;Shaw 4;Waller 4;Barber 3;Fielding 3;Herron 2;Heyes 2 (pens);Turner 2;Bamforth 1;Houghton l(pen;Hughes 1;McDermott 1; Rooke 1;
Own Goals 3;(Total 108)

Other Results:

F.A.Cup:

Prelim Rd	Prescot Cables	Home	2-0	Fielding;Taberner;
Ist Qual	Ashton United	Home	3-2	Hazelden;Houghton(pen);Taberner;
2nd Qual	Marine	Away	5-1	Hazelden 2;Taberner;Heyes;Shaw;
3rd Qual	Skelmersdale United	Away	0-0	
Replay	Skelmersdale United	Home	2-1	Hazelden;Taberner;
4th Qual	Rhyl	Home	1-1	Prescott;
Replay	Rhyl	Away	1-2	Prescott;

Lancashire Combination Cup.

Ist Rd	Earlestown	Home	4-4	Hazelden 2;Lydon;Shaw;
Replay	Earlestown	Away	6-2	Hazelden 2;Shaw 2; Houghton(pen);Lydon;
2nd Rd	Fleetwood	Home	4-1	Hazelden 2(1 pen); Connor;Taberner;
3rd Rd	Chorley	Away	0-0	
Replay	Chorley	Home	2-3	Prescott;Waller;

Lancashire Junior Cup:

Ist Rd	Prescot Cables	Home	2-1	Twidle 2;
2nd Rd	Crompton Recs	Away	4-0	Bamforth 2;Hazelden; Webb;
3rd Rd	Morecambe	Home	1-1	Taberner;
Replay	Morecambe	Away	0-1	

Liverpool Non-League Senior Cup:

Ist Rd	Wigan Rovers	Home	4-2	Twidle 2;Fielding; Taberner;
2nd Rd	South Liverpool	Home	1-1	AET Twidle(pen);
Replay	South Liverpool	Away	1-3	Waller;

Seasons Honours: None.

SEASON 1961-62
Cheshire League:

	Home	Away
Altrincham	2-4	0-0
Bangor City	3-1	1-2
Buxton	1-0	4-1
Chester Reserves	4-0	2-1
Congleton Town	4-0	3-1
Ellesmere Port Town	1-1	2-2
Frickley Colliery	6-1	0-1
Hyde United	3-0	1-1
Macclesfield Town	2-1	2-1
Mossley	1-5	3-5
Northwich Victoria	4-1	0-3
Oswestry Town	3-0	2-1
Rhyl	0-0	1-2
Runcorn	2-1	1-3
Sankeys of Wellington	0-0	1-0
Stafford Rangers	4-0	0-1
Stalybridge Celtic	2-0	2-1
Tranmere Rovers Reserves	5-0	2-2
Winsford United	4-3	2-4
Witton Albion	0-1	2-0
Wrexham Reserves	3-0	1-0

P.	W.	D.	L.	F.	A.	W.	D.	L.	F.	A.	Pts	Pos.
42	15	3	3	54	19	9	4	8	32	32	55	5th

League Appearances:
Arnold 25;Booth 12;Briars 35;Campbell 2;Connor 29;Crank 12; Eastham 4;Gregory 3;Higgins 38;Higham 31;Houghton 29; Lambert 36; Newton 3;J.O'Loughlin 2;W.O'Loughlin 40; Prescott 37;Richardson 38;Roper 22:Schofield 18;Shaw 15; Tucker 23;Williams 8;

League Scorers:
Higham 26;W.O'Loughlin ll;Arnold 8;Booth 7;Lambert 6;Shaw 6; Schofield 5;Briars 4(all pens);Williams 4;Prescott 3;Roper 2; Tucker 2;Houghton l(pen);Own Goals 1;(Total 86)

Other Results:

F.A.Cuip

Ist Qual	Skelmersdale United	Away	4-0	Lambert 2;Prescott; Shaw;
2nd Qual	Prescot Cables	Home	1-1	Campbell;
Replay	Prescot Cables	Away	3-1	J.O'Loughlin;Williams; W.O'Loughlin;
3rd Qual	Altrincham	Away	1-1	Booth;
Replay	Altrincham	Home	3-1	Booth;W.O'Loughlin; Campbell;
4th Qual	Morecambe	Away	0-2	

Lancashire Junior Cup:

Ist Rd	Crompton Recs	Home	3-1	Briars(pen);Tucker; W.O'Loughlin;
2nd Rd	Metherfield	Away	2-1	Higham 2;
3rd Rd	Chorley	Away	0-0	
Replay	Chorley	Home	1-0 (AET)	Higham;
S-F	New Brighton	Home	3-0	Higham 2;W.O'Loughlin:
Final	Morecambe	(at Deepdale)	1-3	Lambert;

Inter League Cup:

Ist Rd	Lancaster City	Away	0-2	

Liverpool Non-League Senior Cup:

Ist Rd	Skelmersdale United	Home	4-1	Briars 2;W.O'Loughlin; Booth;
S-F	Burscough	Away	4-0	Higham 2;Arnold; Schofield;
Final	New Brighton	(at Anfield)	0-2	

Seasons Honours: Lancashire Junior Cup runners-up
Liverpool Non-League Senior Cup runners-up

SEASON 1962-63
Cheshire League:

	Home	Away
Altrincham	0-0	0-2
Bangor City	3-2	2-3
Buxton	3-1	1-2
Chester Reserves	1-1	3-2
Congleton Town	4-0	1-2
Ellesmere Port Town	3-0	3-1
Frickley Colliery	2-0	1-0
Hyde United	1-0	2-1
Macclesfield Town	1-2	2-2
Mossley	3-1	3-1
Northwich Victoria	4-0	1-1
Oswestry Town	2-0	1-0
Rhyl	3-1	0-1
Runcorn	1-2	2-3
Sankeys of Wellington	2-1	3-6
Stafford Rangers	1-0	3-0
Stalybridge Celtic	1-0	0-1
Tranmere Rovers Reserves	1-0	0-1
Winsford United	0-0	0-1
Witton Albion	2-1	1-5
Wrexham Reserves	3-3	1-4

P.	W.	D.	L.	F.	A.	W.	D.	L.	F.	A.	Pts	Pos.
42	15	4	2	41	15	7	2	12	30	39	50	7th

League Appearances:
Arnold 8;Ashurst 4;Bradbury 27;Briars 33;Crank 22;Edmundson 21; Evans 1;Glover 7;Gregory 9;Hennin 38;Higgins 39;Hill 1; Houghton 39;Kinsella 32;Lyon 39;Morgans 40;Nightingale 2; W.O'Loughlin 37; Richardson 35;Roper 19;Schofield 8;Smith 2; Swindells 1;

League Scorers:
Lyon 22;Bradbury 13(3 pens);Kinsella 12;Morgans 10; W.O'Loughlin 6 Houghton 2(1 pen);Arnold 1;Briars 1;Glover 1; Hennin 1;Higgins 1; Schofield 1;(Total 71)

Other Results:

F.A.Cup:

Ist Qual	Corinthians	Home	5-0	Bradbury;Kinsella;og; Hennin;Lyon;
2nd Qual	Fleetwood	Home	8-1	Lyon 2;Morgans 2;og; Garrett; W.O'Loughlin; Kinsella;
3rd Qual	Netherfield	Away	3-0	Lyon 3;
4th Qual	Ellesmere Port T.	Home	2-0	Lyon 2;
Ist Rd	Gateshead	Away	1-2	Bradbury;

Lancashire Junior Cup:

Ist Rd	Marine	Home	1-0	W.O'Loughlin;
2nd Rd	Accrington Stanley	Away	2-1	AET Kinsella;Lyon;
3rd Rd	Lancaster City	Away	3-0	Morgans 2;Kinsella;
S-F	Morecambe	Home	1-2	AET Kinsella;

Inter-League Cup:

Ist Rd	Nelson	Home	3-0	Bradbury;Lyon;og;
2nd Rd	Bacup Borough	Home	4-0	Lyon 2;W.O'Loughlin; Bradbury;
3rd Rd	Horwich RMI	Home	2-0	Hennin;Houghton;
4th Rd	Ashton United	Away	2-0	Morgans;W.O'Loughlin;
S-F	Macclesfield Town	Home	2-1	Kinsella;Lyon;
Final Ist Leg	Winsford United	Away	2-3	Houghton;Lyon;
Final 2nd Leg	Winsford United	Home	0-1	

Liverpool Non-League Senior Cup:

Ist Rd	Earlestown	Home	4-0	Kinsella 2;Bradbury; Lyon;
S-F	Skelmersdale United	Home	3-0	Morgans 2;Lyon;
Final	South Liverpool	Home	1-0	Kinsella;

Seasons Honours: Liverpool Non-League Senior Cup winners
Inter League Cup runners-up

SEASON 1963-64
Cheshire League:

	Home	Away
Altrincham	2-1	1-3
Bangor City	0-1	0-1
Buxton	0-0	1-3
Chester Reserves	4-0	2-1
Congleton Town	5-2	1-1
Ellesmere Port Town	1-1	1-2
Frickley Colliery	4-5	2-2
Hyde United	3-1	1-0
Macclesfield Town	1-4	2-4
Mossley	2-4	1-0
Northwich Victoria	3-2	0-1
Oswestry Town	2-3	2-1
Rhyl	4-5	0-2
Runcorn	3-1	1-5
Sankeys of Wellington	3-0	1-1
Stafford Rangers	8-2	3-2
Stalybridge Celtic	2-3	3-2
Tranmere Rovers Reserves	4-3	0-5
Winsford United	9-0	2-2
Witton Albion	2-3	1-1
Wrexham Reserves	4-1	3-1

P.	W.	D.	L.	F.	A.	W.	D.	L.	F.	A.	Pts	Pos.
42	11	2	8	66	42	7	5	9	28	40	43	12th

League Appearances:
Allen 8;Atherton 4;Bimpson 5;Briars 41;Brown 3;Crank 23;Edmondson 15;Glover 22;Gornall 16;Gregory 4;Grundy 10;Houghton 34;Lyon 40; McKay 17;Morgans 30;Murdoch 33;Neill 35;Roper 26;Seddon 26; Sleight 16;Stewart 17;Welsh 22;Wilson 15;

League Scorers:
Lyon 32(1 pen);Murdoch 13;Morgans 10(1 pen);Welsh 7; Brown 5(1 pen), Houghton 5(1 pen);Neill 5;Edmondson 4; Sleight 4;Bimpson 2;Roper 2;Glover 1; Gornall 1;Grundy 1; Seddon 1;Own Goals 1;(Total 94)

Other Results:

F.A.Cup:

4th Qual	Bangor City	Home	1-1	Morgans;
Replay	Bangor City	Away	0-1	

Cheshire League Cup:

2nd Rd	Stafford Rangers	Away	2-0	Houghton;Morgans;
3rd Rd	Stalybridge Celtic	Away	1-2	Lyon;

Lancashire Junior Cup:

Ist Rd	Wigan Rovers	Home	7-0	Murdoch 3;Morgans 2; Edmondson;Sleight;
2nd Rd	Ashton United	Home	2-1	Houghton;og;
3rd Rd	Netherfield	Away	1-4	Edmondson;

Liverpool Non-League Senior Cup:

Ist Rd	Burscough	Home	2-1	Lyon 2;
2nd Rd	New Brighton	Away	0-2	

Seasons Honours:
None

Season 1963/64
(Back): Briars, Neill, Seddon, McKay, D.Houghton, Crank.
(Front): Wilson, Morgans, Lyon, Murdoch, Sleight.

Season 1964/65
(Back): Wilkinson, Crompton, Barrett, D.Houghton, Gubbins, Crank.
(Front): Campbell, Davenport, Lyon, Brown, Grundy

SEASON 1964-65
Cheshire League:

	Home	Away
Altrincham	1-2	1-0
Bangor City	4-3	0-0
Buxton	5-0	4-0
Chester Reserves	6-2	0-2
Congleton Town	8-1	2-1
Ellesmere Port Town	2-1	3-1
Frickley Colliery	2-0	4-1
Hyde United	3-0	3-0
Macclesfield Town	1-3	2-2
Mossley	4-1	2-0
Northwich Victoria	1-0	3-2
Oswestry Town	3-0	1-3
Rhyl	4-2	2-0
Runcorn	2-1	3-1
Sankeys of Wellington	3-0	1-1
Stafford Rangers	8-0	2-0
Stalybridge Celtic	4-0	3-2
Tranmere Rovers Reserves	2-3	2-4
Winsford United	3-1	4-1
Witton Albion	4-0	0-5
Wrexham Reserves	5-0	3-0

P.	W.	D.	L.	F.	A.	W.	D.	L.	F.	A.	Pts	Pos.
42	18	0	3	76	20	14	3	4	45	26	67	Ist

League Appearances:
Barratt 8;Brown 35;Campbell 41;Craig 21;Crank 12;Crompton 41;Davenport 39;Gornall 2;Grundy 25;Gubbins 30;Halsall 34; Hart 3;D.Houghton 42;S.Houghton 15;Johnstone 1;Lyon 41; Murdoch 7;Roper 7;Stanley 20;Wilkinson 38;

League Scorers:
Lyon 45;Davenport 33;Brown 12;Gubbins 7(6 pens);Crompton 3; Grundy 3;Murdoch 3;Campbell 2;D.Houghton 2;Stanley 2;Own Goals 9; (Total 121)

Other Results:

F.A.Cup:

4th Qual	Stalybridge Celtic	Away	4-2	Davenport 2;Lyon 2;
Ist Rd	Stockport County	Away	1-2	Lyon;

Cheshire League Cup:

Ist Rd	Hyde United	Home	2-1	Gubbins(pen);Lyon;
2nd Rd	Frickley Colliery	Home	7-0	Lyon 5;Campbell; Davenport;
3rd Rd	Bangor City	Home	2-0	Davenport;Lyon;
S-F	Winsford United	Away	3-0	Campbell;Davenport; Lyon;
Final	Runcorn	Home	1-1	Lyon;
Final	Runcorn	Away	2-2	(AET) Davenport;Lyon;

Lancashire Junior Cup:

Ist Rd	Earlestown	Home	3-0	Lyon 2;Crompton;
2nd Rd	Darwen	Away	7-0	Crompton 3;Davenport 3 Brown;
3rd Rd	Ashton United	Home	1-1	Campbell;
Replay	Ashton United	Away	3-1	Brown 2;Lyon;
S-F	Netherfield	Home	1-1	Brown;
Replay	Netherfield	Away	2-1	Lyon;Stanley;
Final	Chorley (at Deepdale)		1-4	Lyon;

Liverpool Non-League Senior Cup:

Ist Rd	Prescot Cables	Away	1-1	AET Murdoch
Replay	Prescot Cables	Home	5-1	Hickson 2;Johnstone; Grundy;Stanley;
S-F	Burscough	Home	2-1	Davenport;Wilkinson;
Final Ist Leg	New Brighton	Away	3-0	Davenport;Lyon; Murdoch;
Final 2nd Leg	New Brighton	Home	3-3	Lyon 2;Davenport;

Seasons Honours: Cheshire League Champions; Liverpool Non-League Senior Cup winners: Cheshire League Cup winners; Lancashire Junior Cup runners-up

SEASON 1965-66
Cheshire League:

	Home	Away
Altrincham	1-1	2-2
Bangor City	4-2	2-2
Buxton	4-3	1-1
Chester Reserves	7-1	4-0
Ellesmere Port Town	1-1	5-4
Frickley Colliery	7-0	3-2
Hyde United	5-1	1-1
Macclesfield Town	0-0	1-0
Mossley	3-0	3-2
New Brighton	7-0	2-1
Northwich Victoria	4-0	0-1
Oswestry Town	7-1	2-1
Rhyl	4-0	5-2
Runcorn	4-0	5-1
Stafford Rangers	3-1	6-1
Stalybridge Celtic	2-0	1-0
Stockport County Reserves	4-0	0-3
Tranmere Rovers Reserves	4-0	3-0
Winsford United	4-0	3-0
Witton Albion	1-1	3-1
Wrexham Reserves	3-2	2-1

P.	W.	D.	L.	F.	A.	W.	D.	L.	F.	A.	Pts	Pos.
42	17	4	0	79	14	15	4	2	54	26	72	2nd

League Appearances:
Barratt 3;Brown 22;Cairns 4;Craig 42;Crompton 40;Darbyshire 1; Grundy 8;Halsall 34;Hart 4;Heath 5;D.Houghton 34; S. Houghton14; Lace 12;Llewellyn 39;Lyon 41;Roberts 42; Ryan 37;Stanley 38; Wilkinson 42;

League Scorers:
Llewellyn 49(7 pens);Lyon 42;Stanley 10(1 pen);Crompton 7; Ryan 5; Brown 4;Roberts 4;Cairns 2(1 pen);D.Houghton 2;Lace 2; Craig 1;Grundy 1;S.Houghton 1;Own Goals 3;(Total 133).

Other Results:

F.A.Cup:

4th Qual	Chorley	Home	4-0	Lyon 3;Llewellyn;
Ist Rd	Doncaster Rovers	Away	1-1	Lyon;
Replay	Doncaster Rovers	Home	3-1	Lyon 3;
2nd Rd	Chester	Away	1-2	Llewellyn;

Cheshire League Cup:

Ist Rd	Tranmere Rovs Res	Home	1-0	Llewellyn;
2nd Rd	Chester Reserves	Away	1-1	Lyon;
Replay	Chester Reserves	Home	2-0	Lyon 2;
3rd Rd	Stalybridge Celtic	Home	4-1	S.Houghton;Llewellyn; Lyon;Lace;
S-F	Macclesfield Town	Away	1-0	Roberts;
Final Ist Leg	Altrincham	Home	3-1	D.Houghton;Llewellyn; Roberts;
Final 2nd Leg	Altrincham	Away	2-0	Brown;Roberts;

Lancashire Junior Cup:

Ist Rd	Fleetwood	Home	2-1	Lyon;Ryan;
2nd Rd	Horwich RMI	Home	2-2	D.Houghton;Llewellyn;
Replay	Horwich RMI	Away	5-0	Lyon 2;D.Houghton; Brown;Llewellyn;
S-F	Morecambe	Away	2-0	Lyon;Ryan;
Final	Netherfield (at Morecambe)		2-0	S.Houghton;Roberts;

Liverpool Non-League Senior Cup:

Ist Rd	New Brighton	Home	3-1	Llewellyn;Lyon;Grundy;
S-F	Guinness Exports	Home	2-0	Lyon 2;
Final	Sth Liverpool(Southport)		2-0	AET Lyon;Roberts;

Seasons Honours:
Edward Case Cup(League) runners-up Cheshire League Cup winners
Lancashire Junior Cup winners; Liverpool Non-League Senior Cup winners

Season 1965/66

(Back): Birchall, Ball, Hitchen, L.Jackson, Bold, Whitter, H.Jackson (Dirs.) Parkinson (Trainer) (Middle): Banks (Train.) D.Houghton, Roberts, S.Houghton, Halsall, Crompton, Wilkinson, Craig, Birkett (Train.) Front: Ryan, Llewellyn, Lyon, Brown, Stanley.

Season 1968/69

(Back): Birkett (Train.), Ryan, McLoughlin, Sutherland, Gaskell, Cairney, Sealey, Shaw. (Front): Gillibrand, Turner, Lynn, McNeill (Manager), Hill, Cairns, Sykes.

SEASON 1966-67
Cheshire League:

	Home	Away
Altrincham	0-2	1-2
Bangor City	5-0	1-4
Buxton	4-0	0-2
Chester Reserves	2-2	3-3
Ellesmere Port Town	6-2	2-2
Frickley Colliery	6-2	0-4
Hyde United	3-1	1-5
Macclesfield Town	0-0	1-6
Mossley	2-1	2-1
New Brighton	2-1	2-1
Northwich Victoria	4-2	2-2
Oswestry Town	1-0	2-1
Rhyl	6-1	2-1
Runcorn	4-3	2-0
Stafford Rangers	1-1	2-2
Stalybridge Celtic	2-0	1-0
Stockport County Reserves	5-1	3-2
Trarimere Rovers Reserves	1-1	5-0
Winsford United	6-0	2-0
Witton Albion	2-0	0-2
Wrexham Reserves	3-0	2-1

P.	W.	D.	L.	F.	A.	W.	D.	L.	F.	A.	Pts	Pos.
42	16	4	1	65	20	10	4	7	36	41	60	2nd

League Appearances:
Allen 2;Brown 5(2);Craig 41;Crompton 40;Grundy 17(2); Halsall 40; Hayes 28(4);D.Houghton 38;S.Houghton 33(4); Howard 3;Jenkins 0(2); Lace 20(3);Lewis 6(2);Llewellyn 40; Lyon 33;Pearson 2(3);Roberts 31;Ryan 38(1);Smith 0(1); Stanley 15(2);Wilkinson 28;

League Scorers:
Llewellyn 28(1 pen);Lyon 27;Lace 8;Hayes 7(1 pen);Roberts 7; Crompton 6;Stanley 4;Lewis 3;Grundy 2;S.Houghton 2; Brown 1; D.Houghton 1;Pearson 1;Ryan 1;Own Goals 3; (Total 101)

Other Results:

F.A.Cup:

4th Qual	Altrincham	Away	4-2	Llewellyn 2;Lyon;Ryan;
Ist Rd	Tranmere Rovers	Away	1-1	Lyon;
Replay	Tranmere Rovers	Home	0-1	

Cheshire League Cup:

Ist Rd	Altrincham	Home	1-0	Crompton;
2nd Rd	Wrexham Reserves	Home	4-1	Llewellyn 2;Hayes;Lyon
3rd Rd	Runcorn	Away	0-0	
Replay	Runcorn	Home	0-1	

Lancashire Senior Cup:

Ist Rd	Preston North End	Home	1-2	Llewellyn;

Lancashire Junior Cup:

2nd Rd	Burscough	Away	1-1	Roberts;
Replay	Burscough	Home	1-2	Roberts;

Liverpool Non-League Senior Cup

Ist Rd	St Helens Town	Home	5-2 (AET)	Smith 2;Stanley 2; Jenkins;
S-F	Burscough	Away	3-1 (AET)	Roberts;Stanley; S.Houghton;
Final	Skelmersdale United	Away	2-0	Llewellyn;Lyon;

Lancashire Floodlit Cup:

Ist Rd Ist Lg	Ashton United	Away	1-2	Grundy;
Ist Rd 2nd Lg	Ashton United	Home	9-1	Houghton2;Llewellyn;Ryan; Lyon;Wilkinson;Stanley;Crompton;og;
S-F Ist Leg	Chorley	Away	1-2	Llewellyn;
S-F 2nd Leg	Chorley	Home	2-1	Lace;Hayes(pen);
Replay	Chorley	Away	2-0	D.Houghton 2;(I pen);
Final Ist Leg	Morecambe	Away	0-1	
Final 2nd Leg	Morecambe	Home	2-0	Llewellyn;Lyon;

Seasons Honours: Cheshire League runners-up Lancashire Floodlit Cup winners Liverpool Non-League Senior Cup winners ; Northern Floodlit League and Cup

SEASON 1967-68
Cheshire League:

	Home	Away
Altrincham	0-3	0-1
Bangor City	3-0	0-1
Buxton	0-2	2-1
Chester Reserves	2-0	1-0
Ellesmere Port	1-1	1-1
Frickley Colliery	1-2	1-0
Hyde United	3-0	2-2
Macclesfield Town	1-1	1-4
Mossley	1-0	1-2
New Brighton	1-1	1-1
Northwich Victoria	2-1	0-3
Oswestry Town	3-0	2-1
Rhyl	3-1	1-1
Runcorn	6-2	1-1
Stafford Rangers	3-3	0-3
Stalybridge Celtic	1-0	4-0
Stockport County Reserves	1-1	0-0
Tranmere Rovers Reserves	0-1	1-2
Winsford United	3-1	3-0
Witton Albion	1-1	0-2
Wrexham Reserves	1-0	3-1

P.	W.	D.	L.	F.	A.	W.	D.	L.	F.	A.	Pts	Pos.
42	11	6	4	37	21	7	6	8	25	27	48	8th

League Appearances:
Blundell 35;Brown 3;Cairns 4;Craig 22;Dumican 23(2);Durrant 15; Floyd 2;Gillibrand 3;Grundy 7(2);Halsall 42;Holden 5(1); D.Houghton 33;A.Jones 28;P.Jones 30;Lace 26(3);Llewellyn 35(1); Lyon 28(1);McLoughlin 7;Melling 10;Partridge 4;Roberts 27;Ryan 9; Sandiford 21;Sandilands 12;Sealey 6; Swarbrick 0(1);Sykes 7; Wilkinson 18(1);

League Scorers:
Llewellyn 19;Sandiford 7;Lace 6;Lyon 6;Blundell 5;D.Houghton 5(4 pens); Roberts 3;McLoughlin 2;Dumican 1; Durrant 1;Grundy 1; Holden 1;Melling 1;Sealey 1;Wilkinson 1; Own Goals 2;(Total 62)

Other Results:

F.A.Cup:

4th Qual	Macclesfield Town	Home	1-1	Dumican
Replay	Macclesfield Town	Away	0-3	

Cheshire League Cup:

Ist Rd	Stockport Reserves	Away	2-1	Holden;Lace;
2nd Rd	Runcorn	Home	2-3	Lyon;Llewellyn;

Lancashire Senior Cup:

2nd Rd	Bury	Home	1-1	Smith
Replay	Bury	Away	0-3	

Lancashire Junior Cup:

Ist Rd	Rossendale United	Home	5-2	Dumican 2;Lyon 2; Llewellyn;
2nd Rd	Ashton United	Home	7-0	Lyon 3;Llewellyn 2; Durrant(pen)Sandilands
3rd Rd	Fleetwood	Away	1-0	Llewellyn;
S-F	St Helens Town	Home	1-0	Llewellyn;
F inal	Marine (at Prescot)		2-0	Blundell;P.Jones;

Lancashire Floodlit Cup:

2ndRd Ist Leg	New Brighton	Home	2-1	Sandiford 2;
2ndRd 2nd Leg	New Brighton	Away	1-3	Sandiford;

Seasons Honours: Lancashire Junior Cup winners.

FINAL LEAGUE TABLES: 1968/69 - 1977/78

Northern Premier League: 1968/69

Macclesfield Town	38	27	6	5	82	38	60
Wigan Athletic	38	18	12	8	59	41	48
Morecambe	38	16	14	8	64	37	46
Gainsborough Trinity	38	19	8	11	64	43	46
South Shields	38	19	8	11	78	56	46
Bangor City	38	18	9	11	102	64	45
Hyde United	38	16	10	12	71	65	42
Goole Town	38	15	10	13	80	78	40
Altrincham	38	14	10	14	69	52	38
Fleetwood d	38	16	6	16	58	58	38
Gateshead	38	14	9	15	42	48	37
South Liverpool	38	12	13	13	56	66	37
Northwich Victoria	38	16	5	17	59	82	37
Boston United	38	14	8	16	59	65	36
Runcorn	38	12	11	15	59	63	35
Netherfield	38	12	4	22	51	69	28
Scarborough	38	9	10	19	49	68	28
Ashington,	38	10	8	20	48	74	28
Chorley	38	8	9	21	46	75	25
Worksop Town	38	6	8	24	34	88	20

Northern Premier League: 1969170

Macclesfield Town	38	22	8	8	72	41	52
Wigan Athletic	38	20	12	6	56	32	52
Boston United	38	21	8	9	65	33	50
Scarborough	38	20	10	8	74	39	50
South Shields	38	19	7	12	66	43	45
Gainsborough Trinity	38	16	11	11	64	49	43
Stafford Rangers	38	16	7	15	59	52	39
Bangor City	38	15	9	14	68	63	39
Northwich Victoria	38	15	8	15	60	66	38
Netherfield	38	14	9	15	56	54	37
Hyde United	38	15	7	16	59	59	37
Altrincham	38	14	8	16	62	65	36
Fleetwood	38	13	10	15	53	60	36
Runcorn	38	11	13	14	57	72	35
Morecambe	38	10	13	15	41	51	33
South Liverpool	38	11	11	16	44	55	33
Great Harwood	38	10	9	19	63	92	29
Matlock Town.	38	8	12	18	52	67	28
Goole Town	38	10	6	22	50	71	26
Gateshead	38	5	12	21	37	94	22

Northern Premier League: 1970/71

Wigan Athletic	42	27	13	2	91	32	67
Stafford Rangers	42	27	7	8	87	51	61
Scarborough	42	23	12	7	83	40	58
Boston United	42	22	12	8	69	31	56
Macclesfield Town	42	23	10	9	84	45	56
Northwich Victoria	42	22	5	15	71	55	49
Bangor City	42	19	10	13	72	61	48
Altrincham	42	19	10	13	50	76	48
South Liverpool	42	15	15	12	67	57	45
Chorley	42	14	14	14	58	61	42
Gainsborough Trinity	42	15	11	16	65	63	41
Morecambe	42	14	11	17	67	79	39
South Shields	42	12	14	16	67	66	38
Bradford (P.A.)	42	15	8	19	54	73	38
Lancaster City	42	12	12	18	53	76	36
Netherfield	42	13	9	20	59	57	35
Matlock Town	42	10	13	19	58	80	33
Fleetwood	42	10	11	21	56	90	31
Great Harwood	42	8	13	21	66	98	29
Runcorn	42	10	5	27	58	84	25
Kirkby Town	42	6	13	23	57	93	25
Goole Town	42	10	4	28	44	98	24

Northern Premier League: 1971/72

Stafford Rangers	46	30	11	5	91	32	71
Boston United	46	28	13	5	87	37	69
Wigan Athletic	46	27	10	9	70	43	64
Scarborough	46	21	15	10	75	46	57
Northwich Victoria	46	20	14	12	65	59	54
Macclesfield Town	46	18	15	13	61	50	51
Gainsborough Trinity	46	21	9	16	93	79	51
South Shields	46	18	14	14	75	57	50
Bangor City	46	20	8	18	93	74	48
Altrincham	46	18	11	17	72	58	47
Skelmersdale United	46	19	9	18	61	58	47
Matlock Town	46	20	7	19	67	75	47
Chorley	46	17	12	17	66	59	46
Lancaster City	46	15	14	17	85	84	44
Great Harwood	46	15	14	17	60	74	44
Ellesmere Port Town	46	17	9	20	67	71	43
Morecambe	46	15	10	21	51	64	40
Bradford (P.A.)	46	13	13	20	54	71	39
Netherfield	46	16	5	25	51	73	37
Fleetwood	46	11	15	20	43	67	37
South Liverpool	46	12	12	22	61	73	36
Runcorn	46	8	14	24	48	80	30
Goole Town	46	9	10	27	51	97	28
Kirkby Town	46	6	12	28	38	104	24

Northern Premier League: 1972/73

Boston United	46	27	16	3	88	34	70
Scarborough	46	26	9	11	72	39	61
Wigan Athletic	46	23	14	9	69	38	60
Altrincham	46	22	16	8	75	55	60
Bradford (P.A.)	46	19	17	10	63	50	55
Stafford Rangers	46	20	11	15	63	46	51
Gainsborough Trinity	46	18	13	15	70	50	49
Northwich Victoria	46	17	15	14	74	62	49
Netherfield	46	20	9	17	68	65	49
Macclesfield Town	46	16	16	14	58	47	48
Ellesmere Port Town	46	18	11	17	52	56	47
Skelmersdale United	46	15	16	15	58	59	46
Bangor City	46	16	13	17	70	60	45
Mossley	46	17	11	18	70	73	45
Morecambe	46	17	11	18	62	70	45
Great Harwood	46	14	15	17	63	74	43
South Liverpool	46	12	19	15	47	57	43
Runcorn	46	15	12	19	75	78	42
Goole Town	46	13	13	20	64	73	39
South Shields	46	17	4	25	64	81	38
Matlock Town	46	11	11	24	42	80	33
Lancaster City	46	10	11	25	53	78	31
Barrow	46	12	6	28	52	101	30
Fleetwood	46	5	15	26	31	77	25

Northern Premier League: 1973/74

Boston United	46	27	11	8	69	32	65
Wigan Athletic	46	28	8	10	96	39	64
Altrincham	46	26	11	9	77	34	63
Stafford Rangers	46	27	9	10	101	45	63
Scarborough	46	22	14	10	62	43	58
South Shields	46	25	6	15	87	48	56
Runcorn	46	21	14	11	72	47	56
Macclesfield Town	46	18	15	13	48	47	51
Bangor City	46	19	11	16	65	56	49
Gainsborough Trinity	46	18	11	17	77	64	47
South Liverpool	46	16	15	15	55	47	47
Skelmersdale United	46	16	13	17	50	59	45
Goole Town	46	14	15	17	60	69	43
Fleetwood	46	14	15	17	48	68	43
Mossley	46	15	11	20	53	65	41
Northwich Victoria	46	14	13	19	68	75	41
Morecambe	46	13	13	20	62	84	39
Buxton	46	14	10	22	45	71	38
Matlock Town	46	11	13	21	50	79	36
Great Harwood	46	10	14	22	52	74	34
Bradford (P.A.)	46	9	15	22	42	84	33
Barrow	46	13	7	26	46	94	33
Lancaster City	46	10	12	24	52	67	32
Netherfield	46	11	5	30	42	88	27

Northern Premier League: 1974/75

Wigan Athletic	46	33	6	7	94	38	72
Runcorn	46	30	8	8	102	42	68
Altrincham	46	26	12	8	87	43	64
Stafford Rangers,	46	25	13	8	81	39	63
Scarborough	46	24	12	10	75	45	60
Mossley	46	23	11	12	78	52	57
Gateshead United	46	22	12	12	74	48	56
Goole Town	46	19	12	15	75	71	50
Northwich Victoria	46	18	12	16	83	71	48
Great Harwood	46	17	14	15	69	66	48
Matlock Town	46	19	8	19	87	79	46
Boston United	46	16	14	16	64	63	46
Morecambe	46	14	15	17	71	87	43
Worksop Town	46	14	14	18	69	66	42
South Liverpool	46	14	14	18	59	71	42
Buxton	46	11	17	18	50	77	39
Macclesfield Town	46	11	14	21	46	62	36
Lancaster City	46	13	10	23	53	76	36
Bangor City	46	13	9	24	56	67	35
Gaisborough Trinity	46	10	15	21	46	79	35
Skelmersdale United	46	13	7	26	63	93	33
Barrow	46	9	15	22	45	72	33
Netherfield	46	12	8	26	43	92	32
Fleetwood	46	5	10	31	26	97	20

Northern Premier League: 1975/76

Runcorn	46	29	10	7	95	42	68
Stafford Rangers	46	26	15	5	81	41	67
Scarborough	46	26	10	10	84	43	62
Matlock Town	46	26	9	11	96	63	61
Boston United	46	27	6	13	95	58	60
Wigan Athletic	46	21	15	10	81	42	57
Altrincham	46	20	14	12	77	57	54
Bangor City	46	21	12	13	80	70	54
Mossley	46	21	11	14	70	58	53
Goole Town	46	20	13	13	58	49	53
Northwich Victoria	46	17	17	12	79	59	51
Lancaster City	46	18	9	19	61	70	45
Worksop Town	46	17	10	19	63	56	44
Gainsborough Trinity	46	13	17	16	58	69	43
Macclesfield Town	46	15	12	19	50	64	42
Gateshead United	46	17	7	22	64	63	41
Buxton	46	11	13	22	37	62	35
Skelmersdale United	46	12	10	24	45	74	34
Netherfield	46	11	11	24	55	76	33
Morecambe	46	11	11	24	47	67	33
Great Harwood	46	13	7	26	58	86	33
South Liverpool	46	12	9	25	45	78	33
Barrow	46	12	9	25	47	84	33
Fleetwood	46	3	9	34	36	131	15

Northern Premier League: 1976/77

Boston United	44	27	11	6	82	35	65
Northwich Victoria	44	27	11	6	85	43	65
Matlock Town	44	26	11	7	108	57	63
Bangor City	44	22	11	11	87	52	55
Scarborough	44	21	12	11	77	66	54
GooleTown	44	23	6	15	64	50	52
Lancaster City	44	21	9	14	71	58	51
Gateshead United	44	18	12	14	80	64	48
Mossley	44	17	14	13	74	59	48
Altrincham	44	19	9	16	60	53	47
Stafford Rangers	44	16	14	14	60	55	46
Runcorn	44	15	14	15	58	50	44
Worksop Town	44	16	12	16	50	58	44
Wigan Athletic	44	14	15	15	62	54	43
Morecambe	44	13	11	20	59	75	37
Gainsborough Trinity	44	13	10	21	sa	74	36
Great Harwood	44	11	14	19	63	84	36
Buxton	44	11	13	20	48	63	35
Macclesfield Town	44	1	15	21	41	68	31
Frickley Athletic	44	11	a	25	53	93	30
Barrow	44	it	6	27	56	87	28
South Liverpool	44	10	8	26	51	104	28
Netherfield	44	9	8	27	47	92	26

Northern Premier League: 1977/78

Boston United	46	31	9	6	85	35	71
Wigan Athletic	46	25	15	6	83	45	65
Bangor City	46	26	10	10	92	50	62
Scarborough	46	26	10	10	80	39	62
Altrincham	46	22	15	9	84	49	59
Northwich Victoria	46	22	14	10	83	55	58
Stafford Rangers	46	22	13	11	71	41	57
Runcorn	46	19	18	9	70	44	56
Mossley	46	22	11	13	85	73	55
Matlock Town	46	21	12	13	79	60	54
Lancaster City	46	15	14	17	66	82	44
Frickley Athletic	46	15	12	19	77	81	42
Barrow	46	14	12	20	58	61	40
Goole Town	46	15	9	22	60	82	39
Great Harwood	46	13	13	20	66	83	39
Gainsborough Trinity	46	14	10	22	61	74	38
Gateshead	46	16	5	25	65	74	37
Netherfield	46	11	13	22	50	80	35
Workington	46	13	8	25	48	80	34
Worksop Town	46	12	10	24	45	84	34
Morecambe	46	11	11	24	67	92	33
Macclesfield Town	46	12	9	25	60	92	33
Buxton	46	13	6	27	60	95	32
South Liverpool	46	9	7	30	53	111	25

SEASON 1968-69
Northern Premier League:

	Home	Away
Altrincham	3-2	3-0
Ashington	1-1	2-1
Bangor City	4-0	3-3
Boston United	0-3	2-1
Chorley	1-0	2-1
Fleetwood	1-1	2-1
Gainsborough Trinity	1-1	0-0
Gateshead	3-0	0-1
Goole Town	1-1	1-1
Hyde United	2-0	2-2
Macclesfield Town	0-0	0-2
Morecambe	1-0	2-2
Netherfield	3-1	1-0
Northwich Victoria	2-3	1-2
Runcorn	3-1	0-1
Scarborough	2-1	2-0
South Liverpool	2-1	1-1
South Shields	1-3	0-1
Worksop Town	3-1	1-1

P.	W.	D.	L.	F.	A.	W.	D.	L.	F.	A.	Pts	Pos.
38	11	5	3	34	20	7	7	5	25	21	48	2nd

League Appearances:
Beattie 32;Brown 10;Cairney 36;Cairns 5;Crompton 1(1); Dooney 1(1) Gaskell 35;Gillibrand 38;Halsall 3;Hill 22;Lynn 20(1);Lyon 24(3); McLoughlin 21(1);McNeill 0(1);Melling 4(1); Parry 17;Ryan 28(1); Salt 15;Sandilands 1;Sealey 15(1);Shaw 9(2); Sutherland 34; Sykes 15:Turner 32(2);

League Scorers:
McLoughlin 17(2 pens);Ryan 13;Cairney 6;Lyon 4;Hill 3 (1 pen); Lynn 3;Sutherland 3;Parry 2(1 pen);Turner 2(1 pen); Beattie 1; Gillibrand 1;Salt 1;Shaw 1;Own Goals 2;(Total 59)

Other Results:

F.A.Cup:

4th Qual	Altrincham	Away	0-2	

Northern Premier League Cup:

Prelim	Chorley	Away	4-5	Cairney 2;Lynn;Sealey;

Lancashire Senior Cup:

Ist Rd	Southport	Away	0-1	

Lancashire Junior Cup:

2nd Rd	Great Harwood	Home	2-2	McLoughlin;Shaw;
Replay	Great Harwood	Away	1-3	AET McLoughlin;

Lancashire Floodlit Cup

Ist Rd	Lancaster City	Home	2-1	Cairney;Lyon;
2nd Rd	South Liverpool	Home	3-0	Cairney;Salt;Shaw;
S-F	Netherfield	Home	0-0	
Replay	Netherfield	Away	1-2	Ryan;

Seasons Honours:
Northern Premier League runners-up

SEASON 1969-70
Northern Premier League:

	Home	Away
Altrincham	2-2	3-1
Bangor City	2-2	1-2
Boston United	4-0	0-0
Fleetwood	0-0	0-1
Gainsborough Trinity	1-0	1-1
Gateshead	3-1	0-0
Goole Town	2-1	1-0
Great Harwood	1-0	1-2
Hyde United	1-0	3-2
Macclesfield Town	2-1	0-0
Matlock Town	0-0	0-5
Morecambe	1-1	1-2
Netherfield	0-0	0-1
Northwich Victoria	1-0	2-1
Runcorn	3-2	4-0
Scarborough	2-0	1-1
South Liverpool	5-1	2-0
South Shields	2-0*	1-1
Stafford Rangers	1-0	2-1

*played at Chorley

P.	W.	D.	L.	F.	A.	W.	D.	L.	F.	A.	Pts	Pos.
38	13	6	0	33	11	7	6	6	23	21	52	2nd

League Appearances:
Bannister 9;Breen 32(1);Brown 1;Cairney 20(3);Coutts 27; Dooney 1; Fielding 22(5);Fleming 37(1);Gillibrand 38;Hill 12(2); Ledgard 31; McLoughlin 30;Milne 15;Molyneux 2;Morris 25; Reeves 36;Ross 6(1); A.Ryan 9(4);Savage 15(4);Sutherland 35;Turner 15(1);

League Scorers:
McLoughlin 17(1 pen);Fleming 7;Ryan 5;Breen 4;Fielding 3; Gillibrand 3;Sutherland 3;Cairney 2;Ross 2;Savage 2;Turner 2; Hill I(pen);Morris 1;Own Goals 4;(Total 56)

Other Results:

F.A.Cup.

Ist Qual	Chorley	Home	1-1	Sutherland;
Replay	Chorley	Away	5-2	McLoughlin 2;Fielding; Breen;Sutherland;
2nd Qual	Droylsden	Home	4-1	McLoughlin 2;Ryan; Savage;
3rd Qual	Burscough	Home	1-1	McLoughlin;
Replay	Burscough	Away	3-2	McLoughlin 2;Fleming;
4th Qual	Skelmersdale Utd.	Home	2-0	Fleming 2;
Ist Rd	Port Vale	Home	1-1	Sutherland;
Replay	Port Vale	Away	2-2	AET Fleming;Fielding;
2nd Rep.	Port Vale (Old Trafford)		0-1	AET

F.A.Troiphy:

Ist Rd	Arnold	Away	5-2	Cairney 3;Coutts; Fielding;
2nd Rd	Telford United	Away	0-1	

Northern Premier League Cup:

Prelim	Great Harwood	Home	2-0	Sutherland;Fielding;
Ist Rd	South Shields	Home	3-0	Fleming 2;Breen;
2nd Rd	Netherfield	Home	0-1	

Lancashire Senior Cup:

Ist Rd	Southport	Home	2-1	McLoughlin;Breen;
2nd Rd	Great Harwood	Home	0-0	
Replay	Great Harwood	Away	0-2	

Lancashire Floodlit CuD:

Ist Rd	Skelmersdale United	Home	1-2	Ryan;

Lancashire Challenge Trophy:

Ist Rd	Prescot Town	Home	2-0	Cairney;Gillibrand;
2nd Rd	Darwen	Home	11-1	McLoughlin 7;Fleming Hill(pen);Fielding;
3rd Rd	Netherfield	Home	2-0	McLoughlin;Breen;
S-F	Rossendale United	Home	2-1	Fleming;Breen;
Final	Skelmersdale United (at Chorley)		1-2	McLoughlin

Seasons Honours:
Northern Premier League runners-up
Lancashire Challenge Trophy runners-up

Season 1969/70

(Back): Molyneux, Birkett (Train.), Cowap (V.Chair.), Horrocks (Chair.), Cairney, Coutts, Tinsley (Sec.), Ryan. (Middle): Turner, Morris, Gillibrand, Farrimond (Dir.), Ledgard, Sutherland, Fielding. (Front): Savage, Breen, Ross, McNeill (Manager), Fleming.

Season 1970/71

(Back): Ledgard, Temple, Sutherland, Roberts, Reeves, Davies, Morris, Breen, Savage. (Front): Coutts, Gillibrand, Milne, Todd, Fleming.

SEASON 1970-71
Northern Premier League:

	Home	Away
Altrincham	1-1	1-1
Bangor City	0-0	5-2
Boston United	2-0	1-2
Bradford Park Avenue	3-0	1-1
Chorley	1-0	1-1
Fleetwood	4-1	1-1
Gainsborough Trinity	5-0	2-2
Goole Town	7-0	1-0
Great Harwood	3-1	2-2
Kirkby Town	3-3	3-1
Lancaster City	4-0	0-0
Macclesfield Town	0-1	3-1
Matlock Town	2-1	4-0
Morecambe	4-1	0-0
Netherfield	1-0	2-1
Northwich Victoria	1-0	2-1
Runcorn	3-1	4-1
Scarborough	1-1	2-0
South Liverpool	1-1	1-0
South Shields	2-1	2-1
Stafford Rangers	4-1	1-0

P.	W.	D	L.	F.	A.	W.	D.	L.	F.	A.	Pts	Pos.
42	15	5	1	52	14	12	8	1	39	18	67	1st

League Appearances:
Bannister 1;Breen 16(3);Cooke 3(1);Coutts 37;Davies 36; Dugdale 0(1);Fleming 30(1);Gillibrand 42;Koo 14(1);Ledgard 6(4);Milne 34(1);Morris 30(1);Oates 25;Reeves 41;Roberts 1; Savage 5(1); Sutherland 40;Temple 33;Todd 40;Turner 28;

League Scorers:
Davies 30;Fleming 16(4 pens);Oates 10;Temple 8;Todd 6;Koo 3; Breen 2;Coutts 2;Milne 2;Savage 2;Sutherland 2;Turner 2; Cooke 1; Own Goals 5;(Total 91)

Other Results:

F.A.Cup:

4th Qual	Skelmersdale United	Away	1-1	Todd
Replay	Skelmersdale United	Home	5-0	Temple(2)Davies(2)og;
Ist Rd	South Shields	Away	1-1	Temple;
Replay	South Shields	Home	2-0	Temple;Todd;
2nd Rd	Peterborough United	Home	2-1	Davies;Fleming(pen);
3rd Rd	Manchester City	Away	0-1	

F.A.Trophy:

Ist Rd	Stafford Rangers	Home	2-0	Oates;Davies;
2nd Rd	Boston United	Away	1-0	Koo
3rd Rd	Hillingdon Borough	Home	0-1	

Lancashire Senior Cup:

Ist Rd	Chorley	Home	0-0	
Replay	Chorley	Away	2-3	Davies;Milne;

Northern Premier League Cup:

Ist Rd	Chorley	Home	1-0	Coutts;
2nd Rd	Scarborough	Home	3-1	Fleming 2(1 pen);Todd;
S-F Ist Leg	Fleetwood	Home	1-1	Oates;
S-F 2nd Leg	Fleetwood	Away	2-4	Fleming;Koo;

Ashworth Trophy:

S-F	Netherfield	Home	2-0	Davies;Templel
Final Ist Leg	Skelmersdale United	Away	0-5	
Final 2nd Leg	Skelmersdale United	Home	2-2	Oates;Cooke;

Lancashire Floodlit Cup:

2nd Rd	Lancaster City	Home	4-0	Savage;Todd;Temple; Morris;
S-F	Netherfield	Home	3-1	Temple(2);Davies;
Final Ist Leg	Skelmersdale United	Home	1-0	Davies;
Final 2nd Leg	Skelmersdale United	Away	2-1	Cooke;Temple;

Lancashire Challenge Trophy:

Ist Rd	Burscough	Home	5-2	Davies(3);Koo;Turner;
2nd Rd	Prescot Town	Home	2-0	Todd;Fleming(pen)
3rd Rd	Great Harwood	Home	2-0	Koo(2);
S-F	Rossendale United	Home	1-0	Oates;
Final	Skelmersdale United (at Chorley)		1-3	Oates

SeasonsHonours; :Northern Premier League Champions
Lancashire Floodlit Cup winners; Lancashire Challenge Trophy runners-up

SEASON 1971-72
Northern Premier League:

	Home	Away
Altrincham	0-0	3-1
Bangor City	0-1	0-1
Boston United	0-0	0-1
Bradford Park Avenue	1-0	0-0
Chorley	0-0	0-2
Ellesmere Port	4-3	1-0
Fleetwood	2-0	1-1
Gainsborough Trinity	2-1	1-0
Goole Town	4-1	3-0
Great Harwood	1-1	3-1
Kirkby Town	1-0	3-1
Lancaster City	2-3	5-2
Macclesfield Town	1-0	0-1
Matlock Town	1-1	3-1
Morecambe	1-0	3-2
Netherfield	1-0	3-0
Northwich Victoria	1-0	2-2
Runcorn	2-1	2-1
Scarborough	1-0	2-2
Skelmersdale United	2-1	1-4
South Liverpool	0-1	3-1
South Shields	2-2	1-0
Stafford Rangers	1-0	0-3

P.	W.	D.	L.	F.	A.	W.	D.	L.	F.	A.	Pts	Pos.
46	14	6	3	30	16	13	4	6	40	27	64	3rd

League Appearances:
Allen 0(1);Atherton 1;Breen14(2);Chadwick 17(1);Coutts 38; Davies 40;Dugdale 1;Fleming 36(2);Fletcher 22;Gillibrand 43; Gregory 1;Hodgkinson 0(1);Hodkinson 1;John King 10(2); Johnny King ll;Koo 21(6);Ledgard 26(3);Milne 21(2);Morris 27; Oates 40(1); Reeves 45;Riordan 2;Rogers 1;Sutherland 45;Tait 1(2);Temple 6(1); Todd 29;Welsby 1;Wilder 6(1);

League Scorers:
Davies 22;Fleming ll(l pen);Fletcher ll;Oates 6;Chadwick 4;Koo 4;Todd 3;Milne 2;Breen 1;Johnny King 1;Ledgard 1;Morris 1; Temple 1; Own Goals 2 (Total 70)

Other Results:

F.A.Cup:

4th Qual	Rhyl	Home	2-1	Oates;Sutherland;
Ist Rd	Halifax Town	Home	2-1	Oates;Sutherland;
2nd Rd	Wrexham	Away	0-4	

F.A.Trophy:

Ist Rd	Witton Albion	Home	1-0	Fletcher;
2nd Rd	Great Harwood	Away	4-3	Fletcher(2);Davies Fleming;
3rd Rd	Barnet	Home	1-2	Fletcher;

Northern Premier League Shield:

	Fleetwood	Home	3-2	Coutts;Davies;Fleming (pen);

Northern Premier League Cup:

Prelim	Netherfield	Away	3-1	Fleming;Koo;Oates;
Ist Rd	South Liverpool	Home	1-1	Oates;
Replay	South Liverpool	Away	2-0	Koo(2);
2nd Rd	Skelmersdale United	Home	2-1	Koo(2);
S-F Ist Leg	Ellesmere Port	Away	0-0	
S-F 2nd Leg	Ellesmere Port	Home	1-0	Chadwick
Fin. Ist Leg	Gainsborough.T.	Away	4-0	Chadwick(2)King;Davies
Fin.2nd Leg	Gainsborough.T.	Home	0-2	

Ashworth Trophy:

Ist Leg	Skelmersdale United	Home	0-1	
2nd Leg	Skelmersdale United	Away	1-2	Allen

Lancashire Challenge Trophy:

Ist Rd	Prescot Cables	Home	7-0	Koo(4);Breen;Davies;Fleming;
2nd Rd	South Liverpool	Home	1-1	Chadwick
Replay	South Liverpool	Away	1-0	Koo(pen);
3rd Rd	Great Harwood	Away	2-1	Allen;Koo;
S-F	Skelmersdale Utd.	Home	2-0	Chadwick;og
Final	Netherfield (At Chorley)		3-1	Coutts;Davies;Fletcher

Lancashire Senior Cup:

Ist Rd	Manchester City	Home	2-0	Davies;Fleming;
2nd Rd	Liverpool	Home	0-2	

Lancashire Floodlit Cup:

2nd Rd	Morecambe	Home	5-2	Chadwick(2);Ledgard; Fletcher(2);
S-F	Netherfield	Home	6-1	Fletcher 3(1 pen); Koo(2);Chadwick;
Fin. Ist Leg	Rossendale United	Away	1-2	Fleming;
Fin. 2nd Leg	Rossendale United	Home	0-1	

Herefordshire Cup (Nv S Challencel):

Ist Leg	Hereford United	Home	1-1	Koo;
2nd Leg	Hereford United	Away	0-1	

Seasons Honours: Northern Premier League Shield winners Lancashire Challenge Trophy winners Northern Premier League Cup winners Lancashire Floodlit Cup runners-up.

Season 1971/72

(Back): Wilder, Koo, Davies, Sutherland, Reeves, Morris, Coutts, Ledgard, Fleming.
(Front): King, Temple, Dugdale, Todd, Milne (P/Manager), Breen, Oates, Gillibrand.

Season 1972/73

(Back): Fletcher, Sutherland, Morris, Jackson, Reeves, Aspinall, King, Gregory, Banks (Train.)
(Front): Chadwick, Oates, Gillibrand, Rigby (Manager), Koo, Worswick, Taylor.

SEASON 1972-73
Northern Premier League:

	Home	Away
Altrincham	4-1	0-2
Bangor City	4-1	0-0
Barrow	1-0	1-0
Boston United	0-0	0-0
Bradford Park Avenue	2-0	1-2
Ellesmere Port	1-1	1-0
Fleetwood	4-0	1-1
Gainsborough Trinity	1-1	3-3
Goole Town	4-2	0-4
Great Harwood	4-0	0-0
Lancaster City	1-0	1-0
Macclesfield Town	2-0	1-0
Matlock Town	4-1	4-1
Morecambe	1-0	0-1
Mossley	2-1	3-1
Netherfield	3-0	2-2
Northwich Victoria	1-0	0-1
Runcorn	3-0	0-1
Scarborough	1-1	0-3
Skelmersdale United	0-0	2-2
South Liverpool	1-2	0-0
South Shields	2-0	2-1
Stafford Rangers	0-0	1-2

P.	W.	D.	L.	F.	A.	W.	D.	L.	F.	A.	Pts	Pos.
46	16	6	1	48	11	7	8	8	23	27	60	3rd

League Appearances:
Aspinall 9(7);Chadwick 19(5);Clements 19;Fletcher 13; Gillibrand 46;Gregory 0(1);Jackson 43;Johnson 22(1);King 30(1); Koo 1(2); McCunnell 19(5);Monks 3;Morris 30;Oates 33(1); Pearson 5(2); Reeves 42;Roberts 0(1);Rogers 37(6); Sutherland 40;Tait 3;Taylor 46;Tinney 0(1);Wallace 1;Welsby 3; Wilson 1(1);Worswick 41(2);
League Scorers:
Oates 14(3 pens);Worswick ll;Jackson 9;Rogers 8;Chadwick 4; Clements 4;Fletcher 4;Aspinall 3;McCunnell 3(1 pen);King 2; Morris 2;Pearson 2;Sutherland 1;Taylor 1;Own Goals 1; (Total 69)

Other Results:
F.A.Cup:
4th Qual Burscough Away 3-1 Fletcher;Worswick; Rogers;
Ist Rd Grimsby Town Away 1-2 Oates(pen);
Northern Premier League Cup:
Ist Rd South Shields Home 2-0 Fletcher;Rogers;
2nd Rd Gainsborough.T. Home 3-0 Fletcher Sutherland Oates;
SF Ist Leg South Liverpool Home 2-1 Clements;Jackson;
SF 2nd Leg South Liverpool Away 3-0 Rogers(2);Clements;
Final Ist Leg Northwich Victoria Home 0-1
Final 2nd Leg Northwich Victoria Away 2-2 King;Rogers;
F.A.Troiphy:
Ist Rd Burton Albion Home 5-0 Worswick(3 pens); Clements;Fletcher;
2nd Rd South Liverpool Home 2-0 Oates;Worswick;
3rd Rd Romford Home 2-0 Clements;Oates(pen);
4th Rd Morecambe Away 1-1 Oates;
Replay Morecambe Home 0-0 (AET)
2nd Rep. Morecambe (at Ewood Pk) 1-0 Oates;
S-F Stafford.R. (at Vale Pk) 0-0
Replay Stafford.R.(at Oldham) 1-0 Oates;
Final Scarborough (at Wembley) 1-2 AET Rogers;
Lancashire Senior Cup:
Ist Rd Great Harwood Home 3-1 Jackson;Rogers;Tinney;
2nd Rd Southport Home 1-0 Taylor;
3rd Rd Liverpool Home 2-3 Jackson;Oates;
Lancashire Challenge Trophy:
Ist Rd Ashton Town Home 2-1 Oates(pen);Rogers;
2nd Rd Clitheroe Home 6-0 Pearson 2;Worswick 2; Jackson;Rogers;
3rd Rd South Liverpool Home 0-1
Northern Premier League Shield:
Stafford Rangers Away 3-0 Chadwick;Oates(pen); Worswick;
Lancashire Floodlit Cup:
2nd Rd Morecambe Home 0-0
Replay Morecambe Away 3-2 Aspinall;Taylor;og;
S-F Great Harwood Home 0-0
Replay Great Harwood Away 2-0 Oates 2(1 pen);
Final South Liverpool Home 6-1 Rogers 3;Jackson; Worswick;og;
Seasons Honours: Lancashire Floodlit Cup winners; Northern Premier League Shield winners; Northern Premier League Cup runners-up; F.A.Trophy runners-up

SEASON 1973-74
Northern Premier League:

	Home	Away
Altrincham	1-0	0-3
Bangor City	2-1	2-1
Barrow	4-1	3-0
Boston United	1-0	2-2
Bradford Park Avenue	4-1	0-0
Buxton	5-0	4-0
Fleetwood	2-0	1-2
Gainsborough Trinity	3-1	1-2
Goole Town	1-1	1-2
Great Harwood	7-0	1-1
Lancaster City	2-0	4-1
Macclesfield Town	2-4	0-0
Matlock Town	7-0	3-2
Morecambe	3-0	2-0
Mossley	4-0	3-0
Netherfield	3-0	0-1
Northwich Victoria	5-3	2-1
Runcorn	2-0	1-0
Scarborough	0-0	0-1
Skelmersdale United	2-0	1-2
South Liverpool	0-0	0-0
South Shields	2-1	2-0
Stafford Rangers	1-2	0-3

P.	W.	D.	L.	F.	A.	W.	D.	L.	F.	A.	Pts	Pos.
46	18	3	2	63	15	10	5	8	33	24	64	2nd

League Appearances:
Aspinall 0(1);Birtwhistle 4(4);Braithwaite 2;Clements 37;Garrett 13(1);Gillibrand 45;Gore 12(1);Hodkinson 1(1);Jackson 45;King 21; Kinsey 5;D.Lyon 28(2);Marsden 23(3);McCunnell 3(10);McHale 2; Morris 44;Reeves 26;Richardson 0(1);Rogers 40(1);Seddon 5; Sutherland 45;Tait 5(2); Tattum 1;Taylor 28(1);Welsby 20;Worswick 40(3);Wright 11;

League Scorers:
Marsden 17(7 pens);Jackson 17;Rogers 16;Worswick 11(5 pens); Clements 8;Lyon 6;Garrett 4;Morris 4;Sutherland 3;Birtwhistle 1; Kinsey 1; McCunnell 1;Seddon 1;Taylor 1;Wright 1;Own Goals 4; (Total 96)

Other Results:
F.A.Cup:
Ist Rd Huddersfield Town Away 0-2
F.A.Trophy:
Ist Rd Boston United Home 2-3 Kinsey(2);
Northern Premier League Cup:
Prelim Buxton Away 4-1 Rogers(2);Jackson;Lyon
Ist Rd Mossley Home 1-1 Worswick
Replay Mossley Away 1-2 Jackson
Ashworth Trophy.
Rossendale United Home 1-0 Jackson
Rossendale United Away 2-1 Rogers(2);
Lancashire Senior Cup:
Ist Rd Blackpool Away 0-2
Lancashire Challenge Trophy:
Ist Rd Formby Home 2-0 Lyon;ROgers;
2nd Rd Blackpool Mechanics Home 1-0 Marsden;
3rd Rd Horwich RMI Home 2-0 Clement;Rogers;
S-F Accrington Stanley Home 2-0 King;Worswick;
Final Skelmersdale United (at Southport) 4-1 Oates 2(lpen)Worswick; Braithwaite:
Seasons Honours:
Northern Premier League runners-up; Ashworth Trophy winners;
Lancashire Challenge Trophy winners.

SEASON 1974-75
Northern Premier League:

	Home	Away
Altrincham	0-1	2-2
Bangor City	3-1	1-1
Barrow	6-1	4-2
Boston United	2-1	1-1
Buxton	3-1	2-0
Fleetwood	1-0	3-1
Gainsborough Trinity	2-1	1-3
Gateshead	3-0	1-0
Goole Town	3-1	2-0
Great Harwood	1-0	3-2
Lancaster City	1-0	3-1
Macclesfield Town	4-1	1-0
Matlock Town	2-1	0-3
Morecambe	5-1	1-1
Mossley	0-0	0-1
Netherfield	5-1	4-0
Northwich Victoria	2-0	0-2
Runcorn	2-0	1-0
Scarborough	3-1	1-0
Skelmersdale United	2-1	1-0
South Liverpool	4-0	1-1
Stafford Rangers	0-1	0-2
Worksop Town	4-0	3-2

P.	W.	D.	L.	F.	A.	W.	D.	L.	F.	A.	Pts	Pos.
46	20	1	2	58	14	13	4	5	36	24	72	Ist

League Appearances:
Aspinall 1;Baker 22;Braithwaite 2(4);Clements 18(6);Critchley 3; Garrett 38(1);Gillibrand 32;Gore 39;Hesketh 1;Jackson 18(2); King 36(1);Melling 3(1);Molyneux 42;Morris 26;Ollerton 2; Reeves 43;Rogers 43;Sutherland 23;Tattum 1;Tiler 10(1); Wilkinson 13(2);Worswick 46;Wright 44(2);

League Scorers:
Rogers 24(3 pens);Worswick 20;Garrett 14;Gore 11(5 pens); Wright 8; King 5;Clements 3;Wilkinson 3;Sutherland 2; Jackson 1;Molyneux 1; Own Goals 2;(Total 94)

Other Results:

F.A.Cup:

4th Qual	Kidderminster.H.	Home	4-0	Worswick(2)Sutherland Rogers
Ist Rd	Shrewsbury	Away	1-1	King
Replay	Shrewsbury	Home	2-1	Gore Jackson
2nd Rd	Mansfield Town	Home	1-1	own goal
Replay	Mansfield Town	Away	1-3	King

F.A.Trophy:

Ist Rd	Altrincham	Home	3-1	Rogers(2)Wright
2nd Rd	Northwich Victoria	Away	4-2	Garret Gore Jackson og
3rd Rd	Lancaster City	Away	2-0	Rogers;Worswick;
4th Rd	Bedford Town	Home	0-1	

Northern Premier League Cup:

Ist Rd	South Liverpool	Away	1-2	Rogers(pen);

Northern Premier League Shield:

	Boston United	Away	1-2	Wright

Ashworth Trophy:

Ist Leg	Rossendale United	Home	1-2	Wright
2nd Leg	Rossendale United	Away	0-1	

Lancashire Challenge Trophy:

Ist Rd	Nelson	Home	3-0	Garrett;KIng;Rogers;
2nd Rd	Bacup	Home	0-0	
Replay	Bacup	Away	0-2	

Seasons Honours: Northern Premier League Champions

SEASON 1975-76
Northern Premier League:

	Home	Away
Altrincham	4-1	0-1
Bangor City	2-0	2-2
Barrow	1-0	4-0
Boston United	6-0	1-2
Buxton	6-0	0-2
Fleetwood	3-0	4-0
Gainsborough Trinity	0-0	0-0
Gateshead	1-0	2-1
Goole Town	1-3	0-0
Great Harwood	0-0	7-3
Lancaster City	1-1	0-0
Macclesfield Town	0-1	1-1
Matlock Town	1-0	2-2
Morecambe	0-0	0-3
Mossley	2-3	1-1
Netherfield	5-2	2-0
Northwich Victoria	1-2	3-1
Runcorn	1-1	0-2
Scarborough	2-1	0-0
Skelmersdale United	4-1	2-1
South Liverpool	2-0	0-0
Stafford Rangers	1-2	2-2
Worksop Town	3-0	1-0

P.	W.	D.	L.	F.	A.	W.	D.	L.	F.	A.	Pts	Pos.
46	13	5	5	47	18	8	10	5	34	24	57	6th

League Appearances:
Aspinall 5(1);Baines 7(1);Baker II;Braithwaite 30(6);Bromley 22(1); Coyne 3;Critchley 2;Eales 44;Garrett 34(5);Gillibrand 46; Gore 45;Hinnigan 37(1);King 29(1);Molyneux 32;O'Hare 3(3); Parle 2(2);Prescott 8;Rogers 38;Wilkinson 33(4);R.Wilson 8(2); Worswick 32(1);Wright 35;

League Scorers:
Rogers 25(1 pen);Worswick II;Wilkinson 8;Braithwaite 6;Garrett 6; Gore 6(4 pens);King 4;R.Wilson 3;Coyne 2;Hinnigan 2;Wright 2; Aspinall 1;Bromley 1; Own Goals 4;(Total 81)

Other Results:

F.A.Cup:

Ist Rd	Matlock Town	Home	4-1	Wilkinson 2;Rogers; Worswick;
2nd Rd	Sheff Wed	Away	0-2	

F.A.Trophy.

Ist Rd	Northwich Vics	Away	2-0	King;Rogers;
2nd Rd	Grantham	Home	1-1	Wright
Replay	Grantham	Away	2-1	Coyne;Worswick;
3rd Rd	Hillingdon Boro	Home	1-3	Coyne

Northern Premier League Shield:

	Runcorn	Home	3-1	Wilkinson;Worswick;Wright

Northern Premier League Cup:

Ist Rd	Lancaster City	Home	3-2	Bromley;Garrett:Rogers:
2nd Rd	Scarborough	Away	0-1	

Lancashire Challeiige Trophy:

Ist Rd	Barrow	Home	1-0	Gore(pen);
2nd Rd	Horwich RMI	Away	4-0	Wilkinson 2;Garrett;og;
3rd Rd	Netherfield	Home	5-0	Coyne;Garrett;Rogers;Gore;Wright;
S-F	Morecambe	Away	2-2	Garrett 2;
S-F Replay	Morecambe	Home	3-0	Rogers 2;Wilkinson;
Final	Chorley	Home	1-2	Rogers

Inter League Cup(North v South Challenge),

Ist Leg	Wimbledon	Home	1-0	Worswick;
2nd Leg	Wimbledon	Away	0-2 (AET)	

Seasons Honours: Northern Premier League Shield winners; Lancashire Challenge Trophy runners-up;

SEASON 1976-77
Northern Premier League:

	Home	Away
Altrincham	1-2	3-1
Bangor City	2-1	0-0
Barrow	5-2	1-4
Boston United	1-1	1-1
Buxton	3-1	3-0
Frickley Athletic	4-1	0-2
Gainsborough Trinity	3-0	0-0
Gateshead	2-0	0-2
Goole Town	1-1	1-0
Great Harwood	1-1	0-2
Lancaster City	2-2	1-1
Macclesfield Town	0-0	2-2
Matlock Town	0-2	1-2
Morecambe	1-1	0-1
Mossley	2-2	3-1
Netherfield	2-0	0-1
Northwich Victoria	0-1	0-1
Runcorn	0-0	1-1
Scarborough	1-3	3-5
South Liverpool	3-0	3-0*
Stafford Rangers	1-2	1-3
Worksop Town	2-0	1-1

*played at Runcorn

P.	W.	D.	L	F.	A.	W.	D.	L.	F.	A.	Pts	Pos.
44	9	8	5	37	23	5	7	10	25	31	43	14th

League Appearances:
Baines 7(4);Bannister 26(1);Braithwaite B;Brown 29;Critchley 15; Davies 8(1);Garrett 8(2);Gillibrand 36;Gore 42;Hinnigan 36;Kenyon 12(1);Larner 2(3);Makin 16(1);Morris 13;Prescott 35(4);Rimmer 7(5);Rogers 8;Rowlands 4;Scott 3;Sweeney 2;Ward 42; Whitehead 6;Wilkie 36(1);D.Wilson 6(2);R.Wilson 1(2);Worswick 41; Wright 32(6);

League Scorers:
Wilkie 13;Worswick 12(4 pens);Hinnigan 4;Rogers 4(2 pens); Davies 3;Gore 3;Makin 3;Wright 3;Kenyon 2;Larner 2;Prescott 2; Ward 2;Bannister 1;Braithwaite 1;Garrett 1;Rimmer 1; Rowlands 1; Sweeney 1;D.Wilson 1;Own Goals 2(Total 62)

Other Results:

F.A.Cup:

Ist Rd	Matlock Town	Away	0-2	

F.A.Trophy:

Ist Rd	Boston Utd	Away	2-2	Prescott;Wilkie;
Replay	Boston Utd	Home	2-1	Makin;Worswick(pen);
2nd Rd	Wimbledon	Away	2-3	Worswick,Own Goal

Northern Premier League Shield:

2nd Rd	Runcorn	Home	1-2	Rogers;

Lancashire Junior Cup:

Ist Rd	Formby	Home	3-0	Hinnigan;Wilkie;Wright;
2nd Rd	Darwen	Away	2-2	Gore 2;
Replay	Darwen	Home	5-1	Makin 2;Wilkie 2;Prescott
3rd Rd	Marine	Home	3-1	Makin 2;Davies;
S-F	Barrow	Home	1-0	Worswick;
Final	Chorley	Away	1-0	Hinnigan

Seasons Honours..
Lancashire Junior Cup winners;

SEASON 1977-78
Northern Premier League:

	Home	Away
Altrincham	1-0	0-0
Bangor City	2-1	0-0
Barrow	4-1	1-1
Boston United	0-2	2-4
Buxton	4-0	2-2
Frickley Athletic	1-0	0-4
Gainsborough Trinity	2-1	2-1
Gateshead	1-0	3-0
Goole Town	2-0	2-0
Great Harwood	0-0	3-2
Lancaster City	2-2	6-1
Macclesfield Town	1-1	4-0
Matlock Town	2-0	1-0
Morecambe	1-1	2-1
Mossley	1-2	3-1
Netherfield	0-0	2-1
Northwich Victoria	1-1	1-1
Runcorn	0-0	2-2
Scarborough	2-4	1-3
South Liverpool	2-0	2-0
Stafford Rangers	1-0	2-2
Workington	4-1	4-1
Worksop Town	3-0	1-1

P.	W.	D.	L.	F.	A.	W.	D.	L.	F.	A.	Pts	Pos.
46	13	7	3	37	17	12	8	3	46	28	65	2nd

League Appearances:
Brown 40;Cole 1(1);Corrigan 13;Critchley 6;Fowles 1; Gallagher 0(1) Gillibrand 46;Gore 46;Grundy 2(2); Hinnigan 46;Houghton 15(2); Makin 4(1);Mitchell 7(3); Moore 28(1);Morris 31(2);Prescott 9(1); Rimmer 2(6); Styles 18(4);Ward 44;Whittle13(2);Wilkey 1;Wilkie 46 Worswick 41(1);Wright 46;

League Scorers:
Wilkie 20;Wright 14;Moore II;Houghton 9;Worswick 8(2 pens);Gore 7 Ward 5;Whittle 3;Hinnigan 2; Corrigan 1;Own Goals 3;(Total 83)

Other Results:

F.A.Cup:

4th Qual	Marine	Away	3-0	Ward;Moore;Gore;
Ist Rd	York City	Home	1-0	Wilkie;
2nd Rd	Sheff Wed	Home	1-0	Whittle;
3rd Rd	Birmingham.C	Away	0-4	

F.A.Trophy:

Ist Rd	Ashton Utd	Away	3-1	Worswick(2);Moore
2nd Rd	Enfield	Home	1-1	Moore;
Replay	Enfield	Away	1-1	AET Whittle(pen);
2nd Replay	Enfield	(at Leicester)	3-0	Ward(2);Worswick
3rd Rd	Leatherhead	Away	0-2	

Northern Premier League Cup:

Ist Rd	Worksop Town	Home	2-1	Workswick(pen);Wilkie;
2nd Rd	Gateshead	Away	2-2	Moore(2);
Replay	Gateshead	Home	3-1	Moore(2);Wilkie;
Q-F	Scarborough	Home	2-1	Wilkie(2);
S-F Ist Leg	Boston Utd	Away	1-3	Styles;
S-F 2nd Leg	Boston Utd	Home	0-2	

Lancashire Junior Cup:

2nd Rd	Rossendale	Away	1-1	Moore;
Replay	Rossendale	Home	7-0	Moore 3(1 pen);Worswick 2: Wright;Whittle;
3rd Rd	Darwen	Home	1-0	Ward;
S-F	Accrington	Home	4-3	Ward 2;Wilkie;Gillibrand;
Final	Chorley	Home	2-0	Houghton;Worswick;

Seasons Honours: Northern Premier League runners-up;
Lancashire Junior Cup winners;

Season 1976/77

Celebrations after the winning of the Lancashire Junior Cup, beating Chorley 1-0. Joe Hinnigan was the goalscorer.

Season 1977/78

(Back): Gore, Ward, Wright, Brown, Morris, Hinnigan.
(Front): Rimmer, Worswick, Wilkie, Gillibrand, Styles, Moore.

SEASON 1978-79

DIVISION 4

No.	Date	Opposition	Res.	Att.	Goalscorers	Brown J.	Hinnigan J.	Gore T.	Gillibrand I.	Ward N.	Davids N.	Corrigan F.	Purdie I.	Houghton P.	Wilkie J.	Wright J.	Gay G.	Smart K.	Crompton A.	Seddon I.	Moore M.	Worswick M.	Brownbill D.	Fretwell D.	Grew M.	Curtis J.
1	19 Aug	Hereford United	0-0	5674		1	2	3	4	5	6	7	8	9	10	11										
2	23	GRIMSBY TOWN	0-3	9227		1	3	2	6	5	4	7	11	9		8	10*		12							
3	26	Reading	0-2	4788		1		2	6	5	4*	7	8	9	10	11		3	12							
4	2 Sep	NEWPORT COUNTY	2-3	5319	Hinnigan, Purdie	1	3*	2	6	5		7	11		10	4				8	9	12				
5	9	Wimbledon	1-2	3217	Corrigan	1	3	4	6	5		7	11			8		2	10		9					
6	13	ROCHDALE	3-0	5746	Wright, Corrigan, Hinnigan	1	3	4	6	5		7	11			8		2	10		9*		12			
7	16	BRADFORD CITY	1-3	7090	Purdie	1	3	4	6	5		7	11			8		2	10*		9		12			
8	23	York City	1-0	3307	Gore	1	3	4		5	6	7	11			8		2			9		10			
9	26	Portsmouth	0-1	13902		1	3	4		5	6	7	11			8		2			9*		10			
10	30	SCUNTHOPRE UNITED	1-0	4459	Brownbill	1	3	4		5	6	7	11			8		2			10		*			
11	7 Oct	Huddersfield Town	1-1	5150	Brownbill	1	3	4		5		7*	11			8		2	12		9		10	6		
12	14	DONCASTER ROVERS	1-0	5788	Ward	1	3	4		5		7	11			8		2			9		10	6		
13	18	HALIFAX TOWN	1-0	5216	Hinnigan	1	3	4		5		7	11	12		8		2			9*		10	6		
14	21	Barnsley	0-0	9841		1	3	4		5		7	11	12		8		2			9		10*	6		
15	28	NORTHAMPTON TOWN	2-0	6264	Purdie(2,1pen)	1	3	4		5		7	11	10		8		2			9			6		
16	3 Nov	Stockport County	1-0	8357	Hinnigan	1	3	4		5		7	11	10		8		2			9			6		
17	10	Newport County	1-2	4142	Houghton	1	3	4		5		7	11*	10		8		2			9		12	6		
18	18	READING	3-0	5858	Houghton(2), Ward	1	3	4		5		7	11	10		8		2			9			6		
19	9 Dec	Darlington	1-1	1967	Moore	1*	3	4		5		7	11	10		8		2			9		12	6		
20	16	Halifax Town	2-1	2437	Moore, Purdie		3	4			5	7	11			8		2			9		10	6	1	
21	26	CREWE ALEXANDRA	1-0	7586	Houghton		3	4		5		7	11	9		8		2			10			6	1	
22	30	ALDERSHOT	3-2	7289	Moore, Houghton(2)		3	4		5		7	11	10		8		2			9			6	1	
23	9 Jan	Port Vale	1-2	3744	Wright			4		5	3	7	11*	9		8		2			10		12	6	1	
24	3 Feb	PORTSMOUTH	2-0	8289	Wright, Corrigan	1	3	4		5		7	11	10		8		2			9			6		
25	14	WIMBLEDON	1-2	6704	Purdie(pen)	1		2		5		7	11	9		8		3	10				4	6		
26	17	HUDDERSFIELD TOWN	2-1	7420	Ward(2)	1	3	4		5		7	11	9		8		2	10					6		
27	24	Doncaster Rovers	1-0	4612	Wright	1	3	4		5		7	11	9		8		2	10*		12			6		
28	28	York City	1-1	5896	Houghton	1	3	2		5		7	11	9*		8			10		4		12	6		
29	3 Mar	BARNSLEY	1-1	9427	Wright	1	3	4		5		7	11			8		2			10		9	6		
30	10	Northampton Town	4-2	2275	Brownbill(2), Purdie, Corrigan	1	3	4		5		7*	11			8		2	12		9		10	6		
31	14	TORQUAY UNITED	3-1	5722	Moore(2), Hinnigan	1	3	4		5		7	11			8		2			10		9	6		
32	17	STOCKPORT COUNTY	2-0	7610	Wright, Smart	1	3	4		5		7	11			8		2			10		9	6		
33	19	Rochdale	2-0	3621	Purdie, Moore	1	3	4		5		7	11			8		2			10		9	6		
34	24	Grimsby Town	1-3	8252	O.G.	1	3*	4		5		7	11	12		8		2			10		9	6		
35	28	HEREFORD UNITED	0-0	4876		1		4		5		7	11*	9		8		3			10		12	6		2
36	31	BOURNEMOUTH	1-0	5527	Houghton	1		4		5		7	11	10		8		3			9			6		2
37	3 Apr	Hartlepool United	1-1	2081	Houghton	1		4		5		7	11	9		8		3			10			6		2
38	7	Torquay United	1-1	2969	Houghton	1		4		5		7	11	10		8		3			9			6		2
39	13	PORT VALE	5-3	8452	Houghton(3), Brownbill, Moore	1	3	4		5*		7	11	9		8		2			10		12	6		
40	14	Crewe Alexandra	1-1	4604	Purdie(pen)	1	3	4		5		7	11	9*		8		2			10		12	6		
41	16	HARTLEPOOL UNITED	2-2	8217	Wright, Purdie	1	6	4		5		7*	11	9		8		3			10		12			2
42	21	Aldershot	0-1	5466		1	3	4		5	6		11			8		7*	12		10		9			2
43	28	DARLINGTON	2-2	6153	Moore, Brownbill	1	3	4		5		7	11			8*		6	12		10		9			2
44	1 May	Scunthopre United	1-0	1582	Gore	1	3	4			5	7	11			8					10		9	6		2
45	5	Bournemouth	1-2	3063	Purdie	1	3	4		5	12	7	11			8		2			10*		9	6		
46	7	Bradford City	1-1	3748	Moore	1	3	4		5	12	7	11			8					10		9	6*		2
					Apps.	42	39	46	7	44	10	45	46	23	3	46	1	40	7	1	40		20	33	4	9
					Subs.						2			3	1				6		1	1	10			
					Goals		5	2		4		4	11	13		7		1			9		6			

F.A. CUP

Rd.	Date	Opposition	Res.	Att.	Goalscorers	Brown J.	Hinnigan J.	Gore T.	Gillibrand I.	Ward N.	Davids N.	Corrigan F.	Purdie I.	Houghton P.	Wilkie J.	Wright J.	Gay G.	Smart K.	Crompton A.	Seddon I.	Moore M.	Worswick M.	Brownbill D.	Fretwell D.	Grew M.	Curtis J.
1R	25 Nov	BURY	2-2	10142	Gore, Houghton	1	3	4		5		7	11	9		8		2			10		12	6		
1Rr	29	Bury	1-4	9339	Moore	1	3	4		5		7	11	9		8		2			10		12	6		

LEAGUE CUP

Rd.	Date	Opposition	Res.	Att.	Goalscorers	Brown J.	Hinnigan J.	Gore T.	Gillibrand I.	Ward N.	Davids N.	Corrigan F.	Purdie I.	Houghton P.	Wilkie J.	Wright J.	Gay G.	Smart K.	Crompton A.	Seddon I.	Moore M.	Worswick M.	Brownbill D.	Fretwell D.	Grew M.	Curtis J.
1R1	12 Aug	Tranmere Rovers	1-1	4402	Gore	1	2	3	4	5	6	7	8	9	10	11										
1R2	16	TRANMERE ROVERS	2-1	8512	Corrigan(2)	1	2	3	4	5		7	8	9	10	11			6							
2R	29	Luton Town	0-2	6618		1		3	4			7	8	9	10	11		2	6	5						

Football League Division 4: 1978/79 Final Table.

		Pl.	Home W	D	L	F	A	Away W	D	L	F	A	F.	A.	Pts
1	Reading	46	19	3	1	49	8	7	10	6	27	27	76	35	65
2	Grimsby Town	46	15	5	3	51	23	11	4	8	31	26	82	49	61
3	Wimbledon	46	18	3	2	50	20	7	8	8	28	26	78	46	61
4	Barnsley	46	15	5	3	47	23	9	8	6	26	19	73	42	61
5	Aldershot	46	16	5	2	38	14	4	12	7	25	33	63	47	57
6	Wigan Athletic	46	14	5	4	40	24	7	8	8	23	24	63	48	55
7	Portsmouth	46	13	7	3	35	12	7	5	11	27	36	62	48	52
8	Newport County	46	12	5	6	39	28	9	5	9	27	27	66	55	52
9	Huddersfield Town	46	13	8	2	32	15	5	3	15	25	38	57	53	47
10	York City	46	11	6	6	33	24	7	5	11	18	31	51	55	47
11	Torquay United	46	14	4	5	38	24	5	4	14	20	41	58	65	46
12	Scunthorpe United	46	12	3	8	33	30	5	8	10	21	30	54	60	45
13	Hartlepool United	46	7	12	4	35	28	6	6	11	22	38	57	66	44
14	Hereford United	46	12	8	3	35	18	3	5	15	18	35	53	53	43
15	Bradford City	46	11	5	7	38	26	6	4	13	24	42	62	68	43
16	Port Vale	46	8	10	5	29	28	6	4	13	28	42	57	70	42
17	Stockport County	46	11	5	7	33	21	3	7	13	25	39	58	60	40
18	Bournemouth	46	11	6	6	34	19	3	5	15	13	29	47	48	39
19	Northampton Town	46	12	4	7	40	30	3	5	15	24	46	64	76	39
20	Rochdale	46	11	4	8	25	26	4	5	14	22	38	47	64	39
21	Darlington	46	8	8	7	25	21	3	7	13	24	45	49	66	37
22	Doncaster Rovers	46	8	8	7	25	22	5	3	15	25	51	50	73	37
23	Halifax Town	46	7	5	11	24	32	2	3	18	15	40	39	72	26
24	Crewe Alexandra	46	3	7	13	24	41	3	7	13	19	49	43	90	26

Season 1978/79
(Back): Smart, Houghton, Davids, Gray, Brown, Corrigan, Ward, Hinnigan, Wright.
(Front): McNeill (Manager), Crompton, Seddon, Gore, Gillibrand, Wilkie, Purdie, Banks (Trainer)

Season 1979/80
(Back): N.Ward, Purdie, Brownbill, Brown, B.Ward, Smart, Quinn, McDermott.
(Middle): Colquhoun (Physio), Hinnigan, Wright, Urquhart, Hart, Davids, Curtis, Corrigan, Houghton, Fretwell, Banks (Train.)
(Front): Gore, Crompton, Wilkie, McNeill (Manager), Horrocks (Chairman), Moore, Wignall, Mayer.

SEASON 1979-80

DIVISION 4

No.	Date	Opposition	Res.	Att.	Goalscorers	Shyne C.	Smart K.	Hinnigan J.	Gore T.	Ward N.	Fretwell D.	Corrigan F.	Moore M.	Houghton P.	Wright J.	Purdie I.	Brownbill D.	Davids N.	Urquhart G.	Hart N.	Crompton A.	Brown J.	Methven C.	McIvor R.	Quinn L.A.	Buckley G.	Whittle M.	Shearer D.	McMullen D.	Quinn M.
1	18 Aug	Darlington	2-2	2063	Purdie, Hinnigan	1	2	3	4	5	6	7	8	9	10	11														
2	22	HUDDERSFIELD TOWN	1-2	6926	Moore	1	2	3	4	5	6	7	10	9	8*	11	12													
3	25	Stockport County	2-1	4000	Houghton, Gore	1	2	3	4	12	6	7	10	9	8	11*		5												
4	1 Sep	PORTSMOUTH	1-2	8198	Moore	1	2	3	4	5*	6	7	10	9	8	11			12											
5	8	Bournemouth	2-1	4390	Brownbill	1	2	3	6		4	7	9	10	8	11	12													
6	15	YORK CITY	2-5	5900	Corrigan, Urquhart	1	2*	3	4		6	7	9		8	11	10	5	12											
7	19	HARTLEPOOL UNITED	2-1	4877	Houghton(2)	1	2	3*	4		6	7	10	11	8	12	9	5		5										
8	22	Hereford United	1-2	3891	Wright	1		3	2		6	7	10	9	8	4*	11	5	12											
9	29	BRADFORD CITY	4-1	8009	Moore, Gore, Hinnigan, Houghton	1		3	2		6	7	10	9	8		11	5	4											
10	6 Oct	TORQUAY UNITED	0-3	6541		1		3	2		6	7	9	11*	8		10	5	4		12									
11	9	Huddersfield Town	0-4	7871				3	2		6	7	10	11	8		9*	5	4			1	12							
12	13	Doncaster Rovers	1-3	4169	McIvor			3	4		6*	7	10	9	8	11			12			1	5	2						
13	20	LINCOLN CITY	2-1	5454	Houghton(2)			3	4		2	7	9*	10	8			6	11			1	5		12					
14	24	ROCHDALE	1-1	5086	Quinn			3	4		2	7		9	8			6	11			1	5		10					
15	27	Newport County	2-3	4910	Methven, Quinn		12	3	4		2	7			8			6	11			1	5		10	9*				
16	3 Nov	DARLINGTON	4-1	5001	O.G., Quinn, Hinnigan(2)			3	4		2	7		9	8			6	11			1	5		10					
17	6	Rochdale	2-0	2936	Quinn, Houghton			3	4		2	7		9	8			6	11			1	5		10					
18	17	SCUNTHORPE UNITED	4-1	4618	Gore, Hinnigan, Urquhart, Quinn			3	4		2	7		11	8			6	9			1	5		10					
19	1 Dec	NORTHAMPTON TOWN	0-0	6158				3	4		2	7		9	8			6	11			1	5		10					
20	8	Walsall	1-1	5261	Quinn			3	4		2	7	12	9*	8			6	11			1	5		10					
21	21	CREWE ALEXANDRA	2-0	4316	Wright, Gore(pen)			3	4		2	7		9	8			6	11			1	5		10					
22	26	Peterborough United	2-1	3312	Gore(pen), Quinn			3	4		2	7	9		8			6	11			1	5		10					
23	29	STOCKPORT COUNTY	3-1	6847	Wright(2), Quinn			3	4		2	7	9*		8		12	6	11			1	5		10					
24	12 Jan	Portsmouth	1-1	15620	Houghton			3	4		2	7		12	8		9	6	11			1	5		10*					
25	2 Feb	York City	2-1	2400	Houghton, Corrigan			3	4		2	7		9	8		10	6	11			1	5							
26	6	BOURNEMOUTH	2-1	5904	Houghton, Wright			3	4		2	7		9	8		10	6	11			1	5							
27	9	HEREFORD UNITED	1-1	6123	Corrigan				4		2		12	9*	8		10	6	11			1	5	3	7					
28	16	Bradford City	1-2	6381	Quinn			3	4		2	7		9	8		10*	6	11			1	5		12					
29	29	Lincoln City	0-4	3644			3		4		6		10	9	8		12	5	11			1		2	7*					
30	5 Mar	ALDERSHOT	2-1	5018	Corrigan, Houghton				4		2	7		9	8			6	11			1	5		10		3			
31	8	NEWPORT COUNTY	0-1	6128					4*		2	7		9	8		12	6	11			1	5		10		3			
32	10	Tranmere Rovers	3-1	3069	Gore, Urquhart, Houghton				4		2	7	12	9	8			6	11			1	5		10*		3			
33	14	Torquay United	2-2	2824	Corrigan, Whittle				4		2	7	10	9	8			6	11			1	5				3			
34	19	Halifax Town	0-0	1406					4		2	7		9	8			6	11			1	5				3	10		
35	22	TRANMERE ROVERS	0-0	5828					4		2	7	12	9	8			6	11*			1	5				3	10		
36	26	PORT VALE	3-1	4854	Shearer(3)				4		2	7		9	8			6	11			1	5				3	10		
37	29	Scunthorpe United	3-1	2140	Gore, Shearer(2)				4		2	7		9	8			6	11			1	5				3	10		
38	4 Apr	Crewe Alexandra	1-2	5632	Corrigan				4		2	7	12	9	8			6	11			1	5		10*		3			
39	5	PETERBOROUGH UNITED	2-1	6094	Gore(pen), Methven				4		2	7		9*	8		12	6	11			1	5				3	10		
40	7	Port Vale	1-1	3814	Shearer				4		2	7	12		8		9	6	11*			1	5				3	10		
41	12	HALIFAX TOWN	3-1	5076	Quinn, Davids, Houghton				4		2	7		9	8			6	11			1	5				3			10
42	15	Hartlepool United	1-1	1840	Gore(pen)				4		2	7		9	8			6	11			1	5				3	10		
43	19	Northampton Town	1-1	2373	Shearer				4		2*			9	8			6	11			1	5				3	10	12	7
44	26	WALSALL	3-0	7720	Urquhart, Houghton(2)				4		2			9	8			6	11			1	5				3	10		7
45	30	DONCASTER ROVERS	0-0	4740					4		2	12		9	8			6	11			1	5				3	10		7
46	3 May	Aldershot	3-0	2683	Corrigan, Shearer(2)				4*		2	7		9	8			6	11			1	5				3	10	12	
					Apps.	10	8	27	46	3	46	41	17	40	46	8	12	41	37	1		36	34	3	17	1	17	11		4
					Subs.		1			1		1	6	1		1	6		4		1		1		2				2	
					Goals			5	9			7	3	15	5	1	2	1	4				2	1	9		1	9		1

F.A. CUP

Rd	Date	Opposition	Res.	Att.	Goalscorers	Shyne C.	Smart K.	Hinnigan J.	Gore T.	Ward N.	Fretwell D.	Corrigan F.	Moore M.	Houghton P.	Wright J.	Purdie I.	Brownbill D.	Davids N.	Urquhart G.	Hart N.	Crompton A.	Brown J.	Methven C.	McIvor R.	Quinn L.A.	Buckley G.	Whittle M.	Shearer D.	McMullen D.	Quinn M.
1R	24 Nov	Blackpool	1-1	11277	Methven			3	4		2	7		9	8			6	11			1	5		10					
1Rr	28	BLACKPOOL	2-0	14589	Corrigan, Gore			3	4		2	7		9	8			6	11			1	5		10					
2R	5 Jan	Northwich Victoria	2-2	5249	Gore, Hinnigan			3	4		2	7		9	8			6	11			1	5		10					
2Rr	7	NORTHWICH VICTORIA	1-0	11298	Brownbill			3	4		2*	7		9	8		12	6	11			1	5		10					
3R	14	Chelsea	1-0	22300	Gore			3	4		2	7		9	8		10	6	11			1	5		12					
4R	26	Everton	0-3	51863				3	4		2	7		9	8		10	6	11			1	5							

LEAGUE CUP

Rd	Date	Opposition	Res.	Att.	Goalscorers	Shyne C.	Smart K.	Hinnigan J.	Gore T.	Ward N.	Fretwell D.	Corrigan F.	Moore M.	Houghton P.	Wright J.	Purdie I.	Brownbill D.	Davids N.	Urquhart G.	Hart N.	Crompton A.	Brown J.	Methven C.	McIvor R.	Quinn L.A.	Buckley G.	Whittle M.	Shearer D.	McMullen D.	Quinn M.
1R1	11 Aug	Stockport County	1-2	6004	Houghton	1	2	3	4	5	6	7		9	8	11	10													
1R2	15	STOCKPORT COUNTY	0-0	7591		1	2	3	4	5	6	7		9	8	11	10													

Football League Division 4 : 1979/80 Final Table.

		Pl.	Home W	D	L	F	A	Away W	D	L	F	A	F.	A.	Pts
1	Huddersfield Town	46	16	5	2	61	18	11	7	5	40	30	101	48	66
2	Walsall	46	12	9	2	43	23	11	9	3	32	24	75	47	64
3	Newport County	46	16	5	2	47	22	11	2	10	36	28	83	50	61
4	Portsmouth	46	15	5	3	62	23	9	7	7	29	26	91	49	60
5	Bradford City	46	14	6	3	44	14	10	6	7	33	36	77	50	60
6	Wigan Athletic	46	13	5	5	42	26	8	8	7	34	35	76	61	55
7	Lincoln City	46	14	8	1	43	12	4	9	10	21	30	64	42	53
8	Peterborough Utd.	46	14	3	6	39	22	7	7	9	19	25	58	47	52
9	Torquay United	46	13	7	3	47	25	2	10	11	23	44	70	69	47
10	Aldershot	46	10	7	6	35	23	6	6	11	27	30	62	53	45
11	Bournemouth	46	8	9	6	32	25	5	9	9	20	26	52	51	44
12	Doncaster Rovers	46	11	6	6	37	27	4	8	11	25	36	62	63	44
13	Northampton Town	46	14	5	4	33	16	2	7	14	18	50	51	66	44
14	Scunthorpe United	46	11	9	3	37	23	3	6	14	21	52	58	75	43
15	Tranmere Rovers	46	10	4	9	32	24	4	9	10	18	32	50	56	41
16	Stockport County	46	9	7	7	30	31	5	5	13	18	41	48	72	40
17	York City	46	9	6	8	35	34	5	5	13	30	48	65	82	39
18	Halifax Town	46	11	9	3	29	20	2	4	17	17	52	46	72	39
19	Hartlepool United	46	10	7	6	36	28	4	3	16	23	36	59	64	38
20	Port Vale	46	8	6	9	34	24	4	6	13	22	46	56	70	36
21	Hereford United	46	8	7	8	22	21	3	7	13	16	31	38	52	36
22	Darlington	46	7	11	5	33	26	2	6	15	17	48	50	74	35
23	Crewe Alexandra	46	10	6	7	25	27	1	7	15	10	41	35	68	35
24	Rochdale	46	6	7	10	20	28	1	6	16	13	51	33	79	27

SEASON 1980-81

DIVISION 4

No.	Date	Opposition	Res.	Att.	Goalscorers	Brown J.	Fretwell D.	Whittle M.	Gore T.	Methven C.	Davids N.	McMullen D.	Wright J.	Houghton P.	Hutchinson R.	Quinn T.	Quinn M.	Curtis J.	Glenn D.	Corrigan F.	Kettle B.	Oliver J.	Ward A.	Urquhart G.	Tierney L.	Cribley A.	Urquhart B.	McAdam S.	Wignall M.	Lloyd L.
1	16 Aug	HARTLEPOOL UNITED	0-3	5233		1	2	3	4	5	6	7	8	9	10	11	12													
2	23	Lincoln City	0-2	3939		1	3	11	4	5	6	12	8	9	10		7*	2												
3	30	ALDERSHOT	1-0	4300	Wright	1	2	3	4	5	6	7	8	9	10	12	11*													
4	6 Sep	PORT VALE	1-0	4678	Gore	1	2	3	4	5	6	7	8	9	10				12	11										
5	13	Darlington	1-3	2321	O.G.	1	2		4	5	6	7	8		10				12	11	3	9*								
6	16	Halifax Town	1-0	2052	T.Quinn	1			4	5	6	7	8		9	10		2		11	3									
7	20	BURY	2-1	6239	Gore(2,1pen)				4	5	6	7	8		9*	10	12	2		11	3		1							
8	27	Mansfield Town	1-3	3402	Hutchinson				4	5	6	7*	8		9	10		2		11	3		1	12						
9	1 Oct	HALIFAX TOWN	4-1	4247	M.Quinn(2), Kettle, G.Urquhart				4	5	6		8		9		10	2		11	3		1	7						
10	4	Rochdale	0-3	3479					4	5	6		8	12	9		10	2		11*	3		1	7						
11	8	DONCASTER ROVERS	3-0	3608	M.Quinn(3)					5	6	7	8		9		10	2		12	3		1	4	11*					
12	11	PETERBOROUGH UNITED	1-1	4851	Corrigan					5	6	7	8		9		10	2		11	3		1	4*	12					
13	18	Torquay United	0-2	2013						5	6	7*	8		9		10	2		11	3		1	4	12					
14	20	Southend United	0-1	5643			4			5	6		8	12	9		10	2		11	3		1		7*					
15	25	TRANMERE ROVERS	1-1	5421	M.Quinn					5	6	7*	8	12	9		10	2		11	3		1	4						
16	29	YORK CITY	1-0	3668	G.Urquhart		6			5			8		9		10	2	7	11*	3	12	1	4						
17	1 Nov	Bournemouth	0-3	2983			6			5			8		9*		10	2	7	12	3		1	11		4				
18	4	Doncaster Rovers	1-1	3625	M.Quinn		3			5		12	8	9			10	2	7		11*		1		4	6				
19	8	BRADFORD CITY	0-1	5155			3			5		12			11*		10	2	7				1	8	4	6	9			
20	12	NORTHAMPTON TOWN	3-0	3375	M.Quinn(2), B.Urquhart		2			5			8				10		7	11			1	4		6	9	3		
21	15	Hartlepool United	1-3	5020	Houghton	1	3			5		12	8	7			10			11				4		6	9	2		
22	29	Hereford United	1-1	2358	Houghton	1	3			5		8		7	9		10	2		11				4		6				
23	6 Dec	SCUNTHORPE UNITED	1-1	3672	McMullen	1	2			5		8		7	9		10			11				4		6		3		
24	13	Crewe Alexandra	2-1	2829	T.Quinn, Houghton		2			5		7		9	10	12				11			1	4		6	8*	3		
25	26	CREWE ALEXANDRA	0-0	5026			2			5		7		9	10	8				11*			1	4		6	12	3		
26	27	Stockport County	1-0	3062	T.Quinn		2			5		7		9	10	8				11			1	4		6		3		
27	3 Jan	SOUTHEND UNITED	0-1	5267			2			5		7		9	10	8*				11			1	4		6	12	3		
28	10	York City	1-2	2028	B.Urquhart		2			5		7	11*	9	10	8							1	4		6	12	3		
29	24	Aldershot	1-0	2932	T.Quinn		2			5		7*	11	9	10	8	12						1	4		6		3		
30	31	LINCOLN CITY	0-2	5190			2			5		7*	11	9	10	8	12						1	4		6		3		
31	3 Feb	Northampton Town	1-1	1708	M.Quinn		2			5			11	9	10	8	7						1	4*	12	6		3		
32	7	DARLINGTON	3-1	3626	Methven, Wright, M.Quinn		2			5			11	9	10	8	7						1			6		3	4	
33	11	HEREFORD UNITED	1-0	3370	Wright		2			5			11	9	10*	8	7		12				1			6		3	4	
34	14	Port Vale	0-3	3214			2			5		12	11	9	4	8	7						1			6	10	3*		
35	21	MANSFIELD TOWN	2-0	4032	M.Quinn, Wright		6			5			11	10		8	9	2					1			4	12	3	7*	
36	28	Bury	0-0	4700			6			5			11	10		8	9	2					1			7		3	4	
37	7 Mar	ROCHDALE	0-1	6029			12			5			11	10		8	9*	2					1			4		3	7	6
38	13	Peterborough United	0-0	3455						5			8	10			9	2		11			1	7		4		3		6
39	21	Torquay United	2-0	3376	Hutchinson, O.G.					5			8	10	12		9	2		11			1	7*		4		3		6
40	29	Tranmere Rovers	3-2	3437	Houghton(3)					5			8	10			9	2		11			1	7		4		3		6
41	31	Wimbledon	0-1	2638						5			8	10			9	2		11			1	7		4		3		6
42	4 Apr	BOURNEMOUTH	0-1	3750			2			5			8			10*	9			11			1	7		4	12	3		6
43	11	Bradford City	3-3	2069	Wright(2,2pens), M.Quinn		6			5			8	10		12	9		7	11*			1			2		3	4	
44	18	STOCKPORT COUNTY	2-1	3980	Hutchinson, T.Quinn		2			5					10	9			7	11			1			4		3	8	6
45	25	WIMBLEDON	1-0	3381	Methven		2			5			11	10	7	12	9						1			4		3*	8	6
46	2 May	Scunthorpe United	4-4	1704	M.Quinn, Wright(pen), Glenn(2)		3			5			8	10	11	12	9		7				1			2			4	6*
					Apps.	9	32	4	10	46	15	20	38	29	34	19	32	23	8	27	14	1	37	26	4	30	5	25	9	9
					Subs.		1					5		3	1	5	4		3	2		1		1	3		5			
					Goals				3	2		1	7	6	3	5	14		2	1	1			2			2			

F.A. CUP

Round	Date	Opposition	Res.	Att.	Goalscorers	Brown J.	Fretwell D.	Whittle M.	Gore T.	Methven C.	Davids N.	McMullen D.	Wright J.	Houghton P.	Hutchinson R.	Quinn T.	Quinn M.	Curtis J.	Glenn D.	Corrigan F.	Kettle B.	Oliver J.	Ward A.	Urquhart G.	Tierney L.	Cribley A.	Urquhart B.	McAdam S.	Wignall M.	Lloyd L.
1R	22 Nov	CHESTERFIELD	2-2	8682	Houghton(2)	1	2			5			8	7	4		10			11						6	9	3		
1Rr	25	Chesterfield	0-2	8372		1	2			5			8	7	4		10			11						6	9	3		

LEAGUE CUP

Round	Date	Opposition	Res.	Att.	Goalscorers	Brown J.	Fretwell D.	Whittle M.	Gore T.	Methven C.	Davids N.	McMullen D.	Wright J.	Houghton P.	Hutchinson R.	Quinn T.	Quinn M.	Curtis J.	Glenn D.	Corrigan F.	Kettle B.	Oliver J.	Ward A.	Urquhart G.	Tierney L.	Cribley A.	Urquhart B.	McAdam S.	Wignall M.	Lloyd L.
1R1	9 Aug	CREWE ALEXANDRA	2-1	5512	Gore(2)	1	2	3	4	5	6	7	8	9	10										11					
1R2	13	Crewe Alexandra	2-2	4063	Gore, Hutchinson	1	2	3	4	5	6		8	9	10	7									11					
2R2	27	Preston North End	0-1	8028		1	3	11	4	5	6	7	8	9	10			2												
2R2	3 Sep	PRESTON NORTH END	1-2	9692	Wright	1	2	3	4	5	6	7	8	9	10		11													

Football League Division 4 : 1980/81 Final Table.

		Pl.	Home W	D	L	F	A	Away W	D	L	F	A	F.	A.	Pts
1	Southend United	46	19	4	0	47	6	11	3	9	32	25	79	31	67
2	Lincoln City	46	15	7	1	44	11	10	8	5	22	14	66	25	65
3	Doncaster Rovers	46	15	4	4	36	20	7	8	8	23	29	59	49	56
4	Wimbledon	46	15	4	4	42	17	8	5	10	22	29	64	46	55
5	Peterborough Utd.	46	11	8	4	37	21	6	10	7	31	33	68	54	52
6	Aldershot	46	12	9	2	28	11	6	5	12	15	30	43	41	50
7	Mansfield Town	46	13	5	5	36	15	7	4	12	22	29	58	44	49
8	Darlington	46	13	6	4	43	23	6	5	12	22	36	65	59	49
9	Hartlepool United	46	14	3	6	42	22	6	6	11	22	39	64	61	49
10	Northampton Town	46	11	7	5	42	26	7	6	10	23	41	65	67	49
11	Wigan Athletic	46	13	4	6	28	16	5	7	11	22	39	51	55	47
12	Bury	46	10	8	5	38	21	7	3	13	32	41	70	62	45
13	Bournemouth	46	9	8	6	30	21	7	5	11	17	27	47	48	45
14	Bradford City	46	9	9	5	30	24	5	7	11	23	36	53	60	44
15	Rochdale	46	11	6	6	33	25	3	9	11	27	45	60	70	43
16	Scunthorpe United	46	8	12	3	40	31	3	8	12	20	38	60	69	42
17	Torquay United	46	13	2	8	38	26	5	3	15	17	37	55	63	41
18	Crewe Alexandra	46	10	7	6	28	20	3	7	13	20	41	48	61	40
19	Port Vale	46	10	8	5	40	23	2	7	14	17	47	57	70	39
20	Stockport County	46	10	5	8	29	25	6	2	15	15	32	44	57	39
21	Tranmere Rovers	46	12	5	6	41	24	1	5	17	18	49	59	73	36
22	Hereford United	46	8	8	7	29	20	3	5	15	9	42	38	62	35
23	Halifax Town	46	9	3	11	28	32	2	9	12	16	39	44	71	34
24	York City	46	10	2	11	31	23	2	7	14	16	43	47	66	33

Season 1980/81

(Back): T.Quinn, M.Quinn, McAllister, Tierney, Wright, Hendry, Tait. (Middle): Gillibrand (Coach), Urquhart, Oliver, Davids, Brown, Ward, Methven, Houghton, Corrigan, Banks (Train./Coach). (Front): Whittle, Wignall, Curtis, Gore, McNeill (Manager), McMullen, Hutchinson, Glenn, Fretwell.

Season 1982/83

(Back):Banks (Trainer), Bradd, Rogers, Barrow, Tunks, Methven, Houghton, Cribley, Langley, McNally (Chief Scout). (Middle): MacMahon, Glenn, Sheldon, Butler, Lloyd (Manager), Williams, O'Keefe, Weston. (Front): Aspinall, Hatton, Phillips.

FINAL LEAGUE TABLES 1981/82 - 1994/95

Football League Division 4 : 1981/82

		Pl.	Home					Away					F.	A.	Pts
			W	D	L	F	A	W	D	L	F	A			
1	Sheffield United	46	15	8	0	53	15	12	7	4	41	26	94	41	96
2	Bradford City	46	14	7	2	52	23	12	6	5	36	22	88	45	91
3	Wigan Athletic	46	17	5	1	47	18	9	8	6	33	28	80	46	91
4	Bournemouth	46	12	10	1	37	15	11	9	3	25	15	62	30	88
5	Peterborough Utd.	46	16	3	4	46	22	8	7	8	25	35	71	57	82
6	Colchester United	46	12	6	5	47	23	8	6	9	35	34	82	57	72
7	Port Vale	46	9	12	2	26	17	9	4	10	30	32	56	49	70
8	Hull City	46	14	3	6	36	23	5	9	9	34	38	70	61	69
9	Bury	46	13	7	3	53	26	4	10	9	27	33	80	59	68
10	Hereford United	46	10	9	4	36	25	6	10	7	28	33	64	58	67
11	Tranmere Rovers	46	7	9	7	27	25	7	9	7	24	31	51	56	60
12	Blackpool	46	11	5	7	40	26	4	8	11	26	34	66	60	58
13	Darlington	46	10	5	8	36	28	5	8	10	25	34	61	62	58
14	Hartlepool United	46	9	8	6	39	34	4	8	11	34	50	73	84	55
15	Torquay United	46	9	8	6	30	25	5	5	13	17	34	47	59	55
16	Aldershot	46	8	7	8	34	29	5	8	10	23	39	57	68	54
17	York City	46	9	5	9	45	37	5	3	15	24	54	69	91	50
18	Stockport County	46	10	5	8	34	28	2	8	13	14	39	48	67	49
19	Halifax Town	46	6	11	6	28	30	3	11	9	23	42	51	72	49
20	Mansfield Town	46	8	6	9	39	39	5	4	14	24	42	63	81	47
21	Rochdale	46	7	9	7	26	22	3	7	13	24	40	50	62	46
22	Northampton Town	46	9	5	9	32	27	2	4	17	25	57	57	84	42
23	Scunthorpe United	46	7	9	7	26	35	2	6	15	17	44	43	79	42
24	Crewe Alexandra	46	3	6	14	19	32	3	3	17	10	52	29	84	27

Football League Division 3 : 1982/83

		Pl.	Home					Away					F.	A.	Pts
			W	D	L	F	A	W	D	L	F	A			
1	Portsmouth	46	16	4	3	43	19	11	6	6	31	22	74	41	91
2	Cardiff City	46	17	5	1	45	14	8	6	9	31	36	76	50	86
3	Huddersfield Town	46	15	8	0	56	18	8	5	10	28	31	84	49	82
4	Newport County	46	13	7	3	40	20	10	2	11	36	34	76	54	78
5	Oxford United	46	12	9	2	41	23	10	3	10	30	30	71	53	78
6	Lincoln City	46	17	1	5	55	22	6	6	11	22	29	77	51	76
7	Bristol Rovers	46	16	4	3	55	21	6	5	12	29	37	84	58	75
8	Plymouth Argyle	46	15	2	6	37	23	4	6	13	24	43	61	66	65
9	Brentford	46	14	4	5	50	28	4	6	13	38	49	88	77	64
10	Walsall	46	14	5	4	38	19	3	8	12	26	44	64	63	64
11	Sheffield United	46	16	3	4	44	20	3	4	16	18	44	62	64	64
12	Bradford City	46	11	7	5	41	27	5	6	12	27	42	68	69	61
13	Gillingham	46	12	4	7	37	29	4	9	10	21	30	58	59	61
14	Bournemouth	46	11	7	5	35	20	5	6	12	24	48	59	68	61
15	Southend United	46	10	8	5	41	28	5	6	12	25	37	66	65	59
16	Preston North End	46	11	10	2	35	17	4	3	16	25	52	60	69	58
17	Millwall	46	12	7	4	41	24	2	6	15	23	53	64	77	55
18	Wigan Athletic	46	10	4	9	35	33	5	5	13	25	39	60	72	54
19	Exeter City	46	12	4	7	49	43	2	8	13	32	61	81	104	54
20	Orient	46	10	6	7	44	38	5	3	15	20	50	64	88	54
21	Reading	46	10	8	5	37	28	2	9	12	27	51	64	79	53
22	Wrexham	46	11	6	6	40	26	1	9	13	16	50	56	76	51
23	Doncaster Rovers	46	6	8	9	38	44	3	3	17	19	53	57	97	38

Football League Division : 1983/84

		Pl.	Home					Away					F.	A.	Pts
			W	D	L	F	A	W	D	L	F	A			
1	Oxford United	46	17	5	1	58	22	11	6	6	33	28	91	50	95
2	Wimbledon	46	15	5	3	58	35	11	4	8	39	41	97	76	87
3	Sheffield United	46	14	7	2	56	18	10	4	9	30	35	86	53	83
4	Hull City	46	16	5	2	42	11	7	9	7	29	27	71	38	83
5	Bristol Rovers	46	16	5	2	47	21	6	8	9	21	33	68	54	79
6	Walsall	46	14	4	5	44	22	8	5	10	24	39	68	61	75
7	Bradford City	46	11	9	3	46	30	9	2	12	27	35	73	65	71
8	Gillingham	46	13	4	6	50	29	7	6	10	24	40	74	69	70
9	Millwall	46	16	4	3	42	18	2	9	12	29	47	71	65	67
10	Bolton Wanderers	46	13	4	6	36	17	5	6	12	20	43	56	60	64
11	Orient	46	13	5	5	40	27	5	4	14	31	54	71	81	63
12	Burnley	46	12	5	6	52	25	4	9	10	24	36	76	61	62
13	Newport County	46	11	9	3	35	27	5	5	13	23	48	58	75	62
14	Lincoln City	46	11	4	8	42	29	6	6	11	17	33	59	62	61
15	Wigan Athletic	46	11	5	7	26	18	5	8	10	20	38	46	56	61
16	Preston North End	46	12	5	6	42	27	3	6	14	24	39	66	66	56
17	Bournemouth	46	11	5	7	38	27	5	2	16	25	46	63	73	55
18	Rotherham United	46	10	5	8	29	17	5	4	14	28	47	57	64	54
19	Plymouth Argyle	46	11	8	4	38	17	2	4	17	18	45	56	62	51
20	Brentford	46	8	9	6	41	30	3	7	13	28	49	69	79	49
21	Scunthorpe United	46	9	9	5	40	31	0	10	13	14	42	54	73	46
22	Southend United	46	8	9	6	34	24	2	5	16	21	52	55	76	44
23	Port Vale	46	10	4	9	33	29	1	6	16	18	54	51	83	43
24	Exeter City	46	4	8	11	27	39	2	7	14	23	45	50	84	33

Football League Division 3 : 1984/85

		Pl.	Home					Away					F.	A.	Pts
			W	D	L	F	A	W	D	L	F	A			
1	Bradford City	46	15	6	2	44	23	13	4	6	33	22	77	45	94
2	Millwall	46	18	5	0	44	12	8	7	8	29	30	73	42	90
3	Hull City	46	16	4	3	46	20	9	8	6	32	29	78	49	87
4	Gillingham	46	15	5	3	54	29	10	3	10	26	33	80	62	83
5	Bristol City	46	17	2	4	46	19	7	7	9	28	28	74	47	81
6	Bristol Rovers	46	15	6	2	37	13	6	6	11	29	35	66	48	75
7	Derby County	46	14	7	2	40	20	5	6	12	25	34	65	54	70
8	York City	46	13	5	5	42	22	7	4	12	28	35	70	57	69
9	Reading	46	8	7	8	31	29	11	5	7	37	33	68	62	69
10	Bournemouth	46	16	3	4	42	16	3	8	12	15	30	57	46	68
11	Walsall	46	9	7	7	33	22	9	6	8	25	30	58	52	67
12	Rotherham United	46	11	6	6	36	24	7	5	11	19	31	55	55	65
13	Brentford	46	13	5	5	42	27	3	9	11	20	37	62	64	62
14	Doncaster Rovers	46	11	5	7	42	33	6	3	14	30	41	72	74	59
15	Plymouth Argyle	46	11	7	5	33	23	4	7	12	29	42	62	65	59
16	Wigan Athletic	46	13	6	5	36	22	3	8	12	24	42	60	64	59
17	Bolton Wanderers	46	12	5	6	38	22	4	1	18	31	53	69	75	54
18	Newport County	46	9	6	8	30	30	4	7	12	25	37	55	67	52
19	Lincoln City	46	8	11	4	32	20	3	7	13	18	31	50	51	51
20	Swansea City	46	7	5	11	31	39	5	6	12	22	41	53	80	47
21	Burnley	46	6	8	9	30	24	5	5	13	30	49	60	73	46
22	Orient	46	7	7	9	30	36	4	6	13	21	40	51	76	46
23	Preston North End	46	9	5	9	33	41	4	2	17	18	59	51	100	46
24	Cambridge United	46	2	3	18	17	48	2	6	15	20	47	37	95	21

Football League Division 3 : 1985/86

		Pl.	Home					Away					F.	A.	Pts
			W	D	L	F	A	W	D	L	F	A			
1	Reading	46	16	3	4	39	22	13	4	6	28	29	67	51	94
2	Plymouth Argyle	46	17	3	3	56	20	9	6	8	32	33	88	53	87
3	Derby County	46	13	7	3	45	20	10	8	5	35	21	80	41	84
4	Wigan Athletic	46	17	4	2	54	17	6	10	7	28	31	82	48	93
5	Gillingham	46	14	5	4	48	17	8	8	7	33	37	81	54	79
6	Walsall	46	15	7	1	59	23	7	2	14	31	41	90	64	75
7	York City	46	16	4	3	49	17	4	7	12	28	41	77	58	71
8	Notts County	46	12	6	5	42	26	7	8	8	29	34	71	60	71
9	Bristol City	46	14	5	4	43	19	4	9	10	26	41	69	60	68
10	Brentford	46	8	8	7	29	29	10	4	9	29	32	58	61	66
11	Doncaster Rovers	46	7	10	6	20	21	9	6	8	25	31	45	52	64
12	Blackpool	46	11	6	6	38	19	6	6	11	28	36	66	55	63
13	Darlington	46	10	7	6	39	33	5	6	12	22	45	61	78	58
14	Rotherham United	46	13	5	5	44	18	2	7	14	17	41	61	59	57
15	Bournemouth	46	9	6	8	41	31	6	3	14	24	41	65	72	54
16	Bristol Rovers	46	9	8	6	27	21	5	4	14	24	54	51	75	54
17	Chesterfield	46	10	6	7	41	30	3	8	12	20	34	61	64	53
18	Bolton Wanderers	46	10	4	9	35	30	5	4	14	19	38	54	68	53
19	Newport County	46	7	8	8	35	33	4	10	9	17	32	52	65	51
20	Bury	46	11	7	5	46	26	1	6	16	17	41	63	67	49
21	Lincoln City	46	7	9	7	33	34	3	7	13	22	43	55	77	46
22	Cardiff City	46	7	5	11	22	29	5	4	14	31	54	53	83	45
23	Wolverhampton W.	46	6	6	11	29	47	5	4	14	28	51	57	98	43
24	Swansea City	46	9	6	8	27	27	2	4	17	16	60	43	87	43

Football League Division 3 : 1986/87

		Pl.	Home					Away					F.	A.	Pts
			W	D	L	F	A	W	D	L	F	A			
1	Bournemouth	46	19	3	1	44	14	10	7	6	32	26	76	40	97
2	Middlesbrough	46	16	5	2	38	11	12	5	6	29	19	67	30	94
3	Swindon Town	46	14	5	4	37	19	11	7	5	40	28	77	47	87
4	Wigan Athletic	46	15	5	3	47	26	10	5	8	36	34	83	60	85
5	Gillingham	46	16	5	2	42	14	7	4	12	23	34	65	48	78
6	Bristol City	46	14	6	3	42	15	7	8	8	21	21	63	36	77
7	Notts County	46	14	6	3	52	24	7	7	9	25	32	77	56	76
8	Walsall	46	16	4	3	50	27	6	5	12	30	40	80	67	75
9	Blackpool	46	11	7	5	35	20	5	9	9	39	39	74	59	64
10	Mansfield Town	46	9	9	5	30	23	6	7	10	22	32	52	55	61
11	Brentford	46	9	7	7	39	32	6	8	9	25	34	64	66	60
12	Port Vale	46	8	6	9	43	36	7	6	10	33	34	76	70	57
13	Doncaster Rovers	46	11	8	4	32	19	3	7	13	24	43	56	62	57
14	Rotherham United	46	10	6	7	29	23	5	6	12	19	34	48	57	57
15	Chester City	46	7	9	7	32	28	6	8	9	29	31	61	59	56
16	Bury	46	9	7	7	30	26	5	6	12	24	34	54	60	55
17	Chesterfield	46	11	5	7	36	33	2	10	11	20	36	56	69	54
18	Fulham	46	8	8	7	35	41	4	9	10	24	36	59	77	53
19	Bristol Rovers	46	7	8	8	26	29	6	4	13	23	46	49	75	51
20	York City	46	11	8	4	34	29	1	5	17	21	50	55	79	49
21	Bolton Wanderers	46	8	5	10	29	26	2	10	11	17	32	46	58	45
22	Carlisle United	46	7	5	11	26	35	3	3	17	13	43	39	78	38
23	Darlington	46	6	10	7	25	28	1	6	16	20	49	45	77	37
24	Newport County	46	4	9	10	26	34	4	4	15	23	52	49	86	37

Football League Division 3 : 1987/88

		Pl.	Home					Away					F.	A.	Pts
			W	D	L	F	A	W	D	L	F	A			
1	Sunderland	46	14	7	2	51	22	13	5	5	41	26	92	48	93
2	Brighton & Hove A.	46	15	7	1	37	16	8	8	7	32	31	69	47	84
3	Walsall	46	15	6	2	39	22	8	7	8	29	28	68	50	82
4	Notts County	46	14	4	5	53	24	9	8	6	29	25	82	49	81
5	Bristol City	46	14	6	3	51	30	7	6	10	26	32	77	62	75
6	Northampton Town	46	12	8	3	36	18	6	11	6	34	33	70	51	73
7	Wigan Athletic	46	11	8	4	36	23	9	4	10	34	38	70	61	72
8	Bristol Rovers	46	14	5	4	43	19	4	7	12	25	37	68	56	66
9	Fulham	46	10	5	8	36	24	9	4	10	33	36	69	60	66
10	Blackpool	46	13	4	6	45	27	4	10	9	26	35	71	62	65
11	Port Vale	46	12	8	3	36	19	6	3	14	22	37	58	56	65
12	Brentford	46	9	8	6	27	23	7	6	10	26	36	53	59	62
13	Gillingham	46	8	9	6	45	21	6	8	9	32	40	77	61	59
14	Bury	46	9	7	7	33	26	6	7	10	25	31	58	57	59
15	Chester City	46	9	8	6	29	30	5	8	10	22	32	51	62	58
16	Preston North End	46	10	6	7	30	23	5	7	11	18	36	48	59	58
17	Southend United	46	10	6	7	42	33	4	7	12	23	50	65	83	55
18	Chesterfield	46	10	5	8	25	28	5	5	13	16	42	41	70	55
19	Mansfield Town	46	10	6	7	25	21	4	6	13	23	38	48	59	54
20	Aldershot	46	12	3	8	45	32	3	5	15	19	42	64	74	53
21	Rotherham United	46	8	8	7	28	25	4	8	11	22	41	50	66	52
22	Grimsby Town	46	6	7	10	25	29	6	7	10	23	29	48	58	50
23	York City	46	4	7	12	27	45	4	2	17	21	46	48	91	33
24	Doncaster Rovers	46	6	5	12	25	36	2	4	17	15	48	40	84	33

Football League Division 3 : 1988/89

		Pl.	Home					Away					F.	A.	Pts
			W	D	L	F	A	W	D	L	F	A			
1	Wolverhampton W.	46	18	4	1	61	19	8	10	5	35	30	96	49	92
2	Sheffield United	46	16	3	4	57	21	9	6	8	36	33	93	54	84
3	Port Vale	46	15	3	5	46	21	9	9	5	32	27	78	48	84
4	Fulham	46	12	7	4	42	28	10	2	11	27	39	69	67	75
5	Bristol Rovers	46	9	11	3	34	21	10	6	7	33	30	67	51	74
6	Preston North End	46	14	7	2	56	31	5	8	10	23	29	79	60	72
7	Brentford	46	14	5	4	36	21	4	9	10	30	40	66	61	68
8	Chester City	46	12	6	5	38	18	7	5	11	26	43	64	61	68
9	Notts County	46	11	7	5	37	22	7	6	10	27	32	64	54	67
10	Bolton Wanderers	46	12	8	3	42	23	4	8	11	16	31	58	54	64
11	Bristol City	46	10	3	10	32	25	8	6	9	21	30	53	55	63
12	Swansea City	46	11	8	4	33	22	4	8	11	18	31	51	53	61
13	Bury	46	11	7	5	27	22	5	6	12	28	45	55	67	61
14	Huddersfield Town	46	10	8	5	35	25	7	1	15	28	48	63	73	60
15	Mansfield Town	46	10	8	5	32	22	4	9	10	16	30	48	52	59
16	Cardiff City	46	10	9	4	30	16	4	6	13	14	40	44	56	57
17	Wigan Athletic	46	9	5	9	28	22	5	9	9	27	31	55	53	56
18	Reading	46	10	6	7	37	29	5	5	13	31	43	68	72	56
19	Blackpool	46	10	6	7	36	29	4	7	12	20	30	56	59	55
20	Northampton Town	46	11	2	10	41	34	5	4	14	25	42	66	76	54
21	Southend United	46	10	9	4	33	26	3	6	14	23	49	56	75	54
22	Chesterfield	46	9	5	9	35	35	5	2	16	16	51	51	86	49
23	Gillingham	46	7	3	13	25	32	5	1	17	22	49	47	81	40
24	Aldershot	46	7	6	10	29	29	1	7	15	19	49	48	78	37

Football League Division 3 : 1989/90

		Pl.	Home					Away					F.	A.	Pts
			W	D	L	F	A	W	D	L	F	A			
1	Bristol Rovers	46	15	8	0	43	14	11	7	5	28	21	71	35	93
2	Bristol City	46	15	5	3	40	16	12	5	6	36	24	76	40	91
3	Notts County	46	17	4	2	40	18	8	8	7	33	35	73	53	87
4	Tranmere Rovers	46	15	5	3	54	22	8	6	9	32	27	86	49	80
5	Bury	46	11	7	5	35	19	10	4	9	35	30	70	49	74
6	Bolton Wanderers	46	12	7	4	32	19	6	8	9	27	29	59	48	69
7	Birmingham City	46	10	7	6	33	19	8	5	10	27	40	60	59	66
8	Huddersfield Town	46	11	5	7	30	23	6	9	8	31	39	61	62	65
9	Rotherham United	46	12	6	5	48	28	5	7	11	23	34	71	62	64
10	Reading	46	10	9	4	33	21	5	10	8	24	32	57	53	64
11	Shrewsbury Town	46	10	9	4	38	24	6	6	11	21	30	59	54	63
12	Crewe Alexandra	46	10	8	5	32	24	5	9	9	24	29	56	53	62
13	Brentford	46	11	4	8	41	31	7	3	13	25	35	66	66	61
14	Leyton Orient	46	9	6	8	28	24	7	4	12	24	32	52	56	58
15	Mansfield Town	46	13	2	8	34	25	3	5	15	16	40	50	65	55
16	Chester City	46	11	7	5	30	23	2	8	13	13	32	43	55	54
17	Swansea City	46	10	6	7	25	27	4	6	13	20	36	45	63	54
18	Wigan Athletic	46	10	6	7	29	22	3	8	12	19	42	48	64	53
19	Preston North End	46	10	7	6	42	30	4	3	16	23	49	65	79	52
20	Fulham	46	8	8	7	33	27	4	7	12	22	39	55	66	51
21	Cardiff City	46	6	9	8	30	35	6	5	12	21	35	51	70	50
22	Northampton Town	46	7	7	9	27	31	4	7	12	24	37	51	68	47
23	Blackpool	46	8	6	9	29	33	2	10	11	20	40	49	73	46
24	Walsall	46	6	8	9	23	30	3	6	14	17	42	40	72	41

Football League Division 3 : 1990/91

		Pl.	Home					Away					F.	A.	Pts
			W	D	L	F	A	W	D	L	F	A			
1	Cambridge United	46	14	5	4	42	22	11	6	6	33	23	75	45	86
2	Southend United	46	13	6	4	34	23	13	1	9	33	28	67	51	85
3	Grimsby Town	46	16	3	4	42	13	8	8	7	24	21	66	34	83
4	Bolton Wanderers	46	14	5	4	33	18	10	6	7	31	32	64	50	83
5	Tranmere Rovers	46	13	5	5	38	21	10	4	9	26	25	64	46	78
6	Brentford	46	12	4	7	30	22	9	9	5	29	25	59	47	76
7	Bury	46	13	6	4	39	26	7	7	9	28	30	67	56	73
8	Bradford City	46	13	3	7	36	22	7	7	9	26	32	62	54	70
9	Bournemouth	46	14	6	3	37	20	5	7	11	21	38	58	58	70
10	Wigan Athletic	46	14	3	6	40	20	6	6	11	31	34	71	54	69
11	Huddersfield Town	46	13	3	7	37	23	5	10	8	20	28	57	51	67
12	Birmingham City	46	8	9	6	21	21	8	8	7	24	28	45	49	65
13	Leyton Orient	46	15	2	6	35	19	3	8	12	20	39	55	58	64
14	Stoke City	46	9	7	7	36	29	7	5	11	19	30	55	59	60
15	Reading	46	11	5	7	34	28	6	3	14	19	38	53	66	59
16	Exeter City	46	12	6	5	35	16	4	3	16	23	36	58	52	57
17	Preston North End	46	11	5	7	33	29	4	6	13	21	38	54	67	56
18	Shrewsbury Town	46	8	7	8	29	22	6	3	14	32	46	61	68	52
19	Chester City	46	10	3	10	27	27	4	6	13	19	31	46	58	51
20	Swansea City	46	8	6	9	31	33	5	3	15	18	39	49	72	48
21	Fulham	46	8	8	7	27	22	2	8	13	14	34	41	56	46
22	Crewe Alexandra	46	6	9	8	35	35	5	2	16	27	45	62	80	44
23	Rotherham United	46	5	10	8	31	38	5	2	16	19	49	50	87	42
24	Mansfield Town	46	5	8	10	23	27	3	6	14	19	36	42	63	38

Football League Division 3 : 1991/92

		Pl.	Home					Away					F.	A.	Pts
			W	D	L	F	A	W	D	L	F	A			
1	Brentford	46	17	2	4	55	29	8	5	10	26	26	81	55	82
2	Birmingham City	46	15	6	2	42	22	8	6	9	27	30	69	52	81
3	Huddersfield Town	46	15	4	4	36	15	7	8	8	23	23	59	38	78
4	Stoke City	46	14	5	4	45	24	7	9	7	24	25	69	49	77
5	Stockport County	46	15	5	3	47	19	7	5	11	28	32	75	51	76
6	Peterborough Utd.	46	13	7	3	38	20	7	7	9	27	38	65	58	74
7	West Bromwich Alb.	46	12	6	5	45	25	7	8	8	19	24	64	49	71
8	Bournemouth	46	13	4	6	33	18	7	7	9	19	30	52	48	71
9	Fulham	46	11	7	5	29	16	8	6	9	28	37	57	53	70
10	Leyton Orient	46	12	7	4	36	18	6	4	13	26	34	62	52	65
11	Hartlepool United	46	12	5	6	30	21	6	6	11	27	36	57	57	65
12	Reading	46	9	8	6	33	27	7	5	11	26	35	59	62	61
13	Bolton Wanderers	46	10	9	4	26	19	4	8	11	31	37	57	56	59
14	Hull City	46	9	4	10	28	23	7	7	9	26	31	54	54	59
15	Wigan Athletic	46	11	6	6	33	21	4	8	11	25	43	58	64	59
16	Bradford City	46	8	10	5	36	30	5	9	9	26	31	62	61	58
17	Preston North End	46	12	7	4	42	32	3	5	15	19	40	61	72	57
18	Chester City	46	10	6	7	34	29	4	8	11	22	30	56	59	56
19	Swansea City	46	10	9	4	35	24	4	5	14	20	41	55	65	56
20	Exeter City	46	11	7	5	34	25	3	4	16	23	55	57	80	53
21	Bury	46	8	7	8	31	31	5	5	13	24	43	55	74	51
22	Shrewsbury Town	46	7	7	9	30	31	5	4	14	23	37	53	68	47
23	Torquay United	46	13	3	7	29	19	0	5	18	13	49	42	68	47
24	Darlington	46	5	5	13	31	39	5	2	16	25	51	56	90	37

Football League Division 2 : 1992/93 (Formerly Division 3)

		Pl.	Home					Away					F.	A.	Pts
			W	D	L	F	A	W	D	L	F	A			
1	Stoke City	46	17	4	2	41	13	10	8	5	32	21	73	34	93
2	Bolton Wanderers	46	18	2	3	48	14	9	7	7	32	27	80	41	90
3	Port Vale	46	14	7	2	44	17	12	4	7	35	27	79	44	89
4	West Bromwich Alb.	46	17	3	3	56	22	8	7	8	32	32	88	54	85
5	Swansea City	46	12	7	4	38	17	8	6	9	27	30	65	47	73
6	Stockport County	46	11	11	1	47	18	8	4	11	34	39	81	57	72
7	Leyton Orient	46	16	4	3	49	20	5	5	13	20	33	69	53	72
8	Reading	46	14	4	5	44	20	4	11	8	22	31	66	51	69
9	Brighton & Hove A.	46	13	4	6	36	24	7	5	11	27	35	63	59	69
10	Bradford City	46	12	5	6	36	24	6	9	8	33	43	69	67	68
11	Rotherham United	46	9	7	7	30	27	8	7	8	30	33	60	60	65
12	Fulham	46	9	9	5	28	22	7	8	8	29	33	57	55	65
13	Burnley	46	11	8	4	38	21	4	8	11	19	38	57	59	61
14	Plymouth Argyle	46	11	6	6	38	28	5	6	12	21	36	59	64	60
15	Huddersfield Town	46	10	6	7	30	22	7	3	13	24	39	54	61	60
16	Hartlepool United	46	8	6	9	19	23	6	6	11	23	37	42	60	54
17	Bournemouth	46	7	10	6	28	24	5	7	11	17	28	45	52	53
18	Blackpool	46	9	9	5	40	30	3	6	14	23	45	63	75	51
19	Exeter City	46	5	8	10	26	30	6	9	8	28	39	54	69	50
20	Hull City	46	9	5	9	28	26	4	6	13	18	43	46	69	50
21	Preston North End	46	8	5	10	41	47	5	3	15	24	47	65	94	47
22	Mansfield Town	46	7	8	8	34	34	4	3	16	18	46	52	80	44
23	Wigan Athletic	46	6	6	11	26	34	4	5	14	17	38	43	72	41
24	Chester City	46	6	2	15	30	47	2	3	18	19	55	49	102	29

Football League Division 3 : 1993/94

		Pl.	Home					Away					F.	A.	Pts
			W	D	L	F	A	W	D	L	F	A			
1	Shrewsbury Town	42	10	8	3	28	17	12	5	4	35	22	63	39	79
2	Chester City	42	13	5	3	35	18	8	6	7	34	28	69	46	74
3	Crewe Alexandra	42	12	4	5	45	30	9	6	6	35	31	80	61	73
4	Wycombe Wanderers	42	11	6	4	34	21	8	7	6	33	32	67	53	70
5	Preston North End	42	13	5	3	46	23	5	8	8	33	37	79	60	67
6	Torquay United	42	8	10	3	30	24	9	6	6	34	32	64	56	67
7	Carlisle United	42	10	4	7	35	23	8	6	7	22	19	57	42	64
8	Chesterfield	42	8	8	5	32	22	8	6	7	23	26	55	48	62
9	Rochdale	42	10	5	6	38	22	6	7	8	25	29	63	51	60
10	Walsall	42	7	5	9	28	26	10	4	7	20	27	48	53	60
11	Scunthorpe United	42	9	7	5	40	26	6	7	8	24	30	64	56	59
12	Mansfield Town	42	9	3	9	28	30	6	7	8	25	32	53	62	55
13	Bury	42	9	6	6	33	22	5	5	11	22	34	55	56	53
14	Scarborough	42	8	4	9	29	28	7	4	10	26	33	55	61	53
15	Doncaster Rovers	42	8	6	7	24	26	6	4	11	20	31	44	57	52
16	Gillingham	42	8	8	5	27	23	4	7	10	17	28	44	51	51
17	Colchester United	42	8	4	9	31	33	5	6	10	25	38	56	71	49
18	Lincoln City	42	7	4	10	26	29	5	7	9	26	34	52	63	47
19	Wigan Athletic	42	6	7	8	33	33	5	5	11	18	37	51	70	45
20	Hereford United	42	6	4	11	34	33	6	2	13	26	46	60	79	42
21	Darlington	42	7	5	9	24	28	3	6	12	18	36	42	64	41
22	Northampton Town	42	6	7	8	25	23	3	4	14	19	43	44	66	38

Football League Division 3 : 1994/95

		Pl.	Home					Away					F.	A.	Pts
			W	D	L	F	A	W	D	L	F	A			
1	Carlisle United	42	14	5	2	34	14	13	5	3	33	17	67	31	91
2	Walsall	42	15	3	3	42	18	9	8	4	33	22	75	40	83
3	Chesterfield	42	11	7	3	26	10	12	5	4	36	27	62	37	81
4	Bury	42	13	7	1	39	13	10	4	7	34	23	73	36	80
5	Preston North End	42	13	3	5	37	17	6	7	8	21	24	58	41	67
6	Mansfield Town	42	10	5	6	45	27	8	6	7	39	32	84	59	65
7	Scunthorpe United	42	12	2	7	40	30	6	6	9	28	33	68	63	62
8	Fulham	42	11	5	5	39	22	5	9	7	21	32	60	54	62
9	Doncaster Rovers	42	9	5	7	28	20	8	5	8	30	23	58	43	61
10	Colchester United	42	8	5	8	29	30	8	5	8	27	34	56	64	58
11	Barnet	42	8	7	6	37	27	7	4	10	19	36	56	63	56
12	Lincoln City	42	10	7	4	34	22	5	4	12	20	33	54	55	56
13	Torquay United	42	10	8	3	35	25	4	5	12	19	32	54	57	55
14	Wigan Athletic	42	7	6	8	28	30	7	4	10	25	30	53	60	52
15	Rochdale	42	8	6	7	25	23	4	8	9	19	44	44	67	50
16	Hereford United	42	9	6	6	22	19	3	7	11	23	43	45	62	49
17	Northampton Town	42	8	5	8	25	29	2	9	10	20	38	45	67	44
18	Hartlepool United	42	9	5	7	33	32	2	5	14	10	37	43	69	43
19	Gillingham	42	8	7	6	31	25	2	4	15	15	39	46	64	41
20	Darlington	42	7	5	9	25	24	4	3	14	18	33	43	57	41
21	Scarborough	42	4	7	10	26	31	4	3	14	23	39	49	70	34
22	Exeter City	42	5	5	11	25	36	3	5	13	11	34	36	70	34

SEASON 1981-82

DIVISION 4

No.	Date	Opposition	Res.	Att.	Goalscorers	Brown J.	McMahon J.	Glenn D.	Cribley A.	Lloyd L.	Methven C.	Sheldon K.	Barrow G.	Bradd L.	Quinn M.	Evans A.	Houghton P.	Wright J.	McAdam S.	Langley K.	Weston J.	Wignall M.	Tunks R.	O'Keefe E.	Taylor B.	Butler J.	Ward A.
1	29 Aug	Bradford City	3-3	4229	Evans(2), Bradd	1	2	3	4	5	6	7*	8	9	10	11	12										
2	5 Sep	SHEFFIELD UNITED	0-1	8001		1	2	3	4*	5	6	7	8		10	11	9	12									
3	12	Hartlepool United	1-2	1715	Houghton	1	2		4	5	6	7	8		10	11	9	12	3*								
4	19	NORTHAMPTON TOWN	3-1	3996	Glenn, Houghton, M.Quinn		2	3	12	5	6	7			10	11	9	4		8*							1
5	23	PORT VALE	2-0	4525	McMahon, Sheldon		2		3	5	6	7	12	8	10*	11	9	4									1
6	26	Tranmere Rovers	0-0	2774			2		3	5	6	7		8*	10	11	9	4		12							1
7	29	Bournemouth	0-0	4952			2			5	6	7	8		10	11	9	4			3						1
8	3 Oct	TORQUAY UNITED	1-0	4876	Houghton		2			5	6	7	8		10	11	9	4			3						1
9	10	STOCKPORT COUNTY	2-1	4873	Houghton, Methven		2			5	6	7	8	9		11	10				3	4					1
10	17	Hull City	2-0	3600	Moughton(2)		2			5	6	7	8	9		11	10				3	4					1
11	20	Bury	3-5	6249	Bradd, Barrow, Methven		2		12	5*	6	7	8	9		11	10				3	4					1
12	24	SCUNTHORPE UNITED	2-1	4553	McMahon, Barrow		2		5		6	7	8	9*	12	11	10				3	4					1
13	30	Colchester United	2-1	3882	McMahon, Houghton	1	2	7	3	5	6		8	9			10				11	4					
14	4 Nov	DARLINGTON	2-1	4512	Barrow, Weston	1	2	7	3	5	6		8	9			10				11	4					
15	7	HEREFORD UNITED	1-1	4715	Barrow		2	7*	3	5	6		8	9		12	10				11	4	1				
16	14	York City	0-0	2780					2	5	6	7	8	9		11	10				3	4	1				
17	28	Rochdale	1-1	2765	Bradd	1	2	3			6	7	8	5	9	11	10					4					
18	5 Dec	HALIFAX TOWN	2-0	4022	Houghton, Bradd		2	3			6	7	8	4	9	11	10*	12				6	1				
19	2 Jan	Mansfield Town	2-1	2173	Lloyd, Bradd		2	3		5	6		8	9		11	10				7	4	1				
20	5	TRANMERE ROVERS	0-0	4133			2	3		5	6		8	9	12	11	10				7*	4	1				
21	19	PETERBOROUGH UNITED	5-0	4111	Methven,Bradd(2),Houghton,Barrw		2*	3		5	6		8	9	7	11	10				12	4	1				
22	23	BRADFORD CITY	4-1	7107	Bradd, M.Quinn, Houghton(2)			3		5	6		8	9	7	11	10	4			2		1				
23	26	Crewe Alexandra	1-0	3874	Methven			2		5	6		8	9	7	11	10	4			3		1				
24	30	Northampton Town	3-2	2418	Lloyd, O'Keefe, Bradd			2	3	5	6		8	9	7		10	4					1	11			
25	6 Feb	HARTLEPOOL UNITED	1-1	6315	M.Quinn			2	3	5	6		8	9	7		10	4					1	11			
26	8	Port Vale	1-1	8775	Barrow			2	3	5	6		8	9	7		10					4	1	11			
27	13	Torquay United	0-0	2524				2	3	5*	6		8	9	7*	12	10					4	1	11			
28	17	ALDERSHOT	1-0	5120	O'Keffe(pen)			2	3		6		8	5	7	11	10				12	4	1	9			
29	26	Stockport County	1-0	5084	M.Quinn(pen)			2	3	5*	6			9	7	11	10				12	4	1	8			
30	6 Mar	HULL CITY	2-1	6008	Bradd(2)			2	5		6			9	12	11	10*	12			3	4	1	8			
31	9	BURY	3-2	7508	Barrow, Methven, O'Keffe		2	3	5		6		8	9		11	10					4	1	7			
32	12	Scunthorpe United	7-2	2511	Bradd(3),Houghtn(2),Methvn,Barrw		2	3	5		6		8	9	12	11	10					4	1	7			
33	16	Darlington	1-3	2147	Glenn		2	3	5		6		8	9		11	10					4*	1	7			
34	20	COLCHESTER UNITED	3-2	6747	Barrow(2), Bradd		2	3	5	4	6		8	9	12	11	10						1	7			
35	23	Sheffield United	0-1	22336			2		5	4	6		8	9*	12	11*	10				3		1	7			
36	27	Hereford United	0-3	4191			2	3		5	6		8	9			10						1	7	4		
37	30	BLACKPOOL	2-1	7329	Bradd, Methven		2	3		5	6		8	9	12		10*				11		1	7	4		
38	2 Apr	YORK CITY	4-2	6029	Barrow, McMahon, Methven(2)		2	3		5	6		8	9			10				11		1	7	4		
39	9	Blackpool	2-1	9439	Houghton, Bradd		2	3		5	6		8	9		12	10				11		1	7	4		
40	10	CREWE ALEXANDRA	3-0	6142	O'Keefe(3,1pen)		2	3	5		6		8	9*			10				11		1	7	4		
41	17	Halifax Town	0-0	3660			2	3	4	5	6		8	9			10				11		1	7			
42	24	ROCHDALE	1-1	6153	Houghton		2	3*	7	4	6		8	9	12		10						1		11	6	
43	1 May	Peterborough United	3-0	6229	Barrow, Bradd(2)		2	3	4	5	6		8	9			10					11	1	7			
44	4	BOURNEMOUTH	0-0	9021			2	3	4	5	6		8	9			10					11	1	7			
45	8	MANSFIELD TOWN	3-1	8517	O'Keefe(3,1pen)		2	3	4	5*	6		8	9			10					11	1	7	12		
46	15	Aldershot	0-2	2493			2	3	4		6			9	12		10				5	11	1	7	8*		
					Apps.	6	36	35	29	36	46	15	40	41	20	29	45	9	1	1	22	25	31	22	7	1	9
					Subs.				2				1		9	3	1	4		1	3				1		
					Goals		4	2		2	9	1	12	19	4	2	15				1			9			

F.A. CUP

Round	Date	Opposition	Res.	Att.	Goalscorers	Brown J.	McMahon J.	Glenn D.	Cribley A.	Lloyd L.	Methven C.	Sheldon K.	Barrow G.	Bradd L.	Quinn M.	Evans A.	Houghton P.	Wright J.	McAdam S.	Langley K.	Weston J.	Wignall M.	Tunks R.	O'Keefe E.	Taylor B.	Butler J.	Ward A.
1R	21 Nov	HARTLEPOOL UNITED	2-2	5303	Methven, Quinn		2		3		6	7	8	5	9		10				11	4	1				
1Rr	25	Hartlepool United	0-1	3739					2		6	7	8	5	9	11	10				3	4	1				

LEAGUE CUP

Round	Date	Opposition	Res.	Att.	Goalscorers	Brown J.	McMahon J.	Glenn D.	Cribley A.	Lloyd L.	Methven C.	Sheldon K.	Barrow G.	Bradd L.	Quinn M.	Evans A.	Houghton P.	Wright J.	McAdam S.	Langley K.	Weston J.	Wignall M.	Tunks R.	O'Keefe E.	Taylor B.	Butler J.	Ward A.
1R1	31 Aug	STOCKPORT COUNTY	3-0	5079	Lloyd, Quinn, Houghton	1	2	3	4	5	6	7	8	9*	10	11	12										
1R2	14 Sep	Stockport County	2-1	2913	Lloyd, Methven		2	3	12	5	6	7			10	11	9	4		8*							1
2R1	6 Oct	Aldershot	2-2	1960	Barrow(2)		2		3	5	6	7	8	9		11	10					4					1
2R2	27	ALDERSHOT	1-0	4926	Barrow	1	2	3	5		6	7	8		9	11	10					4					
3R	11 Nov	CHELSEA	4-2	12063	Wignall(2), Bradd, Evans		2		3	5	6	7	8	9		11	10					4	1				
4R	1 Dec	ASTON VILLA	1-2	15362	Houghton		2	3			6	7	8	5	9	11	10					4	1				

SEASON 1982-83

DIVISION 3

No.	Date	Opposition	Res.	Att.	Goalscorers	Tunks R.	McMahon J.	Glenn D.	O'Keefe E.	Cribley A.	Methven C.	Lodge P. (loan)	Barrow G.	Bradd L.	Houghton P.	Rogers J.	Butler J.	Weston J.	Langley K.	Lloyd L.	Gemmill A.	Williams W.	Lowe D.	Walsh S.	Sheldon K.	Steel W. (loan)	Shaw M.	Young D.
1	28 Aug	Lincoln City	1-2	3196	Bradd	1	2	3	4	5	6	7	8	9	10	11*	12										
2	4 Sep	BRENTFORD	3-2	5019	Houghton,O'Keefe(pen),Lodge(pen)	1	2		6	3	4	7	8	9*	10	11	12	5									
3	7	BRADFORD CITY	3-2	5339	Butler, Houghton, Rogers	1	2		4	5	6	7	8		10	11	9	3									
4	11	Cardiff City	2-3	3850	Houghton, Rogers	1	2		4	5	6	7	8	9	10*	11	12	3									
5	18	BOURNEMOUTH	1-2	4866	O'Keefe	1	2		4	5	6	7		9*	10	12	11	3	8								
6	25	Chesterfield	0-2	2835		1	2		4	3	6			9	11	12	8*		7	5	10							
7	28	Doncaster Rovers	6-3	4457	Methven,Houghtn(3),O'Keefe,Bradd	1	2		4	8	6			9	10			3	7	5	11							
8	2 Oct	PLYMOUTH ARGYLE	3-0	5011	Bradd(2), O'Keefe	1	2	12	9	7	4			10	11			5	6	3*	8							
9	9	SOUTHEND UNITED	4-0	4705	O'Keefe(3,1pen), Houghton	1	2	7	9	4				10	11			5	6	3	8							
10	16	Bristol Rovers	0-4	4439		1	2	7	4	8				9	10			3	6	5	11							
11	19	PORTSMOUTH	0-1	4504		1	2		6*	8	5			9			10	3	7	4	11	12						
12	23	Reading	1-2	2621	Bradd	1	2			8	6			9	10		7	3	12	5	11		4					
13	30	NEWPORT COUNTY	0-1	4108		1	2	3			5			8	9		6	7	12		10		4	11				
14	3 Nov	Exeter City	1-2	2399	Weston	1		4			6			9	10		3	8	2		11			5	7			
15	6	Orient	1-1	2266	Houghton	1		3		2	6			9	10		4	8			11			5	7			
16	13	MILLWALL	3-1	4456	Bradd, Houghton(2)	1	2			3	4			10	9		6	8			7			5		11		
17	27	Gillingham	2-0	3952	Langley, Lowe	1	2			3	6						9	11	4				10	5	7		8	
18	4 Dec	SHEFFIELD UNITED	3-2	5050	Lowe, Steel(2)	1	2			3	6						7	11	4				10	5		9	8	
19	18	OXFORD UNITED	0-1	4008		1	2	7	4	3	6			12			9	11	8				10*	5				
20	24	Wrexham	1-1	4091	O'Keefe	1	2	7	10	3*	6		8	12			9	11	4					5				
21	29	WALSALL	1-3	4564	Langley	1	2	7	10	3	6		8	12			9*	11	4					5				
22	1 Jan	Preston North End	1-4	7685	O'Keefe	1	2	7*	10	3	6		8				9	11	4				12	5				
23	3	HUDDERSFIELD TOWN	2-0	7724	Lowe, O.G.	1	2	3	10	4	6		8				9	11					12	5	7*			
24	8	Brentford	3-1	4939	O'Keefe, McMahon, Butler	1	2	3	10	4	6		8				9	11					7	5				
25	15	LINCOLN CITY	2-1	4731	Lowe, Barrow	1	2	6	10	5	4		8				9	11					7	3				
26	22	Bradford City	1-0	4741	O'Keefe(pen)	1	2	3	10	4	6		8		12		9	11					7*	5				
27	29	DONCASTER ROVERS	0-3	4387		1	2	3	10	4	6		8		12		9	11					7*	5				
28	5 Feb	CHESTERFIELD	2-2	3009	O'Keefe, Lowe	1	2*	3	10	4	6		8		7		9	11					12	5				
29	15	EXETER CITY	1-0	2764	O'Keefe	1	2	3	10	4	6		8		7		9	11						5				
30	18	Southend United	0-2	2277		1	2		10*	3	6		8		12		9	11	4				7	5				
31	26	BRISTOL ROVERS	0-5	3288		1	2	3	10		6		8		12		9	11	4*				7	5				
32	1 Mar	Portsmouth	0-0	16139		1	2	3			6		8		10		4	11					9	5	7			
33	5	READING	2-2	3042	Butler, O'Keefe(pen)	1	2	3	9		6		8		10		4	11						5	7			
34	12	Newport County	0-1	3647		1	2	3	9	11	6		8		10		4						7	5				
35	19	ORIENT	0-1	2954		1	2		10	3	5				12		6	11	7			8*	9	4				
36	27	Millwall	0-2	2772		1	2	11	12	3	6			5	9		4						10		7		8*	
37	2 Apr	Walsall	0-2	2829		1	2	3	9	4	6		8	12	10		11*						7	5				
38	4	WREXHAM	3-1	3377	Cribley, Barrow, Houghton	1		3		8	6		4		11			10	2				9	5	7			
39	9	Sheffield United	0-2	8918		1		3	12	8	6		4		11*			10	2				9	5	7			
40	16	CARDIFF CITY	0-0	4447		1			11	9	4		6				7	5	2				10	3	8			
41	19	Plymouth Argyle	2-0	3097	O'Keefe, Butler	1			10	8	6		4				11	3	2				9	5	7			
42	20	Oxford United	0-2	4596		1			10	8	6		4		12		11	3	2				9	5	7*			
43	30	GILLINGHAM	2-2	3610	O'Keefe(pen), Barrow	1			10	8	6		4		12		11	3	2				9	5	7*			
44	7 May	Bournemouth	2-2	4523	Lowe, Houghton	1			10	5	6			12	11		4	3	2				9		7*			8
45	10	Huddersfield Town	1-1	11093	O.G.	1			10	5	6		4		11		7	3	2				9					8
46	14	PRESTON NORTH END	0-1	7191		1				7	4		6	12	11		9	5*	2				10					8
					Apps.	46	35	25	34	41	44	5	28	16	27	4	37	41	26	7	11	1	25	31	14	2	3	3
					Subs.			1	2					6	7	2	3		2			1	3					
					Goals		1		16	1	1	1	3	6	12	2	4	1	2				6			2		

F.A. CUP

Round	Date	Opposition	Res.	Att.	Goalscorers	Tunks R.	McMahon J.	Glenn D.	O'Keefe E.	Cribley A.	Methven C.	Lodge P. (loan)	Barrow G.	Bradd L.	Houghton P.	Rogers J.	Butler J.	Weston J.	Langley K.	Lloyd L.	Gemmill A.	Williams W.	Lowe D.	Walsh S.	Sheldon K.	Steel W. (loan)	Shaw M.	Young D.
1R	21 Nov	TELFORD UNITED	0-0	4805		1	2			5	6			9	10		4	3	8			11			7			
1Rr	23	Telford United	1-2	5085	Butler	1	2			5	6			9	10		4	3	8			11*	12		7			

LEAGUE CUP

Round	Date	Opposition	Res.	Att.	Goalscorers	Tunks R.	McMahon J.	Glenn D.	O'Keefe E.	Cribley A.	Methven C.	Lodge P. (loan)	Barrow G.	Bradd L.	Houghton P.	Rogers J.	Butler J.	Weston J.	Langley K.	Lloyd L.	Gemmill A.	Williams W.	Lowe D.	Walsh S.	Sheldon K.	Steel W. (loan)	Shaw M.	Young D.
1R1	30 Aug	Stockport County	1-1	3418	O'Keefe	1	2	3	4	5	6		8	9	10	11			7									
1R2	14 Sep	STOCKPORT COUNTY *	1-1	4008	Bradd	1	2		4	5	6			9		11	8	3	7			10						
2R1	4 Oct	MANCHESTER CITY	1-1	12194	O.G.	1	2	7	4	8	6			9	10			3		5	11							
2R2	27	Manchester City	0-2	16083		1	2	7		3	6			9	10		12	8			11		4*	5				

* Won on penalties 6-5

SEASON 1983-84

DIVISION 3

No.	Date	Opposition	Res.	Att.	Goalscorers	Tunks R.	Cribley A.	Cornstive P.	Butler J.	Walsh S.	Methven C.	Bruce A.	Barrow G.	Lowe D.	Taylor S.	Houghton P.	Langley K.	Williams W.	Bailey N.	Kelly T.	Kilner J.	Newell M.	Johnson S.	Aspinall Warren	Schofield M.
1	27 Aug	Plymouth Argyle	0-0	3730		1	2	3	4	5	6	7	8	9	10	11									
2	3 Sep	OXFORD UNITED	0-2	2697		1	2	3	4	5	6	7		9	10	11	8*	12							
3	6	EXETER CITY	1-1	2569	Taylor	1	2	3	4	5	6	7	8	9	10		11								
4	10	Bournemouth	1-0	3161	Houghton	1	2	3	4	5	6		8	9	10	11	7								
5	17	BRENTFORD	2-1	3034	Taylor Bruce	1	2	3	4	5	6	12	8	9	10	11*	7								
6	24	Sheffield United	2-2	10797	Lowe Cribley	1	2	3	4	5	6	11	8	9	10		7								
7	26	Port Vale	1-1	4655	Bruce	1	2	3	4	5	6	11	8*	9	10	12	7								
8	1 Oct	HULL CITY	1-1	4858	Taylor(pen)	1	2	3	4	5	6	8		9	10	11	7								
9	8	LINCOLN CITY	2-0	3864	Taylor(pen), Cornstive	1	2	3*	4	5	6	11	8	9	10		7		12						
10	15	Preston North End	3-2	6622	Taylor, Bruce, Bailey	1	2	3	4	5	6	11	8	9	10		7		12						
11	18	Scunthorpe United	0-0	2345		1	2	3	4	5	6	11	8	9	10		7		12						
12	22	GILLINGHAM	1-2	4189	Bruce	1	2	3	4	5	6	11	8	9	10		7		12						
13	29	Burnley	0-3	7410		1	2	3	4	5	6	11	8	9	10*		7		12						
14	1 Nov	ORIENT	0-1	3362		1	6	3	4	5		11	8	9	10		7		2						
15	5	Millwall	0-2	3850		1	6	3	4	5		11	8	9	10		7		2						
16	12	WIMBLEDON	3-2	3470	Bruce, Barrow, Langley	1	2	3	9	5	6	11	8		10		7		4						
17	26	WALSALL	0-1	3485		1	5	3	4			11	8	9	10		7		6	2					
18	3 Dec	Newport County	3-5	3196	Taylor(pen), Walsh, Lowe	1	4	3*	9	5		11	8	12	10		7		6	2					
19	17	Southend United	0-1	1819		1	4	3	9	5		11	8		10		7		6	2					
20	26	BOLTON WANDERERS	0-1	10045		1	2	3	9	5	6	11	8	12	10		7		4*						
21	27	Bradford City	2-6	5176	Butler, Lowe		2	3*	4	5	6	11	8	9	10		7			12	1				
22	31	ROTHERHAM UNITED	2-1	3526	Bruce, Taylor		2		4	5	6	11	8	9	12		7			3	1	10*			
23	21 Jan	Brentford	1-0	3972	Cornstive	1	5	3	4*		6	11	8	9	10		7		12	2					
24	27	Orient	0-0	2123		1	2	3			6	11	8	9*	10		7		4	5		12			
25	4 Feb	Hull City	0-1	6841		1	3		4	5	6	11*	8	9	10		7		12	2					
26	11	SHEFFIELD UNITED	3-0	5079	Johnson(2), Barrow	1	3		4	5	6	11	8		10		7			2			9		
27	18	BURNLEY	1-0	7509	Barrow	1	3		4	5	6	11	8		10		7			2			9		
28	25	Gillingham	0-3	4013		1	2	3	4	5	6*	11			10		7		8	12			9		
29	3 Mar	SCUNTHORPE UNITED	2-0	3092	Johnson(2)	1	2	3		5	6	11*		12	10		7		8	4			9		
30	6	MILLWALL	0-0	3212		1	2			5	6	12	8	11	10*		7		3	4			9		
31	10	Wimbledon	2-2	2565	Johnson, Lowe	1	2	3		5	6	11*	8	10			7			4		12	9		
32	17	Lincoln City	1-0	2030	Barrow	1		3	2	5	6		8	10			7			4		11	9		
33	20	BOURNEMOUTH	1-3	2910	Kelly	1		3	2	5	6		8	10			7			4		11	9		
34	24	PRESTON NORTH END	1-0	4470	Kelly	1	2			5	6	11*	8	10			7			4		12	9	3	
35	27	Bristol Rovers	1-2	7072	Lowe		2		11	5	6		8	10			7			4	1		9	3	
36	31	PORT VALE	3-	3163	Lowe, Butler(2)	1	2		11	5	6		8	10			7			4			9	3	
37	3 Apr	PLYMOUTH ARGYLE	1-1	2756	Johnson	1	2		11	5	6		8	10			7			4			9	3	
38	7	Exeter City	1-1	2412	Barrow	1	2		11	5	6		8	10					7	4			9	3	
39	14	NEWPORT COUNTY	1-0	2903	Lowe		2		11	5	6		8	10			7		3	4	1		9		
40	17	BRISTOL ROVERS	0-0	2665		1	2		11*	5	6	12	8	10			7		3	4			9		
41	21	Bolton Wanderers	1-0	6142	Johnson	1	2		11	5	6		8	10			7			4			9	3	
42	23	BRADFORD CITY	0-1	3470		1	2		11	5		12	8	10			7			4		6	9	3*	
43	28	Walsall	0-3	3286		1	6		2	5			8	10			7		3	4		11*	9		12
44	2 May	Oxford United	0-0	8967		1	2		3	5	6	11	8	10			7			4			9		
45	7	Rotherham United	1-4	2863	Bruce	1	2		11	5	6	10	8*				7		3	4		12	9		
46	12	SOUTHEND UNITED	1-0	3335	Lowe	1	5	3	2		6	11	8	10			7			4			9		
					Apps.	42	44	29	41	42	39	32	42	37	29	5	44		16	27	4	5	21	7	
					Subs.							4		3	1	1		1	7	2		4			1
					Goals		1	2	3	1		7	5	8	7	1	1		1	2			7		

F.A. CUP

Round	Date	Opposition	Res.	Att.	Goalscorers	Tunks R.	Cribley A.	Cornstive P.	Butler J.	Walsh S.	Methven C.	Bruce A.	Barrow G.	Lowe D.	Taylor S.	Houghton P.	Langley K.	Williams W.	Bailey N.	Kelly T.	Kilner J.	Newell M.	Johnson S.	Aspinall Warren	Schofield M.
1R	19 Nov	Bradford City	0-0	4599		1	5	3	2		6	11	8	9	10		7		4						
1Rr	28	BRADFORD CITY	4-2	3471	Taylor(2), Bruce(2)		4	3*	9	5		11	8	12	10		7		6	2	1				
2R	10 Dec	WHITBY	1-0	4820	Taylor	1	2	3	4	5	6	11	8	9*	10		7		12						
3R		West Ham United	0-1	16000		1	2	3	4	5	6	11	8	9	10		7								

LEAGUE CUP

Round	Date	Opposition	Res.	Att.	Goalscorers	Tunks R.	Cribley A.	Cornstive P.	Butler J.	Walsh S.	Methven C.	Bruce A.	Barrow G.	Lowe D.	Taylor S.	Houghton P.	Langley K.	Williams W.	Bailey N.	Kelly T.	Kilner J.	Newell M.	Johnson S.	Aspinall Warren	Schofield M.
1R1	30 Aug	BURY	1-2	3071	Methven	1	2	3	4	5	6	7		9	10	11	8								
1R2	13 Sep	Bury	0-2	2558		1	2	3	4	5*	6		8	9	10	11	7							12	

ASSOCIATE MEMBERS CUP

Round	Date	Opposition	Res.	Att.	Goalscorers	Tunks R.	Cribley A.	Cornstive P.	Butler J.	Walsh S.	Methven C.	Bruce A.	Barrow G.	Lowe D.	Taylor S.	Houghton P.	Langley K.	Williams W.	Bailey N.	Kelly T.	Kilner J.	Newell M.	Johnson S.	Aspinall Warren	Schofield M.
1R	21 Feb	Bury	0-1	1613		1	4	3	9	5	6	11	8		10		7		12	2*					

Season 1983/84

(Back): Clarke (Res.Manager), Walsh, Barrow, Houghton, Tunks, Langley, Comstive, Cribley, Butler, Crompton (Y.T.Manager).
(Middle): Banks (Train.), Bruce, Young, Taylor, McNally (Manager), Methven, Williams, Lowe.
(Front): Schofield, Deakin, Phillips, Wilkes, Tarpey, Barratt, Mirchell, Gordon, Aspinall

Season 1984/85

(Back): Clarke (R.Coach), Langley, Barrow, Walsh, Methven, Tunks, Stewart, Johnson, Comstive, Newell, Cribley. (Front): Crompton (Y.T.Coach), Redshaw, Bruce, Cook, Kelly, McNally (Manager), Butler, Lowe, Aspinall, Bailey, Banks (Train.)

SEASON 1984-85

DIVISION 3

No.	Date	Opposition	Res.	Att.	Goalscorers	Tunks R.	Butler J.	Comstive P.	Kelly T.	Cribley A.	Methven C.	Bailey N.	Barrow G.	Johnson S.	Lowe D.	Langley K.	Bruce A.	Walsh S.	Newell M.	Jewell P.	Gardner P.	Bennett G.	Stewart W.	Aspinall Wayne	Aspinall Warren	Knowles B.	Schofield M.	Cook P.	Beesley P.	Redshaw R.
1	25 Aug	Bristol City	0-2	7640		1	2	3	4	5	6	7	8	9	10	11*	12													
2	1 Sep	BRADFORD CITY	1-0	3538	Johnson	1	2	3		4	6	7	8	9		11		5	10											
3	8	Brentford	0-2	3724		1	2	3	12	4	6*	7	8	9		11		5	10											
4	15	GILLINGHAM	0-0	3198		1	2	3		6	5	7	8	9		11		4	10											
5	18	LINCOLN CITY	1-0	2518	Johnson(pen)	1	2	3		4	6	7	8	9	10*	11	12	5												
6	22	Millwall	1-4	4400	Johnson(pen)	1	2	3	4	12	6	7*	8	9		11		5	10											
7	29	YORK CITY	1-2	3219	Johnson	1	2		4	3	6	12	8	9		7	11*	5	10										3*	12
8	3 Oct	Reading	1-0	3069	Butler	1	9		4	2	6	11	8			7		5	10											12
9	6	NEWPORT COUNTY	1-1	2601	O.G.	1	9		4	2	6	7	8*			11		5	10							3				11
10	13	Walsall	0-0	3561		1	8		4	2	6			9		7		5	10							3				11
11	19	Cambridge United	1-1	2672	Johnson	1	8		4	2		6		9		7		5	10			12				3				
12	23	BRISTOL ROVERS	1-0	3022	Johnson	1	7		4	2	6			9		11		5	10			8				3				
13	27	ORIENT	4-2	3007	Johnson(2,1pen), Knowles, Newell	1	7		4	2	6			9		11		5	10			8				3				
14	3 Nov	Swansea City	2-2	3883	Barrow, Butler	1	7		4	2	6		12	9		11		5	10*			8				3				
15	6	Bournemouth	0-1	3276		1	7		4	2	6		10*	9		11		5	12			8				3				
16	10	PLYMOUTH ARGYLE	1-0	3121	Newell	1	7		4	2	6		8	9		11		5	10							3				
17	24	Derby County	2-2	10364	Newell(2)	1	3		4	2	6		8	9	7	11		5	10											
18	1 Dec	HULL CITY	1-1	3743	Newell	1	7		4	2	6		8	9		11*		5	10			12				3				
19	14	Doncaster Rovers	1-1	3278	Barrow	1	2		4	5	6	12	8	9	7	11			10							3*				
20	22	Rotherham United	3-3	4462	Barrow(2), Kelly	1	3		4	2	6		8	9		11		5	10	7										
21	26	BOLTON WANDERERS	1-0	8871	O.G.	1	3		4	2	6		8	9	12	11		5	10	7*										
22	29	PRESTON NORTH END	2-0	4503	Johnson, Lowe	1	3		4	2	6		8	9	12	11		5	10*	7										
23	1 Jan	Burnley	2-1	5281	Barrow, Jewell	1	3		4	2	6*		8	9	7	11		5	12	10										
24	12	Bradford City	2-4	6514	Cribley, Newell	1	5		4	6		2			7	11	8*		9	10		12				3				
25	19	BRENTFORD	1-1	3358	Newell	1	8		4	2	6			9*	7	11		5	10	12						3				
26	2 Feb	York City	0-2	10948		1	3		4		6		8	9	7	11		5	10*		2	12								
27	9	MILLWALL	0-1	3127			3		4		6		8	9	7*	11		5		10	2	12	1							
28	166	Lincoln City	0-1	2286			2		4		6		8	9	7*	11	5			10		12	1	3						
29	2 Mar	Orient	1-1	2035	Lowe	1			4		5		8	9	7	11			12	10	2				6	3*				
30	5	Bristol Rovers	0-2	3883			3		4		5		8	9	7				10*	12	2		1		6		11			
31	9	CAMBRIDGE UNITED	3-3	2227	Bennett, Jewell, Kelly(pen)		5		6		4		7	12	8			3	10*	11	2		1							
32	17	WALSALL	1-2	2221	Johnson	1	3		4		6		8	9	12	11		5		10*		9						2		
33	23	Newport County	1-1	1626	Johnson	1	2		4		6		8	9		11		5	10	7		7				3				
34	30	BOURNEMOUTH	1-2	2402	Jewell	1	2		4		6		8		7	11	12	5	9	10*						3				
35	6 Apr	Bolton Wanderers	0-1	6067			2		4*		6		8		7	11	12	5	9	10			1			3				
36	8	BURNLEY	2-0	3517	Jewell, Lowe	1	2		4		6		8		7	11		5	9	12					10*	3				
37	13	Plymouth Argyle	0-1	4159		1	2		4		6		8		7	11		5	9*	10					12			3		
38	2	DERBY COUNTY	2-0	4015	Aspinall(pen), Walsh	1	2				6		8		7	11		5	9*	10		12			4	3				
39	23	BRISTOL CITY	2-2	2423	Bennett, Walsh	1	2		4		6				7	11		5	9	10*		12			8	3				
40	27	Hull City	1-3	8620	Jewell	1	2		4		6		8		7	11		5	9	10		12				3*				
41	30	SWANSEA CITY	2-0	2406	Bennett, Lowe	1	3		4	2	6		8		7	11		5		10		9*			12					
42	3 May	DONCASTER ROVERS	5-2	2660	Jewell(2), Kelly(2,1pen), Lowe	1	3		4	2	6		8		7	11		5		10		9								
43	6	Preston North End	5-2	4875	Barrow(2), Butler, Jewell, Newell	1	3		4	2	6		8		7	11*		5	12	10		9								
44	11	ROTHERHAM UNITED	2-1	3012	Barrow, Jewell	1	3			2	6		8		7	4*		5	9	10		11			12					
45	13	READING	1-1	2382	Newell		3			2	6		8		7			5	9	10*		12	1		4				11	
46	17	Gillingham	1-5	2604	Langley	1	3		4	2					7	8*		5	9	10					12				11	6
					Apps.	40	45	6	39	30	43	10	37	29	26	43	3	40	35	23	5	10	6	1	6	20	1	2	2	2
					Subs.				1	1		2	1	1	3		4		4	3		10			4					2
					Goals		3		4	1			8	11	5	1		2	9	9		3			1	1				

F.A. CUP

Rd	Date	Opposition	Res.	Att.	Goalscorers	Tunks R.	Butler J.	Comstive P.	Kelly T.	Cribley A.	Methven C.	Bailey N.	Barrow G.	Johnson S.	Lowe D.	Langley K.	Bruce A.	Walsh S.	Newell M.	Jewell P.	Gardner P.	Bennett G.	Stewart W.	Aspinall Wayne	Aspinall Warren	Knowles B.	Schofield M.	Cook P.	Beesley P.	Redshaw R.
1R	17 Nov	Wrexham	2-0	2527	Langley, Newell	1	2		4	5	6		8	9	7	11		5	10											
2R	8 Dec	NORTHWICH VICTORIA	2-1	5099	Newell, Johnson(pen)	1	2		4	5	6	12		9		11		5*	10	7					8					
3R	5 Jan	Chelsea	2-2	16220	Newell, Jewell	1	2		4	5		6	8		7	11	5		10	9										
3Rr	26	CHELSEA	0-5	9708		1	2		4	5*	6	11	8	9	7		12	5	10											

LEAGUE CUP

Rd	Date	Opposition	Res.	Att.	Goalscorers	Tunks R.	Butler J.	Comstive P.	Kelly T.	Cribley A.	Methven C.	Bailey N.	Barrow G.	Johnson S.	Lowe D.	Langley K.	Bruce A.	Walsh S.	Newell M.	Jewell P.	Gardner P.	Bennett G.	Stewart W.	Aspinall Wayne	Aspinall Warren	Knowles B.	Schofield M.	Cook P.	Beesley P.	Redshaw R.
1R1	28 Aug	Wrexham	3-0	1423	Newell, Johnson(2,1pen)	1	2	3		4	6	7	8	9		11		5	10											
1R2	4 Sep	WREXHAM	2-0	1202	Johnson, Langley	1	2	3	4	5	6	7	8	9		11			10											
2R1	25	WEST BROMWICH ALBION	0-0	6209		1	2	3	4	6			8	9	11	7		5	10											
2R2	9 Oct	West Bromwich Albion	1-3	8133	Methven	1	7		4	2	6	8		9		11		5	10*							3				12

FREIGHT ROVER TROPHY

Rd	Date	Opposition	Res.	Att.	Goalscorers	Tunks R.	Butler J.	Comstive P.	Kelly T.	Cribley A.	Methven C.	Bailey N.	Barrow G.	Johnson S.	Lowe D.	Langley K.	Bruce A.	Walsh S.	Newell M.	Jewell P.	Gardner P.	Bennett G.	Stewart W.	Aspinall Wayne	Aspinall Warren	Knowles B.	Schofield M.	Cook P.	Beesley P.	Redshaw R.
1R	29 Jan	Wrexham	2-2	736	Newell(2)	1	2		4		6	11#	8	9*	7			5	10			12		14		3				
1Rr	5 Feb	WREXHAM	3-1	1544	Jewell(2), Johnson		2		4		6		8	9	7	11		5		10			1			3				
2R	2 Apr	Bury	1-0	2141	Kelly(pen)	1	2		4		6		8		7	11		5	10	9*					12	3				
NQF	11	TRANMERE ROVERS	3-1	2027	Lowe(2), Kelly	1	2		4		6		8		7	11		5	10	9						3				
NSF	8 May	LINCOLN CITY	3-1	1782	Lowe, Barrow, Bennett	1	3		4	2	6		8		7*	11#		5	14	10		9			12					
NF	20	Mansfield Town	1-1	5214	O.G.	1	3*		4	2	6		8		7	11		5	10	14		9			12					
F	1 June	Brentford	3-1	39897	Newell, Kelly, Lowe	1			4	2	6		8		7	11		5	10#	14		9			12	3				

SEASON 1985-86

DIVISION 3

No.	Date	Opposition	Res.	Att.	Goalscorers	Tunks R.	Butler J.	Knowles B.	Kelly T.	Cribley A.	Methven C.	Lowe D.	Barrow G.	Newell M.	Langley K.	Griffiths I.	Aspinall Warren	Cook P.	Beesley P.	Jewell P.	Stewart W.	Bailey N.	Walsh S.
1	17 Aug	Swansea City	1-0	4700	Barrow	1	2	3	4	5	6	7	8	9	10	11							
2	24	DERBY COUNTY	2-1	4707	Newell, Lowe	1	2	3	4*	5	6	7	8	9	10		12	11					
3	26	York City	1-4	4067	Aspinall	1	2	3	4		6	7		9	10	11	12		5	8*			
4	31	BRENTFORD	4-0	2871	Kelly(pen), Aspinall, Newell(2)	1	2	3	4		6	7		9	10	11	8*		5	12			
5	7 Sep	Bristol City	0-1	5673			2	3			6	7		9	10	11	8	12	5	4*	1		
6	14	DARLINGTON	5-1	3694	Newell(3), Bailey, Cribley	1	2	3		5	6	7		9	10*		8	11		12		4	
7	17	Gillingham	0-2	3401		1	2	3		5	6	7		9	10		8	11		12		4*	
8	21	BOURNEMOUTH	3-0	3057	Aspinall(2pens), Newell	1	2	3		5	6	7		9	10	11	8			12		4*	
9	28	Chesterfield	1-1	3518	Newell	1	2	3	4*	5	6	7		9	10	11	8	12					
10	1 Oct	WALSALL	2-0	4818	Kelly, Jewell	1	2	3	4	5	6	7		9	10	11	8*						
11	5	Bury	0-0	4610		1	2	3	4	5	6	7		9	10	11	8						
12	12	BLACKPOOL	1-1	5993	Cribley	1	2	3	4	5	6	7		9	10	11*	8	12					
13	19	Cardiff City	1-3	2020	Griffiths	1	2	3	4	5	6	7		9	10*	11	12			8			
14	22	NOTTS COUNTY	3-1	3555	Newell(2), Kelly	1	2	3	4	5	6	7		9	10	11	12			8			
15	26	NEWPORT COUNTY	0-0	3719		1	2	3	4	5	6	7		9	10	11	12			8			
16	2 Nov	Reading	0-1	5378		1	2	3	4	5		7	12	9	10	11			6	8*			
17	5	Doncaster Rovers	2-2	2069	Newell, Aspinall	1	2	3	4	5		7		9	10	11	8		6				
18	9	ROTHERHAM	2-0	3084	Barrow, Newell	1	2	3	4	5	6	7	8	9	10	11*	12						
19	23	Plymouth Argyle	1-2	6714	Methven	1	2	3	4	5	6	7	8	9	10			11					
20	30	LINCOLN CITY	3-2	3014	Kelly, Newell, Methven	1	2	3	4	5	6	7	8	9	10	11							
21	14 Dec	Wolverhampton Wanderers	2-2	2982	Kelly, Newell	1	2	3*	4	5	6	7	8	9		11	12					10	
22	22	Derby County	0-1	14047		1	2		4		6	7*	8	9		11	5		3	12		10	
23	26	BRISTOL ROVERS	4-0	3711	Aspinall, Kelly(p), Griffiths, Newell	1	2	3	4		6	7	8	9		11	10*		5			12	
24	1 Jan	Bolton Wanderers	2-1	9252	Newll, Barrow	1	2	3	4		6	7	8	9	12	11	10*		5				
25	11	Brentford	3-1	4048	Aspinall(2), Barrow	1	2	3	4	5	6	7*	8		10		9	11		12			
26	18	SWANSEA CITY	5-0	3308	Aspinall, Cook, Methven(2), Kelly	1	2	3	4	5	6	7	8		10		9	11					
27	1 Feb	BRISTOL CITY	1-1	3402	Cook	1	2	3	4*	5	6	7	8		10		12	11		9			
28	4	Notts County	1-1	3369	Barrow	1	2	3		4	6	7	8		10			11		9			5
29	8	CARDIFF CITY	2-0	3428	Aspinall, Lowe	1	2	3	4	5	6	7	8		10	11	9						
30	15	GILLINGHAM	3-3	5017	Kelly, Aspinall, Griffiths	1	2	3	4	5	6	7	8		10	11	9						
31	22	Bournemouth	2-0	3949	Methven, Jewell	1	2	3	4	5	6	7	8		10	11*	9			12			
32	1 Mar	CHESTERFIELD	2-0	3209	Aspinall, Methven	1	2	3	4		6	7	8		10	11*	9			12			5
33	11	BURY	1-0	3521	Aspinall	1	2	3				7	8		10	11	9	4*	6	12			5
34	15	Blackpool	2-1	6218	Langley, Jewell	1	2	3		5	6	7	8		10	11	9*			4			12
35	18	York City	1-0	4307	Aspinall	1	2	3	4	5	6	7	8		10	11	9						
36	22	Newport County	4-3	1700	Kelly(pen), Langley, Lowe, Aspinall	1	2	3	4	5	6	7	8		10	11	9						
37	29	BOLTON WANDERERS	1-3	8009	Methven	1		3	4	2	6	7	8		10*	11	9			12			5
38	1 Apr	Bristol Rovers	1-1	3428	Barrow	1		3	4	2	6	7	8		10	11	9			12			5*
39	5	DONCASTER rOVERS	0-1	4143				3	4	2	6	7	8		10	11	9*		5	12	1		
40	12	Rotherham United	0-0	3004				3		2	6	7			10	11	9	4*	5	8	1		12
41	15	Walsall	3-3	4293	Jewell, Lowe, Aspinall			3		2	6	7			10	11	9	4*	5	8	1		12
42	19	PLYMOUTH ARGYLE	3-0	9485	Jewell(2), Lowe			3		2	6	7	12		10	11	9		5	8	1		4*
43	22	READING	1-0	6056	Aspinall(pen)			3		2	6	7	12		10	11	9		5	8*	1		4
44	26	Lincoln City	0-0	3074				3		2	6	7	8		10	11	9*		5	12	1		4
45	29	Darlington	1-1	2013	Aspinall(pen)			3		2	6	7	12		10	11	9		5	8*	1		4
46	3 May	WOLVERHAMPTON WANDS.	5-3	4029	Aspinall(3,2pens), Walsh, Barrow	1		3		2	6	7	8		10	11	9		5	12			4*
					Apps.	38	36	45	32	38	43	46	26	24	42	38	33	11	17	14	8	5	10
					Subs.								4		1		8	3		15		1	3
					Goals				9	2	7	5	7	16	2	3	21	2		6		1	1

F.A. CUP

Rd	Date	Opposition	Res.	Att.	Goalscorers	Tunks R.	Butler J.	Knowles B.	Kelly T.	Cribley A.	Methven C.	Lowe D.	Barrow G.	Newell M.	Langley K.	Griffiths I.	Aspinall Warren	Cook P.	Beesley P.	Jewell P.	Stewart W.	Bailey N.	Walsh S.
1R	16 Nov	DONCASTER ROVERS	4-1	3315	Lowe(2), Aspinall, Newell	1	2	3	4	5	6	7		9	10	11	8						
2R	7 Dec	Runcorn	1-1	3310	Knowles	1	2	3	4	5	6	7	8	9*	10	11	12						
2Rr	10	RUNCORN	4-0	3390	Newell(2), Methven, O.G.	1	2	3	4	5*	6	7	8	9	10	11	12						
3R	4 Jan	BOURNEMOUTH	3-0	4185	Kelly, Methven, Aspinal	1	2	3	4		6	7*	8	9	10	11	12		5				
4R	25	Southampton	0-3	14462		1	2	3	4	5	6	7	8		10			11		9			

LEAGUE CUP

Rd	Date	Opposition	Res.	Att.	Goalscorers	Tunks R.	Butler J.	Knowles B.	Kelly T.	Cribley A.	Methven C.	Lowe D.	Barrow G.	Newell M.	Langley K.	Griffiths I.	Aspinall Warren	Cook P.	Beesley P.	Jewell P.	Stewart W.	Bailey N.	Walsh S.
1R1	20 Aug	PORT VALE	2-1	2227	Kelly(2)	1	2	3	4	5	6	7	8	9	10	11							
1R2	2 Sep	Port Vale	0-2	2772		1	2	3	4		6	7		9	10	11	8		5				

FREIGHT ROVER TROPHY

Rd	Date	Opposition	Res.	Att.	Goalscorers	Tunks R.	Butler J.	Knowles B.	Kelly T.	Cribley A.	Methven C.	Lowe D.	Barrow G.	Newell M.	Langley K.	Griffiths I.	Aspinall Warren	Cook P.	Beesley P.	Jewell P.	Stewart W.	Bailey N.	Walsh S.
Pre	22 Jan	Chester City	2-0	1375	Aspinall(2)	1	2	3	4	5	6	7	8		10		9*	11		12			
Pre	28	ROCHDALE	6-0	2106	Lowe(2),Barrow(2),Kelly,Griffiths	1	2*	3	4	5	6	7	8		10#	12		11		9		14	
1R	18 Feb	ROTHERHAM UNITED	3-0	2597	Lowe, Barrow, Aspinall	1	2	3	4	5	6	7	8		10	11	9						
NSF	26 Mar	Port Vale	2-1	4832	Barrow, Aspinall	1	2	3	4	5	6	7*	8		10	11	9#			12		14	
NF1	6 May	BOLTON WANDERERS	0-1	6975		1		3		2	6	7	8		10	11		12	5	9*		4	
NF2	9	Bolton Wanderers	1-2	12120	Jewell	1		3*		2	6	7	8		10	11			5	9		4	12

Season 1985/86

(Back): Aspinall, Knowles, Lowe, Stewart, Butler, Cook, Mitchell. (Middle): Banks (Train.), Mathias (A.Manager), Schofield, Wewell, Barrow, Cribley, Langley, Beesley, Tunks (Coach), Crompton, Bingham (Physio). (Front): Bailey, Kelly, Methven, Hamilton (Manager), Griffiths, Wilkes, Jewell.

Season 1986/87

(Back): Tunks (A.Manager), Knowles, Beesley, Lowey, Adkins, Schofield, Thompson, Cook. (Middle): Hamilton, Houston, Butler, Mathias (Manager), Cribley, Griffiths, Jewell. (Front): Lowe, Mitchell.

SEASON 1986-87

DIVISION 3

No.	Date	Opposition	Res.	Att.	Goalscorers	Tunks R.	Butler J.	Knowles B.	Cook P.	Cribley A.	Beesley P.	Lowe D.	Jewell P.	Hamilton D.	Lowey J.	Houston G.	Griffiths I.	Thompson C.	Hilditch A.	Adkins N.	Campbell R.	Holden A.	Whitehead A.
1	23 Aug	Notts County	0-2	3533		1	2	3	4	5	6	7	8	9	10	11*	12						
2	30	MIDDLESBOROUGH	0-2	2904		1	2	3	10	5	6	7	8	4			11	9					
3	6 Sep	Bristol City	1-2	6729	Griffiths	1	2	3	10*	5	6	7	9	4			11	8	12				
4	13	NEWPORT COUNTY	1-2	2163	Hamilton	1	2	3	10	5	6	7	9	4			11*	8	12				
5	16	WALSALL	5-1	2185	Lowe, Thompson(3,1pen), Hilditch	1	2		10	5	6	7	9	4			11	8	3				
6	20	Blackpool	1-5	4905	Cribley(pen)		2	3	12	5	6	7	9	4			11	8*	10	1			
7	26	BOLTON WANDERERS	2-1	4986	Thompson, Cook	1	2		11	5	6	7	9	4		10		8	3				
8	30	Rotherham United	2-0	2417	Hilditch, Lowe	1	2		11	5	6	7	9	4		10		8	3				
9	5 Oct	Swindon Town	1-3	6450	Campbell	1	2	12		5	6	7	10	4		11*		8	3		9		
10	11	BRISTOL ROVERS	4-3	2438	Houston(2), Lowe, Griffiths	1	2*			5	6	7	12	4		10	11	8	3		9		
11	18	FULHAM	2-0	2495	Campbell, Thompson	1	2	3		5	6	7		4		10	11	8			9		
12	21	Chesterfield	3-4	1804	Campbell(2), Thompson	1	2	3		5	6	7		4		10	11	8			9		
13	25	Bournemouth	1-3	4911	Thompson	1	2	3		5	6	7		4	12	10*	11	8			9		
14	1 Nov	CARLISLE UNITED	2-0	2982	Griffiths, Houston		2			5	3	7		4		10	11	8		1	9	6	
15	4	DONCASTER ROVERS	1-1	2388	Hamilton		2			5	3	7		4		10*	11	8	12	1	9	6	
16	8	Port Vale	1-0	3289	Houston		2	3		5	6	7	9	4		10	11	8		1			
17	22	Darlington	0-1	1612			2	3		5		7	9	4		10*	11	8		1	12	6	
18	29	GILLINGHAM	3-1	2492	Campbell(2), Lowe	1	2	3		5		7	10	4			11	8	12		9*	6	
19	13 Dec	BRENTFORD	1-1	2411	Lowe	1	2	3	4	5		7	10				11	8			9	6	
20	21	Mansfield Town	5-1	3035	Lowe(3), Campbell, Jewell	1	2	3	4	5		7	10				11	8			9	6	
21	26	CHESTER CITY	2-2	4187	Campbell, Thompson	1	2	3	4*	5		7	10	12			11	8			9	6	
22	27	York City	1-1	3237	Cribley(pen)	1		3	4	5		7	10	2		11		8			9	6	
23	1 Jan	Bury	3-1	3324	Cribley(pen), Jewell, Cook	1		3	4	5	6	7	10	2			11	8			9		
24	3	DARLINGTON	1-1	3154	Hilditch	1		3	4*	5	6			2		10	11	8	12		9		
25	24	BRISTOL CITY	3-1	3092	Hilditch, Campbell(2)	1		3	4	5		7	10	2			11	8	7		9	6	
26	7 Feb	Walsall	3-2	6959	Hilditch, Holden, Lowe	1		3	4	2	5	7	10		12		11	8	9*			6	
27	13	BLACKPOOL	4-1	6857	Cribley(2pens), Hilditch, Jewell	1		3	4	5	6	7	10	2				3	11		9		
28	28	ROTHERHAM UNITED	2-1	3917	O.G., Lowe	1		3		5	12	7	10	2			11	8	4		9	6#	
29	3 Mar	Carlisle United	2-0	2278	Thompson, Jewell	1		3		5	6	7	10	2			11	8	4		9		
30	17	CHESTERFIELD	1-1	2553	Lowe	1	12	3		5	6	7	10	2			11*	8	4		9		
31	21	Bristol Rovers	0-1	2635		1	2	3		5	6	7	10	4			11*	8	12		9		
32	24	NOTTS COUNTY	1-0	3171	Jewell		2	3	11	5	6	7	10	4				8		1	9		
33	28	SWINDON TOWN	3-1	4424	Campbell, Cribley(pen), Cook		2	3	11	5	6	7	10	4				8		1	9		
34	31	Newport County	2-1	1428	Cook, Jewell		2		11	5	6	7	10	4				8		1	9		6
35	4 Apr	PORT VALE	2-1	3567	Campbell(2)	1	2	3		5	6	7	10	4			11		8		9		
36	7	Bolton Wanderers	2-1	5321	Jewell, Campbell	1	2	3		5	6	7	10	4			11		8		9		
37	14	BOURNEMOUTH	0-2	4672		1	2	3		5	6	7	10	4			11*	12	8		9		
38	17	BURY	1-0	3892	Hilditch	1	2	3	11	5	6	7	10	4				8	12		9#		
39	20	Chester City	2-1	3813	Hilditch, Cribley(pen)	1	2	3	11	5	6	7	10*	4				8	9		12		
40	22	Doncaster Rovers	1-1	1470	Lowe	1	2	3	11	5	6	7				4		8	10		9		
41	25	MANSFIELD TOWN	3-0	3395	Lowe, Campbell, Jewell	1	2	3	11	5	6	7	10			12		8	4		9*		
42	28	Fulham	2-2	3609	Lowe, Jewell	1	2	3	11*	5	6	7	10	12				8	4		9		
43	2 May	Gillingham	0-0	5376		1	2	3		5	6	7	10	4			11	8			9		
44	4	YORK CITY	3-2	3816	Campbell, Lowe*, Hamilton	1	2	3		5	6	7	10	4			11	8			9		
45	6	Middlesborough	0-0	18523		1		3	11		6	7	10	4				8	2		9		5
46	9	Brentford	3-2	4235	Lowe, Cribley(pen), Knowles	1		3	11	5	6	7	10	4		9		8	2				
					Apps.	38	35	38	26	45	38	45	38	39	1	16	30	42	21	8	33	11	2
					Subs.		1	1	1		1		1	2	2	1	1	1	7		2		
					Goals			1	4	8		16	9	3		4	3	9	8		16	1	

F.A. CUP

Round	Date	Opposition	Res.	Att.	Goalscorers	Tunks R.	Butler J.	Knowles B.	Cook P.	Cribley A.	Beesley P.	Lowe D.	Jewell P.	Hamilton D.	Lowey J.	Houston G.	Griffiths I.	Thompson C.	Hilditch A.	Adkins N.	Campbell R.	Holden A.	Whitehead A.
1R	15 Nov	LINCOLN CITY	3-1	3547	Griffiths, Lowe(2)		2	3		5	6	7	9	4		10	11	8		1			
2R	6 Dec	Darlington	5-0	2552	Campbell(2),Jewell(2),Thompson	1	2	3	4	5		7	10			11		8			9	6	
3R	19 Jan	GILLINGHAM	2-1	3459	Thompson, Campbell	1		3	4	5			10	2			11	8	7		9	6	
4R	31	NORWICH CITY	1-0	8095	Jewell	1		3	4	5		7	10	2				8	11		9	6	
5R	21 Feb	HULL CITY	3-0	11453	Thompson, Jewell, Campbell	1		3		5		7	10	2			11	8	4		9	6	
6R	15 Mar	LEEDS UNITED	0-2	12250		1		3		5	6	7	10	2			11	8	4		9		

LEAGUE CUP

Round	Date	Opposition	Res.	Att.	Goalscorers	Tunks R.	Butler J.	Knowles B.	Cook P.	Cribley A.	Beesley P.	Lowe D.	Jewell P.	Hamilton D.	Lowey J.	Houston G.	Griffiths I.	Thompson C.	Hilditch A.	Adkins N.	Campbell R.	Holden A.	Whitehead A.
1R1	26 Aug	BLACKBURN ROVERS	1-3	2368	Cribley	1	2	3		5	6	7	8	4		11	10	9					
1R2	2 Sep	Blackburn Rovers	0-2	2831		1	2	3	10	5	6	7		4		8	11	9					

FREIGHT ROVER TROPHY

Round	Date	Opposition	Res.	Att.	Goalscorers	Tunks R.	Butler J.	Knowles B.	Cook P.	Cribley A.	Beesley P.	Lowe D.	Jewell P.	Hamilton D.	Lowey J.	Houston G.	Griffiths I.	Thompson C.	Hilditch A.	Adkins N.	Campbell R.	Holden A.	Whitehead A.
Pre	16 Dec	WREXHAM	2-2	1465	Knowles, Cribley	1	2	3	4	5		7	10				11	8			9	6	
Pre	3 Feb	Tranmere Rovers	3-2	1217	Cook, Jewell, Lowe	1		3	4	2	5	7	10				11	8			9	6	
1R	10	Bury *	1-1	1112	Jewell	1		3			5	7	10	1			11	8	4		9	6	

* After extra time and penalty shoot-out.

SEASON 1987-88

DIVISION 3

No.	Date	Opposition	Res.	Att.	Goalscorers	Tunks R.	Butler J.	Knowles B.	Hamilton D.	Cribley A.	Beesley P.	Storer S.	Thompson C.	Campbell R.	Jewell P.	Cook P.	Hilditch A.	Ainscow A.	Griffiths B.	Holden A.	Redfern D.	Adkins N.	Thompson D.	Atherton P.	Senior S.	Hughes P.	Pilling A.	Wilson A.	Smith B.	Kennedy A.	McEwan S.
1	15 Aug	Notts County	4-4	6344	Thompsn,Campbll,Knwles,Crbley(p)	1	2	3	4	5	6	7*	8	9	10	11	12														
2	29	Preston North End	1-0	7057	Cook	1	2	3	4	5	6		8	9	10	11	7														
3	31	GILLINGHAM	1-1	3412	Cribley(pen)	1	2	3	4	5	6	12	8	9	10*	11	7														
4	5 Sep	Bristol Rovers	3-2	3168	Beesley, Hamilton, Campbell	1	2	3	4	5	6	7*	8	9	10	11	12														
5	12	DONCASTER ROVERS	2-1	2764	Campbell, Ainscow	1	2	3	4	5	6	7	8#	9	10	11*	12	14													
6	15	Mansfield Town	1-0	3261	Cribley(pen)	1	2	3	4	5	6	7		9	10	11	8														
7	19	Walsall	2-1	5353	Jewell(2)	1	2	3	4	5	6	7		9	10	11	8														
8	26	BURY	0-2	3664		1	2	3	4	5	6	7	14	9	10	12	8#		11*												
9	29	Aldershot	2-3	2529	Campbell, Hilditch	1	2	3*	4	5	6	7#		9	10	11	8		14	12											
10	3 Oct	YORK CITY	1-1	2878	Butler		2	12	4	5	3	7#	8	9	10		8	14	11*	6	1										
11	10	Sunderland	1-4	13974	Jewell		2	12	4	5*	3	7	8		10		9	14	11#	6	1										
12	17	FULHAM	1-3	2806	Campbell		2	3	4		5	12	8	9	10		7	11*		6		1									
13	20	BRIGHTON & HOVE ALBION	3-3	2392	Hilditch(2), C.Thompson		2	3	4		5	12	8	9	10		11	14		6		1#	7*								
14	24	Blackpool	0-0	4821		1	2	3	4		5		8	9	10		11			6				7							
15	31	ROTHERHAM UNITED	3-0	3004	Jewell, Campbell(2)		2	3	4		5		8	9	10*	12	11			6	1				7						
16	3 Nov	Chesterfield	1-0	1725	Cook		2	3	4		5		8	9		10	11*			6					7	1					
17	7	SOUTHEND UNITED	1-0	3081	Cook		2	3	4		5			9	12	10	11			6					7	1					
18	21	Brentford	1-2	3625	Pilling		2	3	4		5			9	10	11		14	8*					6*	7	1	12				
19	28	BRISTOL CITY	1-1	2879	Holden		2	3	4		5			9	10*	11		12		6					7	1	8				
20	12 Dec	Grimsby Town	2-0	2196	O.G., Cook			3	4		5				10	11	2	9		6					7	1	8				
21	19	NORTHAMPTON TOWN	2-2	2692	D.Thompson, Pilling				4		5				10	11		9*					6	3	7	1	8	2	12		
22	26	Bury	2-0	4555	Holden, McEwan				4						10	11		9		6			7		2	1	8			3	5
23	28	CHESTER CITY	1-0	4394	Hilditch				4							11	10	9		6			7	12	2*	1	8			3	5
24	1 Jan	PRESTON NORTH END	2-0	6872	Hilditch(2)				4					12		11	10	9		6			7	2		1	8			3	5
25	2	Doncaster Rovers	4-3	2464	D.Thompson,Jewell,Cook,Ainscow				4		12				10	11		9		6*			7	2		1	8			3	5
26	16	WALSALL	3-1	5063	McEwan, Ainscow(2)				4		5				10	11		9					7	2		1	8			3	5
27	23	Gillingham	1-0	4256	Hamilton				4		6				10	11	12	9*					7	2		1	8			3	5
28	30	Northampton Town	1-1	4825	Pilling				4		6		12		10	11	9*						7	2		1	8			3	5
29	6 Feb	BRISTOL ROVERS	1-0	3827	Cook				4		6				10	11	9						7	2		1	8			3	5
30	13	Chesterfield	0-1	3088					4		6		12		10	11	9						7	2		1	8*			3	5
31	20	NOTTS COUNTY	2-1	5182	D.Thompson, Jewell				4		6		12		10	11	9						7	2	14	1	8			3	5
32	27	York City	1-3	2366	Jewell				4		6		12	14	10	11	9						7	2	5	1	8*			3	
33	1 Mar	ALDERSHOT	4-0	3017	Jewll(3), Hilditch				4		6		8	12	10	11	9*						7	2	5	1				3	5
34	5	Fulham	2-3	3860	D.Thompson, Hilditch				4		6		8	12	10	11#	9*		14				7	2		1				3	5
35	12	SUNDERLAND	2-2	6949	Cook, Senior		12		4		6		8	9*	10	11#			14				7			1				3#	5
36	19	Rotherham United	1-1	3288	McEwan		12		4		6		8	14	10	11	9*						7		2	1				3	5
37	25	BLACKPOOL	0-0	4505			2		4		6		8	9	10	11*			12				7		2	1				3	5
38	28	MANSFIELD TOWN	2-1	3217	McEwan, Griffiths		2		4				8	9	10	11*			12				7		6	1				3	5
39	1 Apr	Southend United	2-3	5003	Cook, Campbell				4		6		8	9	10	11			14				7		2	1	12			3	5
40	4	BRENTFORD	1-1	3597	Campbell						6		8	9	10	11			4				7		2	1	12			3	5
41	9	Brighton & Hove Albion	0-1	9423					4		6		8	9*	10	11			12				7		2	1				3	5
42	12	PORT VALE	2-0	3750	C.Thompson, Campbell				4		6		8	9	10	11							7		2	1				3	5
43	23	CHESTERFIELD	1-2	3303	Campbell				4		6		8	9	10	11*			12				7	2		1				3	5
44	25	Port Vale	1-2	3044	O.G.		14	3	4		6		8*	9	10	11#							7		2	1	12				5
45	30	Bristol City	1-4	7340	Jewell		11	3	4		6		8#	12	10	14							7		2*	1	9				5
46	2 May	GRIMSBY TOWN	0-1	2715			2	3	4		6		12	9	10	11							7		14	1	8				5#
					Apps.	10	23	21	45	11	41	9	25	28	40	38	25	9	5	14	3	2	27	14	20	31	16	1		22	23
					Subs.		3	2			1	3	6	6	1	3	4	6	8	1				1	2		4		1		
					Goals		1	1	2	3	1		5	11	11	8	8	4	1	2			2		1		3				4

F.A. CUP

Rd	Date	Opposition	Res.	Att.	Goalscorers	Tunks R.	Butler J.	Knowles B.	Hamilton D.	Cribley A.	Beesley P.	Storer S.	Thompson C.	Campbell R.	Jewell P.	Cook P.	Hilditch A.	Ainscow A.	Griffiths B.	Holden A.	Redfern D.	Adkins N.	Thompson D.	Atherton P.	Senior S.	Hughes P.	Pilling A.	Wilson A.	Smith B.	Kennedy A.	McEwan S.
1R	14 Nov	Altrincham	2-0	4004	Butler, Campbell		2	3	4		5		8	9	10	11				6					7	1					
2R	5 Dec	WOLVERHAMPTON W.	1-3	5879	Hilditch		2	3	4		5			9		11	10			6					7	1	8				

LEAGUE CUP

Rd	Date	Opposition	Res.	Att.	Goalscorers	Tunks R.	Butler J.	Knowles B.	Hamilton D.	Cribley A.	Beesley P.	Storer S.	Thompson C.	Campbell R.	Jewell P.	Cook P.	Hilditch A.	Ainscow A.	Griffiths B.	Holden A.	Redfern D.	Adkins N.	Thompson D.	Atherton P.	Senior S.	Hughes P.	Pilling A.	Wilson A.	Smith B.	Kennedy A.	McEwan S.
1R1	18 Aug	BOLTON WANDERERS	2-3	4115	Thompson, Campbell	1	2	3	4		6	7	8	9	10	11	12		5*												
1R2	25	Bolton Wanderers	3-1	5847	Campbell(3)	1	2	3	4	5	6	7*	8	9	10	11#	14		12												
2R1	22 Sep	LUTON TOWN	0-1	5108			2	3	4	5	6	7		9	10	11*	8		12			1									
2R2	6 Oct	Luton Town	2-4	4227	Hamilton, O.G.		2		4	5	3	7		9*	10		8	12	11	6	1										

FREIGHT ROVER TROPHY

Rd	Date	Opposition	Res.	Att.	Goalscorers	Tunks R.	Butler J.	Knowles B.	Hamilton D.	Cribley A.	Beesley P.	Storer S.	Thompson C.	Campbell R.	Jewell P.	Cook P.	Hilditch A.	Ainscow A.	Griffiths B.	Holden A.	Redfern D.	Adkins N.	Thompson D.	Atherton P.	Senior S.	Hughes P.	Pilling A.	Wilson A.	Smith B.	Kennedy A.	McEwan S.
Pre	13 Oct	CREWE ALEXANDRA	2-2	1552	Hamilton(pen), Thompson		2	3	4		5		8	9	10		7	11		6		1									
Pre	24 Nov	Bury	2-5	1620	Jewell(2)		2	3	4		5			9	10	11				6					7	1	8				

Season 1987/88

(Back): Philpotts (Coach), Thompson, Hilditch, Campbell, Adkins, Holden, Beesley, Cook, Tunks (A.Manager). (Front): Ainscow, Butler, Jewell, Hamilton, Mathias (Manager), Cribley, Griffiths, Storer, Knowles.

Season 1988/89

(Back): Philpotts (Coach), Beesley, Ainscow, Hughes, Hilditch, Senior, Adkins, McEwan, Holden, Cribley (Physio).(Front): Atherton, Tankard, Hamilton, Pilling, Russell, Mathias (Manager), Thompson, Butler, Rimmer, Crompton.

SEASON 1988-89

DIVISION 3

No.	Date	Opposition	Res.	Att.	Goalscorers	Hughes P.	Atherton P.	Tankard A.	Butler J.	Beesley P.	Holden A.	Pilling A.	Senior S.	Hilditch A.	Russell C.	Rimmer N.	Thompson D.	Hamilton D.	Parkinson J.	McEwan S.	Adkins N.	Entwistle W.	Diamond B.	Griffiths B.	Wilson A.	Ainscow A.	Johnson A.	Hemming C.	Woods R.	Ramage C.	Page D.	Fallon S.	Crompton J.
1	27 Aug	Bristol Rovers	2-3	4080	Rimmer, Russell	1	2	3	4	5	6	7	8	9	10	11																	
2	3 Sep	MANSFIELD TOWN	0-0	2514		1		3	4	5	6	8	2	9	10	11	7																
3	10	Brentford	1-1	4081	Rimmer	1		3	4	5	6	8	2	9	10	11	7																
4	17	READING	3-0	2534	Russell(2), Hilditch	1		3	4	5	6	8	2	9	10	11	7																
5	24	Fulham	1-1	3431	Butler	1		3	4	5	6	8	2	9	10*	11	7	12															
6	30	BLACKPOOL	2-1	4141	Rimmer(pen), Butler	1	2	3	4	5	6	8		9*		11	7	10	12														
7	4 Oct	Aldershot	1-3	1527	O.G.	1	2	3	4	5	6	8	9		7	11		10															
8	8	PORT VALE	0-2	3976		1	2	3	4	5*	6	8	9		7	11		10		12													
9	15	Wolverhampton Wanderers	1-2	10320	Hilditch	1	12		2	5	6	8	3	9*	10	11	7	4															
10	22	Sheffield United	1-2	11363	Atherton		12		2	5	6	8	3	9*		11	7	4			1	10											
11	25	BOLTON WANDERERS	1-1	4438	Entwistle		2		9	5	6	8	3			11	7	4			1	10											
12	28	Southend United	2-1	3120	Hamilton, Butler		2		8	5	6	12	3			11	7	4*			1	9	10										
13	1 Nov	SWANSEA CITY	1-2	2432	Diamond		2	12	8	5	6	4	3			11*	7				1	9	10										
14	5	NORTHAMPTON TOWN	1-3	2472	Entwistle		2		8	5	6	4	3			14	7			12	1	9*	10	11#									
15	8	Preston North End	2-2	8396	Thompson, Diamond			3	8	5	6	4	2			11	7				1	9	10										
16	12	BRISTOL CITY	0-1	2675				3	8	5			2			11	7	4		6	1	9	10										
17	26	HUDDERSFIELD TOWN	0-2	2779			4		8	3	5	7*	2							6	1	9	10		12	11							
18	3 Dec	Bury	1-1	3121	Entwistle		2		3	5	6	8	4	10			7				1	9				11							
19	10	SOUTHEND UNITED	3-0	2027	Thompson, Griffiths, Holden		2		3	5	6	8	4				7				1	9		11		10							
20	18	NOTTS COUNTY	0-1	3016			2		3	5	6	8*	4	14			7	12			1	9#		11		10							
21	26	Chester City	0-1	3262			2			5	6		3	8			7	4			1	9		11		10							
22	30	Cardiff City	2-2	4621	Entwistle, Griffiths		2*	12		5	6	8	3	10			7	4			1	9		11									
23	2 Jan	GILLINGHAM	3-0	3090	Hamilton, Entwistle, Hilditch		2			5	6	8	3	10			7	4			1	9		11									
24	7	CHESTERFIELD	0-2	2249			2	3		5	6	8		10			7	4			1	9*		11		12							
25	14	Mansfield Town	1-0	2788	Parkinson		2	3				8	6	10			7		4		1	9		11			5						
26	21	BRENTFORD	1-1	2514	Thompson		2	3		6		8	10				7		4		1	9		11				5					
27	4 Feb	Blackpool	0-2	4221			2#	3		6		8	10				7	12	4*		1	9		11			14	5					
28	11	ALDERSHOT	2-1	2132	Thompson, Griffiths		2	3*		6		8	10				7	12	4		1	9		11				5					
29	18	Port Vale	1-2	6100	Griffiths		2	3		6		8	10				7	4*	12		1	9#		11			14	5					
30	4 Mar	SHEFFIELD UNITED	1-2	3966	Senior		2	3		6		8	10	12			7		4		1	9#		11			5*		14				
31	11	Northampton Town	1-1	3443	Pilling	1	2	3		5		8	10	6			7		4					11						9			
32	24	Gillingham	1-2	3244	Griffiths	1	2	3		5		8	4	6			7							11					12	9*	10		
33	27	CHESTER CITY	3-0	3132	Senior, Griffiths, Ramage	1	2	3		5		8	4	6			7		12					11*						9	10		
34	1 Apr	Notts County	0-1	4929		1	2	3		5		8	4	6			7		14			12		11						9*	10#		
35	4	Chesterfield	1-1	3179	Beesley	1	4			5			3	6		8	7		2			12		11						9*	10		
36	7	CARDIFF CITY	1-0	2083	Ramage	1	4			5			3	6		8	7		2					11						9	10		
37	15	Swansea City	2-1	3719	O.G., Page	1	4	3					2	6		8	7					12		11*			5			9	10		
38	19	Reading	3-0	3821	Thompson, O.G., Page		4	3		5			2	6		8	7				1			11						9	10		
39	22	FULHAM	0-1	3056			4	3		5			2	6		8	7				1	12		11						9*	10		
40	29	Bristol City	1-0	5156	Tankard		4	3		5		6	2			8	7				1	9		11							10		
41	1 May	PRESTON NORTH END	1-1	5671	Beesley		4	3		5		6	2			8	7				1			11					12	9*	10		
42	3	BRISTOL ROVERS	3-0	2529	Griffiths, Thompson, Pilling		4	3		5		6	2			8	7				1			11					9		10		
43	6	BURY	1-0	3045	Johnson		4	3		5		6	2			8#	7				1			11*		12	14		9		10		
44	9	Bolton Wanderers	1-1	6166	Thompson		4	3		5		6#	2				7			14	1	12		11			8		9		10*		
45	13	Huddersfield Town	1-1	4225	Entwistle		4	3		5		6	2				7			8	1	10		11*					9		12		
46	16	WOLVERHAMPTON WANDS.	1-1	5531	Griffiths(pen)		4	3		5		6	2				7				1	10		11			14		9*		12	8#	
					Apps.	16	38	31	20	44	23	38	44	23	8	24	42	13	8	3	30	24	6	29		5	4	4	5	10	13	1	
					Subs.		2	2				1		2		1		4	4	3		5			1	2	4		3		2		
					Goals		1	1	3	2	1	2	2	3	3	3	7	2	1			6	2	8			1			2	2		

F.A. CUP

Rd	Date	Opposition	Res.	Att.	Goalscorers	Hughes P.	Atherton P.	Tankard A.	Butler J.	Beesley P.	Holden A.	Pilling A.	Senior S.	Hilditch A.	Russell C.	Rimmer N.	Thompson D.	Hamilton D.	Parkinson J.	McEwan S.	Adkins N.	Entwistle W.	Diamond B.	Griffiths B.	Wilson A.	Ainscow A.	Johnson A.	Hemming C.	Woods R.	Ramage C.	Page D.	Fallon S.	Crompton J.
1R	19 Nov	Hartlepool United	0-2	2476					8	3	5	10	2			11*	7	4		6	1	9				12							

LEAGUE CUP

Rd	Date	Opposition	Res.	Att.	Goalscorers	Hughes P.	Atherton P.	Tankard A.	Butler J.	Beesley P.	Holden A.	Pilling A.	Senior S.	Hilditch A.	Russell C.	Rimmer N.	Thompson D.	Hamilton D.	Parkinson J.	McEwan S.	Adkins N.	Entwistle W.	Diamond B.	Griffiths B.	Wilson A.	Ainscow A.	Johnson A.	Hemming C.	Woods R.	Ramage C.	Page D.	Fallon S.	Crompton J.
1R1	29 Aug	PRESTON NORTH END	0-0	4035		1	2	3	4	5	6	7*	8	9	10	11																	12
1R2	6 Sep	Preston North End	0-1	4945		1		3	4	5	6		2	9	10*	11	7			12													

SHERPA VAN TROPHY

Rd	Date	Opposition	Res.	Att.	Goalscorers	Hughes P.	Atherton P.	Tankard A.	Butler J.	Beesley P.	Holden A.	Pilling A.	Senior S.	Hilditch A.	Russell C.	Rimmer N.	Thompson D.	Hamilton D.	Parkinson J.	McEwan S.	Adkins N.	Entwistle W.	Diamond B.	Griffiths B.	Wilson A.	Ainscow A.	Johnson A.	Hemming C.	Woods R.	Ramage C.	Page D.	Fallon S.	Crompton J.
Pre	13 Dec	Rochdale	2-0	1134	Griffiths, Entwistle		2		3	5	6	8	4				7				1	9		11		10							
1R	17 Jan	Tranmere Rovers	1-0	2915	Thompson		2	3				8	6	10*			7		4		1	9		11		12		5					
NQF	21 Feb	CREWE ALEXANDRA	0-1	3004			2	3		5		8	9						4*		1	11		10			12	6		14			7#

SEASON 1989-90

DIVISION 3

No.	Date	Opposition	Res.	Att.	Goalscorers	Adkins N.	Senior S.	Tankard A.	Rimmer N.	Atherton P.	Beesley P.	Thompson D.	Parkinson J.	Hilditch A.	Page D.	Carberry J.	Patterson D.	Fallon S.	Johnson A.	Griffiths B.	Pilling A.	Nugent S.	McGarvey S.	Crompton J.	Ward R.	Daley P.	Kelly A.	Hughes P.	Rogerson L.	Taylor C.	Whitworth N.	Baraclough I.
1	19 Aug	Blackpool	0-0	4561		1	2	3	4	5	6	7	8	9	10	11*				12												
2	26	ROTHERHAM UNITED	0-3	2659		1	2		4	5	6	7	8*	9	10	11#		3	12	14												
3	2 Sep	Bury	2-2	3122	Hilditch(2)	1	2	3	4	5	6	7	8	9	10*	14				11#	12											
4	9	NORTHAMPTON TOWN	0-0	2459		1	2	3	4	5	6	7	8	9	10*	12				11												
5	16	Leyton Orient	0-1	4280		1	2*	3	4	5	6	7	8		10#	9	12			11		14										
6	23	CARDIFF CITY	1-1	2345	Pilling	1	2	3	4	5	6	7	8		10#	9*	12			11	14											
7	26	TRANMERE ROVERS	1-3	3136	Griffiths(pen)	1	2	3	4	5	6	7	8		10#	14	12			11	9*											
8	30	Brentford	1-3	4647	Pilling	1	2	3	4*	5	6	7			14		12			11	8		9	10#								
9	7 Oct	Bolton Wanderers	2-3	6462	Hilditch, O.G.	1		3	4	5	6			10		14	5	12		11#	8		9		7*							
10	14	SHREWSBURY TOWN	0-0	2279		1	2	3	4	5	6	7		8	10					11	12					9*						
11	17	Huddersfield Town	0-2	5119		1	2	3	4	5	6	7		9	10#	14	12			11	8*											
12	21	WALSALL	3-0	2229	Carberry, Dalcy, O.G.	1	2	3	4	5				8		7	6			11			9*		12	10						
13	28	Bristol City	0-3	6365		1	2	3	4	5		7*		9			6		12	11					8#	10	14					
14	31	READING	3-1	2029	Hilditch, Ward, Tankard(pen)		2	3		5				8	10	7	6			11*					4	9	12	1				
15	4 Nov	CREWE ALEXANDRA	1-0	2727	Daley		2	3		5		10		8#		7*	6		12	11					4	9	14	1				
16	11	Notts County	1-1	5449	Carberry		2	3		5				8	10	7*	6		12	11					4#	9	14	1				
17	25	Fulham	0-4	3156			2	3		5		14		8*	10#	7	6		12	11					4	9		1				
18	1 Dec	BIRMINGHAM CITY	1-0	2600	Ward		2	3	8	5					14	7*	6		12	11#	9				4	10		1				
19	16	SWANSEA CITY	2-0	2034	Daley(2)		2	3	8	5		7	4			12	6			11	9*					10		1				
20	26	Chester City	0-0	3165			2#	3	8	5		7	4	9			6*		12	11	14					10		1				
21	30	Preston North End	1-1	7220	Rimmer		2	3	8	5		7	4	9		12			6	11*						10		1				
22	1 Jan	Mansfield Town	4-0	2477	Thompson, Hilditch(3)		2	3	8	5		7#	4	9		12			6	11*	14					10		1				
23	13	Rotherham United	2-1	6055	Daley, Pilling		2	3	8	5		7	4*						6	11	9					10		1				
24	20	BLACKPOOL	1-1	3179	Pilling		2	3		5		7	4			12			6*	11	9					10		1	14			
25	3 Feb	Cardiff City	1-1	3218	Pilling		2#	3	8	5		7			4*	11			6	12	9					10		1		14		
26	10	LEYTON ORIENT	0-2	2396				3	8	5		7			9*	12			6	11#	4					10		1	14			
27	13	BURY	0-0	2104				3	8	5		7	2		9#	11*			6	12	4					10		1			2	
28	17	Birmingham City	0-0	5473			2	3	8	5		7	4			11	12		6		9					10		1				
29	24	FULHAM	2-1	2163	Griffiths(2,1pen)		2	3	8	5		7	4#			11*	14		6	12	9					10		1				
30	3 Mar	Bristol Rovers	1-6	5169	Carberry		2	3		5		7	4			12	14		6	11#	9					10		1	8*			
31	6	BRENTFORD	2-1	2052	Pilling, Thompson		2	3	8	5		7	4						6	11	9					10		1				
32	9	Tranmere Rovers	0-2	9604			2	3	8	5		7	4			12	14		6	11#	9*					10		1				
33	13	Northampton Town	1-1	2172	Daley		2	3	8	5		7	4				12		6	11	9					10*		1				
34	16	BOLTON WANDERERS	2-0	6850	Griffiths, O.G.		2	3	8	5		7	4						6	11	9					10		1				
35	20	Shrewsbury Town	3-1	2297	Thompson(3)		2	3	8	5		7	4			12	14		6	11*	9					10#		1				
36	24	HUDDERSFIELD TOWN	1-2	3167	Parkinson		2	3	8	5		7	4						6	11	9*					10#		1			14	12
37	31	Walsall	2-1	3182	Griffiths, O.G.		2	3	8	5			4	14		12			6	11*	7#					10		1				9
38	4 Apr	BRISTOL ROVERS	1-2	2352	Baraclough		2	3		5			4	8	14	7*	12		6	11						10#		1				9
39	7	BRISTOL CITY	2-3	3281	Baraclough, Parkinson		2	3		5		7	4	10	12		8		6	11*								1				9
40	10	Reading	0-2	3099			2	3	8	12		7	4	10#			5		6	11						14		1				9*
41	14	Mansfield Town	0-1	2421			2	3	8	5		7	4	10#	12		14		6	11								1				9*
42	16	CHESTER CITY	1-0	2277	Griffiths(pen)		2	3	8	5		7	4		12				6	11						10		1				9*
43	21	Swansea City	0-3	3141			2	3	8	5		7	4		12		14		6	11						10#		1				9*
44	24	PRESTON NORTH END	0-1	4454			2	3	8	5		7	4		10	12#	14		6	11								1				9*
45	28	NOTTS COUNTY	1-1	2433	Patterson		2	3	8	5		7	4		10	12	14		6	11*						9#		1				
46	5 May	Crewe Alexandra	2-3	3389	Griffiths, Johnson		2	3	8	5		7	4		10*	12	14		6	11						9#		1				
					Apps.	13	43	45	38	45	11	38	33	20	18	15	12	1	26	40	21		3	1	8	32		33	1		1	8
					Subs.					1		1		1	7	17	17	1	7	5	5	1			3	1	4		2	1	1	1
					Goals			1	1			5	2	7		3	1		1	7	6				2	6						2

F.A. CUP

Rd	Date	Opposition	Res.	Att.	Goalscorers	Adkins N.	Senior S.	Tankard A.	Rimmer N.	Atherton P.	Beesley P.	Thompson D.	Parkinson J.	Hilditch A.	Page D.	Carberry J.	Patterson D.	Fallon S.	Johnson A.	Griffiths B.	Pilling A.	Nugent S.	McGarvey S.	Crompton J.	Ward R.	Daley P.	Kelly A.	Hughes P.	Rogerson L.	Taylor C.	Whitworth N.	Baraclough I.
1R	19 Nov	MANSFIELD TOWN	2-0	3087	Page, Hilditch		2	3		5		12		8	10	7	6			11					4	9*		1				
2R	9 Dec	CARLISLE UNITED	2-0	4151	Johnson, Griffiths		2	3	8	5		11	4			7*	6		12	14	9#					10		1				
3R	6 Jan	Watford	0-2	10069			2	3	9*	5		7	4	8		11#			6	14	12					10		1				

LEAGUE CUP

Rd	Date	Opposition	Res.	Att.	Goalscorers	Adkins N.	Senior S.	Tankard A.	Rimmer N.	Atherton P.	Beesley P.	Thompson D.	Parkinson J.	Hilditch A.	Page D.	Carberry J.	Patterson D.	Fallon S.	Johnson A.	Griffiths B.	Pilling A.	Nugent S.	McGarvey S.	Crompton J.	Ward R.	Daley P.	Kelly A.	Hughes P.	Rogerson L.	Taylor C.	Whitworth N.	Baraclough I.
1R1	22 Aug	Wrexham	0-0	2042		1	2	3	4	5	6	7	8	9	10	11*				12												
1R2	29	WREXHAM	5-0	1871	Hilditch,Page,Prkinsn,Snior,Thmpsn	1	2	3	4	5	6	7	8	9	10*					11	12											
2R1	19 Sep	Liverpool	2-5	19231	Griffiths, Thompson	1		3	4	2	6	7	8		10#	9*	5		14	11		12										
2R2	3 Oct	LIVERPOOL *	0-3	17954		1	2	3	4	5	6	7*		9#	10	12	14			11	8											

* played at Anfield

LEYLAND DAF CUP

Rd	Date	Opposition	Res.	Att.	Goalscorers	Adkins N.	Senior S.	Tankard A.	Rimmer N.	Atherton P.	Beesley P.	Thompson D.	Parkinson J.	Hilditch A.	Page D.	Carberry J.	Patterson D.	Fallon S.	Johnson A.	Griffiths B.	Pilling A.	Nugent S.	McGarvey S.	Crompton J.	Ward R.	Daley P.	Kelly A.	Hughes P.	Rogerson L.	Taylor C.	Whitworth N.	Baraclough I.
Pre	5 Dec	BOLTON WANDERERS	1-0	2306	Daley		2	3	8	5		11				7	6		12	14	9#					10		1		4*		
Pre	19	Crewe Alexandra	0-1	1984			2	3	8	5		7	4			12	6			11	9*					10		1				
1R	9 Jan	Preston North End	2-1	4539	Daley, Rimmer		2	3	8	5		7	4						6	11	9					10		1				
NGF	30	DONCASTER ROVERS *	1-2	2742	Carberry		2	3		5		7	4*			14			6	11	9#				8	10		1	12			

* after extra time

Season 1989/90

(Back): Philpotts (Coach), Patterson, Beesley, Parkinson, Hughes, Johnson, Tankard, Atherton, Cavanagh (Coach). (Middle): D.Crompton, J. Crompton, Pilling, Senior, Banford, Hamilton (Manager), Adkins, Rimmer, Thompson, Woods, Cribley (Physio). (Front): Fallon, Ward, Griffiths, Andrews, Page, Carberry.

Season 1990/91

(Back): Patterson, Daley, Hughes, Philpotts (A.Manager), Adkins, Rogerson, Johnson. (Middle): Cribley (Coach/Physio), Fairclough, Tankard, Parkinson, Atherton, Page, Woods, Crompton (Y.T.Coach). (Front): Musker, Eyre, Pilling, Rimmer, Hamilton (Manager), Griffiths, Carberry, Phoenix, Hunter.

SEASON 1990-91

DIVISION 3

No.	Date	Opposition	Res.	Att.	Goalscorers	Adkins N.	Parkinson J.	Tankard A.	Atherton P.	Johnson A.	Hildersley R.	Woods R.	Rimmer N.	Daley P.	Fairclough D.	Griffiths B.	Patterson D.	Griffiths J.	Page D.	Appleton S.	Rogerson L.	Langley K.	Carberry J.	Pilling A.	Paladino J.	Pennock T.	Boughey D.	Hughes P.	Jones P.	Powell G.	Worthington G.
1	25 Aug	MANSFIELD TOWN	0-2	2049		1	2	3	4	5*	6	7	8	9	10	11	12	14													
2	1 Sep	Grimsby Town	3-4	5162	Woods, Page(2)	1	2	3	4		6*	7	8	9		11#	5	14	10	12											
3	8	BOURNEMOUTH	2-0	2159	Daley, Patterson	1	2	3	4			7	8	9		14	5	11#	10	6											
4	15	Rotherham United	1-5	4341	Page	1	2	3	4	12		7*	8	9#		14	5	11	10	6											
5	18	Fulham	2-1	3041	Daley(2)	1	2	3	4	12		7	8	9		11	5		10	6*											
6	22	BIRMINGHAM CITY	1-1	3907	Page	1	2	3	4	6		7	8	9		11	5		10												
7	28	BOLTON WANDERERS	2-1	4366	Patterson, Griffiths(pen)	1	2	3	4			7	8	9*	14	11	5		10#		12	6									
8	1 Oct	Tranmere Rovers	1-1	7030	Page	1	2	3	4	5		7	8	9	12	11*			10			6									
9	6	Crewe Alexandra	0-1	3771		1	2	3	4	5		7	8	9*	12	11#		14	10			6									
10	13	READING	1-0	2576	Daley	1	2	3	4	5		7		9		11			10			6	8								
11	20	SOUTHEND UNITED	4-1	2691	Page, Daley, Griffiths(2,1pen)	1	2	3	4	5		7		9		11	12		10			6	8*								
12	23	Cambridge United	3-2	4500	Johnson, Daley, Page	1	2	3	4	5		7		9		11	8		10			6									
13	27	Bradford City	1-2	6803	Woods	1	2#	3	4	5		7	8	9		11	12		10			6*		14							
14	3 Nov	PRESTON NORTH END	2-1	4728	Woods, Page	1	2*	3	4	5		7	8	9		11#	12		10			6	14								
15	10	Stoke City	0-2	12756		1	2	3	4	5		7	8	9*		11#	12		10			6	14								
16	24	LEYTONN ORIENT	1-2	2260	Johnson	1	2	3	4	5		7*	8			11	9#	12	10			6		14							
17	1 Dec	BURY	1-2	2878	Tankard	1	2	3	4	5			8	9*	7#	11	12	14	10			6									
18	15	Shrewsbury Town	0-0	2275		1	2	3	4	12		7	8			11	5		10*			6	14	9#							
19	23	Brentford	0-1	6495			2	3	4	6		7	8	9		11*	5		10			12			1						
20	26	EXETER CITY	4-1	2045	Page, Daley, Griffiths(2)		2	3	4	5		7	8	9		11			10			6			1						
21	29	SWANSEA CITY	2-4	2525	Page, Patterson		2	3	4	5	7*		8	9#		11	12		10			6	14		1						
22	1 Jan	Huddersfield Town	0-1	4887			2	3	4	5			8	9		11			10			6	7		1						
23	12	GRIMSBY TOWN	2-0	2893	Griffiths, Fairclough		2	3	4	5		7	8		9*	11#	12		10			6	14			1					
24	19	Mansfield Town	1-1	2166	Boughey		2	3	4	5			8		9*	11	12		10			6	14			1	7#				
25	26	Reading	1-3	3416	Boughey			3	4	5			8	9		11	2		10			6	14		1		7*				
26	3 Feb	FULHAM	2-0	2256	Griffiths, Pilling			3	4	5	10*		8	9		11#	2	7				6		14				1	12		
27	5	Birmingham City	0-0	5319				3	4	5			8	9		11*	2	7				6		12				1	10		
28	23	STOKE CITY	4-0	3728	Daley(2), Patterson, Page			3	4	5			8	9		11	2		10			6						1	7		
29	26	Chester City	2-1	1014	Johnson, Rimmer			3	4	5			8	9		11*	2		10			6	12					1	7		
30	2 Mar	Bury	2-2	2967	Johnson(2)			3	4	5			8	9					10			6	11	2				1	7		
31	5	Bournemouth	3-0	4662	Pilling, Daley, Page			3	4	5				9				8	10			6	11	2				1	7		
32	9	SHREWSBURY TOWN	2-2	2269	Langley, Pilling			3	4	5				9		12	14	8*	10#			6	11	2				1	7		
33	12	TRANMERE ROVERS	0-1	2912				3	4	5				9		11			10*			6	8	2				1	7	12	
34	16	Bolton Wanderers	1-2	7812	B.Griffiths(pen)			3	4	5						12	2		10*			6	11	8				1	7	9	
35	23	CREWE ALEXANDRA	1-0	2426	Carberry			3	4	5				9		11	2					6*	12	8#				1	7	10	14
36	26	ROTHERHAM UNITED	2-0	2171	Powell, Carberry			3	4	5				9		11*	2					6	8#	14				1	7	10	12
37	30	Exeter City	0-1	4510				3	4	5				9		12				14		6	8	2*				1	7	10	11
38	1 Apr	BRENTFORD	1-0	2160	Worthington			3	4	5				9		11*			12			6	8					1	7	10	2
39	6	Swansea City	6-1	2869	Carbrry, Wrthingtn(2), Grffths, Dley, Jnes			3	4	5				9		11*				14		6	8					1	7	10#	2
40	13	HUDDERSFIELD TOWN	1-1	4642	Worthington			3	4	5			8	9		11*			14	12			6					1	7	10*	2
41	16	CHESTER CITY	2-0	2131	Griffiths(pen), Powell			3	4	5			8	9		11*						6	12					1	7	10	2
42	19	Southend United	2-0	7550	Worthington, Rimmer			3	4	5			8	9		11*						6	12					1	7	10	2
43	23	Leyton Orient	1-1	2613	Langley			3	4	5			8	9		11						6	12					1	7	10	2*
44	27	CAMBRIDGE UNITED	0-1	3273				3	4	5			8	9		11				12		6	14					1	7*	10	2#
45	4 May	BRADFORD CITY	3-0	3267	Griffiths(2,1pen), Powell			3	4	5			8	9		11*				12		6	14		1				7#	10	2
46	11	Preston North End	1-2	5917	Powell			3	4	5			8	9					14	12		6	11		1					10	2#
					Apps.	18	25	46	46	40	4	20	34	41	4	38	18	6	31	3		38	14	8	7	2	2	19	19	13	10
					Subs.					3					3	5	10	5	3	7	1	1	14	5					1	1	2
					Goals			1		5		3	2	11	1	12	4		12			2	3	3			2		1	4	5

F.A. CUP

Round	Date	Opposition	Res.	Att.	Goalscorers	Adkins N.	Parkinson J.	Tankard A.	Atherton P.	Johnson A.	Hildersley R.	Woods R.	Rimmer N.	Daley P.	Fairclough D.	Griffiths B.	Patterson D.	Griffiths J.	Page D.	Appleton S.	Rogerson L.	Langley K.	Carberry J.	Pilling A.	Paladino J.	Pennock T.	Boughey D.	Hughes P.	Jones P.	Powell G.	Worthington G.
1R	17 Nov	CARLISLE UNITED	5-0	3947	Griffiths(2), Woods, Rimmers(2)	1	2	3	4	5		7	8	9*		11	12		10			6									
2R	8 Dec	HARTLEPOOL UNITED	2-0	2492	Page, Griffiths	1	2	3	4	5*		7	8			11	12		10			6		9							
3R	5 Jan	Coventry City	1-1	10802	Patterson		2	3	4	5		7	8		9*	11	12		10			6				1					
3Rr	8 Jan	COVENTRY CITY	0-1	7429			2	3	4	5		7	8		9*	11#	12		10			6	14			1					

LEAGUE CUP

Round	Date	Opposition	Res.	Att.	Goalscorers	Adkins N.	Parkinson J.	Tankard A.	Atherton P.	Johnson A.	Hildersley R.	Woods R.	Rimmer N.	Daley P.	Fairclough D.	Griffiths B.	Patterson D.	Griffiths J.	Page D.	Appleton S.	Rogerson L.	Langley K.	Carberry J.	Pilling A.	Paladino J.	Pennock T.	Boughey D.	Hughes P.	Jones P.	Powell G.	Worthington G.
1R1	28 Aug	BARNSLEY	0-1	2714		1	2	3	4	12	6	7	8	9	10*	11#	5	14													
1R2	4 Sep	Barnsley *	1-0	4588	Page	1	2*	3	4			7	8	9		14	5	11#	10	6	12										

* lost 4-3 on penalties

LEYLAND DAF CUP

Round	Date	Opposition	Res.	Att.	Goalscorers	Adkins N.	Parkinson J.	Tankard A.	Atherton P.	Johnson A.	Hildersley R.	Woods R.	Rimmer N.	Daley P.	Fairclough D.	Griffiths B.	Patterson D.	Griffiths J.	Page D.	Appleton S.	Rogerson L.	Langley K.	Carberry J.	Pilling A.	Paladino J.	Pennock T.	Boughey D.	Hughes P.	Jones P.	Powell G.	Worthington G.
Pre	6 Nov	CHESTER CITY	4-0	1809	Griffiths, Page(3)	1		3	4	5		7	8	9		11	2		10			6									
Pre	11 Dec	Bury	1-2	1025	Johnson	1	2	3	4	12		7	8*			11	5		10#			6	14	9							
1R	22 Jan	ROCHDALE	2-0	1200	Johnson, Griffiths		2	3	4	5			8	9		11			10			6	7		1						
NQF	29	BURY	2-0	1982	Langley, Daley			3	4	5			8	9		11	2	7	10			6						1			
NSF	19 Feb	TRANMERE ROVERS	0-3	4417				3	4	5			8	9		11	2*	7#	14			6		12				1	10		

SEASON 1991-92

DIVISION 3

No.	Date	Opposition	Res.	Att.	Goalscorers
1	18 Aug	Shrewsbury Town	0-1	3834	
2	23	CHESTER CITY	2-1	2637	Worthington(2)
3	31	West Bromwich Albion	1-1	12053	Worthington
4	3 Sep	STOCKPORT COUNTY	1-3	3567	Powell
5	7	Peterborough United	0-0	4488	
6	14	HULL CITY	0-1	2445	
7	17	HUDDERSFIELD TOWN	1-3	3531	Powell
8	21	Bolton Wanderers	1-1	6923	O.G.
9	28	DARLINGTON	1-2	2034	Powell
10	5 Oct	Hartlepool United	3-4	3047	Powell, Daley(2)
11	11	READING	1-1	1817	Griffiths
12	19	Birmingham City	3-3	9662	Jones, Daley(2)
13	26	EXETER CITY	4-1	1761	Johnson, Powell, Connelly, Daley
14	1 Nov	SWANSEA CITY	1-0	2092	Johnson
15	5	Preston North End	0-3	3657	
16	9	Brentford	0-4	6675	
17	22	BURY	2-0	2268	Worthington, Griffiths
18	30	LEYTON ORIENT	1-1	2066	Powell
19	14 Dec	Stoke City	0-3	8419	
20	26	WEST BROMWICH ALBION	0-1	5068	
21	28	SHREWSBURY TOWN	1-1	2276	Daley
22	1 Jan	Stockport County	3-3	4149	Connelly, Daley(2)
23	11	BRADFORD CITY	2-1	2548	Langley, Daley
24	18	Bournemouth	0-3	4338	
25	28	Fulham	1-1	2466	Taylor
26	8 Feb	Exeter City	1-0	3036	Griffiths
27	11	Leyton Orient	1-3	3142	Taylor
28	15	STOKE CITY	1-0	5695	Griffiths(pen)
29	18	Chester City	0-1	1065	
30	22	Bradford City	1-1	5621	Worthington
31	28	FULHAM	0-2	2202	
32	3 Mar	BOURNEMOUTH	2-0	1790	Johnson, Worthington(pen)
33	7	Torquay United	1-0	2198	Daley
34	10	PRESTON NORTH END	3-0	3364	Worthington(2), Daley
35	14	Swansea City	0-3	3726	
36	20	BRENTFORD	2-1	2371	Pilling, Parkinson
37	28	Bury	4-1	2618	Worthingtn(p),Parkinsn,Daley,Pwell
38	31	Hull City	1-1	3385	Worthington
39	3 Apr	PETERBOROUGH UNITED	3-0	2485	Johnson, Langley, Worthington
40	7	TORQUAY UNITED	0-0	1970	
41	11	Huddersfield Town	1-3	7058	Daley
42	18	BOLTON WANDERERS	1-1	3557	Worthington
43	20	Darlington	1-0	1223	Worthington
44	24	HARTLEPOOL UNITED	1-1	2002	Daley
45	28	BIRMINGHAM CITY	3-0	5950	Worthington(2), Pilling
46	2 May	Reading	2-3	2748	Patterson, Parkinson

No.	Adkins N.	Appleton S.	Parkinson J.	Atherton P.	Patterson D.	Langley K.	Powell G.	Rimmer N.	Daley P.	Worthington G.	Griffiths B.	Jones P.	Gray P.	Johnson A.	Tankard A.	Pilling A.	Carberry J.	Smith J.	Widdrington T.	Nugent S.	Smyth J.	Connelly D.	Williams W.	Edwardson B.	Sharratt C.	Collins D.	Taylor R.D.	Skipper P.	Dolan J.
1	1	2*	3	4	5	6	7	8	9	10	11#	12	14																
2	1	12	2		5	6*	7	8	9	10	11#	3	14	4															
3	1				5	6	9	8		10	11*	2		4	3	7	12												
4	1				5	6	9	8		10	11*	2		4	3	7		12											
5	1				5	6#	9	8		10	11	2	14	4	3	7*	12												
6	1				5	6	7	8		10	11*	2	9#	4	3			12	14										
7	1				5		7	8		10		6		4	3	14	11*	12	2	9#									
8	1				9	6	7	8		10	11*	2		4	3		12		5										
9	1				2	6	7	8#	9	10*	11			4	3	12			5		14								
10	1	2			5	6	7		9		11		10*	4	3			12	8										
11	1					6	7		9		11			4	3			12	5	10*	2	8							
12	1	12				6	7		9		11#	10		4	3						2	8	5	14					
13	1		2			6	7		9		11	10		4	3						12	8	5*						
14	1		2			6	7		9	14	11#	10*		4	3						12	8	5						
15	1		2		5	6	7		9	11*		10#		4	3			14			12	8							
16	1		2		10*	6	7		9	14	11			4	3						12	8	5						
17	1		2		5	6	7			10	11	4			3	9*					12	8							
18	1		2		5	6	7			10	11	4		12	3	9*						8							
19	1		2		5	6	7#		14	10*	11	4		12	3	9						8							
20	1		2		5	6	14		9	10*	11#	4		12	3	7						8							
21	1		2		5	6	14*		9	10	11	7#		4	3							8			12				
22	1		2		5	6			9	10	11	7		4	3							8							
23	1		2		5	6	10#		9		11	7*		4	3	12									14	8			
24	1		2		5	6	10*		9	14	11#	7		4	3	12										8			
25	1	12	2		5	6			9	14	11	7		4	3											8*	10#		
26	1		2		5	6			9	12	11	7		4	3											8	10*		
27	1		2		5	6			9	12	11	7		4	3											8	10*		
28	1		2		5#	6			9	12	11	7		4	3											8	10	14	
29	1		2			6			9	11	11*	7		4	3	12										8*	10	5	
30	1		2			6			9	11		7		4	3											8	10	5	
31	1		2		14	6			9	11#		7		4	3										12	8	10*	5	
32	1		2		11	6#	14		9	10		7		4	3	8#									12			5	
33	1		2		11	6	12		9	10*		7		4	3	8												5	
34	1		2		11	6	12		9	10		7		4	3	8*												5	
35	1		2		11	6	12		9	10*		7		4	3	8												5	
36	1	5	2		11	6	12		9	10		7		4	3	8*												#	
37	1	5#	2		11	6*	12		9	10		7		4	3	8													
38	1	14	2		11	6	12		9	10		7*		4	3	8#												14	
39	1	14	2		11	6			9	10*	12	7		4	3	8#												5	
40	1		2		11	6			9	10		7		4	3	8												5	
41	1		2		11	6	12		9	10*		7		4	3	8												5	
42	1		2		11	6	12		9	10*		7		4	3	8												5	
43	1		2		11	6			9	10		7		4	3	8												5	
44	1		2		11	6	8*		9	10	12	7#		4	3	14												5	
45	1		2		11	6			9	10				4	3	8												5	7
46	1		2		11	6#	12		9	10		5		4	3	8*												14	7
Apps.	46	4	36	1	39	45	22	9	37	34	26	40	2	41	44	21	1		5	2	2	12	4			8	7	15	2
Subs.		5			1		12		1	7	2	1	3	3		6	4	6	1		6			1	14			3	
Goals			5		1	2	7		14	15	4	1		4		2						2					2		

F.A. CUP

Round	Date	Opposition	Res.	Att.	Goalscorers
1R	15 Nov	Scarborough	2-0	1889	Pilling, Worthington
2R	7 Dec	STOCKPORT COUNTY	2-0	4168	Griffiths, Powell
3R	5 Jan	Notts County	0-2	5913	

Round	Adkins N.	Appleton S.	Parkinson J.	Atherton P.	Patterson D.	Langley K.	Powell G.	Rimmer N.	Daley P.	Worthington G.	Griffiths B.	Jones P.	Gray P.	Johnson A.	Tankard A.	Pilling A.	Carberry J.	Smith J.	Widdrington T.	Nugent S.	Smyth J.	Connelly D.	Williams W.	Edwardson B.	Sharratt C.	Collins D.	Taylor R.D.	Skipper P.	Dolan J.
1R	1		2		5	6	7		9*	10	11			4	3	12#					14	8							
2R	1		2		5	6	7		12	10*	11	4		14	3	9						8#							
3R	1		2		5	6	12		9	10	11*	7		4	3							8							

LEAGUE CUP

Round	Date	Opposition	Res.	Att.	Goalscorers
1R1	20 Aug	BURNLEY	3-1	2826	Patterson,Griffiths(p),Worthingtn
1R2	27	Burnley	3-2	3876	Patterson, Rimmer, Jones
2R1	24 Sep	SHEFFIELD UNITED	2-2	3647	Worthington, Patterson
2R2	8 Oct	Sheffield United	0-1	6608	

Round	Adkins N.	Appleton S.	Parkinson J.	Atherton P.	Patterson D.	Langley K.	Powell G.	Rimmer N.	Daley P.	Worthington G.	Griffiths B.	Jones P.	Gray P.	Johnson A.	Tankard A.	Pilling A.	Carberry J.	Smith J.	Widdrington T.	Nugent S.	Smyth J.	Connelly D.	Williams W.	Edwardson B.	Sharratt C.	Collins D.	Taylor R.D.	Skipper P.	Dolan J.
1R1	1		2	4	5	6	7	8	9	10*	11	3	12																
1R2	1	12	2*		5	6		8	9#	10	11	7	14	4	3														
2R1	1				9	6	7	8		10	11	2		4	3	12			5										
2R2	1	2			5*	6	7		9		11		10#	4	3			14	8		12								

AUTOGLASS TROPHY

Round	Date	Opposition	Res.	Att.	Goalscorers
Pre	22 Oct	HUDDERSFIELD TOWN	0-1	1214	
Pre	8 Jan	Scarborough	1-1	636	Sharratt

Round	Adkins N.	Appleton S.	Parkinson J.	Atherton P.	Patterson D.	Langley K.	Powell G.	Rimmer N.	Daley P.	Worthington G.	Griffiths B.	Jones P.	Gray P.	Johnson A.	Tankard A.	Pilling A.	Carberry J.	Smith J.	Widdrington T.	Nugent S.	Smyth J.	Connelly D.	Williams W.	Edwardson B.	Sharratt C.	Collins D.	Taylor R.D.	Skipper P.	Dolan J.
Pre	1	5*				6	7		9		11	10		4	3	12	14				2	8#							
Pre	1		2		5	6			9	10*	11	7		4	3							8			12				

Season 1991/92

(Back): Pilling, Adkins, Langley, Patterson, Daley, Worthington, Pennock, Powell. (Middle): Philpotts (Coach), Griffiths, Carberry, Page, Tankard, Johnson, Atherton, Parkinson, Appleton, Crompton (Y.T.Coach). (Front): Lyons (Coach), Gray, Jones, Rimmer, Hamilton (Manager), Smith, Edwardson, Nugent, Cribley (Physio).

Season 1992/93

(Back): Robertson, Parkinson, Johnson, Pennock, Adkins, Doolan, Appleton, Daley. (Middle): Crompton (Y.T.Coach), Rimmer, Tankard, Pilling, Powell, Worthington, Jones, Gray, Cribley (Physio). (Front): Griffiths, Nugent, Philpotts, Langley, Hamilton (Manager), Sharratt, Roberts.

SEASON 1992-93

DIVISION 2 (Formerly Division 3)

No.	Date	Opposition	Res.	Att.	Goalscorers	Adkins N.	Parkinson J.	Tankard A.	Johnson A.	Doolan J.	Langley K.	Jones P.	Pilling A.	Daley P.	Worthington G.	Griffiths B.	Powell G.	Appleton S.	Robertson J.	Sharratt C.	Wilson I.	Makin C. (loan)	Kirwan P.	Skipper P.	Nugent S.	Pennock A.	Cooper S.	Woods R. (loan)	Connelly D.	Brolly R.	Garnett S.	White	Ogden N.	Rimmer N.
1	15 Aug	STOCKPORT COUNTY	1-2	3360	Griffiths	1	2	3	4	5	6	7	8	9	10*	11	12																	
2	22	Stoke City	1-2	12902	Griffiths	1	2	3		5	6*	7		9	10#	11	8	14	4	12														
3	29	SWANSEA CITY	2-3	1565	Griffiths(2,1pen)	1				5	6	7		9	10	11	8		4		2	3												
4	1 Sep	FULHAM	1-3	1591	Daley	1	2	3	4	5	6	7*		9	10#	11	12		8			14												
5	5	Rotherham United	3-2	3806	Griffiths(2,1pen), Daley	1	2		4	5	6			9		11	10		8	12	7	3												
6	11	HARLTEPOOL UNITED	2-2	2073	Makin, Johnson	1	2	3	4	5	6			9		11	10		8	12	7	3												
7	15	Exeter City	0-0	2393		1	2	12	4	5	6			9		11	10		8		7	3												
8	18	Reading	0-4	3084		1	2	12	4	5	6			9	14	11	10		8		7	3												
9	26	BURNLEY	1-1	4032	Griffiths	1	2	3	4	5		7		9	12	11	10		8			6												
10	3 Oct	MANSFIELD TOWN	2-0	1644	Griffiths(2)	1	2	3	4	5		7		9		11	10		8			6												
11	10	Brighton & Hove Albion	0-1	5784		1		3	4	5	6	7			9	11	10	12	8			2												
12	14	WEST BROMWICH ALBION	1-0	4408	Makin	1	2	3	4		6	7	12	9	10	11			8			5												
13	24	Plymouth Argyle	0-2	5967		1	2		4		6	7	12	9	10	11	14	5	8			3												
14	31	BOURNEMOUTH	0-0	1803		1	2		4		6	7	10	9		11		5	8			3												
15	3 Nov	BRADFORD CITY	1-2	2070	Pilling	1	2	3	4		6	7	10	9		11	12					8		5										
16	7	Preston North End	0-2	4442		1		3	4		6	7	10	9		11	8			12		2		5										
17	21	LEYTON ORIENT	3-1	1806	Daley(2), Tankard	1		3	4		6		10	9		11	8		5			2		7										
18	28	Chester City	2-1	2395	Griffiths, Pilling	1		3	4		6		10	9		11	8	2	5	12				7										
19	12 Dec	BLACKPOOL	2-1	2492	Powell, Daley	1		3	4		6	2	10	9		11	8	12	5					7										
20	19	Port Vale	2-2	6647	Pilling, Griffiths			3	4		6		10	9		11	8	2	5					7	12	1								
21	26	Bolton Wanderers	1-2	11493	Powell			3	4	2	6		10		14	11	8	12	5					7		1	9							
22	10 Jan	EXETER CITY	0-1	1882		1		3	4	14	6		9			11	12	2	5					7			10	8						
23	16	Burnley	1-0	9154	Griffiths(pen)	1		3	4		6		5			11	8	2						7			10	9						
24	24	READING	1-1	1860	Powell	1		3	4		6		5			11	8	2						7			10	9						
25	30	STOKE CITY	1-1	4775	Pilling	1		3	4		6	9	5			11	8	2	12					7				10						
26	5 Feb	Stockport County	0-3	4799		1		3	4		6	9	5			11		2	8	12				7				10						
27	13	ROTHERHAM UNITED	1-1	1902	Sharratt	1		3	4		6	9	5			11	14	2		8				7	12			10						
28	16	HUDDERSFIELD TOWN	1-0	2474	Brolly	1		3	4		6	9	5				14	12		8				7				10	2	11				
29	20	Fulham	0-1	3502		1		3	4		6		5				14	9		8				7	12			10	2	11				
30	27	BRIGHTON & HOVE ALBION	1-2	2003	Skipper	1		3			6			9		11	12	5		8				7				10	2		4			
31	2 Mar	Hartlepool United	0-0	1791				3			6	10		9		11		5		8				7		1			2		4			
32	6	Mansfield Town	0-2	3024				3				10	6	9		11	14	5		8				7	12	1			2		4			
33	9	Hull City	0-0	3394				3			6	12				11	9	5		10				7		1		8	2		4			
34	12	PRESTON NORTH END	2-3	3562	Powell(2)			3			6	12	14			11	9	5		10				7		1		8	2		4			
35	20	Bradford City	1-2	4748	Robertson			3			6	5	8	9		11	10	2	4	12				7		1		14						
36	23	CHESTER CITY	1-2	1861	Appleton			3			6	5		9		11		2		10				7		1		8			4			
37	27	Leyton Orient	2-1	4104	Garnett, Powell	1		3			6	5	8	9		11	14	2	12					7							4	10		
38	3 Apr	HULL CITY	1-0	1872	White	1		3	4			5	8	9		11	12	2						7							6	10		
39	6	Blackpool	1-2	5095	Griffiths	1		3	4			5	8	9		11	12	2						7							6	10		
40	10	BOLTON WANDERERS	0-2	5408		1		3	4			5	8	9		11	14	2		12				7							6	10		
41	12	Huddersfield Town	1-2	6822	Sharratt	1		3	4		6			9		11	8	2		12				7							5	10		
42	17	PORT VALE	0-4	3743		1		3	4		6		12	9		11		2						7							5	10		
43	24	West Bromwich Albion	1-5	14867	Daley	1			4	3	6		2	9		14			12					7							5	11		
44	1 May	PLYMOUTH ARGYLE	0-2	1432		1		3	4	2	6		5			11				10				7								8		
45	4	Swansea City	1-2	7361	Sharratt	1		3	4	2	6		5			11				10				7								8	12	
46	8	Bournemouth	0-0	3838		1		11	4	2	6		5			10								7								8	3	12
					Apps.	38	13	39	36	16	40	25	27	31	7	43	22	24	21	11	5	14		32	5	8	4	12	7	2	13	10	1	
					Subs.			2		1		2	4		3	1	14	5	3	9		1			4			1					1	1
					Goals			1	1				4	6		13	6	1	1	3		2		1						1	1	1		

F.A. CUP

Rd	Date	Opposition	Res.	Att.	Goalscorers	Adkins N.	Parkinson J.	Tankard A.	Johnson A.	Doolan J.	Langley K.	Jones P.	Pilling A.	Daley P.	Worthington G.	Griffiths B.	Powell G.	Appleton S.	Robertson J.	Sharratt C.	Wilson I.	Makin C. (loan)	Kirwan P.	Skipper P.	Nugent S.	Pennock A.	Cooper S.	Woods R. (loan)	Connelly D.	Brolly R.	Garnett S.	White	Ogden N.	Rimmer N.
1R	14 Nov	CARLISLE UNITED	3-1	2963	Powell, O.G.(2)	1		3	4		6	7*	10	9		11	8	2	5				12											
2R	15 Dec	BURY	1-1	3764	Griffiths(pen)	1		3	4		6		10	9		11	8	2	5	12			7*											
2Rr	2 Jan	Bury	0-1	5136				3	4		6		7		10*	11	8#	2	5	9			14		12	1								

LEAGUE CUP

Rd	Date	Opposition	Res.	Att.	Goalscorers	Adkins N.	Parkinson J.	Tankard A.	Johnson A.	Doolan J.	Langley K.	Jones P.	Pilling A.	Daley P.	Worthington G.	Griffiths B.	Powell G.	Appleton S.	Robertson J.	Sharratt C.	Wilson I.	Makin C. (loan)	Kirwan P.	Skipper P.	Nugent S.	Pennock A.	Cooper S.	Woods R. (loan)	Connelly D.	Brolly R.	Garnett S.	White	Ogden N.	Rimmer N.
1R1	18 Aug	Shrewsbury Town	2-1	1337	Daley, Tankard	1	2	3		5	6	7	8*	9	10	11	12		4															
1R2	25	SHREWSBURY TOWN	0-1	1308		1	2#	3		5	6	7		9	10	11*	8	12	4	14														
2R1	22 Sep	IPSWICH TOWN	2-2	2684	Johnson, Worthington	1	2	3	4	5	6*	7		9	12	11	10		8															
2R2	6 Oct	Ipswich Town	0-4	7325		1	2*	3	4	5	6	7		9	14	11	10#		8		12													

AUTOGLASS TROPHY

Rd	Date	Opposition	Res.	Att.	Goalscorers	Adkins N.	Parkinson J.	Tankard A.	Johnson A.	Doolan J.	Langley K.	Jones P.	Pilling A.	Daley P.	Worthington G.	Griffiths B.	Powell G.	Appleton S.	Robertson J.	Sharratt C.	Wilson I.	Makin C. (loan)	Kirwan P.	Skipper P.	Nugent S.	Pennock A.	Cooper S.	Woods R. (loan)	Connelly D.	Brolly R.	Garnett S.	White	Ogden N.	Rimmer N.
Pre	8 Dec	Blackpool	2-3	1658	Griffiths, Daley	1		3			6		10	9		11	8*	2	5	12			4	7										
Pre	6 Jan	PRESTON NORTH END	2-1	1932	Skipper, Pilling			3	4		6		9		12	11	8*	2	5					7		1	10							
2R	19	Rotherham United *	3-3	1704	Powell(2), Johnson	1		3	4		6		5*			11	8	2		12				7			10	9						
NQF	9 Feb	SCUNTHROPE UNITED	2-1	1512	Langley, Sharratt	1		3	4		6	10	5			11		2		8				7				9						
NSF	23	HUDDERSFIELD TOWN	5-2	2978	Woods(3), Griffiths, Daley	1		3	4*		6		12	9*		11	14	5		8				7				10	2					
NF1	16 Mar	STOCKPORT COUNTY	2-1	4136	Daley, Griffiths			3	4*		6	5		9		11	10		12	14				7		1		8	2#					
NF2	20 Apr	Stockport County	0-2	6315		1		3		8	6		4*	9		11		2	5	12				7	10									

SEASON 1993-94

DIVISION 3

No.	Date	Opposition	Res.	Att.	Goalscorers
1	14 Aug	SCUNTHORPE UNITED	0-2	2353	
2	21	Torquay United	1-1	3465	Morton
3	28	WYCOMBE WANDERERS	1-1	2388	Rennie
4	31	Rochdale	2-1	2628	McKearney, Langley
5	4 Sep	Doncaster Rovers	1-3	3075	Strong
6	11	SCARBOROUGH	1-2	1682	Daley
7	18	Northampton Town	2-0	2235	Gavin, Skipper
8	25	Hereford United	0-3	1813	
9	2 Oct	CHESTER CITY	6-3	1889	Johnsn,McKearney,Gvin,Gillespie(2),Rnnie
10	9	Bury	0-3	2729	
11	16	PRESTON NORTH END	2-2	3741	McKearney(2)
12	23	Colchester United	1-3	2814	Gillespie
13	30	MANSFIELD TOWN	4-1	1434	Gavin(2), Gillespie, Morton
14	2 Nov	Chesterfield	0-1	2758	
15	6	CARLISLE UNITED	0-2	2411	
16	20	Gillingham	2-2	2727	Daley, Lyons
17	27	SHREWSBURY TOWN	2-5	1498	Daley, O.G.
18	11 Dec	TORQUAY UNITED	1-3	1232	Kennedy
19	18	Scunthorpe United	0-1	2873	
20	4 Jan	ROCHDALE	0-0	1912	
21	11	WALSALL	2-2	1561	Lyons, Skipper
22	15	Preston North End	0-3	7728	
23	22	BURY	3-1	2476	Kilford(2), Morton
24	25	Darlington	0-0	1837	
25	29	Mansfield Town	3-2	2285	Gavin, Connelly, Duffy
26	5 Feb	COLCHESTER UNITED	0-1	1695	
27	12	Lincoln City	1-0	2534	Lyons
28	19	Wycombe Wanderers	1-0	4846	Lyons
29	5 Mar	Scarborough	1-4	1390	Furlong
30	12	NORTHAMPTON TOWN	1-1	1855	Wright
31	19	HEREFORD UNITED	3-4	1542	Lyons(2), Gavin
32	22	DONCASTER ROVERS	0-0	1438	
33	26	Chester City	1-2	3542	Lyons
34	29	LINCOLN CITY	0-1	1349	
35	2 Apr	CREWE ALEXANDRA	2-2	2335	Lyons, Kilford
36	5	Walsall	1-1	3815	Lyons
37	9	DARLINGTON	2-0	1709	Skipper, Lyons
38	16	CHESTERFIELD	1-0	1998	Robertson
39	19	Crewe Alexandra	1-4	3396	Langley
40	23	Carlisle United	0-3	3796	
41	30	GILLINGHAM	2-0	1346	Lyons(pen), Morton
42	7 May	Shrewsbury Town	0-0	7686	

No.	Farnworth S.	Rennie P.	Duffy C.	Robertson J.	Skipper P.	Johnson A.	Strong G.	McKearney D.	Gavin P.	Morton N.	Langley K.	Hollis S.	Vaughan D.	Ogden N.	Kennedy M.	West P.	Gillespie K.	Daley P.	Rimmer M.	Lyons A.	Carragher M.	Wright M.	Kilford I.	Connelly D.	Furlong C.	Thorne P.	Patterson I.	Dowe J.
1	1	2	3	4*	5	6	7	8	9	10	11	12																
2	1	2		4	5	6	7	8	9	10	11		3*	12														
3	1	2	12	4	5	6	7*	8	9	10	11				3													
4	1	2	7	4	5	6		8	9	10	11				3*	12												
5	1		3	4	5	6*	12	8	9	10	11			14		2#	7											
6	1	2	6	4	5*			3	9	10	11		14		8#		7	12										
7	1	2	6	4	5			3	9	10	11		12				7*		8									
8	1	2		4*	5	6		3	9	10			11				7	12	8									
9	1	8	2	4	5	6*		3	9	10							7			11	12							
10	1	6	2	4	5			3	9*	10*	7							12	8	11	14							
11	1	2*	7	4	5#		6	3	9	12								10	8	11	14							
12	1		14	4			5*	3	9		12				6		7#	10	8	11	2							
13	1	4	12		5			3	9	10					6		7*		8	11	2							
14	1	4*	12	10	5			3	9	14					6		7		8	11	2#							
15	1	4	2*	8#	5			3	9	10	7				6					11	12	14						
16	1	2			5	6		8		10	12				4*			9		11	7	3						
17	1	2	14		5	6		8		10*	12				4#			9		11	7	3						
18	1	2	12		5*	6		8	10		4#				14			9		11	7	3						
19	1	2		4	5*	6		8	9	10	14							12		11	7	3						
20	1			4	5	6		8	9*	10#	7							12		11	2	3	14					
21	1			4	5	6		8	12	10	7							9		11	2	3*						
22	1	2*		4	5	6		8		10	7							9		11	12		3					
23	1	3	8	4	5				12	10*	7				14			9		11	2		6					
24	1	3	8	4	5				9	10	7				6					11	2							
25	1	3	8	4	5				9	10*	7				6					11	2			12				
26	1	12	8	4	5*	3			9	10	7				6#					11	2			14				
27	1	8	12	4	5	3			9	10	7				6*					11	2			14				
28	1	2	12	4	5				9	10	7				6					11		3		8				
29	1	2		4	5						7				6*				12	11	10	3		8	9			
30	1	2*	12	4	5					10	7									11	6	3		8		9		
31	1			4	5		14		9	12	7#								6	11	2	3*		8		10		
32	1		14	4	5		3		9	12	7*								6	11	2			8		10#		
33	1			4*	5		3		9#	8	7								10	11	2		6	12		14		
34	1			4	5*		3	7	9	14									10	11	2		6	12		8#		
35	1				5		3	7	9	12	6								10*	11	2		4			8		
36	1		12	4	5		3	7		8*									10	11	2		6			9		
37	1		12	7	5		3	4		8									10	11	2		6		14*	9#		
38	1			7	5		3	4		8*								12	10	11	2					9		
39	1		7		5		3			8*	4							12	10	11	2					9	14	
40	1				5		6*			12	14							9	10	11	2	3#				8	4	
41	1			4	5		6			8	7							9	10	11	2	3					12	
42	1		11		5		6	2		8	7							9	10			3					4	
Apps.	42	25	15	34	41	16	16	28	28	32	28		2		15	1	8	11	19	33	27	13	7	8	1	10	2	
Subs.		1	12				2		2	7	5	1	2	2	2	1		7	1		5	1	1	5	1	1	2	
Goals		2	1	1	3	1	1	4	6	4	2				1		4	3		11		1	3	1	1			

F.A. CUP

Round	Date	Opposition	Res.	Att.	Goalscorers
1R	12 Nov	Leek	2-2	2785	Skipper, Morton
1Rr	30	LEEK	3-0	1804	McKearney(pen), Duffy, O.G.
2R	4 Dec	SCARBOROUGH	1-0	1837	Gavin
3R	8 Jan	Grimsby Town	0-1	4488	

Round	Farnworth S.	Rennie P.	Duffy C.	Robertson J.	Skipper P.	Johnson A.	Strong G.	McKearney D.	Gavin P.	Morton N.	Langley K.	Hollis S.	Vaughan D.	Ogden N.	Kennedy M.	West P.	Gillespie K.	Daley P.	Rimmer M.	Lyons A.	Carragher M.	Wright M.	Kilford I.	Connelly D.	Furlong C.	Thorne P.	Patterson I.	Dowe J.
1R	1	3	7	14	5	6		11	9	10#	12				4				8*		2							
1Rr	1	2	11		5	6		8	10		4			12				9#			7	3*			14			
2R	1	2			5	6		8	10		4							9		11	7	3						
3R	1			4	5	6		8	14	10#	7							9		11	2	3*	12					

LEAGUE CUP

Round	Date	Opposition	Res.	Att.	Goalscorers
1R1	16 Aug	ROTHERHAM UNITED	0-1	1531	
1R2	24	Rotherham United	2-4	2009	Gavin, Morton

Round	Farnworth S.	Rennie P.	Duffy C.	Robertson J.	Skipper P.	Johnson A.	Strong G.	McKearney D.	Gavin P.	Morton N.	Langley K.	Hollis S.	Vaughan D.	Ogden N.	Kennedy M.	West P.	Gillespie K.	Daley P.	Rimmer M.	Lyons A.	Carragher M.	Wright M.	Kilford I.	Connelly D.	Furlong C.	Thorne P.	Patterson I.	Dowe J.
1R1	1	2	3*	4	5	6	7	8	9	10	11																	12
1R2	1	3		4	5	6		8	9	10	11		7			2												12

AUTOGLASS TROPHY

Round	Date	Opposition	Res.	Att.	Goalscorers
Pre	27 Sep	Stockport County	0-2	2393	
Pre	18 Oct	BURY	1-3	983	McKearney(pen)

Round	Farnworth S.	Rennie P.	Duffy C.	Robertson J.	Skipper P.	Johnson A.	Strong G.	McKearney D.	Gavin P.	Morton N.	Langley K.	Hollis S.	Vaughan D.	Ogden N.	Kennedy M.	West P.	Gillespie K.	Daley P.	Rimmer M.	Lyons A.	Carragher M.	Wright M.	Kilford I.	Connelly D.	Furlong C.	Thorne P.	Patterson I.	Dowe J.
Pre	1	2	12	4	5	6		3	9	10#							7	11	8*		14							
Pre	1		11	4			5	3		10	6						7	9	8		2							

Season 1993/94

(Back): Skipper, McKearney, Dowe, Strong, Robertson, Daley, Kennedy, Doolan. (Middle): Crompton (Y.Coach), Gavin, Langley, Pennock, Haley, Farnworth, Johnson, Duffy, Cribley (Coach/Physio). (Front): Ogden, Rimmer, Hollis, Vaughan, Swain (Manager), Morton, Connelly, Dixon. (Front Kneeling): Saint, Carragher, Brooks, Newton, Dowds, Furlong, O'Hara, Marshall.

Season 1994/95

(Back): Wright, Adekola, Duffy, Tait, Ogden. (Middle): Hinnigan (Coach), Leonard, Patterson, Robertson, Statham, Farnworth, Strong, Millar, Kilford, Cribley (Coach/Physio). (Front): McKearney, Lyons, Rimmer, Doolan, Barrow (Manager), Gage (Chairman), Crompton (Youth Devt.), Rennie, Farrell, Carragher, Jakub

SEASON 1994-95

DIVISION 3

No.	Date	Opposition	Res.	Att.	Goalscorers	Farnworth S.	Rennie P.	Wright M.	West P.	Robertson J.	Kilford I.	Campbell D.	Morton N.	Gavin P.	Rimmer N.	Lyons A.	Duffy C.	Strong G.	Carragher M.	Ormsby B.	Harford P.	Tait P.	McKearney D.	Jakub Y.	Leonard M.	Farrell A.	Benjamin I.	Miller D.	Adekola D.	Doolan J.	Rodwell A.	Furlong C.	Whitney J.	Black A.	Ogden N.
1	13 Aug	Carlisle United	1-2	6231	O.G.	1	2	3	4#	5	6	7*	8	9	10	11	12	14																	
2	20	GILLINGHAM	0-3	1514		1	2	3		5	6	7*	8	9	10	11		12	2																
3	27	Fulham	0-2	4241		1	2	3		5	6	7*	8	9		11	12	4	10																
4	30	CHESTERFIELD	2-3	1231	Morton, Gavin	1	2	3*		5	6	7	8	9		11#	12	14	10	4															
5	3 Sep	BARNET	1-2	1438	Gavin	1	2			5	6		8	9			12	3	10	4	7	11*													
6	10	Hereford United	2-1	2771	Rennie(pen), Rimmer	1	2	3		5	6		8*	9	10			4	11		7	12													
7	13	Lincoln City	0-1	2030		1	2	3		5	6		8*	9	10			4	11		7		12												
8	17	CARLISLE UNITED	0-2	3003		1	2			5	6		8*	9	10			4	11				12	3	7										
9	24	Scunthore United	1-3	2602	McKearney	1	2			5	6	7	8*	9	10			4	11			14	12#			3									
10	1 Oct	SCARBOROUGH	1-1	1403	Kilford	1				5	8	7		12	10			4	2					3	9*	6	11								
11	8	Doncaster Rovers	3-5	2060	Leonard (2,1pen), Benjamin	1	14				8	7*		12		11		4#	2					3	9	6	10	5							
12	15	ROCHDALE	4-0	2118	Kilford(2), Strong, Benjamin	1					7				10	11		4	2			12		3	9	6	8*	5							
13	22	Northampton Town	0-1	6379		1				12	7				10	11		4	2*					3#	9	6	8	5	14						
14	29	COLCHESTER UNITED	1-2	1621	Robertson	1	12			5	7					11		4	2*					3#	9	6	8	10	14						
15	5 Nov	Hartlepool United	1-0	1683	McKearney	1	2			5	7					11			8				10	3	9	6		4							
16	19	DARLINGTON	4-1	1785	Strong, Lyons(3,1pen)	1	2*			5	7					11		12	8				10	3	9	6		4							
17	26	Torquay United	0-0	2509		1				5	7				4	11		2	8				10	3	9	6									
18	10 Dec	Gillingham	1-0	2257	Leonard	1				5	7				10	11			2				8	3	9	6		4							
19	17	FULHAM	1-1	1791	Leonard	1				5	7				10	11		12	2				8*	3#	9	6		4	14						
20	26	Bury	3-3	3616	Lyons(2), Leonard	1		12		5					10	11			2			14		3	9	7		6	8*	4#					
21	7 Jan	NORTHAMPTON TOWN	2-1	1911	Rimmer, Kilford	1				5	7				10	11			8					3	9	6		4		2					
22	14	Mansfield Town	3-4	2618	Kilford, Rimmer, Lyons	1	12	3		5	7				10	11			8#						9	6	14	4		2*					
23	24	PRESTON NORTH END	1-1	3618	Lyons	1		3		5					10	11*			2				8		9	6	12	4			7				
24	28	Colchester United	1-0	3067	Doolan	1		3		5						11			2				8		9	6		4		10	7				
25	4 Feb	TORQUAY UNITED	1-1	1609	Miller	1		3		5					10	11			2				8		9	6*	12	4			7				
26	11	Darlington	3-1	1780	Rodwell, Benjamin, Lyons	1				5					10	11			2				8	3		6	9	4			7				
27	18	MANSFIELD TOWN	0-4	1884		1				5					10	11			2*				8#	3		6	9	4		12	7	14			
28	21	Exeter City	4-2	2370	Lyons,McKearney(pen),Benjamin(2)	1		12		5	7*				10	11			2				8	3			9	4		6					
29	25	Scarborough	1-0	1416	Lyons	1		3		5	7				10	11			2				8				9	4		6					
30	28	HARTLEPOOL UNITED	2-0	1452	McKearney, Lyons	1		3		5	7				10	11			2				8		12	14	9*	4		6#					
31	18 Mar	Chesterfield United	0-0	3808		1		11		5					10				2				8		9	7		4		6			3		
32	25	Barnet	1-1	2362	McKearney	1		11*		5	7				10				2				8		9	6		4		12			3		
33	29	HEREFORD UNITED	1-1	1492	Benjamin	1				5	8				10				2				11*		9	6	12	4					3	7	
34	1 Apr	LINCOLN CITY	0-1	1696		1				5	8				10				2						9	6*	11	4		12			3	7	
35	4	SCUNTHORPE UNITED	0-0	1307		1				5	8				10	11*			2						9	6		4					3	7	12
36	8	EXETER CITY	3-1	1417	Miller, Lyons, Rimmer	1				5	8				10	11			2				12		9	6		4					3	7*	
37	11	WALSALL	1-0	2176	Lyons	1				5	8				10	11			2						9	6		4					3	7	
38	15	Preston North End	0-1	10238		1				5	8				10	11			2						9	6*		4		12			3	7	
39	18	BURY	0-3	2531		1				5	8				10	11			2						9	6		4		12			3	7*	
40	22	Walsall	0-2	3508		1+				5	8				10	11			2				7*		9	6#		4		12			3		
41	29	Rochdale	0-1	1949						5	8#				10	11			2						9		14	4		12			3	7	
42	6 May	DONCASTER ROVERS	3-2	1576	Lyons(2,1pen), Miller	1				5	8			12		11			2							6	10	4		9			3*	7#	
					Apps.	41	11	14	1	39	35	7	9	9	33	32		12	41	2	3	1	17	16	28	30	12	31	1	9	5		12	9	
					Subs.		3	2		1				3			4	5				4	4		1	1	5		3	7		1			1
					Goals		1			1	5		1	2	4	15		2					5		5		6	3		1	1				

Additional players: Statham M. - Sub.(no.15) match 40 and no.1, match 41. Millett M. - Sub (no.14), match 40, no 6(*), match 41, Sub.(no.14), match 42.

F.A. CUP

Rd	Date	Opposition	Res.	Att.	Goalscorers	Farnworth S.	Rennie P.	Wright M.	West P.	Robertson J.	Kilford I.	Campbell D.	Morton N.	Gavin P.	Rimmer N.	Lyons A.	Duffy C.	Strong G.	Carragher M.	Ormsby B.	Harford P.	Tait P.	McKearney D.	Jakub Y.	Leonard M.	Farrell A.	Benjamin I.	Miller D.	Adekola D.	Doolan J.	Rodwell A.	Furlong C.	Whitney J.	Black A.	Ogden N.
1R	11 Nov	SPENNYMORE UNITED	4-0	2183	Leonard, Carragher(2), Kilford	1	2			5	7					11			8				10	3	9*	6		4	12						
2R	3 Dec	Altrincham	0-1	3020		1				5	7				10	11		2*	8					3	9	6	12	4							

LEAGUE CUP

Rd	Date	Opposition	Res.	Att.	Goalscorers	Farnworth S.	Rennie P.	Wright M.	West P.	Robertson J.	Kilford I.	Campbell D.	Morton N.	Gavin P.	Rimmer N.	Lyons A.	Duffy C.	Strong G.	Carragher M.	Ormsby B.	Harford P.	Tait P.	McKearney D.	Jakub Y.	Leonard M.	Farrell A.	Benjamin I.	Miller D.	Adekola D.	Doolan J.	Rodwell A.	Furlong C.	Whitney J.	Black A.	Ogden N.
1R1	15 Aug	Crewe Alexandra	1-2	3054	Gavin	1	2	3		5	6	7	8	9*	10	11	12	4																	
1R2	23	CREWE ALEXANDRA	3-0	1421	Gavin, Rennie, Carragher	1	2	3		5	6	7	8	9		11		4	10																
2R1	21 Sep	Aston Villa	0-5	12433		1	2			5	6	7	8	9	10			4	11				12	3*											
2R2	5 Oct	ASTON VILLA	0-3	2633		1	12			5	8	7	14	9	10	11#		4	2*					3		6									

AUTOWINDSCREEN SHIELD

Rd	Date	Opposition	Res.	Att.	Goalscorers	Farnworth S.	Rennie P.	Wright M.	West P.	Robertson J.	Kilford I.	Campbell D.	Morton N.	Gavin P.	Rimmer N.	Lyons A.	Duffy C.	Strong G.	Carragher M.	Ormsby B.	Harford P.	Tait P.	McKearney D.	Jakub Y.	Leonard M.	Farrell A.	Benjamin I.	Miller D.	Adekola D.	Doolan J.	Rodwell A.	Furlong C.	Whitney J.	Black A.	Ogden N.
1R	18 Oct	Rochdale	0-1	1004		1	5				7		8*		10	11		4	2					3	9	6			12						
1R	1 Nov	BLACKPOOL	1-0	1161	Leonard	1+	2			5	7					11		12	8				10	3	9	6		4*						15	
2R	28	Rotherham United	3-1	1587	Rimmer, Leonard, Kilford	1				5	7				10	11		2	8					3	9	6		4							
NQF	7 Feb	CREWE ALEXANDRA	1-3	2063	Farrell	1		3#		5					10	11			2*				8	14	9	6	12	4		7					

SEASON 1995-96

DIVISION 3

No.	Date	Opposition	Res.	Att.	Goalscorers	Felgate D.	Butler J.	Farrell A.	Miller D.	Robertson J.	Martinez R.	Seba J.	Lightfoot C.	Leonard M.	Doolan J.	Lyons A.	Carragher M.	Diaz I.	Pender J.	Mutch A.	Farnworth S.	Rimmer N.	Kilford I.	Black T.	Ogden N.	Greenall C.	Benjamin I.	Kelly T.	Biggins W.	Sharp K.	Johnson G.	Lancashire G.	Lowe D.	Barnwell-EdinboroJ.
1	12 Aug	Gillingham	1-2	3901	Martinez	1	2*	3	4	5	6	7	8	9	10	11	12	14																
2	19	SCUNTHORPE UNITED	2-1	3151	Seba, Lightfoot	1		3		5	6	7	8	9		10	2	11	4															
3	26	Preston North End	1-1	6837	Mutch	1	3	10		5	6		8			11	2	7	4	9														
4	29	CHESTER CITY	2-1	2555	Daiz, Lyons		3	10		5	6		8			11	2	7	4	9	1													
5	2 Sep	Scarborough	0-0	1949			3	10		5	6	14	8			11*	2#	7	4	9	1	12												
6	9	BURY	1-2	3128	Kilford		3	10		5		14			12	11*	2	7	4	9	1	8*	6#	13										
7	12	BARNET	1-0	1745	Kilford		2	4		5	6			10		12		11		9	1	8*	7		3									
8	16	Torquay United	1-1	2188	Diaz		2	10		5	6					12		11	4	9	1	8*	7		3									
9	23	PLYMOUTH ARGYLE	0-1	2631			2				6	14	8			12		11	5	9#	1	10*	7*		3	4	13							
10	30	Hereford United	2-2	2198	Diaz, Greenall						7				2		4	8	6		1	11			3	5	10	9						
11	7 Oct	MANSFIELD TOWN	2-6	2084	Diaz(2)		2				6			9		11#		7	5		1	10		14	3*	4	12	8						
12	14	Exeter City	4-0	3870	Diaz, Seba(2), Leonard		2			5	6	11	10#	9				7	12		1	14	8		3*	4								
13	21	HARTLEPOOL UNITED	1-0	2107	Diaz		2			5	6	11#		9*		14		7	10		1		8	12	3	4								
14	28	Leyton Orient	1-1	4562	Martinez		2			5	6	11		9				7	10		1		8		3	4								
15	31	Darlington	1-2	2076	Butler		2			5	6	11*		9		14		7	10		1		8#	12	3	4								
16	4 Nov	FULHAM	1-1	2438	Robertson		2			5	6*		13	9		11		7	10#		1		8	14	3	4								
17	18	Northampton Town	0-0	4102			3	13		5	10						2	7	6		1		8	11		4*			9					
18	25	DONCASTER ROVERS	2-0	2879	Leonard, Biggins		3	5			8		4	9		11	2	7#	6		1			14					10					
19	9 Dec	Plymouth Argyle	1-3	5931	Farrell		3#	6			8			9			2	7*	5		1		12	13		4			10	11				
20	16	HEREFORD UNITED	2-1	1962	Sharp, Martinez		2	6			8			9					5		1		7	12		4			10*	11	3			
21	23	LINCOLN CITY	1-1	2334	Martinez						8			9		11	2	13	5		1	12	10*	7#		4				6	3			
22	26	Cambridge United	1-2	2855	Kilford			7#	6		8			9		11	2	13	5		1		14			4				10	3			
23	2 Jan	ROCHDALE	2-0	2624	Diaz, Martinez						8			9		11	2	7	5		1	10				4				6	3			
24	13	Scunthorpe United	1-3	2288	Sharp			14	12		8*	13		9*		11#	2	7	5		1					4				6	3	10		
25	20	GILLINGHAM	2-1	2873	Lancashire, Diaz						3*			9		14	2	7	5		1	11				4				6	3	10		
26	30	COLCHESTER UNITED	2-0	2101	Johnson(2)						8			9			2	7	5		1	11				4			14	6	3	10*		
27	3 Feb	PRESTON NORTH END	0-1	5567							8			9			2	7	5		1	11				4			10	6*	3			14
28	10	Colchester United	2-1	3082	Lancashire(2)			7			8						2		5		1	11				4			10*	6	3	9		12
29	17	Barnet	0-5	2059				7			8			9			2		5		1	11				4			10*	6	3			12
30	20	SCARBOROUGH	2-0	2208	Martinez(2)		2				8			9				7	5		1	11		10*		4				6	3			13
31	24	TORQUAY UNITED	3-0	2687	Diaz, Black, Pender		2				8*			9				7	5		1	11	12	14		4			10#	6	3*			13
32	27	Bury	1-2	3800	Black		2				8		7#	9				12	5		1	11		10		4				6*	3			13
33	2 Mar	CAMBRIDGE UNITED	3-1	2528	Martinez,Sharp,Barnwell-Edinboro		2#				8		14	9				7	5*		1	11	12	10*		4				6	3			13
34	5	Cardiff City	0-3	1612					14		8		5	9*			2	7			1	11		10		4				6	3			
35	9	Lincoln City	4-2	3282	Greenwell,Johnson,Sharp,Leonrd(p)		2	8					11	12				14	5		1			7#		4			10	6	3	9*		
36	16	CARDIFF CITY	3-1	2789	Sharp(2), Leonard		2	8*				13		9				7	5		1	11#	14	10		4				6	3			
37	19	Chester City	0-0	2835			2	6			8			9*					5		1	11	7			4			10		3			14
38	23	Rochdale	2-0	2870	Riggins(pen), O.G.		2	6			8*						13		5		1	11	7	12		4			10		3			9#
39	30	Mansfield Town	0-1	2369			2	6*			8#	13					14		5		1	11	9	12#		4			10		3		7	
40	2 Apr	EXETER CITY	1-0	2744	Leonard		2				8	12		13				7*	5		1	11	6#			4			10		3		9	
41	6	LEYTON ORIENT	1-0	3081	Lowe		2					7		9			13		5		1	11	12			4			10#	6*	3		8	
42	8	Hartlepool United	2-1	1877	Lowe, Leonard		2	12			6*	13		9			10		5		1	11	7#			4					3		8	
43	13	DARLINGTON	1-1	4473	Lowe		2*		14		6	12		9			10	7#	5		1	11				4					3		8	
44	20	Fulham	0-1	4657				10*	8		6	14		9#			2		5		1	11	3			4					3		7	
45	27	Doncaster Rovers	1-2	2122	Martinez		9	5			6	7					2				1	11	8			4			10		3			
46	4 May	NORTHAMPTON TOWN	1-2	5089	Leonard		2				6	14		9			12	7	5		1	11#				4				8	3*		10	
					Apps.	3	32	21	3	14	42	8	11	32	2	13	23	31	41	7	43	28	18	8	10	37	1	2	15	20	27	5	7	1
					Subs.			3	3			11	2	2	1	6	5	5	1			3	7	11			2		1					8
					Goals		1	1		1	8	3	1	7		1		10	1	1			3	2		2			2	6	3	3	3	1

F.A. CUP

Rd	Date	Opposition	Res.	Att.	Goalscorers	Felgate D.	Butler J.	Farrell A.	Miller D.	Robertson J.	Martinez R.	Seba J.	Lightfoot C.	Leonard M.	Doolan J.	Lyons A.	Carragher M.	Diaz I.	Pender J.	Mutch A.	Farnworth S.	Rimmer N.	Kilford I.	Black T.	Ogden N.	Greenall C.	Benjamin I.	Kelly T.	Biggins W.	Sharp K.	Johnson G.	Lancashire G.	Lowe D.	Barnwell-EdinboroJ.
1R	11 Nov	Runcorn	1-1	2844	Martinez		3			5	6		8	9		14	2	7	10		1			11#		4								
1Rr	21	RUNCORN	4-2	1471	Leonard, Diaz, Martinez, O.G.		3	12		5*	10	14	4	9		11	2	7	6		1		8*											
2R	2 Dec	Barrow	4-0	3500	Black(2), Diaz, Martinez		3	5			8			9		11	2	7	6*		1		12	10		4								
3R	6 Jan	Walsall	0-1	5672				6#			8	12		9		11	2	7	5		1	10*			14	4				3				

LEAGUE CUP

Rd	Date	Opposition	Res.	Att.	Goalscorers	Felgate D.	Butler J.	Farrell A.	Miller D.	Robertson J.	Martinez R.	Seba J.	Lightfoot C.	Leonard M.	Doolan J.	Lyons A.	Carragher M.	Diaz I.	Pender J.	Mutch A.	Farnworth S.	Rimmer N.	Kilford I.	Black T.	Ogden N.	Greenall C.	Benjamin I.	Kelly T.	Biggins W.	Sharp K.	Johnson G.	Lancashire G.	Lowe D.	Barnwell-EdinboroJ.
1R1	15 Aug	Chester City	1-4	2621	Martinez	1	3#	2	4	5	6	7	8	9	10*	12	14#	11																
1R2	22	CHESTER CITY	1-3	2061	Lyons(pen)	1		3	4	5	6	7	8	9		10	2	11																

AUTOWINDSCREEN SHIELD

Rd	Date	Opposition	Res.	Att.	Goalscorers	Felgate D.	Butler J.	Farrell A.	Miller D.	Robertson J.	Martinez R.	Seba J.	Lightfoot C.	Leonard M.	Doolan J.	Lyons A.	Carragher M.	Diaz I.	Pender J.	Mutch A.	Farnworth S.	Rimmer N.	Kilford I.	Black T.	Ogden N.	Greenall C.	Benjamin I.	Kelly T.	Biggins W.	Sharp K.	Johnson G.	Lancashire G.	Lowe D.	Barnwell-EdinboroJ.
1R	26 Sep	SCUNTHORPE UNITED	1-1	1061	Benjamin		2						8			11		7	5		1		10		3	4	9	6						
1R	14 Nov	Bury	0-0	1471			3				6		10	9		11	2	7#	5		1		8	14		4								
2R	28	Rotherham United *	0-0	1008			3	5#	13		8	10	4*	9		11	2	7	6		1					12								

* Lost 1-4 on penalties

Season 1995/96

(Back): Farrell, Kilford, Benjamin, Ogden, Greenall, Leonard, Tait, Lightfoot, Pender.
(Middle): Rimmer, Miller, Lyons, Cribley (Coach/Physio),
Deehan (Manager), Benson (Assist.Manager), Kelly, Doolan, Biggins.
(Front): Black, Seba, Martinez, Farnworth, Felgate, Diaz, Sharp, Carragher.

1995/96 Division 3 Final Table

		Pl.	Home					Away					F.	A.	Pts
			W	D	L	F	A	W	D	L	F	A			
1	Preston North End	46	11	8	4	44	22	12	9	2	34	16	78	38	86
2	Gillingham	46	16	6	1	33	6	6	11	6	16	14	49	20	83
3	Bury	46	11	6	6	33	21	11	7	5	33	27	66	48	79
4	Plymouth Argyle	46	14	5	4	41	20	8	7	8	27	29	68	49	78
5	Darlington	46	10	6	7	30	21	10	12	1	30	21	60	42	78
6	Hereford United	46	13	5	5	40	22	7	9	7	25	25	65	47	74
7	Colchester United	46	13	7	3	37	22	5	11	7	24	29	61	51	72
8	Chester City	46	11	9	3	45	22	7	7	9	27	31	72	53	70
9	Barnet	46	13	6	4	40	19	5	10	8	25	26	65	45	70
10	Wigan Athletic	46	15	3	5	36	21	5	7	11	26	35	62	56	70
11	Northampton Town	46	9	10	4	32	22	9	3	11	19	22	51	44	67
12	Scunthorpe United	46	8	8	7	36	30	7	7	9	31	31	67	61	60
13	Doncaster Rovers	46	11	6	6	25	19	5	5	13	24	41	49	60	59
14	Exeter City	46	9	9	5	25	22	4	9	10	21	31	46	53	57
15	Rochdale	46	7	8	8	32	33	7	5	11	25	28	57	61	55
16	Cambridge United	46	8	8	7	34	30	6	4	13	27	41	61	71	54
17	Fulham	46	10	9	4	39	26	2	8	13	18	37	57	63	53
18	Lincoln City	46	8	7	8	32	26	5	7	11	25	47	57	73	53
19	Mansfield Town	46	6	10	7	25	29	5	10	8	29	35	54	64	53
20	Hartlepool United	46	8	9	6	30	24	4	4	15	17	43	47	67	49
21	Leyton Orient	46	11	4	8	29	22	1	7	15	15	41	44	63	47
22	Cardiff City	46	8	6	9	24	22	3	6	14	17	42	41	64	45
23	Scarborough	46	5	11	7	22	28	3	5	15	17	41	39	69	40
24	Torquay United	46	4	9	10	17	36	1	5	17	13	48	30	84	29

ADVANCED SUBSCRIBERS

Philip, Christmas 1996
Stephen J. Halliwell, Aspull
Garry McAllister, Newtown, Wigan
Owen Mathews, Shevington, Wigan
Griff
James Southam, Hindley, Wigan
David Nicholas, Monifiethe, Angus
Mark Lee's
Ray Howie, Bromleycross, Bolton
Thomas Platt, Scholes, Wigan
Albert Storey, Wigan
Cyril Unsworth, Wigan
Noel S. Dean, Wigan
Frank Armstrong, Wigan
Bernard Ramsdale, Aspull, Wigan
Tom Batson, Newton-le-Willows
William Andrew Taylor, Hindley
David M. McKellen, Westhoughton
Alan and Graham Foster
Royston James Pugh, Wigan
Walter H. Johnson, Coppull
Peter Naylor, Standish
Catherine Louise Meredith, Tyldsley
Eric Corless, Golborne
Barry Gray
Kiera P.J. Sumner, Standish
Andrew Naylor, Shevington Moor
Paul Fairhurst, Earby-in-Pendle
Robert Willis
Stuart James Hayton, Pemberton
Mark Wallis, Appley Bridge
Robert Granville Crompton, Whelley, Wigan
Stephen P. Weston, Bolton
David Moverley, Wigan
Paul Benbow, Appley Bridge
Gill Mates, Merseyside
Andrew Silcock, Abram, Wigan
Kevin Mackenzie, Worsleymesnes, Wigan
Rod & Josie Prescott, Appley Bridge
Gary Marsden, Highfield, Wigan
Graham Bradley Unsworth, Standish
Leslie Riley, Wigan
Shaun Quinlan, Upholland
Graham Paul Hill, Ashton-in-Makerfield
John Pendlebury, Hindley Green
Adrian Brookes, Colby, I.O.M.
Ryan Barlow, Eccles, Manchester
Ben Barlow, Eccles, Manchester
Andrew Prescott, Orrell, Wigan

Philip Rall, Kitt Green
Clive Wareing, Bryngates, Bamfurlong
David Trencher, Orrell
Ian Trencher, Orrell
Peter Trencher, Orrell
Happy Christmas David from Grandad
Tracey Shearer, Appley Bridge
Clare Bennett, Springfield, Wigan
Neil "Eddie" Brennan, Standish
Ralph Brimelow, Wigan
Robert Miller, Billinge, Wigan
Phil Hilton, Winstanley, Wigan
Gareth Edwards, Newbiggin-by-the-Sea
Shaun Connelly, Whelley, Wigan
Lawrence Connelly, Whelley, Wigan
Michael Rhead, Springfield, Wigan
Liam Prescott, Wigan
To Mervyn, Love Mum
Alistair Pope, Preston
Allan Woodward, Ashton , Wigan
John Reece, Horsham, Sussex
Brian Duffy, Hindley Green
Roy Highton, Wigan
John Hampson, Wigan
To Neil Christmas 1996
Jeff Fishwick, Billinge, Wigan
Martin Rhys Davies
Brian Parkes, Swinley, Wigan
Louise Kumar, Whitley, Wigan
John Pennington, Whitley, Wigan
Brian Barnes, Wigan
Kath Rimmer, Wigan
Terry Knowles, Springfield, Wigan
George Cross, Orrell, Wigan
John Abram, Newburgh, Wigan
Moira and Frederick Furness
David Keats
G.T. Allman
Robert M. Smith
Paul Johnston, Birmingham City
L.A. Zammit
David Downs and Marion
Bob Lilliman
Derek Hyde, Cardiff
Chris Harte
Martin Cripps
Raymond Shaw
Graham Speckman
Chris Marsh, Chesterfield
John Treleven

J.A. Motson
Steve Emms
Ray Bickel
Michael John Griffin
Gareth A. Evans
Richard Ainsley
John Ringrose
Peter Savage
A. & J.A. Waterman
S. Metcalfe
John Byrne
Fred Lee, Plymouth Argyle
B.H. Standish
Alan Davies
Richard Wells
Brian Tabner
Gordon Macey, Q.P.R. Historian
Peter Baxter
Phil Hollow
Keith Coburn
Jonny Stokkeland, Kvinesdal, Norway
Association of Sports Historians
R.H. White, Saudi Arabia
Willy Østby, Norway
Alan
Richard Shore
W.D. Phillips
Geoffrey Wright
David Lumb
Martin Simons, Belgium
Roger Wash
Richard W. Lane, Newark
George Mason
Jonathan Hall
David and Matthew Fleckney
Gunnel and Leif Hansson
Trond Isaksen, Norway
David Jowett
Mr. D.M. McPherson
Gerald Hill
John Rawnsley
Peter Cogle, Aberdeen
Roy Banks, Appley Bridge
Ben Hayes, Bolton
Elaine Hayes, Bamber Bridge
Ronnie King, Wigan
Colin Walls, Abram
Jim Gaskell, Wigan
Arran and Nicholas Matthews